Michael Chiorazzi
Gordon Russell
Editors

Law Library Collection Development in the Digital Age

Law Library Collection Development in the Digital Age has been co-published simultaneously as *Legal Reference Services Quarterly*, Volume 21, Numbers 2/3 and 4 2002.

Pre-publication REVIEWS, COMMENTARIES, EVALUATIONS . . .

"A MUST-HAVE, MUST-READ REFERENCE for every law librarian responsible for collection development. AN EXCEPTIONAL COLLECTION . . . ENLIGHTENS AND INFORMS the profession on the current state of the art. Moreover, this single volume captures the future vision faced by law librarianship. It offers significant insights about the short- and longer-term impacts of digital technology on our library collections. It provides probing, challenging descriptions and critiques of current and anticipated practices."

Roger F. Jacobs
Director of the Law Library
and Professor of Law
Kresge Library
Notre Dame Law School

Law Library Collection Development in the Digital Age

Law Library Collection Development in the Digital Age has been co-published simultaneously as *Legal Reference Services Quarterly,* Volume 21, Numbers 2/3 and 4 2002.

Legal Reference Services Quarterly Monographic "Separates"

Below is a list of "separates," which in serials librarianship means a special issue simultaneously published as a special journal issue or double-issue *and* as a "separate" hardbound monograph. (This is a format which we also call a "DocuSerial.")

"Separates" are published because specialized libraries or professionals may wish to purchase a specific thematic issue by itself in a format which can be separately cataloged and shelved, as opposed to purchasing the journal on an on-going basis. Faculty members may also more easily consider a "separate" for classroom adoption.

"Separates" are carefully classified separately with the major book jobbers so that the journal tie-in can be noted on new book order slips to avoid duplicate purchasing.

You may wish to visit Haworth's website at . . .

http://www.HaworthPress.com

. . . to search our online catalog for complete tables of contents of these separates and related publications.

You may also call 1-800-HAWORTH (outside US/Canada: 607-722-5857), or Fax 1-800-895-0582 (outside US/Canada: 607-771-0012), or e-mail at:

getinfo@haworthpressinc.com

Law Library Collection Development in the Digital Age, edited by Michael Chiorazzi and Gordon Russell (Vol. 21, No. 2/3/4, 2002). *Examines recent changes in law library collection development that were brought about by advances in publishing and digital technology.*

Teamwork and Collaboration in Libraries: Tools for Theory and Practice, edited by Marc B. Silverman (Vol. 20, No. 3, 2001). *"A superb collection of insightful works on one of the profession's most timely and most vexing topics. A thorough compendium of shared experiences and research, Silverman's work is a clear example of the very process it endeavors to explore." (John J. DiGilio, MLIS, JD, Legal & Business Research Librarian, Kirkpatrick & Lockhart, LLP, Pittsburgh, Pennsylvania)*

Public Services Issues with Rare and Archival Law Materials, edited by Michael Widener, BJ, MLIS (Vol. 20, No. 1/2, 2001). *An essential reference for law librarians and archivists, this helpful book gives practical advice and information on providing access to rare and archival law collections and promoting their use by scholars, teachers, and students.*

Teaching Legal Research and Providing Access to Electronic Resources, edited by Gary L. Hill, JD, MLL, BA, Dennis S. Sears, JD, MA, MLIS, MBA, and Lovisa Lyman, MA, MLIS, BA (Vol. 19, No. 3/4, 2001). *"A unique mixture of historical, theoretical, and practical approaches to legal research instruction in one convenient location." (Gail A. Partin, MSLS, JD, Associate Law Librarian, Sheely-Lee Law Library, The Dickinson School of Law of the Pennsylvania State University)*

Emerging Solutions in Reference Services: Implications for Libraries in the New Millennium, edited by John D. Edwards, JD, MALS (Vol. 19, No. 1/2, 2001). *"The authors provide practical advice on how to cope with everything from tight budgets to training needs to knife wielding patrons. I highly recommend that law school reference librarians purchase and read this outstanding work." (Bill Draper, BA, MS, JD, Reference Librarian and Lecturer, Biddle Law Library, University of Pennsylvania, Philadelphia)*

Law Librarians Abroad, edited by Janet Sinder, AB, JD, MS (Vol. 18, No. 3, 2000). *"A pure pleasure! Law librarians seeking information on how to find professional work abroad and useful advice on how to survive in a foreign land will be amply rewarded. Delightful." (Peter C. Schanck, JD, MLS, Law Library Director and Professor of Law, Marquette University Law Library, Milwaukee, Wisconsin)*

The Political Economy of Legal Information: The New Landscape, edited by Samuel E. Trosow (Vol. 17, No. 1/2, 1999). *Through this informative book you will gain new insights into such important issues as how industry consolidation will affect small legal publishers and the possibility that the law that governs public access to judicial opinions mandates citation reform.*

Symposium of Law Publishers, edited by Thomas A. Woxland, MLS, JD (Vol. 11, No. 3/4, 1991). *"Librarians involved in collection development would find the symposium useful as it provides an insider's view of the legal publishing industry." (Canadian Law Libraries)*

The Legal Bibliography: Tradition, Transitions, and Trends, edited by Scott B. Pagel, JD, MLS (Vol. 9, No. 1/2, 1989). *"An excellent introduction to major bibliographic titles and future concerns for the novice law librarian or student of legal librarianship. . . . A useful addition to the reference shelf of the private law or acquisitions librarian." (Legal Information Alert)*

Practical Approaches to Legal Research, edited by Kent C. Olson, JD, MLS, and Robert C. Berring, JD, MLS (Supp. #01, 1988). *"A long overdue book–a legal research manual for librarians. . . . A readable and entertaining text on locating and using law books. . . . Almost everything a law librarian needs to know about legal research is covered in this book." (Legal Information Alert)*

ALL HAWORTH INFORMATION PRESS
BOOKS AND JOURNALS ARE PRINTED
ON CERTIFIED ACID-FREE PAPER

Law Library Collection Development in the Digital Age

Michael Chiorazzi
Gordon Russell
Editors

Law Library Collection Development in the Digital Age has been co-published simultaneously as *Legal Reference Services Quarterly,* Volume 21, Numbers 2/3 and 4 2002.

The Haworth Information Press
An Imprint of
The Haworth Press, Inc.
NewYork • London • Oxford

Published by

The Haworth Information Press®, 10 Alice Street, Binghamton, NY 13904-1580 USA

The Haworth Information Press® is an imprint of The Haworth Press, Inc., 10 Alice Street, Binghamton, NY 13904-1580 USA.

Law Library Collection Development in the Digital Age has been co-published simultaneously as *Legal Reference Services Quarterly,* Volume 21, Numbers 2/3 and 4 2002.

Cover design Jennifer Gaska.

Library of Congress Cataloging-in-Publication Data

Law library collection development in the digital age / Michael Chiorazzi, Gordon Russell, editors.
p. cm.
Co-published simultaneously as Legal reference services quarterly, v. 21, nos. 2/3 and 4, 2002.
Includes bibliographical references and index.
ISBN 0-7890-2022-X (alk. paper) – ISBN 0-7890-2023-8 (pbk : alk. paper)
1. Law libraries–Collection development. 2. Law–Electronic information resources. 3. Legal literature–Publishing–Technological innovations. I. Chiorazzi, Michael G. II. Russell, Gordon, 1954- . III. Legal reference services quarterly.
Z675.L2 L387 2002
025.2′18634–dc21

2002151038

Indexing, Abstracting & Website/Internet Coverage

This section provides you with a list of major indexing & abstracting services. That is to say, each service began covering this periodical during the year noted in the right column. Most Websites which are listed below have indicated that they will either post, disseminate, compile, archive, cite or alert their own Website users with research-based content from this work. (This list is as current as the copyright date of this publication.)

Abstracting, Website/Indexing Coverage	Year When Coverage Began
• *CNPIEC Reference Guide: Chinese National Directory of Foreign Periodicals*	**1995**
• *Current Cites [Digital Libraries] [Electronic Publishing] [Multimedia & Hypermedia] [Networks & Networking] [General]*	**2000**
• *Current Law Index*	**1992**
• *FINDEX <www.publist.com>*	**1999**
• *Hein's Legal Periodical Checklist: Index to Periodical Articles Pertaining to Law <www.wshein.com>*	**1992**
• *IBZ International Bibliography of Periodical Literature <www.saur.de>*	**1995**
• *Index Guide to College Journals (core list compiled by integrating 48 indexes frequently used to support undergraduate programs in small to medium sized libraries)*	**1999**
• *Index to Legal Periodicals & Books <www.hwwilson.com>*	**1992**
• *Index to Periodical Articles Related to Law*	**1992**

(continued)

- *Information Science Abstracts <www.infotoday.com>* **1992**
- *Informed Librarian, The <http://www.infosourcespub.com>* **1993**
- *InfoTrac Custom <www.galegroup.com>* **1996**
- *INSPEC <www.iee.org.uk/publish/>* **1992**
- *Journal of Academic Librarianship: Guide to Professional Literature, The* **1997**
- *Konyvtari Figyelo (Library Review)* **2000**
- *LegalTrac on InfoTrack web <www.galegroup.com>* **1984**
- *Library & Information Science Abstracts (LISA) <www.csa.com>* **1992**
- *Library and Information Science Annual (LISCA) <www.lu.com/arba>* **1998**
- *Library Literature & Information Science* **1992**
- *OCLC Public Affairs Information Service <www.pais.org>* **2000**
- *Sage Public Administration Abstracts (SPAA)* **1992**
- *SwetsNet <www.swetsnet.com>* **2002**

Special Bibliographic Notes related to special journal issues (separates) and indexing/abstracting:

- indexing/abstracting services in this list will also cover material in any "separate" that is co-published simultaneously with Haworth's special thematic journal issue or DocuSerial. Indexing/abstracting usually covers material at the article/chapter level.
- monographic co-editions are intended for either non-subscribers or libraries which intend to purchase a second copy for their circulating collections.
- monographic co-editions are reported to all jobbers/wholesalers/approval plans. The source journal is listed as the "series" to assist the prevention of duplicate purchasing in the same manner utilized for books-in-series.
- to facilitate user/access services all indexing/abstracting services are encouraged to utilize the co-indexing entry note indicated at the bottom of the first page of each article/chapter/contribution.
- this is intended to assist a library user of any reference tool (whether print, electronic, online, or CD-ROM) to locate the monographic version if the library has purchased this version but not a subscription to the source journal.
- individual articles/chapters in any Haworth publication are also available through the Haworth Document Delivery Service (HDDS).

Law Library Collection Development in the Digital Age

CONTENTS

Preface xiii

Books, Bytes, Bricks and Bodies: Thinking About Collection Use in Academic Law Libraries 1
Michael Chiorazzi

Re-Engineering the Law Library Resources Today for Tomorrow's Users: A Response to "How Much of Your Print Collection Is Really on WESTLAW or LEXIS-NEXIS?" 29
Gordon Russell

Availability of Works Cited in Recent Law Review Articles on LEXIS, Westlaw, the Internet, and Other Databases 55
Simon Canick

Strategic Planning for Distance Learning in Legal Education: Initial Thoughts on a Role for Libraries 69
Richard A. Danner

Web Mirror Sites: Creating the Research Library of the Future, and More . . . 87
Claire M. Germain

Legal Scholarship and Digital Publishing: Has Anything Changed in the Way We Do Legal Research? 105
E. Dana Neacsu

Trust v. Antitrust: Consolidation in the Legal Publishing Industry 123
John Dethman

Access versus Ownership: A Changing Model of Intellectual Property 153
Scott Matheson

A Law Library in the New Century: The Creation of the University of St. Thomas Law Library 177
Edmund P. Edmonds
Margaret Maes Axtmann

Electronic Journals in the Academic Law Library–Law Reviews and Beyond 189
Marguerite Most

Book Selection Services: One Law Library, Two Vendors 259
Maureen Garmon

Changes in the Courthouse–Electronic Records, Filings and Court Dockets: Goals, Issues and the Road Ahead 275
Julie C. Turner

The Changing Role of Law Library Vendors: The William S. Hein & Company Perspective 301
Kevin M. Marmion
Richard J. Spinellii

Index 307

ABOUT THE EDITORS

Michael Chiorazzi is Director of the Law Library and Professor of Law at the James E. Rogers College of Law at the University of Arizona. He holds a joint appointment as Professor in the School of Information Resources and Library Science of the College of Social and Behavioral Sciences. His scholarship interests include legal history and law library administration. Mr. Chiorazzi is Editor of *Legal Reference Services Quarterly* and is active in AALL, AALS, and the ABA Section on Legal Education and Admission to the Bar. Prior to his appointment at the University of Arizona, he worked at the Boston College and Duke University Law Libraries. In the summer of 2002, he was a visiting professor at the University of Washington Information School.

Gordon Russell is Law Library Director and Associate Professor of Law at the St. Thomas University Law Library in Miami, Florida. He has taught first year legal research and writing, advanced electronic research for upper classes and online computer-assisted legal research courses in the LLM Tax Program. He has presented papers and spoken at international professional conferences, and received an award from Lexis for "Advanced Legal Research Folio Database." Mr. Russell wrote "NAFTA & Mexico" and prepared a Folio Views database for the United States-Mexico Law Institute's Fifth Annual Conference. He is a member of the American Association of Law Schools, the American Bar Association, the Canadian Association of Law Libraries, the International Association of Law Libraries, and the Southeast Association of Law Libraries.

Preface

The idea for this book grew from a paper presented by Professor Penny Hazelton, "How Much of Your Print Collection Is Really on WESTLAW or LEXIS-NEXIS?" Professor Hazelton's empirical look at the availability of electronic alternatives to the print law collection couldn't have come at a better time. Many of us were considering similar investigations and Professor Hazelton offered us a starting point. It was the topic of much discussion in the law librarianship profession and Professor Hazelton was asked to speak at a number of conferences on the subject.

The affect of digital publishing on legal research and law libraries has been profound. While the overused term *paradigm shift* causes some to shutter, it does accurately describe the situation we currently face in building legal collections and Hazelton's article seemed to capture the zeitgeist of the law librarianship profession.

A February 2000 conference, "Not a Box but a Window," hosted by the Faculty of Law of the University of Toronto, provided me with an opportunity to begin to collect my own thoughts on the implications of Hazelton's article. I presented my initial reactions to the Hazelton article; those thoughts eventually evolved into the first article in this collection. More importantly, that conference served as the incubator for this book. At the Toronto conference I spent some time discussing my article with Professor Gordon Russell. He also had spent some time considering the issues presented in the Hazelton article and was considering writing a response for an upcoming program at the American Association of Law Libraries (AALL) annual meeting. I proposed creating a work dealing with the issues surrounding digital law library collection development. (Little did I realize at the time that the project would grow to a book of this size!) Gordon agreed to assist as co-editor of the proj-

[Haworth co-indexing entry note]: "Preface." Chiorazzi, Michael. Co-published simultaneously in *Legal Reference Services Quarterly* (The Haworth Information Press, an imprint of The Haworth Press, Inc.) Vol. 21, No. 2/3, 2002, pp. xv-xvi; and: *Law Library Collection Development in the Digital Age* (ed: Michael Chiorazzi, and Gordon Russell) The Haworth Information Press, an imprint of The Haworth Press, Inc., 2002, pp. xiii-xiv. Single or multiple copies of this article are available for a fee from The Haworth Document Delivery Service [1-800-HAWORTH, 9:00 a.m. - 5:00 p.m. (EST). E-mail address: getinfo@haworthpressinc.com].

ect. His article in this work, the second of three that respond to Hazelton, is an outgrowth of his AALL panel discussion. Simon Canick adds the third, a further empirical examination of digital legal collection development entitled "Availability of Works Cited in Recent Law Review Articles on LEXIS, Westlaw, the Internet, and Other Databases."

Earlier versions of four additional articles in this collection were all presented at the Toronto conference: Richard Danner's "Strategic Planning for Distance Learning in Legal Education: Initial Thoughts on a Role for Libraries"; Claire Germain's "Web Mirror Sites: Creating the Research Library of the Future, and More . . ."; Dana Neacsu's "Legal Scholarship and Digital Publishing: Has Anything Changed in the Way We Do Legal Research?"; and finally, Ed Edmonds' and Margie Axtmann's "A Law Library in the New Century: The Creation of the University of St. Thomas Law Library," which appears later in the collection. Quite a distinguished group!

Three articles in this collection began as research papers in Professor Hazelton's Current Issues in Law Librarianship course at the University of Washington. All three deal with important considerations in building law library collections–John Dethman's "Trust v. Antitrust: Consolidation in the Legal Publishing Industry," Scott Matheson's "Access versus Ownership: A Changing Model of Intellectual Property" and Julie Turner's "Changes in the Courthouse–Electronic Records, Filings and Court Dockets: Goals, Issues and the Road Ahead." (If we include Simon Canick, there are four authors who are recent graduates of the University of Washington School of Information's law librarianship program–Professor Penny Hazelton's influence yet again!)

The remaining three papers are perhaps best described as the most practice oriented in this collection. Marguerite Most has written a comprehensive examination of the growth of e-journals as they relate to legal publishing. Maureen Garmon has written an empiric analysis of the Hein Greenslips and Blackwell North America's Bookservice to determine their coverage on Anglo-American, foreign and international legal materials. Finally, Kevin Marmion and Dick Spinelli of Hein Publishing discuss the past, present and future role of law specialized book jobbers.

Gordon and I are quite proud of this book. It covers a wide variety of issues of legal collection development, a subject near and dear to all legal reference librarians' hearts. It will be particularly useful to legal reference librarians new to collection development and the legal publishing industry. We hope you enjoy it.

Michael Chiorazzi

Books, Bytes, Bricks and Bodies: Thinking About Collection Use in Academic Law Libraries

Michael Chiorazzi

SUMMARY. This article builds on Professor Penny Hazelton's examination of "how much of your collection is really available on Lexis and Westlaw?" While Hazelton examined the question from the perspective of space occupied, Professor Chiorazzi looks at the question from the perspective of collection use. Using the economic theory called the Pareto Principle, Chiorazzi argues that over 80% of the use of all legal materials is accounted for by the 20% of all legal materials that are available online. This has significant implications for law librarians seeking to expand or build new facilities. The legal research environment has changed to a point where most research can in fact be done online and large research paper collections may become harder to defend against administrators using potentially shortsighted cost-benefit analyses while making library budgeting decisions. *[Article copies available for a fee from The Haworth Document Delivery Service: 1-800-HAWORTH. E-mail address: <getinfo@haworthpressinc.com> Website: <http://www.HaworthPress.com> © 2002 by The Haworth Press, Inc. All rights reserved.]*

KEYWORDS. Collection development, computer assisted legal research, Pareto Principle, collection use, online legal materials

---

Michael Chiorazzi is Director of the Law Library and Professor of Law and Information Resources & Library Science, James E. Rogers College of Law, University of Arizona.

[Haworth co-indexing entry note]: "Books, Bytes, Bricks and Bodies: Thinking About Collection Use in Academic Law Libraries." Chiorazzi, Michael. Co-published simultaneously in *Legal Reference Services Quarterly* (The Haworth Information Press, an imprint of The Haworth Press, Inc.) Vol. 21, No. 2/3, 2002, pp. 1-28; and: *Law Library Collection Development in the Digital Age* (ed: Michael Chiorazzi, and Gordon Russell) The Haworth Information Press, an imprint of The Haworth Press, Inc., 2002, pp. 1-28. Single or multiple copies of this article are available for a fee from The Haworth Document Delivery Service [1-800-HAWORTH, 9:00 a.m. - 5:00 p.m. (EST). E-mail address: getinfo@haworthpressinc.com].

INTRODUCTION

At the March 1999 AALL/Duke Law Library conference, "Space Planning and Technology for Academic Law Libraries," Professor Penny Hazelton presented a paper that begins to answer the question asked of every librarian beginning a new building project: "But it all will be online. Why do you need so much space for books?" In her study of the collection of the University of Washington Gallagher Law Library, she determined that if she were to remove the hard copies of everything that was available on Lexis or Westlaw, only 13% of the collection could be withdrawn.

Her talk and accompanying handout intrigued me. Every so often we read something that causes us to stop and reassess our view of things–I call it "things that make you go hmmm!" I asked her to let me publish it in *Legal Reference Services Quarterly (LRSQ).*[1] Here was the first attempt of which I was aware to quantify the perceived move from paper to digital law collections. Yet, something was not quite right. Why was it, that in spite of Hazelton's numbers, use of our paper collections appears to decline while more and more research seems to occur in an online environment? We all see it in our libraries–for far too many students, if it is not online, it doesn't exist. This is not unique to academic law libraries. To see what is happening in law firms, one need only monitor the listserv *law-lib*, where withdrawn sets of the National Reporter System, offered for the cost of shipping, go begging. We spend increasing amounts of time reminding students, and sometimes even faculty, what is available in our paper collections.

Shortly after the Duke conference, a discussion arose on the law library directors' listserv *lawlibdir* concerning the relocating of infrequently used collections into off-site storage. Professor Roger Jacobs of Notre Dame School of Law Library wrote a thoughtful, cautionary email describing the pitfalls of off-site storage in which he quoted Karl Llewellyn's *threat of the available*:

> This is the lesson from the almost inevitable tendency in any thinking, or in any study, first to turn to the most available material and to study that–to study it exclusively–at the outset; second, having once begun the study of the available, to lose all perspective and come shortly to mistake the merely available, the easily seen, for all there is to be seen.[2]

Hmmm. Does that ever ring true! How often have we been at the reference desk helping a student who "has looked everywhere, but can't find anything on X," only to find that she has not bothered to visit the online catalog or periodical indexes in her research. Their initial reaction is to avoid anything in print in favor of the electronic. Increasingly, we feel fortunate if the student has at the very least searched Lexis or Westlaw rather than rely on a "cruise" with an Internet search engine. An exaggeration? Perhaps, but not much.

Shortly after Professor Jacobs' posting came an email with the subject line, *In Defense of Remote Storage*,[3] from Professor Harry (Terry) Martin, of Harvard Law Library.[4] It is, in my opinion, the best single submission ever posted on the lawlibdir listserv[5]–a brilliant, three page defense of the Harvard Law Library's decision to store over 400,000 volumes off-site during the renovation of the library. He cites Professor Hazelton's article, along with the Pareto Principle, Bradford's law of scatter, and Garfield's law of concentration,[6] to support the proposition that most of these materials are so rarely used that off-site storage is a viable option.

Professor Martin articulated many of my concerns (things that make me go hmmm!) about what Hazelton's numbers did not say. All books and periodicals are not equal. The Pareto principle, along with Bradford's and Garfield's laws, seem to put the numbers in a more meaningful context. I asked Professor Martin to consider working his email into an article for *LRSQ*. He politely declined, and I was now hooked.

I decided to expand the analysis beyond the context of off-site storage. What about the design of new library space or the redesign of existing space? Do we need to fundamentally reexamine the way we think about space? That is, is it important to now focus on the use of the collection, rather than the space collections occupy? Will this affect collection development? Have we turned the digital corner; is the totally digital academic law library now a practical and necessary reality for those brave enough to create one? I decided to educate myself and began a literature search in the library literature, first that of Pareto, Bradford, and Garfield, then bibliometrics and library science.[7]

Next, I looked for other hard data that might support the use of the Pareto Principle for collection planning, and might also help explain the apparent disconnect between use and collection development. There is very little useful statistical data out there for space planning, and the little that there is has not been examined in law library literature, with the notable exceptions of Professor Hazelton's article, an article by George Grossman and a book by Stephen Margeton.[8] I looked to ABA and ARL statistics to determine if their statistical gatherings could provide any insights. Perhaps there was enough data to further develop these laws and principles to assist in both library space and collection design.

This paper is the result of my examination of the available data. It is only a beginning; it is neither systematic nor scientific. It is my hope that it will, however, present some useful data and act as a primer and starting point in the discussion and development of models to anticipate library growth in this new century, particularly as they relate to collection development and library space. Will libraries soon be viewed as the train stations of the 21st century–wonderful, romantic statements of a time long since past?

This article does not describe my vision of the future; the beginning of the new millennium brought us much of that.[9] Rather, I will attempt to assemble some objective measures and data, which may be useful in forecasting change. This is merely an attempt to accumulate the useful and perhaps examine a few speculations; it is also a call to those who are looking for worthwhile research projects and further empirical research. At worst, it may provide you with some information or things that make you go Hmmm!

SOME PRELIMINARY DEFINITIONS

The Pareto Principle states that 80% of use (or need) is met by 20% of the available resources. Dr. J. M. Juran has written that it is a shorthand for a phenomenon that in any population which contributes to a common effect, a relatively few of the contributors account for the bulk of the effect. Or, stated a third way: the vital few and the trivial many. The principle is actually incorrectly attributed to the Italian socio-economist, Vilfredo Pareto.[10] It has been used and misused in every imaginable business context. In meetings: 80% of decisions come from 20% of meeting time. In management: 80% of your managerial problems and headaches are caused by 20% of your staff; and 80% of your manager's interruptions come from the same 20% of people. A search of the Web even revealed its use by a vacuum cleaner company, which stated that 80% of vacuuming takes place on 20% of the carpet. Pareto's thesis was simply that the majority of wealth was in the hands of a few individuals, and that distribution was unchanged from country to country.

Bradford's Law (sometimes called Bradford's law of scatter) states, "that the most significant articles to any given field of investigation are found within a relatively small group of publications. A few journals publish a high percentage of the articles in the field; and, there are many journals that publish only a few articles."[11] This supports the Pareto Principle as well as the arguments for the practicality of off-site storage. The law is named after its creator, librarian Samuel Clements Bradford.

Garfield's Law of Concentration argues that there is a large overlap between disciplines and that material only tangentially related to a particular discipline often comprises the core of another discipline. The Law of Concentration was developed by Eugene Garfield, the founder of the Institute for Scientific Information (ISI) and creator of the *Science Citation Index* (SCI). Interestingly, Garfield's work in bibliometrics was inspired by his examination of Shepard's Citations.

Bibliometrics (or as Garfield preferred, Citationology) and Cybermetrics: Bibliometrics is a standard method of information analysis that seeks to quantify the process of written communication. It has evolved over time. It often involves the statistical analysis of citations by author, subject or publication to determine the work's impact on scholarly communication and the development of the literature of a subject area. Shepard's and Keycite are two examples of bibliometric tools that analyze legal citations. Cybermetrics is a subset of bibliometrics that deals with analysis of information on the World Wide Web. Bradford's and Garfield's Laws are considered bibliometric laws.[12]

PARETO AND DIGITAL COLLECTION DEVELOPMENT

Intuitively, the Pareto Principle makes sense to law librarians. It also goes a long way toward answering the question posed to Professor Hazelton by her law school's faculty and administration. If one assumes that the electronic publishers have made their decisions on what to digitize and make commercially available based on use–that which is most heavily used will be most profitable–then Professor Hazelton's numbers tell us something. If we look a little bit closer at what she excluded in her study and add it to the formula, it is easy to argue that we may have already reached Pareto's 20%.[13] That is, 80% of the research needs of the law library's patrons (students, faculty and lawyers) are met by 20% of the library's collections that are available digitally. It may even be arguable that given the nature of legal research, and the amount of time attorneys spend on cases, statutes and regulations, it might be more accurate to say that 90% of the use is on 10% of the materials.

This may be viewed as little more than educated guessing. There is little in the way of hard data. In addition to the Hazelton study there are a few articles and book chapters that shed some light on law library use, which I will describe later. A relative goldmine of information could be provided in the marketing studies of Lexis and Westlaw, if only they were willing to make these trade secrets available to researchers.

We do have a large body of library literature dealing with use in university and medical library settings, which offers us insights, but little that is directly applicable to our unique setting. What little information on legal publishing is available comes from Dan Dabney, Senior Director of Research and Development at West Group:

> I don't know that marketing has the kind of information you imagine that we have, but if we do it probably is considered highly confidential. I can contribute a little data on the concentration of use, however, and it shows that the use of legal databases is very top-heavy indeed. If you look at the distribution of queries run among our databases, you find that 91.8% of the queries are run in only 8.2% of the databases.
>
> But that may understate the concentration a little. Some documents are to be found in more than one database. For example, Supreme Court cases can be found in SCT, ALLFEDS, and ALLCASES, and all three of those databases are among the top dozen on the query frequency list. If you look at "finds" (a count that included KeyCite jumps and other hypertext links as well as explicit find commands typed by the user), you see that 95.16% of the finds go to the top 4.84% of the find databases.[14]

Think about that! While this is only one snapshot of use, it does confirm the general impression of use of legal materials by researchers. Unfortunately, I have been unable to collect more meaningful data from West, and nothing from Lexis. I can only assume they are afraid of revealing trade secrets.[15]

Exhibit 2, the core of Hazelton's article is entitled, "One Law Library's Attempt to Analyze the Size of the Law Library Collection and the Impact of Westlaw and Lexis."[16] Professor Hazelton operated from the following perspective: What part of her hard copy (paper) collection could be removed because it was available on Lexis and Westlaw? Would there be a significant space savings if the new law library relied on digital materials? She was dealing with an immediate future: Planning was underway, and ground was to be broken within two years. She developed formulas to try to anticipate future growth of the collections she measured, but wisely "punted" and made no effort to forecast new digital initiatives. Ultimately, her report was a defense of the space that had already been allocated to the new law library.

There is an implicit assumption in Hazelton's study that all legal materials are created equal–she made no attempt to empirically study use (a time consuming and near Herculean task). While her study was not meant to be a cost-benefit analysis, shouldn't collection use be considered in such an analysis? Isn't future use a critical element missing from her answer to the question posed by her faculty? Weren't they really asking for a cost-benefit analysis?

This is not to say that Professor Hazelton ignores use. She mentions collection use several times in her discussions.[17] Rather, without some sort of empirical analysis of use, her conclusions are based on incomplete data. Ultimately, while her conclusions ring true to librarians, they are merely informed judgments.

Her research also begs the question: What about the other 80% of our collections? Do we really need it? Given the cost of new space and the cost of acquiring all this seldom used material, is it time to rethink our law libraries' collection development policies? Does the use of our various collections justify the expense? I will now attempt to look more deeply into the available data to see if it tells us anything useful.

THE DIGITAL LIBRARY–IS IT VIABLE?

Let's look at this collection development issue from a digital perspective. Can we create a digital law library that will meet the majority of our patrons' legal research *needs*? I am not just talking about those legal materials available on Lexis and Westlaw, but also other major digital collections and the Internet. For purposes of this argument I will focus on academic law libraries, because I think this is the toughest case. Law firm, state and court libraries may not be fair measures, because, with rare exception, their primary focus is on practice-oriented rather than research-oriented materials.

First, let's look at primary legal materials. Virtually all of American case law is available electronically. In fact, Lexis and Westlaw make more case law available electronically than in hard copy. The current codes of all fifty states, the District of Columbia, the American territories and the federal government are all available electronically. Most of the state and the federal codes are annotated. State and federal session laws are available for the last ten years;[18] federal and state bills from 1991. The last twenty years of the Federal Register and the Code of Federal Regulations are also available digitally.[19] Many cities' municipal codes are also available electronically through state and city Web sites.

There is also an increasing array of valuable secondary sources. Congressional Universe contains the full text of legislative history beginning with 1986 and has the indexing and abstracting back to 1789. It also contains bill tracking and commentary on current legislation.

For case finding tools, the *American Law Reports* (ALR) and the West's digests are available electronically. *U.S. Supreme Court Records and Briefs* and oral arguments are available beginning in 1991. Docket information is also increasingly available–something that has always been extremely difficult and time consuming to search. While the electronic version of Shepard's does not duplicate the paper version, the electronic version that is available is infinitely preferable to the paper. KeyCite is only available electronically. The print version of Shepard's Citations is rapidly disappearing from our reading rooms.

Legal periodical literature is also widely available electronically–although at present a good rule of thumb is that the coverage only extends to the last ten years or so. This is changing with the introduction of Hein-On-Line, a digitization project that hopes to make available complete runs of all university law review and journals. Hein hopes to complete the project by 2010.[20]

Other types of legal commentary, such as encyclopedias, treatises, loose-leaf services, practice manuals, newsletters and continuing legal education materials have also made their electronic presence felt. American Jurisprudence 2d and portions of Corpus Juris Secundum[21] are available through Westlaw, as are Black's and Ballentine's Law Dictionaries. The publishers CCH, RIA and BNA dominate the loose-leaf publication business and most, if not all, of their products are available in electronic format. All of the AmJur practice materials,[22] PLI's, CEB's, and many other bar publications are now available online.[23] The families of Mealey's and Anderson newsletters are all available through Lexis and Westlaw. And, perhaps most importantly for many researchers, Matthew Bender treatises are now available in electronic format. Serious, exhaustive, scholarly commentary in the law is now available electronically and continues to grow at an almost exponential rate.

Access to government information also seems to be growing exponentially. The state and federal governments have made major commitments to developing their Web sites. And they are expanding beyond the delivery of primary legal authority. Significant commentary is now often included. The EEOC Web site, for example, has materials that clearly explain the law and how to file a discrimination complaint. The EPA Web site offers a stunning array of environmental sources. While there is good reason to worry about the government's ability to properly archive this material, these things have a way of working themselves out. After all, the Web is really less than ten years old, and it has only matured in the last five.

International and foreign law research is also evolving. Many international law scholars can now operate almost totally in a digital environment. The UN is a major producer of digitally available international legal materials, but many other organizations are entering the market. The National Center for Inter-American Trade, for example, offers text to Latin American materials and translation services through its Web site.[24]

All of this is actually less than 20% of the average law library hard copy collection and it may account for more than 90% of the use. I think it is fair to say that the legal materials available digitally exceed Pareto's Principle. Projects like the Hein Company's Hein-On-Line are proof of this proposition. The niche publishers are going after the smaller pieces of the legal publishing pie. While Vilfredo Pareto is no longer with us, I will take his name to identify what I consider a core collection of legal materials for an academic law library. This core, Pareto's Law Library, easily contains the 20% of the average academic law library that receives 80% of the use.

Pareto's Law Library Collection of 25,000 Volumes

COLLECTION	VOLUMES
West's *National Reporter System, L.Ed. and U.S. Reports*	12,000
USC, USCA, USCS, USCCAN and CFR	1,000
State codes	3,000
ALR	900
Digests (combination of state and federal)	2,000
Legal encyclopedias	400
Shepard's, CLI and ILP	400
Treatises and loose-leaf (BNA, CCH, RIA)	1,300
Law reviews and journals	4,000
TOTAL	25,000

Let's look at how I developed this core collection. Using Hazelton's numbers from her article, let me start with the volume count of West's

National Reporter System combined with the official U.S. and L. Ed. Reports: just under 12,000 volumes. All fifty state codes total 2,790 volumes–let's round up to 3,000. One copy of the USC, USCA, USCS, USCCAN and CFR combined works out to approximately 1,000 volumes.[25] Now we're at 16,000 volumes. Add 2,000 volumes of digests (using some locally developed formula of state and federal digests),[26] the ALR series with just under 900 volumes, and 2,100 volumes for treatises and loose-leafs (PLI's, Matthew Bender, West treatises, CCH, BNA, RIA, etc.),[27] encyclopedias (CJS and AmJur2d–under 400 vols.), the Current Law Index (LegalTrac), and Shepards (together, under 400 vols.). Now we're up to 21,000 volumes. Finally, we add 4,000 volumes for law reviews and legal periodicals. While the number is one of convenience–it gets me to a nice round number–it is also, I would argue, defensible. (I'll go into more detail about this later in the paper.) We now have an excellent core collection of 25,000 volumes–almost all of which is available online, predominantly through both Lexis and Westlaw.

Why only 4,000 volumes for law reviews and periodicals for this core collection when as much as 90% of our book budget is serial acquisition? Is it enough? Four thousand volumes equals the last ten years of 400 law reviews, journals and legal newspapers. The legal bibliometric literature seems to argue that this formula accounts for the heaviest use of periodical collections. We all know that all legal periodicals have a short shelf life. After 5 years on the shelf their use plummets and all of the major journals, and many of the minor, have been available digitally for the last 10-20 years through the online providers.[28] In my own library, we keep the ten most recent years of law periodicals in the main reading room and the older volumes in the basement. Students and faculty rarely seek out this collection. While this may not be a good thing, and it may merely reflect students' dependence on Lexis, Westlaw and LegalTrac, the fact is that the collection collects dust.

In addition, many schools are beginning to offer free full-text access to their law reviews and journals on the law schools' own Web sites. Isn't this yet another reason we may soon not need recent issues in paper? With projects like Hein-On-Line and interlibrary loan, we may no longer need to keep these old runs. Finally, and very sadly for most in the academy, most law reviews go unread, or at best skimmed on publication, forever forgotten except by the author, his or her parents, and a dozen or so scholars who share the same interests. While the death knell of the student edited law school law review may not yet have sounded, it is under serious attack.[29] How long, in their current form, can they last?

MEASURING COLLECTION USE

What about use? Isn't it a relatively easy argument to say that Pareto's law library, this core collection of 25,000 volumes in our libraries, easily receives 80%, perhaps even 90% of the use? Is it not easier still to argue that 90% of research *time* is spent on this core 6.25% of the collection? Where is the proof? This gets us to the problem of measuring use.

I think it fair to say that most law librarians and legal scholars would agree that the bulk of research is still the reading of cases and statutes. Dan Dabney's numbers, mentioned earlier in this article, seem to confirm this and are worth repeating: 91.8% of the queries entered in Westlaw are run in only 8.2% of the databases. What better proof than the introduction of another federal case reporter, the *Federal Appendix*. The use by attorneys of unpublished opinions made available through Lexis and Westlaw has resulted in the publishing of unpublished opinions! While law librarians immediately reacted to the announcement of the *Federal Appendix* with a combination of amusement and annoyance, many of us placed our orders because we knew that these cases are already out there and easily available. The creation of the *Federal Appendix* just further validated these cases as precedent.

While it is easier to argue that the Pareto Law Library meets the needs of the average lawyer or law student, it may not meet 80% of law school faculty needs. For some it may be sufficient, but for a growing number of law faculty, with their broad research needs, more than 20% of their research time may take place outside of this core literature of the law library. They still are the exception that proves the rule. This is not the place to discuss the rise of cross-disciplinary research, but it is arguable that this rise may begin to work against the efficacy of the Pareto Law Library. Still, these observations are experiential and anecdotal, at best.

We don't have much in the way of data. A notable exception is the work of Simon Canick, published elsewhere in this volume. Simon's examination of the footnotes of seven recent law review articles states that 77% of all cited resources were available in full-text electronic form! Over half of the citations (53.3%) were to cases.[30] A larger study, one that included interdisciplinary and subject specific law-related articles would provide further insights.

Measuring use of legal materials in libraries has been primitive at best. Law libraries routinely track circulation and reference statistics;

interlibrary loans; Lexis and Westlaw use; and book and serial orders–all of which tell us something of use, but they are little more than snapshots. Are there other ways to effectively capture use statistics? Printing vs. photocopying statistics? Count books that need to be reshelved? Randomly pick researchers and track them in the library to develop user profiles? Patron interviews? Create survey instruments and poll users? The sad truth is any effective measure would be incredibly time consuming and expensive.

Law librarians Gary Bravy and Celeste Feather have come closest to providing an empirical glimpse of law library use in their article, "The Impact of Electronic Access on Basic Library Services: One Academic Law Library's Experience." Bravy and Feather studied photocopying, circulation and reshelving statistics over a ten year period at the Georgetown University Law Library. From 1989-90 to 1998-99 photocopying decreased 44%, student checkout transactions decreased 19%, and the number of books reshelved decreased 53%.[31] They make it clear that "there is no way to directly link the circulation, shelving and vending photocopying usage declines to electronic resources. Nevertheless, there are some strong indicators that the increased availability of electronic resources has been at least one of the factors contributing to these declines."[32] The results surprise no one and validate widely held law librarians' perceptions.

As academic law librarians, we anticipate use through examining the research interests of our faculty and the courses our schools offer or there is a clearly defined institutional interest by subject: intellectual property or environmental law; philosophy: law and economics, interdisciplinary or law and society; or regional or practice focuses. These help us anticipate use, but do little to gauge actual use. Geography and demographics may also offer insights. For example, at the University of Arizona, water, immigration, mining, indigenous peoples, elder and community property law-related materials are much more in demand and more heavily used than labor, government contract or admiralty law-related materials. Interestingly, the growing emphasis on interdisciplinary and cross-disciplinary research throughout the country is taking more of our faculty out of the law library and into the university's other libraries. Law libraries have traditionally never collected the esoteric non-legal materials that law faculty now increasingly look for, and use of our law collections by at least some law faculty appears to be decreasing. Arguably, this decline is being countered by an increase in use by faculty from across campus.

This is no small matter. Most academic law libraries increasingly find themselves building collections based on the curriculum and faculty interest. It is not the students who push the limits of our collections, but the faculty. If law faculties have less need of our law collections, will the rise of use by university faculties be enough to save us? It will be interesting to monitor the inter/multi/cross disciplinary movement; it may have some significant implications for library growth.

Perhaps most dangerous, if we move to a digital law library, we take the art and science of collection development out of the hands of librarians who understand the specific needs of their institutions and into the hands of vendors. They are motivated by profit rather than the advancement of human knowledge. To quote Star Trek's Dr. Spock, they seek to serve "the needs of the many over the needs of the few."[33] Or, to quote the *Pareto Principle*: the vital few and the trivial many.[34] The needs of research law libraries run the risk of being viewed as trivial by those whose interests are driven exclusively by profit. The money is to be made at the law firm level, not in academic law libraries. Undoubtedly, new vendors and services will rise to meet the needs of research law libraries, but at what cost?

I will never forget a comment by Professor Dick Danner, early in my career at the Duke Law Library, that collection development was the only pure intellectual work in the law library. While he may have been using hyperbole to impress upon me the importance of my collection development responsibilities, the underlying truth was, and is, that collection development is a core, critical task for law librarians as mediators of information. As mentioned previously, we build for our faculty and students–one size does not fit all!

COMPARING THE COSTS OF DIGITAL AND PAPER COLLECTIONS

A look at the *ABA Comprehensive Law Library Statistical Tables* (1999-2000) provides some interesting insights to the costs of academic law library collections. The average law library budget represents approximately 15%-17% of law school budgets.[35] There is a clear economy of scale based on student enrollment for law school library budgets. There are 22 ABA accredited law schools with more than 1,000 FTE J.D. students. The mean percentage of those law schools' budgets spent on the library is 8.89%, with a median of 8.2%. The range goes from

5.6%-13.3%. Compare that with the 30 ABA accredited law schools with 400-500 FTE J.D. students. The mean percentage of these law schools' budgets spent on the library is 18.34%, with a median of 16.15%. The range within the 30 schools is from 10.0%-35.8%.[36]

Also, as the following chart illustrates, as collection size goes up, the cost per student goes down:

Library Materials Spent Per FTE Student

Volumes/No. of Libraries Reporting	Mean	Median
100,000-200,000 vols. (12)	$1,847	$1,771
200,000-300,000 vols. (45)	$1,680	$1,587
300,000-400,000 vols. (52)	$1,536	$1,364
400,000 or more vols. (74)	$1,493	$1,400
All reporting (183)	$1,575	$1,430

When one considers the cost of Lexis and Westlaw, some interesting numbers emerge. While it is arguable that either system meets most (80%) of our research needs, even if we subscribe to both services, it only costs us $100-$110 per FTE student. That's less than 10% of our overall acquisition budget for both Lexis and Westlaw and only 5% if you chose one of the services. In some schools it may be fair to say that a much higher percentage of use (90-95%?) could be accommodated by 5% of the acquisition budget. No wonder schools like the Massachusetts School of Law challenge ABA accreditation standards.[37] It is a fair question to ask: Do we really need all this stuff to provide a quality legal education? Granted if everyone went digital, the cost of these digital collections would undoubtedly rise, but would it ever equal the current level of material budgets? And what happens when we factor in the cost of square footage requirements to house these collections?

Seventy-four of the 183 accredited schools reporting to the ABA have volume counts in excess of 400,000.[38] So, Pareto's law library of 25,000 volumes is less than 6.25% of 40% of all academic law library collections, *and less than 10% of every academic law library in the country!* While most, if not all of these libraries have multiple copies of many of the titles in Pareto's Law Library, the digital library in effect provides us with as many "copies" as we will ever need at a price of $100-$110 per FTE law student. More copies, less space, lower cost–what's not to love?

The savings would vary from institution to institution, but they would all be varying degrees of *enormous!*

Digital law libraries also offer some significant staff savings. Periodicals do not need to be shelved or bound. Several people can use the same item at once, an enormously important factor for schools with large first year research and writing and moot court courses. No fighting for limited resources, no hidden or incorrectly shelved volumes. Loose-leaf services need no filing. Printing from electronic sources is quicker than photocopying from books. Finally, there is the efficiency and convenience of the desktop, no traveling to the library, and 24/7 access.

Still, digital collections have their own hidden costs and it is important not to ignore or make light of them. Dean Montgomery of the Drexel University's W.W. Hagerty Library has done a comparison of the costs of digital vs. paper collections at her library. As part of the library's strategic plan, the Dean and library staff decided to go as nearly digital as possible. This meant that in 2001, the library subscribed to 300 print-only journals and over 6,000 electronic ones. She found that there were significant costs associated with the maintenance of a digital collection;[39] and while there were also significant cost savings in technical services, circulation and document delivery, these costs were offset by the increase of infrastructure (network, hardware, software, printing, maintenance, etc.) and administrative costs (contract negotiation, change management, budgeting, oversight, etc.). Reference questions decreased while the need for training increased. A higher, better trained, level of staff involvement was required. Overall, the change at Drexel was a positive one. It was anticipated that costs would go down as expertise is gained and patrons and staff become more comfortable with the digital collection. Use of the library's collections increased, which added to the cost benefit.[40]

Many of the problems faced by Drexel are avoided in law libraries because of our reliance on flat pricing contracts with the two major vendors. Our relationship with Lexis and Westlaw is nothing, if not economically efficient: one contract for thousands of databases, on site training staff and excellent telephone technical support. (At least in relation to other vendors. Think about it, a human being answers the phone, they almost always know the answer, and will quickly refer you or get back to you if they do not have an immediate answer!) They provide hardware, printers and sometimes computers, paper and ink supplies for the printers, and service contracts for the printers should they break down. Where else in this service economy do we get offers of more training and help desk assistance than we need or want? Even if they do have ulterior motives, it is of enormous benefit to our library's mission.

While we all agree that both Lexis and Westlaw give us much we will never need, the sheer enormity of these databases is mind-boggling. In advertising claims, Lexis-Nexis states that they provide access to over 2.8 billion documents and 30,700 databases. Lexis and Westlaw's database directories are approaching the size of the Manhattan phone book. And then there are the Internet's commercial and free Web sites. Could anyone have predicted the explosion of governmental and other free Web sites on the Internet? I believe Professor Bob Berring is right: form does mold substance. Our students' and faculty's research decisions are based upon what is easily available in Lexis, Westlaw and the Internet.[41]

That is not to say that our reliance on two major vendors is without its concerns. The recent decision of BNA to withdraw from the Lexis and Westlaw databases and only allow access through its own Web site is a great example of a sudden hidden cost of relying on only the two major vendors. Should there be any significant move to reliance on online sources rather than paper, the costs of the online services would no doubt skyrocket. Any savings are likely to be short-lived as vendors look to recover losses caused by declining sales in paper products through their online services.

The BNA example also highlights another dilemma. All law school libraries are now looking at a significant cost increase for an electronic service that will still not be available to any of our patrons other than law students and law faculty. We are effectively limiting our missions in a way we have not in the past. The uncertainty of the legal publishing landscape cannot be overemphasized. As Professor Hazelton noted in her article, there is incredible uncertainty if we rely on purely digital sources–and every new electronic service seeks to limit those who can use it. A reliance on digital resources may isolate us from the rest of our universities, our alumni, the local bar and all of the others we allow to use our collections.

THE HYBRID LIBRARY–HOW LONG?

Much of the library literature on the future of digital libraries does not involve law libraries; rather, the focus has been on public and academic libraries. Law libraries are a unique subset of special libraries. In the academic environment, law libraries are almost always separate from the university library system, created to serve the law school's teaching and scholarly missions.

While academic law libraries tend to have a broader mission than law firm libraries, law firm libraries are our canary in the mine. Many of the large law firms are dismantling their hard copy libraries and moving to a totally digital environment. Every week on the law-lib listserv comes offers of law libraries available for the cost of shipping. No longer do firm libraries try and create collections equal to academic collections. Do academic libraries need to create collections that mirror those that students will find in law firms?

We often hear from attorneys that they want their law students well grounded in "paper research."[42] When you talk to them, you realize what they are really saying is that new attorneys fail to properly analyze the cases they find online. By failing to read carefully that which they have found, the young attorney fails to reenter the digital research universe to search for more relevant case and statutory law. Their failure is not their reliance on digital legal research, but rather a failure to carefully read and analyze that which they have found–the complaint of seasoned attorneys since the beginnings of the profession.[43]

Even those lawyers who rely predominantly on online legal research still express a preference for particular paper sources, particularly statutes and secondary sources. But how long will this last? Convenience and efficiency have always affected legal research decisions. Should an attorney come to the law library to use the hard copy annotated code or can she rely on a cheaper online version from a state Web site? Is it worth the time spent driving, finding parking for a trip to the local law library to read a paper secondary source (is it on the shelf, will I have to photocopy a lot?), or would the time be better spent grappling with the available case law? All research decisions ultimately involve a cost-benefit analysis, and the online approach is increasingly proving to be the better choice in the final analysis. As online efficiencies increase, even if there is a small loss in effectiveness, lawyers will choose the online route; particularly young attorneys who find online legal research more in their comfort zone.

Many would say that law libraries are fundamentally different from other types of libraries. And in many ways they are. With the possible exception of medical libraries, it is hard to imagine a type of library that offers more of its core collections in digital format than the law library. It is not just the commercial publishers who have pushed us into this direction. The federal government and its Government Printing Office (GPO) has made a serious, almost total, commitment to digital information. Currency of information is also vital, a serious shortcoming of the print medium. If the best printing processes delay the transmittal of digital information by weeks, how can they hope to compete with the digital?

Why is it then, that all of the building to date has been of hybrid law libraries–part digital, part paper, with the emphasis on paper? No one has taken the bold step of going "as nearly digital as possible." Even new law schools like Ave Maria in Michigan and St. Thomas in Minneapolis, while necessarily focusing on digital collections more than most law schools, still look much like their ancient counterparts. Perhaps this is because it is viewed as risky to hook oneself to an uncertain future. They avoid potential accreditation risks. Ownership of a collection seems more permanent than providing access–however reliable that access point may be. As librarians, the shift from ownership to access is unsettling; there is a loss of control of collections in a way previously unknown to librarians. If we build a great paper collection and fiscal calamity strikes, the collection still retains *some* value–it is an asset. The day the law library cancels a digital subscription, the collection vanishes without a trace; there is nothing to show for years of spending. Or as previously mentioned in the BNA example, costs suddenly and unexpectedly, skyrocket. One can only wonder what will happen if many of the publishers who provide text to Lexis and Westlaw decide to unbundle their services from these two major legal database providers.

As we add databases, search access also becomes an issue. While the future is bright, at present most of these digital collections are not cataloged. The online catalog is a wonderful current awareness device in the hands of a moderately sophisticated researcher. The database choices currently available, at least in a research university, are mind-boggling. Yet, in spite of aggressive public relations efforts to make them aware of the availability of these databases, the lack of cataloging often leaves many of our most proficient researchers unaware of this vast array of databases at their disposal. We need to do a better job promoting these resources, if not through cataloging, then through locally created research guides and pathfinders.

The electronic publishers continue to look to limit access. Our contracts only provide for Lexis and Westlaw access to law students and law faculty. CCH, BNA and Loislaw, all demand similar limitations. Electronic databases have the effect of limiting interaction with other members of the academy and the general public. Can we afford this–both politically and ethically? For public institutions this may result in a lack of public support, for private institutions a drop in donations. "What have you done for me lately?" may be the question we are increasingly forced to answer.

We also need to ask ourselves a fundamental question: Do great law schools need great law libraries? The answer is not as certain as it once was.[44] Will we become more like business school's libraries with small working collections of current materials and only a small collection of classics? Will law schools with great university libraries gain in prominence over schools with lesser university libraries?

If one looks at the budgets of the top twenty-five law school libraries, we see that budgets vary widely. While the "better" schools tend to have larger budgets, some of the best have what can only be considered modest budgets. There is no strong link between law library budget and law school ranking. Given the relatively small part library resources play in the *U.S. News and World Reports* law school rankings,[45] a rational decision can be made to slash a library's budget to add faculty. Or, given the emphasis at many schools on improving rankings, why not hire every grad without a job as a research assistant just before the six-month reporting deadline for *U.S. News and World Reports*? Rumors are, it's been done!

Our greatest asset and hope may be our faculty–their genetic makeup is such that they tend to love libraries. And from these faculties come our deans, university provosts and presidents. But deans, university provosts and presidents are also increasingly concerned with the bottom line; at some point cutting library budgets in favor of more faculty positions, a bigger development office or creating competitive salaries will be considered. Our survival is not as certain as it once was.

OK, BUT WE OWN THEM, WHAT DO WE DO WITH ALL THESE BOOKS?

There seems to be a combination of four choices: (1) install compact shelving; (2) store off-site; (3) toss them; or, (4) redesign stacks and collection placement in our libraries. Let's look at all four, starting from what I believe is the easiest to that which is the most interesting, realizing that the best solution will probably be a combination of two or more of these approaches.

First, compact shelving. The advantages are obvious: we increase useable square footage in existing space; we maintain necessary adjacencies (and often improve them); we provide immediate access to the collection and easy ability for patrons to browse the collection; compact shelving has matured into a reliable technology; and, it keeps our volume counts up. The disadvantages: it is expensive; your library's floors must be constructed to withstand the weight (which few are); and, the development office will complain that it does not make for a good naming opportunity; it is most definitely not sexy and it can be downright ugly.

A former dean of mine could not resist making one bad compact shelving joke after another. He viewed compact shelving as the ultimate in librarian weirdness. I think at its core, his comments reflect the fact that compact shelving is ugly, uninspiring, and creates a feeling of working in a warehouse. It does not invite the reader to browse, reflect, freely explore–it is anti-scholar and anti-democratic. The aesthetic of open stacks are very real. Most stacks have aisles of 36 inches. In my library the aisles are 42 inches. That extra six inches makes the stacks much more appealing and allows for more light. They are less claustrophobic. They encourage the reader to pause and shelf read.

Still, much of our collection use would probably be only marginally affected if they were placed in compact shelving. Reporters, older law review and journal runs, government documents, superceded materials, and state materials like reporters and session laws (other than the jurisdiction in which the school is located) are obvious candidates. Treatises may be best housed in stacks that can be easily browsed, but older editions can easily be placed in compact shelving.

Now let's consider the second option: off-site storage. Here it gets a little trickier. It is the concern voiced by Roger Jacobs in his email, in which he quoted Llewellyn's *threat of the available*. Simply stated, will we face the paradigm of out of sight, out of mind? While a 24 or 48 hour turn around for retrieval may be acceptable to some, is it good service? Once we start down the road of providing less, rather than more, we run the risk of becoming marginalized. Our strength has always come from anticipating research needs, not making scholarship more difficult. Terry Martin's Harvard experience may be a bit of an anomaly. In fact, everything about Harvard is probably different. It is the biggest law library in the country, has the largest staff, and the best known. Off-site storage at Harvard just makes the Harvard stacks look more like other not so large academic research collections–it separates the wheat from the chaff.

There is little doubt that the availability of electronic resources has caused use of certain areas of our collection to plummet. In the past, many law libraries would keep the unbound issues of law reviews in a reserve collection. This is now rarely the case. Many libraries keep their older journals and law reviews in compact shelving or off-site storage–with little or no apparent inconvenience to the user. They seem like good candidates for off-site storage, especially those that are available online. Duplicate sets of reporters can also go with little difficulty.

Either of the previous solutions offers great advantages given the costs of new construction and the difficulty in finding the space for new construction on most campuses. For whatever the reason, for many schools new construction is not an option and renovation may be problematic. Less than ideal options may be the only real solution. As university libraries add storage space there is often the possibility of piggybacking onto the larger project.

What about the third option, tossing them? For all the reasons mentioned earlier in this article, this is a risky business. Even the most digitally focused law librarian would want to take a wait and see approach. While the law firms may choose to dump their paper collections, there has been no indication that any academic law library is willing to do so on a major scale. Granted some law schools have removed their print Shepards collections for the electronic version or KeyCite, and many have dumped or closed their state collections; but most have tended to stay the course. Do we look to the firms to foretell our future? Law schools are, after all, in the business of preparing students for practice. The pressure to digitize may come from the firms. If we look at what the last ten years have brought us, it is impossible to correctly predict what the next ten will bring. One can't help but believe the forecasters are correct when they talk about society becoming or "being digital."[46]

Yet it is tempting–toss the books; rely on digital collections and electronic reference–no need for students to come to the library. We free up more room for classrooms, a cafeteria, maybe a gym! My office will consist of a Jacuzzi and waterproof laptop! Most library literature now talks within the context of library services rather than collections and physical space. The library may not be viewed as a separate physical space, but it is still viewed as a separate function. The academic law library is still seen as an independent, ascertainable entity. In the academy its uniqueness is recognized through reporting structure–in the vast majority of cases, the law library is under the control of the dean of the law school, not the university library system. So change would not, in most cases, require university approval; just a dean willing to face a potential ABA accreditation challenge. What if a law school with a reputation that ranked it in the top two tiers of American law schools made such a decision; does anyone really believe they would lose their accreditation?

How about the fourth option, redesign of new or existing buildings? In fact, much of this has been going on for years. Reserve collection space is constantly reinvented. The reference desk continues to change. Compact shelving is used in many libraries. Group study space has expanded and the great reading rooms have shrunken or disappeared. Study carrels have grown larger. Computer labs have been created and expanded. IT departments grow within our libraries and without.

But it may be time for more radical redesign. We have yet to fully grasp the changes brought about by technology, hence the problem. Radical redesign may look foolish in a few years. The example of the bunker-like computing room at the University of Iowa Law Library comes to mind. They built a secure environment for a main frame that was never meant to be. The architects guessed wrong on the rise of the personal computer. Or did they? As our servers grow in size and number, perhaps a separate climate controlled, secure server room is needed in the modern law school!

Is there some way to fundamentally reexamine library space? How has the emerging digital environment changed what the architects call adjacencies? We no longer think of libraries as just a space; can we *unbundle* the academic law library in the law school? A few schools have done this in a modified fashion: faculty offices in the law library or the IT department. The faculty are our heaviest users; shouldn't they be closer to the intellectual action? While the jury is still out on the question, most law library directors, and perhaps law school deans, believe that the law library should run IT. As IT and AV departments merge, where should their place be? By this I mean physical, rather than intellectual or organizational. What about other groups? Law reviews? Student organizations? Career services? Should we think of creating *the new adjacencies*?

Libraries have always had single entrances to cut down on theft and ensure that books were properly checked out. Automated self-check out systems resolve the need for a central place to check out materials from the library and you can't steal digital collections. Why not build the law library in the core of the law school building with several library entrances and exits.

Others have talked and written about using retail design in the creation of law libraries–law library as Barnes & Noble or Borders.[47] Why not have a coffee shop, or better yet, a cafeteria section of the law library? 24-7 is the mantra of the day–should we, could we?[48]

We need to consider noise in new design. Digital resources need to be explained and our training function continues to expand. We need areas where we can talk and areas where quiet reigns–and something in between. Group study rooms are one answer. Smaller, and more reading rooms are another. Computers need to be fed and housed. Not only are they an ongoing expense, but also in this era of cheaper, faster computers with less support, the library has become the primary means of troubleshooting for students and faculty. There are lines of students waiting to talk to the electronic services librarian and his assistant to help them with hardware or software problems with their computers–but that the lines were that long at the reference desk!

I will conclude here; I hope to further explore the topic of law library redesign in a future article. As my own institution begins the process of planning for a new library and information commons, I may get the chance to develop and realize some of these new adjacencies.

CONCLUSION–IN WHICH NOTHING IS CONCLUDED

The time is not yet ripe for a move from paper to digital resources–but the paradigm is most definitely shifting. While the current interpretation of ABA standards[49] may provide reason to avoid a totally digital environment, one wonders for how long this interpretation can survive. The digital legal information environment has significantly changed since August of 1996; would the current *ABA Interpretation 606-3* survive a legal challenge?

For those schools that do not serve larger university or alumni communities, and hence do not have a responsibility to provide legal materials outside the law school community, the time for change to a more (totally?) digital law collection may be at hand. As mentioned earlier in this article, the cost savings of relying on Lexis, Westlaw and the other major electronic legal resources would be enormous. For institutions with public missions, at present the political costs of limiting access to the secondary and peripheral communities may be too expensive, but changing economic conditions may necessitate the need to reconsider the amount of support law libraries can give to their secondary clienteles.

Any cost benefit analysis will need to consider not only the library's mission, but also the space needed and collection use to determine what is best for the institution. As collection space grows tighter in each institution, the analysis must also include an accurate assessment of the current legal publishing environment. For example, since Professor Hazelton's article there has been an explosion of secondary sources available electronically. There is no reason to believe this will not continue, although at what cost? Filling library space with books will become increasingly viewed as inefficient. Other alternatives will be sought.

Will we fall prey to the currently popular business mantra of just-in-time delivery of products? It may cause us to rethink our collection development decisions. Book providers like Amazon.com provide quick and easy delivery of many, if not most, legal titles. Do we continue to build for assumed demand, or rely on actual demand? Anticipating demand is clearly less economically efficient that reacting to demand; we all know we have books on our shelves that no one has read. Yet what about the threat of the easily available? We've all seen the results of students who limit their research to materials available on the Internet: a remarkable, skewed mix of valuable information and gaping holes of missing information you can ride a semi-truck through. Yet the fact remains that an enormous amount of previously hard to find information is now available in seconds. The time needed to collect the information necessary to write an article or brief has collapsed into the almost meaningless; when coupled with electronic publishing, the result has been scholarship on demand. It is changing the academy in ways we cannot even begin to comprehend.

We need to reinvent our future–and we will need help. Patterns of use have radically changed in the last few years; the pressure to innovate is enormous. Whether or not our future is exclusively digital, there can be little doubt that there has been a fundamental shift in the use, organization and content of academic law libraries. If we fail to change, we will become little more than reminders of a time long past. "The ivory towers, which have always looked a little like gothic palaces, seem set to become gothic ruins."[50] And this view is not limited to the academic setting. The U.S. Capital architect would like to convert the U.S. Supreme Court Library into a museum! Why is that? Clearly in his view, the law library has become peripheral to the function of the court. Fortunately, the Court itself seems to know better.

We need to do a better job in determining use patterns in our libraries; identify those uses that may be transitory, and those uses that will remain relatively unchanged. We need to identify, in the words of the business gurus, our core competencies. Why are we needed? What do we do well? How are we different, or better than Amazon.com and Internet search engines? Viscerally, we know the answers, but do our communities? We are not just a delivery mechanism for information, be it digital or paper. It's not that the faculty who asked Professor Hazelton, "Why do you need all those books?" were asking the wrong question; rather, they should have first asked, how do I use the library, how do my colleagues, my students? How does a law library work, what should our law school library contain?

And ultimately, we will need to reexamine our societal mission. If we do not collect the less heavily used materials, Pareto's 80%, if we do not preserve our cultural heritage, who will? We run the risk of relying on others until there are no others to rely upon. If every library were to rely on interlibrary loan to supplement its own collections, the system collapses. Is the Internet the solution? In copyright law we speak of fixed media at present, there seems to be no media less fixed than the Internet.

This discussion needs to be held in our law schools, with university administration, at professional programs like the ABA Bricks & Bytes conference and the AALL and AALS annual meetings, with architects, alumni and donors. Is the law library still the heart of the law school, or is it the circulatory system? Is it a laboratory, information commons or educational technology center? How has the academic mission of our schools changed and what is the effect of that change on our libraries?

Early in this paper I promised that I would not make any predictions. I lied; I will make one safe prediction. I'm betting on a far from paperless digital future. There is a yet to be developed killer application out there that will render Professor Hazelton's faculty's question moot. I wish I knew what that next "killer app" was: the perfect e-book, electronic paper, information receiving implants; but it will happen, and sooner than one might think. We are currently dealing with the digital incunabula. If nothing else, Gutenberg taught us that the consequences of revolutionary technology cannot be accurately understood when in the midst of revolution. Still, we know the direction we are headed; or to put it in a late 20th century perspective: "You don't need a weatherman to know which way the wind blows."

NOTES

1. Penny A. Hazelton, *How Much of Your Print Collection is Really on WESTLAW or LEXIS-NEXIS?* 18 LRSQ 3 (no. 1, 1999).

2. Karl Llewellyn, *Legal Tradition and Social Science Method–A Realist's Critique*, in *Jurisprudence: Realism in Theory and Practice* 82 (1962). He continues, "The simple available thing in law consists in the rules laid down on the statute books by the legislature, or laid down authoritatively by the supreme court of any given jurisdiction. The statute book is in print. The reports of the Supreme Court are in print. Both are collected and arranged in libraries. And the easiest thing to extract from either or both is

the set of rules that they purport to contain. What wonder, then, that these have been the subject matter of our study? What wonder, either, that once the study is begun we come to think of them as occupying the whole field? At the same time, what an absurdity."

3. Copy with author.

4. For another interesting article by Terry, see Harry S. Martin, III, *Can You Really Store a Library in Cyberspace? Renovating Langdell Hall & Other Tales*, 3 Australian Law Librarian 57 (April/June 1995).

5. Granted, some may consider this damning by faint praise! The email passes my "I wish I had written that" test. This may also account for my willingness to label the email brilliant.

6. I will define these terms later in this article.

7. The Web has been particularly helpful in this search. Information and Library School Web sites have dozens of their faculty's articles available in full text. For those of you like me, who have been out of school for twenty years or so, it is a real eye opener; we were educated in very different places.

8. George Grossman, *Housing Books*, 79 L. Lib. J. 521 (1987). A must read for anyone starting a building project. Stephen G. Margeton, *Introduction to Academic Library Design: A Features Approach* (Fred B. Rothman, 2000).

9. See, e.g., Nicholas P. Terry, *Bricks Plus Bytes: How "Click and Brick" Will Define Legal Education Space*, 46 Vill. L. Rev. 95 (2001); John Mayer, *Alternative Futures: The Future of Legal Education*, 1 J. L. School Computing; Steve Sheppard, *The Role of the Professor in the High-Tech Law School*, 1 J. L. Sch. Computing; and, James L. Hoover, *A Vision of Law Schools of the Future*, 1 J. L. Sch. Computing *<http://www.cali.org/jlsc/>*.

10. J.M. Juran, *The Non-Pareto Principle: Mea Culpa*, *<http://www.juran.com/research/articles/SP7518.html>* (viewed 9/21/01).

11. Diodato, Virgil. *The Dictionary of Bibliometrics.* (The Haworth Press, Inc. 1994).

12. This is not the place for a lengthy discussion of bibliometrics or cybermetrics. Both disciplines have a growing literature, much of it available on the Internet. A simple Web search of either term will deliver several interesting examples. Bibliometrics is also beginning to receive the attention of legal scholars. The work of Fred Shapiro of the Yale Law Library and Brian Leiter at University of Texas School of Law are particularly intriguing. See, e.g., Brian Leiter, *New Educational Quality Rankings of U.S. Law Schools for 2000-2002*, *<http://www.texas.edu/law/faculty/bleiter/LGOURMET.HTM>*.

13. For a detailed look at what was excluded in the University of Washington study see Hazelton, id. at 6. (Official state reports, state digests, state administrative codes, state citators, English Reports, USCCAN, regional, federal and topical citators, looseleaf services, treatises, legal newspapers and newsletters, etc.)

14. Email to author from Dan Dabney, October 11, 2001.

15. Interestingly, in a recent visit, a Lexis representative announced that Lexis now has added core concepts (headnotes) to one million Lexis cases. These one million cases represent the 20% of cases in Lexis that are retrieved in 80% of Lexis searches.

16. Hazelton, at 7.

17. For example, "We are a research Law Library. We serve the Law School as well as the rest of the UW, the legal profession and the public. Even if all library patrons had access to Westlaw and Lexis-Nexis, we would need to OWN most primary and secondary sources that are online. A research library must support the work of scholars, not

practitioners. We can guarantee access to important legal literature if we can control or own it." Id. at 12.

Or another, "If the collection were to shrink as a result of technology and use, the Law Library space is planned to be very flexible. More library user spaces could be created or the space could be used for other law school purposes, such as classrooms, offices, institutes and centers, clinics, administration, and more." Id. at 13.

18. *Congressional Universe* has federal public laws since 1988; Westlaw since 1973.

19. *Congressional Universe* has the *CFR* from 1981 and the *Federal Register* from 1980; Westlaw has the *CFR* from 1984 and the *Federal Register* from 1980.

20. Lexis has over 550 law reviews and journals, Westlaw over 600. While there is very significant overlap, both systems have periodicals not available on the other database. Coverage varies, but generally, they are only comprehensive beginning in the mid-1990s.

21. Interestingly, while West owns *C.J.S.* and *Am. Jur. 2d*, it has not chosen to make all of *C.J.S.* available electronically. One wonders what this means about the long-term viability of the product.

22. *AmJur Proof of Facts, Pleading and Practice Forms*, etc.

23. For example, Arizona State Bar publications are available exclusively in electronic format through Loislaw.

24. *<http://www.natlaw.com/>*

25. *USC* = 50 vols.; *USCA* = 250 vols.; *USCS* = 150 vols.; *CFR* = 300 vols.; *USCCAN* = 200 vols.

26. The Decennial digest system is approximately 700 vols.; the Federal Digest is approximately 500 vols.; the five regional digests are approximately 900 vols.; and the individual state digests are anywhere from 75-150 vols.

27. There has been an explosion in the number of treatises available online since Hazelton completed her study. Most Matthew Bender publications are now available online, either through Lexis, Bender's own Web site or the Authority CD-ROMs.

28. Lexis has over 550 law reviews and journals, Westlaw over 600. While there is very significant overlap, both systems have periodicals not available on the other database. Coverage varies, but generally, they are only comprehensive beginning in the mid-1990s.

29. Bernard Hibbitts, Last Writes? Reassessing the Law Review in the Age of Cyberspace, 71 N.Y.U. L. Rev. 615 (1996).

30. Simon Canick, *Availability of Works Cited in Recent Law Review Articles on Lexis-Nexis, Westlaw, the Internet and Other Databases*, 6 Spectrum 13 (October, 2001) (an earlier abbreviated version).

31. Gary J. Bravy and K. Celeste Feather, *The Impact of Electronic Access on Basic Library Services: One Academic Library's Experience*, 93 L. Lib. J. 261, 264-5 (2001).

32. Id. at 266.

33. *Star Trek: The Wrath of Khan* (Paramount 1982) (motion picture).

34. Or, non-Pareto Principle, Juran, at 1.

35. For an interesting, but somewhat dated look at law library budgets as a percentage of law school budgets, see, Jane L. Hammond, *Library Costs as a Percentage of Law School Budgets*, 80 L. Lib. J. 439 (1988).

36. Based on numbers from the *1999-2000 ABA Library Statistics* (April 9, 2001).

37. *Standards for Approval of Law Schools (ABA, 2001). Interpretation 606-3:* At present, no single publishing medium (electronic, print, microform, or audio-visual)

provides sufficient access to the breadth and depth of recorded knowledge and information needed to bring a law school into compliance with Standard 606. Consequently, a collection that consists of a single format may violate Standard 606. (August 1995; August 1996). *<http://www.abanet.org/legaled/standards/standards.html>*.

Those schools who seek to become members of The Association of American Law Schools (AALS) will also need to adhere to a less specific, but seemly more strict, standard: *AALS Bylaws, Section 6-10. Library.*

a. A member school shall maintain a library adequate to support and encourage the instruction and research of its faculty and students. A law library of a member school shall possess or *have ready access to a physical collection* [emphasis mine] and other information resources that substantially:

i. Meet the research needs of its students, satisfy the demands of its curricular offerings, particularly in those respects in which student research is expected, and allows for the training of its students in the use of various research methodologies;
ii. Support the individual research interests of its faculty members;
iii. Serve any special research and educational objectives expressed by the school or implicit in its chosen role in legal education.

<http://www.aals.org/bylaws.html>.

38. Based on *1999-2000 ABA Library Statistics* (April 9, 2001).

39. Carol Hansen Montgomery, *Measuring the Impact of an Electronic Journal Collection on Library Costs*, 6 D-Lib Mag. at 1 (October 2000). *<http://dbib/october00/montgomery/10montgomery/html>*.

40. I have found two electronic journals to be particularly helpful in monitoring the digital library literature: Digital Libraries, at *<http://www.dlib.org>*; and, Journal of Digital Libraries at *<http://jodi.ecs.soton.ac.uk>*.

41. Robert Berring, *Legal Research and Legal Concepts: When Form Molds Substance*, 75 Cal. L. Rev. 15 (1987).

42. For an interesting story see, Bob Berring, *Thinkable Thoughts*, 3:3 Law Librarians in the New Millenium 4 (2001).

43. For a fascinating article on the potential effect of technology on the study and practice of law see, Molly Warner Lien, *Technocentrism and the Soul of the Common Law Lawyer*, 48 Am. U. L. Rev. 85 (1998).

44. But see, Daniel Golden, *Opening Arguments: As Law School Begins, It's Columbia vs. NYU: Rival Deans Court Students, Faculty: and Controversy; Whose Library is Bigger?* Wall Street Journal, Aug. 28, 2001.

45. *Best Graduate School 2002, Law Rankings Methodology*, U.S. News & World Reports, *<http://www.usnews.com/usnews/edu/beyond/gradrank/gblawmet.htm>*.

46. Nicholas Negroponte, *Being Digital* (Knopf, 1995).

47. Tom Steele, *Duke Reprise: Retail Store Design and Law School Planning*, in *ABA Conference on Bricks, Bytes and Constant Renovation*, March 12, 2000.

48. It's been done. Electronic identification cards allow for easy 24/7 access and at least one law library has its own coffee bar.

49. See footnote 36.

50. John Seely Brown and Paul Duguid, *The Social Life of Information* 211 (Harvard Business School Press, 2000).

Re-Engineering the Law Library Resources Today for Tomorrow's Users: A Response to "How Much of Your Print Collection Is Really on WESTLAW or LEXIS-NEXIS?"

Gordon Russell

SUMMARY. The emergence of rich and diverse digital resources requires re-visualization of traditional law library space design and usage patterns. The structure and form of extant libraries–architectural edifices that house our beloved information artifacts–serve our pedagogic purposes less well. The use of digital straw men to justify outmoded library space design impedes the timely arrival of the law library of the future. (Professor Hazelton posits that only 13% of her collection is available on Lexis and Westlaw as justification for a request for 50% of a projected new facility.) Building larger library space merely to house physical material should be reconsidered and a course of action planned and implemented that acknowledges technology's import today. *[Article copies available for a fee from The Haworth Document Delivery Service: 1-800-HAWORTH. E-mail address: <getinfo@haworthpressinc.com> Website: <http://www.HaworthPress.com>* © *2002 by The Haworth Press, Inc. All rights reserved.]*

KEYWORDS. E-books, space planning, collection development, digital libraries, law libraries–management, technological innovations–influence, law libraries–automation

Gordon Russell is Associate Professor and Law Library Director, St. Thomas University Law Library, Miami, FL.

[Haworth co-indexing entry note]: "Re-Engineering the Law Library Resources Today for Tomorrow's Users: A Response to 'How Much of Your Print Collection Is Really on WESTLAW or LEXIS-NEXIS?' " Russell, Gordon. Co-published simultaneously in *Legal Reference Services Quarterly* (The Haworth Information Press, an imprint of The Haworth Press, Inc.) Vol. 21, No. 2/3, 2002, pp. 29-54; and: *Law Library Collection Development in the Digital Age* (ed: Michael Chiorazzi, and Gordon Russell) The Haworth Information Press, an imprint of The Haworth Press, Inc., 2002, pp. 29-54. Single or multiple copies of this article are available for a fee from The Haworth Document Delivery Service [1-800-HAWORTH, 9:00 a.m. - 5:00 p.m. (EST). E-mail address: getinfo@haworthpressinc.com].

> These days, novels are most often composed not on bound leaves but on computer screens. There is no reason to believe our culture will be poorer even in amorphous ways when people absorb them from screens as well. And in definite and obvious ways, readers and writers alike will be richer for the access they will gain to an electronic version of Borges's infinite "Library of Babel." In the near future, books will cost little or nothing, never go out of print and remain eternally available throughout the wired world. Can anyone really be against that?
>
> –Jacob Weisberg[1]

Professor Penny Hazelton, library director at the University of Washington, was asked by the building committee at the University of Washington Law School to answer a series of questions to help them understand why 50% of a proposed new building was devoted to law library space. In response to pressure to reduce the size of the library, Hazelton analyzed her collection and prepared a report. She distributed a copy of her report at the AALL Space Planning and Technology for Academic Law Libraries workshop held at Duke University School of Law in March, 1999 and published it in *Legal Reference Services Quarterly*.[2] Hazelton wanted her findings to be available to support the professional judgment of academic law librarians forced to deal with administrators echoing the common refrain "we don't need books anymore,[3] it's all on the Internet."

At the time of her study Hazelton found that only 13% of her collection was available on Westlaw and Lexis; however, developments over the last two years[4] show that Hazelton's analysis and underlying assumptions may suffer from a myopic condition as common to librarianship as nearsightedness. Clearly, the design of new library space should accommodate flexible reconfiguration for purposes other than rote maximization of linear board feet for projected acquisitions.[5] Just as clearly, building larger library space merely to house physical material should be reconsidered and a course of action planned and implemented that acknowledges technology's import today.[6]

We librarians and law school administrators will see clearly that "less is more" in the context of collection development only when we as a profession are prepared to honestly, rather than dismissively, appraise the import of technology on libraries and society as a whole. The Alexandrian library of the future will be digital, for the masses of our day demand access to society's cultural riches wherever and whenever they please. If we embrace technology now, our collections, our services, and our stature as a profession will grow in quality and sustainability even as our board feet shelving needs decrease accordingly.

During the 1998 American Association of Law Libraries conference in Anaheim, I attended the Academic SIS evening reception. We boarded buses and drove to L.A. to visit the newly renovated law libraries at UCLA and Southwestern School of Law. Southwestern's law library was housed in a lovingly restored classic art deco department store listed in the National Register of Historic Places.[7] As I wandered through the library, I was overcome with the sense of a passing era. As digital information makes the physical book less necessary and less efficient as a research tool, the book itself is well on its way to becoming the icon of knowledge and wisdom.[8]

We stand at a crossroads; just as the Kentucky Derby honors the horse, so the Bullock Wiltshire building pays homage to law books. The architectural splendor, lavish details, aesthetics and workmanship provide a magnificent setting in which to pay homage to the creations of John West,[9] James Briggs,[10] and Frank Shepard.[11] Finally, at the end of the 20th century, in creating libraries like Southwestern's, we have succeeded in creating a legal Taj Mahal to the law book, a magnificent mausoleum for the vestiges of the American legal publishing empire. The law library has a more important role to play than a tomb to the law book.

The Guttenberg world is being transformed by the digital world. Annual book title production in the United States in 1997 (last year statistics available) was 64,711 or roughly 177 books being added every day–representing growth of 10% a year.[12] However, Arlington, Va. based Cyveillance found about 2 billion pages on the Web and estimated that it is increasing at the rate of 7.3 million a day,[13] which projects to a growth rate of 200% growth a year.

Over 110 years ago Dean C.C. Langdell reminded members of the Harvard Law School Association that "printed books are the ultimate source of all legal knowledge"[14] and that law libraries were the laboratory of the law:

> We have . . . constantly inculcated the idea that the library is the proper workshop of professors and students alike; that it is to us all that the laboratories of the university are to the chemists and physicists, the museum of natural history to the zoologist, the botanical garden to the botanists.[15]

I have not been able to shake the feeling that the convergence of art deco architecture and the law library is a fitting symbolic gesture, signifying the ending of the 20th century tradition in the law library.

Hazelton's assumptions, built upon the printed book tradition, will result in law libraries serving the role of archives for the book.[16] The rapid and continuing technological developments since her report was published call into question Hazelton's underlying assumptions: First, that "many legal materials currently owned by the Law Library will never be in electronic format because it will never be economical to convert them."[17] Second, that libraries will need space for growth over the next fifteen years because for now and the near term future online treatises are not "likely to be a good substitute for the printed version."[18] Third, that microforms will play a limited role in the development of the library because "it has never been a favored format for users."[19] Fourth, that reading "online is tedious and, for most users, is not conducive to good analysis and synthesis of legal doctrine and precedents."[20] Fifth, that treatises have an "hierarchal arrangement that is not well-suited for online searching and reading."[21] I will now examine each of these assumptions.

DIGITALIZATION OF THE LAW LIBRARY COLLECTION

Let's examine Hazelton's first assumption that much of the law libraries current collection will never be digitalized.[22] Michael K. Buckland stated that "it would appear that almost any material of interest to library users could become available in electronic form and offer, in principle, a credible alternative to the assembling of local collections."[23] Digitalization may be more cost effective than the storage of the print volumes.

While Hazelton understands that "the Law Library would need to decide if it wanted to replace print materials with electronic publications or other formats like microform or CD ROM,"[24] she has not embraced the belief that much of what is currently held in paper can be, and indeed will be, replaced. Such underlying assumptions dramatically alter the considerations one makes in planning and designing a new building. Costs for replacement of materials must be factored into any equation involving construction of new library space. The cost of replacing print materials in other formats may be less than the per foot cost of new construction.

For example, the benefits of online searching and retrieval might result in a cost benefits analysis that would favor replacing the printed English Reports with one CD, even though the replacement cost is $12,000. This is just one example of a traditional print source that could be replaced. If the new medium lends itself to easier access and use by our primary clientele, the expense may be justified. Such an analysis should also consider the hidden costs of storage.

The Association of Research Libraries in a 1996 Report by the task force on Preserving Digital information provides an extensive analysis of the hidden costs of maintaining a library collection. The study found that it cost a library $0.25 per year to store a volume and every time a book circulated, was checked out and returned, it cost $0.70.[25] Let's assume that in 1998, 10% of Hazelton's print collection of 342,000 volumes circulated. If we use the RLG numbers it would cost the library $109,340 to store and circulate the collection. Assuming that the percentage of the collection circulating remains at 10%, the per volume cost to store the collection and the cost to circulate will increase as the collection grows.

Hazelton's assumption that the libraries' "treatises from the 19th century through the 1980s" will not be available in digital format because "it never will be economical to convert them"[26] is being challenged. There are a number of non law initiatives–The Making of America,[27] Project MUSE,[28] JSTOR,[29] and Early Canadiana Online[30]–that are successfully digitizing print and microform and offering access to digital texts over the Internet to millions of potential users.

These collections provide full text searching and the ability to print the pages quickly while freeing the library from continuing to store older materials in print. The most striking feature of these projects is the wide range of the subject matter. Yale University Library's Project Open Book's goal to create a digital image library of 10,000 volumes by digitizing microfilm provides an opportunity to evaluate issues of selection, quality and cost[31] through a large scale conversion project.[32] The result of such ongoing archival projects is to recreate the print library into a digital library.

The first large-scale legal digitalization project for law is Hein-On-Line. The William S. Hein Company, working with Cornell University, has made use of processes to effectively digitize older law reviews. Scanning and conversion began in late 1998. As of March, 2002 the project has 181 journals available or in production, 3,905,340 total pages available resulting in potential shelf space savings of 896 linear feet (approximately 265 standard shelves). Hein is projecting 5.5 million pages by the end of 2002.[33] Their ultimate goal is to digitally reproduce all law school journals and make them available online in their original print format.

This project will have significant impact on the storage of law reviews. Law libraries are being offered an alternative to maintaining a significant part of their collection in print. Print runs of law journals are an anachronism. It is possible to plan for the replacement of the print copies as they become available through Hein-On-Line. If ownership and access are an issue, back issues could be maintained in microformat.

For the most part, law reviews and journals are available to law school students and faculty on Westlaw and Lexis. Westlaw and Lexis started to place issues of law reviews online in the late 1980s and they selectively began and now aggressively seek to add all university law reviews, as well as including all articles for every journal that they make available online.[34] Hein has announced plans to make digitally available the following historical treatise titles: Classics of International Law and The Nuremberg Trials. This is a natural outgrowth of Hein's significant microform publishing. Hein has developed a significant microfiche collection of law treatises from the 19th century and the Classics of International Law will be the first segment of this microform collection to be made available in digital format. This is the first commercial example of the historic 19th and 20th century law treatises being digitized.

The Hein-On-Line project provides access to digital reproductions of the page–that is, exact images rather than OCR (optical character recognition) representation of the original document.[35] Their subscription structure allows for IP addressing and access to the entire university community, rather than the more restrictive access policies of vendors such as Lexis and Westlaw. Librarian concerns about preservation and continued access to the information if Hein were to cease operation or substantially increase the cost of the product can be addressed by rethinking traditional library practices.

For example, let us examine the well-established library practice of binding legal journals and law reviews. (Why do we bind journals? Wasn't it a way to protect and preserve the information and make it available for future users?) The rapid increase of online versions of journal articles suggests that law libraries rethink the policy of purchasing journals and binding them. By shifting the binding budget to cover the cost of standing orders for microformat version of the journals and implementing collection development policies that would keep five to ten years of unbound journals on the shelf,[36] there would be an initial downsizing of the space required to house the print journals. Academic law libraries would be able to plan for a stasis in the journal collection. Archival ownership and preservation would be achieved by microformat storage. This would balance concerns regarding preservation and ownership while providing users with the material in a digital format. Eventually, certain libraries could decide to rely solely on the digital collection.

Another way to expand the access to law review articles would be for academic law libraries and the American Association of Law Libraries to take a leadership role in indexing and creating Web access to the full text of law school journals. The American Association of Law Libraries (AALL) Indexing of Legal Periodicals Advisory Committee serves as the advisory organization to Gale's Current Law Index and recommends journals to be indexed. It might be possible to expand this product to provide links to full copies of the articles. AALL might play a role in the development of free electronic versions of law school journal articles.

Most law school journals have a limited subscription base which does not cover the cost of production. A concerted effort to provide online indexing and linking to the articles using the Web-based LegalTrac could provide a new model for the access and storage of law reviews. A commercial example of this linking of LegalTrac to the full text can be seen on Westlaw. Westlaw has integrated links from the abstracts of the Westlaw version of LegalTrac (LRI database) to the full text of articles in the Westlaw databases. AALL needs to work with Gale to provide links on the Web-based LegalTrac to the full text of the articles on the Web. This might provide the impetus for the development of a concerted plan by academic law libraries to ensure that their school's law review(s) are available online. Such integration would provide a level of access to the full text of articles through a controlled vocabulary and indexing that is not possible in full text searching. In addition, by creating links from the indexing source to the full text document on the Web would provide the flexibility and quick access that researchers desire.

DIGITALIZATION'S EFFECT ON THE FUTURE GROWTH OF THE COLLECTION

Hazelton's second assumption, that over the next fifteen years online legal treatises will not be a good substitute for the printed book, is being challenged by recent publishing initiatives. The ability to collect and store current treatises and monographs in electronic format is changing the need for print materials. How long buildings remain the principle repository of information is a question that must be discussed. Is there really a need to have the space to collect treatises over the next 15 years?

The publishing world appears to be embracing digitalization and offering opportunities for law libraries to build digital collections of legal treatises and move away from just-in-case ownership to just-in-time collection development policies. Commercial publishers are moving to develop a digital or electronic version of their books, including older materials. Random House, the nation's largest book publisher, announced that it has converted 5,000 of its book titles and has embarked on a two-year project to digitize all of the 50,000 titles books on its backlist.[37] Simon & Schuster is formatting all of its new books in digital form and is preparing to digitize at least 4,000 of its 20,000 backlist titles in the next year.[38]

Publishers of print books constantly must determine how many copies of a book to print to satisfy demand and avoid unsold stock. Retailers rely on "sale-or-return" policies, which enable them to return most unsold books. The "sale-or-return" policy means that publishers carry all the risk, plus freight costs and cost to pulp the unsold books. If a publisher underestimates a book's potential they will either miss out on sales or be forced to undertake a costly reprint.

Today the "shelf-life" of a hardback book, the time it normally remains in a bookstore before it's replaced by a newer book, is usually less than two months. Before the Thor Power-Tool[39] decision in the late '70s, books returned to publishers continued to remain in print; publishers stored the books in warehouses and depreciated them for tax credit. The Thor decision rescinded that tax credit, forcing publishers to allow slower-selling titles to go out of print very quickly.[40] The current tax laws, therefore, provide an incentive for publishers to move to digitize their back inventory because warehousing runs of books raises costs for the publisher.

The ability to reduce the return of unsold books and the historical increased cost of limited runs will be replaced by cost effective printing of single copies on demand. Digital technology has made it possible for the U.S. book publishing industry ($24 billion in sales in 1998),[41] to print on demand, which up until now has not been profitable. In the past, publishers usually allowed rights to revert to the author when sales dried up. However, with print on demand technology, publishers will be able to hold onto book rights indefinitely by filling single copy requests.

A striking development in the area of digital books was the model presented by netLibrary. netLibrary entered into agreements with publishers to sell electronic copies of books. netLibrary had agreements with over 150 publishers to convert their books to digital form and converted over 40,000 books and was adding 100 books a day. Libraries could choose the titles they wished to purchase. Access was provided through a Web browser. The electronic books were priced the same as the print copy. The company responded to concerns that online systems will not be here forever. Libraries, by paying a 50% surcharge, were guaranteed access to the book in perpetuity.[42]

The netLibrary model gave libraries the opportunity to both own the digital collection and maintain access to the information. The private library was maintained by netLibrary. Individual libraries provided access to the netLibrary titles through their OPAC with a link to the full text. Full text could be searched individually or globally. In addition it was possible to hyperlink within a book using the table of contents or the index. The software was designed to assure publishers and librarians that copyrights would be respected. When a netLibrary book was borrowed from a participating library the customers read as much as she or he wanted, even made marginal notes, but only limited portions could be copied or printed. However, only as many copies as the library bought could be checked out at one time. The netLibrary model provided the ability to search the full text of a book, and provides the text of that book anywhere and any time, which is arguably what our faculty and students value most.

The printed book allows users to browse the shelf, choose the title they wish, check it out and take it with them. These attributes are improved with digital storage because the users can full text search throughout the complete library and not be confined to the limitations of browsing the stacks and relying upon the decision of a librarian to identify and classify the contents of a book so that it can be physically located in one place with other books that cover the same topic. Additionally, the digital library is never closed and there are no misshelved or lost books.

netLibrary had over 50 university presses as well as other publishers. Since much of law libraries' non serial book purchasing is spent on monographs from university presses, as netLibrary expanded its publisher holdings, more and more of these would be available online. The netLibrary model provided law libraries with an opportunity to reduce the physical growth of the treatise collection. This was enhanced when netLibrary allowed library consortiums to access the netLibrary collection, providing an interesting model for academic law libraries–access to a large number of titles at a small cost per volume.

Solinet, the regional consortium of libraries in the south, initially purchased 14,000 titles that members of the consortium could subscribe to based on a per student cost of about $1.00 per full-time student equivalent. The consortium made a second purchase of over 1,000 more titles.[43] Our library has joined the Solinet consortium and at the same time purchased the legal material that Solinet did not purchase to enhance our digital book collection.

However, in 2001 netLibrary was effected by the dot.com shakeout and eventually declared bankruptcy. This event could be seen as justifying concerns about reliance on digital licensing agreements. However, because of the access safeguards that netLibrary had implemented–maintenance of the digital collection with OCLC–those who purchased the digital titles and paid the surcharge had ensured continued access to the information.

In fact in November 2001, OCLC announced that it made an offer to purchase netLibrary. Jay Jordon, CEO, OCLC stated:

> This potential alliance with netLibrary would advance our strategic directive to deliver technologies and services that support, extend and enhance the OCLC membership cooperative. eBooks complement out e-journal collection and provide exciting new synergies for our cataloging, resource sharing, reference and preservation services.[44]

On January 25, 2002, the sale of netLibrary to OCLC was completed.[45] OCLC and netLibrary will be working together to bring to libraries a collection of eBooks, grow catalog contents and provide new and innovative learning opportunities in libraries.

As a collection development tool, the new acquisitions list of netLibrary can be used to add new volumes to a library's digital collection. Academic law libraries have the opportunity to buy a print copy or digital version of the book. An academic law consortium composed of ABA accredited law schools much like the regional consortiums could share costs and manage a growing netLibrary collection of online e-books that could in turn be accessed by all law students and faculty.

The netLibrary model has proved to be highly successful and meets the needs of library patrons. The University of Texas initially purchased a collection of 6,000 titles from netLibrary. "No one was sure whether anyone was going to read any digital books," said Dillon, the university's head of collections and information resources. "We were somewhat skeptical. Usually a book has a one-third chance of being checked out. So to have some title checked out 25 times in two months–that's shocking."[46] At a time when circulation and the number of students going into the library at the University of Texas was down, the student use of the digital collection was high. This happened with little advertising of the digital collection.

Many other libraries, including law libraries, are experiencing a decline in circulation numbers and fewer students coming into the library.

The need to obtain necessary information no longer requires the borrowing of a large number of books, or carrying them around. We need to ask ourselves, do we need to purchase a large number of books in the hope that we have on the shelf the one book our patron needs? Can we instead do collection development on the fly? It is a simple matter to add a digital book to the collection when it is requested, just log in, order the book and have it magically appear in your digital library collection, the ultimate just-in-time service. Users have the opportunity to perform full text searches, access the relevant text and the ability to copy or print portions of the book from anywhere at any time. If faculty or students want an actual copy of the book, the book can be quickly ordered and added to the physical collection.

The book publishing world appears to be moving toward a distribution model for delivering books on demand that allows for the instant delivery of books printed on the spot. A number of companies offer some type of instant printing of books.[47] The file would be sent to digital printers. The machinery prints the cover and the pages. The two pieces are then assembled in a book-binding machine. A trimmer cuts the book to size and it is ready to be processed. The process of downloading and printing the book takes 15 minutes.[48] Jim Hamilton, a senior consultant with CAP Ventures, specialists in on demand printing, said, "Perhaps 100,000 of the world's several million books were now in easily printable digital form."[49] Perhaps the libraries' role will change. Patrons searching our digital collections will identify material they need in print format and the item will be ready for them when they arrive at the library. Libraries might decide to become book retailers, allowing customers the option of purchasing or borrowing a desired work. Maybe, given the realities of limited space and valuable time, it would prove cheaper to give the book away rather than paying the cost of processing and storage.

Making the change from just-in-case to just-in-time may mean that we have many formats for our digital information. If our primary clientele are not browsing our collection but finding information globally, then our role is to educate our users to identify the relevant material and provide quick access to that information. We may soon be storing books to download to portable readers or to in-house printing presses, offering full text of books on the Web, providing the digital capabilities to access microformats stored in the library and developing digital archives of our existing print collections.

Even those wedded to ownership of the physical book can see how the net has reshaped the old paradigm. Today, books that are out of print are nonetheless available. It is easy to do a global search of the holding of used and rare bookstores on the Web. Sites such as Bookfinder.com <*http://bookfinder.com*>, abebooks.com <*http://www.abebooks.com/*>, and amazon.com <*http://www.amazon.com*>, provide access to thousands of rare and out of print books. Online ordering, credit card authorization and overnight Federal Express means that you can have the book the next day. The challenge is not ownership but the ability to provide patrons with the opportunity to identify relevant material. OCLC's new FirstSearch provides our faculty with a global database to track down relevant material. Law libraries must decide if providing the resources for our faculty quickly is better than continuing to warehouse materials just in case they are needed.

EXPANDING THE ROLE OF MICROFORMAT IN LAW LIBRARIANS

Hazelton reminds us that "[m]icroformat (film and fiche) has been around for decades" but has "never been a favored format for users" and consequently librarians have been reluctant to get "rid of the print copy because the print copy is clearly a more user-friendly format."[50] In the past, the poor quality of the image on microformat readers and the even poorer quality of the print duplications made the decision to retain print format an easy choice. However, the historical aversion to microformat may be overcome because of the new technologies and the expectations fostered by our users that everything is available to them online. Hazelton's third assumption that microformat will play a limited role in the development of the law library collection may well not be the case.

The myth that everything is available online may provide the impetus for libraries to store in microformat and provide the user with a digital image.[51] Technological developments are providing law libraries with the equipment to store material in microformat while providing digital access to the information.

Newer law libraries have incorporated an integrated format approach that includes the holding of information in microformat. Often for younger law libraries it was the only cost effective way to obtain older materials. Large collections by UPA, LLMC and Hein provided older books, law reviews and primary sources in microformat. Though customers have never liked the format, it has proven to be a good medium for preservation and storage.[52] However, in the process of accessing digital collections we may want to revisit microformat.

The ability to identify and provide access to individual microform materials in our library catalogs increases the accessibility to the information. New developments have made it relatively inexpensive to digitally copy the information from the fiche/film and electronically deliver the relevant material to our primary clientele. This provides an opportunity to extend accessibility of microfiche collections to the desktop. The price of microform digital copiers has fallen and they are now a relatively affordable investment. Unlike full scale conversion projects, digital imaging on demand allows libraries to create an image of the page and electronically forward the file to themselves or others and print out clean copies on laser printers. The copy of the image is often superior to the quality of a regular photocopy of a page.

There are opportunities to develop ongoing archival microfilming of library collections. Libraries will soon be able to preserve their collections while shrinking the hard copy collection and creating digital images of the material. By investing in a microform camera to capture paper, a microfilm scanner to produce digital images, and a computer output to microfilm (COM) to gather scanned images, it is possible to electronically create files and print them onto microfilm. The result is that every library will have the opportunity to selectively remove print copies from the collection.[53] It may mean, for example, that University of Washington's rich collection of Japanese legal materials[54] will be available to a worldwide audience through links in the online catalog.

READING ONLINE FOR EFFECTIVE LEGAL ANALYSIS

Hazelton has in some ways understated the problem of reading materials online–it is more than just tedious–it is difficult. The differentiation on the screen causes greater eye strain than reading from a book and the amount of text on the screen is less than the normal page. The glare, the bad layout, the annoyances of reading on screen, all need to be resolved if we are going to read long documents online. However, this fourth assumption that the problems of reading from a screen and the organization structure of information on the screen will limit the use of electronic resources by law students and faculty requires law libraries to collect in print is also being challenged by technology developments.

We have seen in law libraries over the last 20 years that students are not reading online and they are for the most part not reading the cases in our case reporters. Rather, they are copying the case and articles and parts of books from the material in the library or they print the information they find online to read at their leisure. Students want to read a case, highlight it, add comments, and dissect it. Reading the case in a reporter, an article in law journal, or a chapter in a library book, precludes a student from doing this. The result is that users are printing the documents that they want to read. By implementing printing solutions such as networked copiers that allow for high speed two sided copying, the need for digital access to printed information becomes more critical.

The development of digital reading devices that provide for information to be easily downloaded, easily read, marked up, marginal notes added, and shared with others will provide a resource for the development of good legal analysis and synthesis. Good analysis and synthesis requires our students to write and write and write. The wireless digital world opens up opportunities for law professors to require law students to craft meaningful responses. A digital library provides the laboratory for students to be involved in legal research and analysis. Opportunities for students to research and provide written answers to casebook hypotheticals could offer a framework for gauging how the students are grappling with the legal concepts being taught while developing effective research skills.

At the same time, technology is working to address the problems associated with reading on a screen. For example, several initiatives are currently under way to improve the readiblity of LCD monitors. Microsoft's ClearType[55] and ClearView from Ductus[56] are two ongoing projects to improve the LCD screen's readibility. Microsoft claims that ClearType will improve text clarity by up to 300 percent. ClearView uses anti-aliasing that strategically turns adjacent white pixels along the edges of letters gray. With these and other initiatives to improve readability and increase the size of the screen, I am confident there will be a number of solutions to this problem.

The second development is the digital book.[57] A new generation of electronic books attempts to resolve the problem of portability and readability by requiring a specially designed hardware reader into which selected texts are downloaded electronically. SoftBook Press and NuvoMedia introduced their electronic readers SoftBook Reader and Rocket eBook. The companies were jointly purchased by Gemstar.[58] These first generation electronic books offer a number of features that would provide libraries with instant delivery, lower retrieval costs and reduced space needs. The reader's ability to store a number of books and to download additional books offers a way for libraries to store books digitally and to check out the book to patrons.

The development of the ebook will depend on the development of open standards. Much like the VHS/BETA struggles or the development of the DOS standard, there must be universal standards for digitized books. The process of formulating standards began with the Open Book Initiative.[59] For the digital book to replace the cheap paperback it must be as easy to carry, as easy to read, and available at the same cost. Once competitive, the recreational digital book and the digital textbook or casebook will be very attractive.

Remember, Gutenberg's revolution was not just about movable type. The Chinese had been using movable type for centuries before Gutenberg.[60] Moveable type multiplied the efficiency of another technology–the alphabet–and brought about the revolution of mass literacy to Europe. Today we are seeing the revolution of the digital word. The result may be as revolutionary. The future may result in a new type of book. "A little company called E Ink, spun out of the Massachusetts Institute of Technology, . . . will be able to make electronic paper" that "will look and feel just like real paper printed with good old ink. Except that the ink on the electronic paper could change, much like the characters on a computer screen."[61] Imagine binding e-paper coated with e-ink; it will look, feel and be read just like any other book in the library, but when you're finished reading, plug it in and change the entire content.

RESTRUCTURING THE HIERARCHAL ARRANGEMENT

The use of hypertext, multimedia and the restructuring of hierarchically arranged materials will overcome Hazelton's fifth assumption that "treatises are difficult to use online because they have a hierarchical arrangement that is not well-suited for online searching or reading."[62] There needs to be a concerted effort to make use of the Web's strength and not try to superimpose the linear structure of the book online. One approach to developing information on the Web is through the use of concept mapping.

Prof. Joseph D. Novak developed the concept at Cornell University in the 1960s. His work was based on the theories of David Ausubel[63] who stressed the critical importance of prior knowledge in being able to learn or adapt to new concepts. Novak concluded that "[m]eaningful learning involves the assimilation of new concepts and propositions into existing cognitive structures."[64]

Mind Mapping is a popular related technique, invented (and copyrighted) by Tony Buzan in the UK. "A mind map consists of a central word or concept, around the central word you draw the 5 to 10 main ideas that relate to that word. You then take each of those child words and again draw the 5 to 10 main ideas that relate to each of those words."[65] A mind map has only one main concept, while a concept map may have several. There is Java-based software that can be downloaded to create concept maps that allow for the linking of text, images, audio.[66] The results provide some early examples of the potential development of structured information on the Web that is more than just the mere linear translation of print to the Web.

Our paradigms are shifting as we speak and the basic nature of legal research is being transformed. Dan Dabney's "The Mangy Dog and Other Stories My Computer Told Me" presentation at the CALI conference in Eugene, Oregon focused on the way free text and enhanced citation searching provide new ways of interacting with legal texts, and encourages us to ask new kinds of questions and accept new kinds of answers. Understanding how the new answers are systematically different from the old ones results in a fundamental change in approaching legal research–focusing on the relevant factual information instead of the legal concepts. Concept mapping may offer the online scaffolding to create information that links legal concepts.

RE-VISUALIZING THE 21ST CENTURY LAW LIBRARY

Build it and they will come. For over 50 years the ABA standards have required the building of law libraries to support legal education and academic research. However, building libraries has not resulted in students and faculty coming to the library. In fact, as we enter the 21st century they are looking elsewhere for the information they seek–particularly the computer in front of them and the material available to them through their personal Internet connection.

Today's librarians must be prepared to serve users who believe that if everything they need is not on the Web it should at least be available to them online. We must build libraries that meet the needs of fluid flexible learners[67] who expect libraries to provide them access to the library collection from their desktop. To respond to this expectation, libraries need to function as just-in-time providers instead of just-in-case storage systems.

We have the capability to reinvent the library, our services, and even our profession, today, for tomorrow's users. We must become pioneers, leaders in building a library of the future that our faculty and students will both want and need. Hazelton reminds us that each library must decide if it wants to replace print materials with other formats, including electronic, and that "the Law Library considers these questions on a regular basis as new formats are made available whether digital or microformat."[68]

If the primary role of a library is collection development, librarians must balance the twin competing notions of demand and value. If there is no demand for material, then there can be no value for the material. Yet, librarians may choose to provide shelf space for certain documents for reasons other than demand.[69]

If the underlying premise that guided libraries to collect books was that it would not be possible to obtain the item quickly for the user, the paradigm has changed and we need to ask ourselves what our role is now and in the future. Before we build archival space for the book we should consider whether we can provide a better service at less cost. Librarians have given a value to information artefacts–a sort of good housekeeping seal of approval by putting the book on the library shelves. Can we do the same thing with our library catalog by providing links to information about the book, the table of contents, the index, book reviews and perhaps actual full text searching that would identify relevant matches?

It is my view that collection development was built on the assumption that there was only a narrow window of opportunity to obtain a book. After that time the book was out of print. Collection development and acquisitions created a collection for present and future users should they require the information. Librarians were asked to acquire the material and value its present and future worth so it would be available when our primary clientele wanted to access the information. Do we not all have a gut feeling that we have not done a very good job in selecting materials that are actually used by our faculty and students? If materials do not go out of print, law libraries do not need to buy and store them until needed.

The opportunity to improve our understanding of collection use is now readily available to us; we can actually inventory all materials taken off our shelves. Using portable bar code readers and asking our patrons not to shelve materials could provide us with a better understanding of how our collections are being used. Such information may provide the impetus for us to revise our collection development policies and support digital collection building and just-in-time services. Law librarians need to stop discussing the process of collection development and focus on the underlying rationale.

The acquisitions process has been built on developing a collection that is available when needed. However, there may be a new on demand model. For this to be viable, there must be ways to locate the information. Services such as Worldcat and Firstsearch should allow our customers to self-selector. The library needs to provide the ability to search large holdings that integrate book reviews and word of mouth comments that help users in the selection process. The library must provide links to the wheat that is out there. The World Wide Web is the ultimate disorganized library of full text information. Collection development balances demand and value: "The books placed in the shelves, in the reader's face, so to speak, carry an implicit endorsement. These you should read; these books are good for you; or, these are books you will like."[70]

The challenge, as a large amount of full text material becomes available on the Web, is to evaluate and determine what information should be linked. The ability to provide access through the online catalog is to extend the seal of approval to information in the same way that putting books on the shelf carried an implicit endorsement. There are new ways to develop digital links. For non-depository libraries it is possible to create a MARCHIVE profile that allows the library to obtain all records that have a URL in the MARC 856 field.

Legal looseleaf services have been a staple of legal publishing,[71] but the multi volume looseleaf migrated easily to the digital world. The 1980s and early '90s saw the introduction of the CD-ROM in the law market place. A number of companies produced CD-ROM products that copied the looseleaf publication. This technology required the library to purchase networked CD players, either through traditional players or mirroring the CD information on hard drives.

CD-ROM technology was not without its problems; mirroring technology required the reloading of the information every time a new disc was received. The sheer number of CDs presented challenges. At one point we were involved in running 150 CDs on the network. The daily, weekly, monthly and quarterly updates; the loading of the CDs; and the tweaking of client software because of changes in the product were all challenges. The upkeep of the CD was as time consuming as filing updates in looseleafs. However, as companies have moved to Web-based services, the opportunity to reduce maintenance and filing costs, the reduction in lost pages and instant updating while reducing the hard copy material in the library, is a real option today.

It may require making some alternative choices in the products to which the library subscribes. A number of schools have entered into global licensing agreements with Matthew Bender to provide access to all their Web-based products. It is possible to subscribe to CCH products online; LRP offers online access to a number of their products as does BNA and Aspen. An aggressive policy to eliminate looseleaf format with online versions allows for access to updated material and frees libraries from tedious filings, misfilings and lost pages.

Libraries will continue to access CD-ROM products that replace parts of the traditional paper collection. The ability to purchase CDs for historical materials that do not need to be updated as illustrated by the purchase of the English Reports provides an example of the development of retrospective digitization of information. This trend will continue to develop in the near future.

Hazelton's analysis of the University of Washington's collection is helpful, but its conclusions fail to address the opportunities that are now before us. We have quickly arrived at the point where the library can and must be re-engineered. The next few years will bring a sea of changes in the dynamics of collection development and change the physical structure of the law library. I believe that the resulting integrated collection will better meet the needs of our clientele. Understanding the role of electronic and digital materials in the law library of the 21st century is a far more complex and nuanced process than merely comparing an index of shelved monograph titles against the resources available on Westlaw and Lexis.

To fully comprehend technology's role may be impossible at this early moment in the evolution of digital information transfer. However, to begin to understand this sea change, one must be willing to return to the fundamental principle underlying libraries and library services–the provision of information. We must stop fixating on the book to the detriment of our constituencies. The printed book was merely the prevailing technology for providing information for the last five hundred or so years. Thus, librarians became keepers of the book. And libraries became institutions for the organization, storage, preservation, and retrieval of the information stored in books.

We are the keepers of the book because the book has been the prevailing technology (or "institutional artefact"[72]) for providing information for the past five hundred years. Our structures, libraries, became institutions, monuments, to the organization, storage, preservation, and retrieval of data stored in books. The 21st century law library will increasingly be involved in providing access to information that is not in paper format. But libraries will continue to use organizational structures to provide access to information. The shift in format provides an opportunity to re-engineer the library by creating an integrated collection, rather than just an archive of historical legal materials that will never be digitized. The role of the printed book will change dramatically over the next few years and librarians must move to redefine the library.

Hazelton states that "if the collection could shrink by a replacement program . . . the present configuration of the Law Library will permit other kinds of use."[73] As we revisualize the law school library and its role we should be reconsidering the design of the library. The structure and form of the libraries that we have been building–the architectural edifices that house our information artefacts–serve us less well. Our planning needs to be about more than cutting up space designed for the book to function in another manner. The future library should be designed to meet the desired outcomes of our clients and that is not an emphasis on housing and providing access to books. Integrating the library with the law school to provide maximum use of group space is critical.

By bringing seminar rooms and classrooms within the library, the library itself would become a natural extension of the formal instruction process. Assuming these rooms are wired and equipped with electronic whiteboards, the library would maximize its emerging role as a conduit through which group learning is facilitated. This synergy between the faculty, students, and library promises an exciting and vital role for our profession in the future.

NOTES

1. Jacob Weisberg, "*The Good E-Book*." NYT Sunday June 4, available at <*http://www.nytimes.com/library/magazine/home/20000604mag-ebook.html*> (visited February 28, 2002).

2. Penny A. Hazelton, *How Much of Your Print Collection Is Really on WESTLAW or LEXIS-NEXIS?* 18:1 LRSQ 3 (1999).

3. *Id.* at 4.

4. The Lexis/Westlaw fixation causes law librarians to dismiss as tangential the innovative, formidable online products of publishers like Hein, CCH, BNA, Matthew Bender, Aspen, Oceana et al. Are we willing to stake our professions' future on the stubborn belief that this massive digital migration is but a passing fancy?

5. Historically, library space analyses and needs projections began and ended with arithmetic linear shelf expansion computations.

6. Technology is a rhetorical device with which to argue the need for more space for paper based sources: ". . . if the collection were to shrink as the result of technology." Hazelton, supra note 1, 13.

7. The *Bullocks Wilshire Building* was constructed in 1929, designated as Los Angeles Cultural Monument #56 in 1969, and has been listed on the National Register of Historic Places since 1978. If you would like information about the building go to <*http://www.swlaw.edu/bullockswilshire/historictreasure.html*> (visited February 28, 2002).

8. The response to the death of the book exhibits this love affair with the image of the book. Jerome Stern has written of the book "[a]nd so in the face of the future I must sing the song of the book, nothing more voluptuous do I know than sitting with bright pictures, fat upon my lap, and turning glossy pictures of giraffes and Gauguins, penguins, and pyramids." J. Stern Booklove. *The Book of the Future.* available at <*http://www.archival.com/text/booklove.html*> (visited December 22, 2001). Society has embraced the book and gilded it in a mysticism that obscures its true identity. As the digital world threatens the book we become like the Luddites trying to hold back the demise of the weaver. We eloquently hold on to the book and eulogize its form and function. James Billington writes that "The book, that most user-friendly communications medium, has a long life ahead of it. I do not believe that our great-grandchildren will be reading the plays of Shakespeare or 'Moby Dick' on computer screens." James Billington, *The Library of Congress and the Information Age*, Daedalus, 125(4) 35-51. See also, Walter Crawford and Michael Gorman's, Future Libraries Dreams of Madness & Reality (1995). They wrote:

> The debate about the future of print is really not about print-on-paper versus electronic technology . . . It is about reading and the best means to read. To state a simple, central theme of this book; reading is important to individuals and to society, and print-on-paper is best for sustained reading leading to the acquisition of knowledge.

Many imbue the functional form of the book with mystical powers. Bernard Hibbitts reminds us that the same debate took place at the time of Guttenberg, and quotes from Martin Lowry of Filippo di Strata . . . "The world has got along perfectly well for six thousand years without printing, and has no need to change now" and Johannes Trithemius, in his tract "In Praise of Scribes" declaring "Printed books will never be the equivalent of handwritten codices . . . The simple reason is that copying by hand involves more diligence and industry." Bernard J. Hibbitts, *Yesterday Once More: Skeptics, Scribes and the Demise of Law Review*, para.. 1.2 (Version 1.0, created March 6, 1997) available at <*http://www.law.pitt.edu/hibbitts/akron.htm*>.

9. The explosion in the number of cases and the lament of 19th century lawyers to the over-publication of cases gave rise to entrepreneurial interest in organizing and marketing legal information. John West was not the inventor of reporters and digests but developed a business model for "the reporting and digesting of judicial decisions" that would "enable the legal profession to examine the American case law on any given subject, as easily, exhaustively, and economically as possible." *Symposium of Legal Publishers*, 23 Am. L. Rev. 396, 400 (1889). John B. West had been a law book salesman and developed a product to meet the needs of his market–a national reporter published on a regular basis that lawyers subscribed to and the development of a universal indexing system for the cases within the reporter set. See Erwin C. Surrency, A History of American Publishing, 237-242 (1990).

10. James E. Briggs of Lawyers Co-op, looked at the multiplicity of jurisdictions and the multiplicity of cases and determined that completeness of all opinions was made up of "useless repetitions" (*Symposium of Legal Publishers*, 23 AM. L. REV. 396, 411 (1889)) and that the "current work of all the courts, with which every enterprising lawyer wishes to keep up, must be combined, reported, annotated, condensed and arranged with such consummate skill as to be a constant addition to all that is good and useful in a practical working library of an every-day practitioner who has not the

time to wade through great quantities of matter, but who needs his time for the practice of his profession" (*Symposium*, 414).

Briggs' plan was to selectively provide the current decisions needed by the profession, limit the number of volumes, provide notes and updates to keep costs low, and save lawyers time (Surrency, at 242-245).

11. Frank F. Shepard published his Illinois citations in 1875. He did not create citation indexing and his was not the first American citation service. See Patti Ogden, *'Mastering the Lawless Science of Our Law': A Story of Legal Citation Indexes*, 85 LAW LIBR. J. 1 (1993). Shepard was a law book salesman and businessman who in the course of selling books to lawyers saw lawyers writing in the margin of cases reports references to cases that had modified the case in the reporter (Surrency, at 181-185). He saw a market need, developed a product, and focused on providing lawyers with current information that was accurate and complete and available for all jurisdictions. Lawyers learned how to use it once and it would serve then for any citation research.

12. See *International Publishers Association Annual Book Title Production,* available at *<http://www.ipa-uie.org/statistics/annual_book_prod.html>* (visited February 27, 2002).

13. Brian H. Murray and Alvin Moore. *Sizing the Internet: A White Paper.* available at: *<http://www.cyveillance.com/web/us/corporate/white_papers.htm>* (visited February 28, 2002).

14. Charles Langdell, *The Harvard Law School*, 3 Law Q. Rev. 123, 124 (1887).

15. *Id.*, at 124.

16. If select law libraries wish to assume the mantle of "archivist" or "curator" so be it, but how can the rest of us hope to disabuse the ABA and AALS of the notion that volume counts and multiple copies remain the sin quo non of law library valuation when we cry that the computer is a mirage and the book real? The end result of Hazelton's plea for more space and more monographs is the unsubtle reinforcement of a primitive "size counts" mentality. I would argue that more physical books plus greater linear feet of shelving does not equal better service, greater access, or a law library more worthy of ABA and AALS accreditation in the 21st century.

17. Hazelton, supra note 1, at 13. Hazelton also states that "Few legal treatises are online at all . . . There are thousands of legal treatises published, those for legal practitioners and those that are not (included here are biographies, essays, historical works, government reports, interdisciplinary works)." Id. at 9.

18. *Id.*, at 9.

19. *Id.*, at 1.

20. *Id.*, at 9.

21. *Id.*, at 9.

22. Hazelton, supra. at 13.

23. Michael K. Buckland, *Redesigning Library Services: A Manifesto 6: Supplement,* at *<http://sunsite.berkeley.edu/Literature/Library/Redesigning/supplement.html>* (visited February 28, 2002).

24. Hazelton, supra note 1, at 14.

25. These costs are taken from Appendix 2 of Preserving Digital Information: Report of the Task Force on Archiving of Digital Information, May 1, 1996 available at *<http://www.rlg.org/ArchTF/tfadi.apx2.htm>*. There are also comparisons on the cost to store and access a print library with a digital library. Denise A. Troll, Associate University Librarian, Carnegie Mellon, in a presentation at the Computing & Philosophy

Conference, August, 9-11, 2001 stated in her presentation that the cost of storage and circulation per volume is $20 to $40 for every book on the library's shelf reflect current thinking on the hidden maintenance costs of print items. See "The Philosophy of Digital Libraries: Parsing the Issues Making Tough Choices" (visited February 28, 2002) *<http://www.library.cmu.edu/Libraries/ThePhilosophyOfDLrev2.ppt>*.

26. Hazelton, supra note 1, at 13.

27. The Making of America *<http://moa.umdl.umich.edu/>* project is a digital library of primary sources in American social history from the antebellum period through reconstruction. The collection currently contains 1,600 books and 50,000 journal articles covering the period from 1800 to 1925.

28. Project Muse *<http://muse.jhu.edu/proj_descrip/index.html>* provides access to well over 100 journal titles covering the fields of literature and criticism, history, the visual and performing arts, cultural studies, education, political science, gender studies, and many others.

29. "JSTOR's mission is to help the scholarly community take advantage of advances in information technologies." For further information about JSTOR go to *<http://www.jstor.org/about/>* and to understand the need for archival collection of scholarly journals go to *<http://www.jstor.org/about/need.html>*.

30. Early Canadiana Online (ECO) *<http://www.canadiana.org/cgi-bin/ECO/mtq>* is a full text online collection of more than 3,000 books and pamphlets documenting Canadian history from the first European contact to the late 19th century. The collection is particularly strong in literature, women's history, native studies, travel and exploration, and the history of French Canada.

31. For information on the project and equipment requirements go to *<http://www.library.yale.edu/preservation/pobequip.htm>*. See also Paul Conway, *Yale University Library's Project Open Book: Preliminary Research Findings*, 2(2) D-LIB MAG., available at *<http://www.dlib.org/dlib/february96/yale/02conway.html-as-return>* (visited February 28, 2002) and Anne R. Kenney & Oya Y. Rieger, *Moving Theory into Practice* (2000) RLG; Bruce R. Kingma, *The Cost of Print, Fiche, and Digital Access: The Early Canadiana Online Project*, 6(2) D-LIB MAG., available at *<http://www.dlib.org/dlib/february00/kingma/02kingma.html-Note1>* (visited February 28, 2002).

32. Paul Conway, *Yale University Library's Project Open Book: Preliminary Re search Findings*, D-Lib Magazine, February 1996, available at *<http://www.dlib.org/dlib/february96/yale/02conway.html#as-return>* (visited February 28, 2002). See also Anne R. Kenney & Oya Y. Rieger, *Moving Theory into Practice* (2000) RLG; Bruce R. Kingma, *The Cost of Print, Fiche, and Digital Access: The Early Canadiana Online Project*, 6(2) D-Lib Magazine available at *<http://www.dlib.org/dlib/february00/kingma/02kingma.html#Note>* (visited February 28, 2002).

33. See *<http://heinonline.org/HeinDocs/TitlesCurrently Available.htm>* for updated numbers and a list of titles currently available.

34. Currently the full text of 627 legal journals are available on Westlaw and 502 journals on Lexis.

35. The reader software is available for free at *<http://www.adobe.com/>*.

36. This is not a unique idea–due to space concerns Syracuse University Law Library identifies and keep full print runs of approximately 40 law reviews. For all other law reviews the library keeps 10 years of unbound issues and maintains earlier volumes in microformat. Conversation with Louis Lantzy, Director of the Law Library, Spokane Washington (June 16, 1999).

37. Matthew Rose, *A New Chapter: Book Publishing Is Finally Entering the Digital Age; It Had No Choice.* WALL ST. J. Mar. 20, 2000, available at 2000 WL-WSJ 3022151 "Now, the book industry's leading publisher, Random House Inc., has embarked on an ambitious program to transform many of its titles into a new digital format. Random House, owned by Germany's Bertelsmann AG, has spent millions of dollars over the past two years developing a system through which almost all of the 3,500 new titles it publishes annually are stored in a new digital database. This year, it's starting the mammoth process of adding to that archive as many as 50,000 books on its backlist–a collection of older titles still in print as well as some that are out of print."

38. Doreen Caravajal, *Racing to Convert Books to Bytes Evolving Market for E-Titles*, N. Y. TIMES, Dec. 9, 1999 at C1. This development is the result of a long term commitment to digitalization. In 1994 Simon and Schuster reengineered its editing, production, and even certain accounting processes to develop custom publishing–see John W. Verity, *A Model Paperless Library: Simon & Schuster is at Archiving's Leading Edge.* BUS. WK. Dec. 23, 1996, available at <*http://www.businessweek.com/1996/52/b3507105.htm*> (visited February 28, 2002).

39. *Thor Power Tool Co. v. Commissioner*, 439 U.S. 522, 532 (1979).

40. See Kevin O'Donnell, Jr., *How Thor Power Hammered Publishing* (last updated 1993) available at <*http://www.sfwa.org/bulletin/articles/thor.htm*> to better understand why "more titles see print every year, but the average title sells fewer copies, and goes out of print more quickly, than its late '70s counterpart."

41. *Trade Book Publishing: Review, Forecast & Segment Analysis* Wilton CT. (1999).

42. This addressed one of Hazelton's concerns. netLibrary dealt with this by working with OCLC to provide an archival site for all of its books in the event that the company were to cease to exist.

43. See information on the Solinet Shared collection at <*http://www.solinet.net/lps/specialpromo/netLibrary/netLibrary.htm*> (visited February 28, 2002).

44. *OCLC Makes Offer to Purchase Assets of NetLibrary.* Press Release, November 15, 2001, available at <*http://www.oclc.org/oclc/press/20011115.shtm*> (visited February 28, 2002).

45. *OCLC Closes Deal on netLibrary Sale.* Press Release, January 28, 2002, available at <*http://www.oclc.org/oclc/press/20020128.shtm*> (visited February, 28, 2002).

46. Caravajal, supra, note 39.

47. See Danny Shaw, *Print-on-Demand: The Best Bridge Between New Technologies and Established Markets,* available at <*http://www.u-publish.com/pod2.htm*> (visited February28, 2002) and Jason Epstein, *Reading the Digital Future*, July 5, 2001. N.Y. Rev. Books, available at <*http://www.nybooks.com/articles/14318*> (visited February 28, 2002).

48. U.S. book retailer Barnes & Noble and online book retailer Amazon.com have teamed with Ingram Book Group's Lightening Print Unit, <*http://www.lightningsource.com/index2.html*>. Random House has bought a stake in Xlibris <*http://www2.xlibris.com/*> a Philadelphia online self publishing company.

49. Ian Simpson, *Publishing Turns New Page With Instant Books*, available at <*http://www.iran-central.net/iran-news/archive/79-01-20/todayac.htm-ac4*> (visited February 28, 2002).

50. Hazelton, supra note 1, at 11.

51. To better understand the option available for the storage of text on microformat and the digitalization of microformat information read Peggy Lunt, *The Ageless Allure*

of Microfilm, Imaging & Document Solutions Oct., 1998, available at <*http://www.imagingmagazine.com/db_area/archs/1998/October/The_4_1584.htm*> (visited February 28, 2002).

52. Microformat offer an ideal storage medium–it is estimated that wet film has a life expectancy of 500 years and dry film 100 years. See, *Id.*

53. "[I]n looking at what should be in the new Law Library, the print volumes duplicated in microform will require close scrutiny." Hazelton, supra note 1, at 11.

54. Hazelton, supra note 1, at 13. An example of such a project is the Chicago Kent project to digitalize the collection of ILO materials.

55. For updated information on ClearType Font Technology and LCD Displays you may go to Microsoft's ClearType page: <*http://www.microsoft.com/typography/cleartype/*> (visited February 13, 2002).

56. For updated information on Ductus ClearView you may go to Ductus's homepage at <*http://www.ductus.com/*> (visited February 28, 2002).

57. For a history of ebooks see Stephanie Ardito, *Electronic Books: To "E" or Not to "E"; That is the Question*, 8(4) SEARCHER, Apr., 2000 available at <*http://www.infotoday.com/searcher/apr00/ardito.htm*> (visited February 28, 2002).

58. For an overview see Darcy DiNucci, *Electronic Publishing: The Future of Publishing?* available at <*http://www.creativepro.com/story/feature/0,1819,1538,00.html*> (visited February 28, 2002).

59. The Open eBook Initiative is sponsored by the National Institute of Standards and Technology <*http://www.openebook.org/*> (visited February 28, 2002).

60. The Chinese carved wood. Gutenberg was a goldsmith adept at shaping, engraving and casting. What he invented was a cheap way to produce individual pieces of type. The rediscovery of the ancients and the rise of learning, the trade of Italian cities, etc., was already underway pre-Gutenberg. It was part of the pressure that led to Gutenberg. The Peccia system for mass producing handwritten manuscripts (i.e., disbinding the book and having a group of scribes each making multiple copies of the same page and then binding them up again) grew out of the demands at Italian universities that led to Gutenberg.

61. Kevin Maney, *E-novel Approach Promise New Chapter For Book Lovers,* USA Today B1 Tuesday May 9, 2000. The company is already producing indoor signs using the technology. Currently the technology only allows for the formation of large chunky letters.

62. Hazelton, supra note 1, at 9.

63. See David P. Ausbel, The Psychology of Meaningful Verbal Learning: An Introduction to School Learning. (1963).

64. Joseph D. Novak, and D. B. Gowin. Learning How to Learn. (1984). See also The Concept Mapping Homepage <*http://users.edte.utwente.nl/lanzing/cm_home.htm*> (visited February 28, 2002).

65. Tony Buzan, Use Both Sides of Your Brain. 3rd ed. (1991).

66. The Institute for Human and Machine Cognition Concept Map Software allows users to construct, navigate, and share knowledge models. The toolkit allows users to build, and collaborate during the construction of concept maps. The software can be downloaded <*http://cmap.coginst.uwf.edu/index.html*> (visited February 28, 2002).

67. "This means that individuals will be able to access the intranet, either from a distance (e.g., home) or, . . . from points within the School. Flexible learning implies a total rethinking of the curriculum, rewriting it and placing it upon the network is a huge task," Tony Carrucan, *The Virtual School: Emancipating the Curriculum*, available at

<http://ausweb.scu.edu.au/aw99/papers/carrucan/paper.html> (visited February 28, 2002).

68. Hazelton, supra at 14.

69. Michael K. Buckland described this as "deliberately privileging some documents over others as a separate matter from the anticipation of demand" Michael K. Buckland, Redesigning Library Services: A Manifesto: Supplement available at *<http://sunsite,berkeley.edu/Literature/Library/Redesiging/supplement.html>* (visited February 28, 2002).

70. Buckland, id.

71. Howard T. Senzel. *Looseleafing the Information Highway: An Anecdotal History of One Technology for Updating* available at *<http://www.snesl.edu/senzel/htsframe.htm>* (visited February 28, 2002).

72. Gaynor Austen, *What is My Core Business? The Academic Librarian As Partner in the Teaching and Research Process*, available at *<http://library.brandeis.edu/beijing_conference/GaynorAusten.doc>* (visited February 28, 2002).

73. Hazelton, supra note 1, at 13.

Availability of Works Cited in Recent Law Review Articles on LEXIS, Westlaw, the Internet, and Other Databases

Simon Canick

SUMMARY. In this study, a group of recent law articles was examined to determine the proportion of cited resources that are easily findable online. Searches were conducted in databases such as LEXIS and Westlaw, and on the Internet, for full-text versions of every source cited in seven articles. The results have been broken down into 13 categories, including "federal cases," "books," "foreign law," and "legal periodicals pre-1990." Not surprisingly, coverage differs widely between the categories. Overall, the study found that 77% of the 1,984 citations in the articles reviewed are available online. The article concludes with a general discussion of why the percentage is likely to increase in the future. *[Article copies available for a fee from The Haworth Document Delivery Service: 1-800-HAWORTH. E-mail address: <getinfo@haworthpressinc.com> Website: <http://www.HaworthPress.com> © 2002 by The Haworth Press, Inc. All rights reserved.]*

KEYWORDS. Footnotes, LEXIS, Westlaw, citations, fulltext, law review articles

---

Simon Canick is Reference Librarian, Arthur W. Diamond Law Library, Columbia University.

[Haworth co-indexing entry note]: "Availability of Works Cited in Recent Law Review Articles on LEXIS, Westlaw, the Internet, and Other Databases." Canick, Simon. Co-published simultaneously in *Legal Reference Services Quarterly* (The Haworth Information Press, an imprint of The Haworth Press, Inc.) Vol. 21, No. 2/3, 2002, pp. 55-67; and: *Law Library Collection Development in the Digital Age* (ed: Michael Chiorazzi, and Gordon Russell) The Haworth Information Press, an imprint of The Haworth Press, Inc., 2002, pp. 55-67. Single or multiple copies of this article are available for a fee from The Haworth Document Delivery Service [1-800-HAWORTH, 9:00 a.m. - 5:00 p.m. (EST). E-mail address: getinfo@haworthpressinc.com].

INTRODUCTION

In recent years, online resources have become compelling alternatives to traditional, print-based legal research for many attorneys and law students. This trend will surely continue as LEXIS, Westlaw, and the Internet broaden their coverage and become more reliable. So far, databases and Web sites have featured commonly used materials like statutes and case law. The wide availability of primary legal information and practice materials may lead some attorneys to believe that they no longer need to visit law libraries.

Legal scholarship is fundamentally different, however. Work produced by law school faculty and students, for instance, often relies upon obscure or historical sources that are available only in print. For Westlaw and LEXIS to keep scholars out of libraries, they will have to aggressively expand their coverage.

The purpose of this study was to assess the scope of various online databases with respect to a particular type of research. Specifically, a group of recent law review articles was examined to determine the proportion of cited resources that are easily findable online. Searches were conducted in several databases and on the Internet for full-text versions of every source cited in seven articles. The selection of the seven articles was arbitrary; no effort was made to ensure consideration of particular subjects, authors, or journals.

In the future, we may read online law review articles with direct links to the full text of each of the works to which they cite. It may be many years before this vision is achieved, however. This study found that a more modest, but still substantial 77% of the 1,984 citations in the articles reviewed are available online.

METHODOLOGY

For this study, seven recent law review articles were selected at random:

- Stephen R. Barnett, *"The Right to One's Own Image": Publicity and Privacy Rights in the United States and Spain*, 47 Am. J. Comp. L. 555 (1999).
- John T. Boese & Beth C. McClain, *Why* Thompson *is Wrong: Misuse of the False Claims Act to Enforce the Anti-Kickback Act*, 51 Ala. L. Rev. 1 (1999).
- William W. Bratton & Joseph A. McCahery, *Comparative Corporate Governance and the Theory of the Firm: The Case Against Global Cross Reference*, 38 Colum. J. Transnat'l L. 213 (1999).

- John C. Coffee, Jr., *Class Action Accountability: Reconciling Exit, Voice, and Loyalty in Representative Litigation*, 100 Colum. L. Rev. 370 (2000).
- Andrew L. Kaufman, *Benjamin Cardozo as Paradigmatic Tort Lawmaker*, 49 DePaul L. Rev. 281 (1999).
- Joseph P. Monteleone & Emy P. Grotell, *Coverage for Employment Practices Liability Under Various Policies: Commercial General Liability, Homeowners', Umbrella, Workers' Compensation, and Directors' and Officers' Liability Policies*, 21 W. New Eng. L. Rev. 249 (1999).
- Laurence C. Nolan, *"Unwed Children" and Their Parents Before the United States Supreme Court From* Levy *to* Michael H.: *Unlikely Participants in Constitutional Jurisprudence*, 28 Cap. U.L. Rev. 1 (1999).

These articles had little in common. Their subject areas ranged from the Civil False Claims Act, to Spanish publicity rights, to class action lawsuits, to the treatment of children born out of wedlock. As expected, this diverse body of articles included citations to a wide variety of resources, including cases, statutes, periodicals, working papers, treatises, government documents, and foreign law.

Each citation was coded according to its type. The following categories were created:

- *Legal Periodicals 1990-present:* Including law review articles, legal newspapers, and bar journals.
- *Legal Periodicals pre-1990:* Including law review articles, legal newspapers, and bar journals.
- *Non-Legal Periodicals 1990-present:* Including newspapers, magazines, and journals from other fields.
- *Non-Legal Periodicals pre-1900:* Including newspapers, magazines, and journals from other fields.
- *Books:* Including legal and non-legal treatises and looseleaf services.
- *Reports/Working Papers:* Including studies and reports issued by think-tanks, non-profit organizations, university groups, and governmental/quasi-governmental bodies.
- *Federal Cases:* All years, all court levels.
- *State Cases:* All years, all court levels.
- *Federal Law:* Including statutes and administrative material.
- *State Law:* Including statutes and administrative material.

- *Uniform Laws:* Including Uniform Codes, Model Codes, and Restatements.
- *Foreign/International Law:* Including primary material, and government reports.
- *Court Filings/Transcripts:* Including pleadings and trial transcripts.

For each footnote, it was determined whether the cited material could be found using LEXIS or Westlaw. If unavailable there, other databases (e.g., JSTOR, ABI-INFORM, etc.) or the World Wide Web were consulted. If full-text could not be located in any online format, then that fact was noted.

Every citation in every article was counted, whether or not the resources encountered had been previously cited. This series of footnotes should illustrate the methodology employed:

> 73. *See* Orsini v. Blasi, 423 U.S. 1042 (1976).
> 74. 42 U.S.C. § 512(b) (1994).
> 75. *See id.* § 512(a)-(c).
> 76. *See,* e.g., Douglas W. Diamond, *Financial Intermediation and Delegated Monitoring*, 51 Rev. Econ. Stud. 393 (1984).

If confronted with this list, LEXIS or Westlaw would first be checked to make sure *Orsini* was available there. If so, the case would be coded as found on Westlaw/LEXIS without inquiring whether, for example, the case existed on the Web. The same process would be followed for the two *United States Code* citations.[1] For the journal article, Westlaw or LEXIS would be checked first. If unavailable there, other databases would be consulted. In this case, the article was found on JSTOR, so it was unnecessary to inquire whether a Web site had its text as well.

GENERAL FINDINGS

As previously noted, 77% of the works cited were found online. LEXIS and Westlaw have the broadest coverage, providing access to 73%. Roughly 4% (79 out of 1,984 total citations) could be found only on another database or the Internet.

The percentage of citations available online varied widely from article to article. For instance, 98% of the cited works from Monteleone and Grotell were found, compared to only 48% from Bratton and McCahery. The difference lies in the types of material most frequently footnoted. Monteleone and Grotell relied heavily on case-law, while Bratton and McCahery routinely cited relatively hard-to-find items, like books and non-legal periodicals.

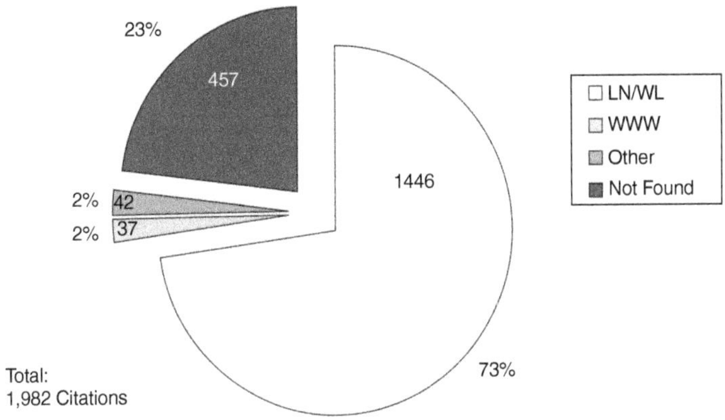

SPECIFIC FINDINGS

- *Legal Periodicals 1990-Present:* Of 163 citations to recent legal periodicals, 150 (92%) were found on LEXIS or Westlaw. The remaining 13 were unavailable in any online source.

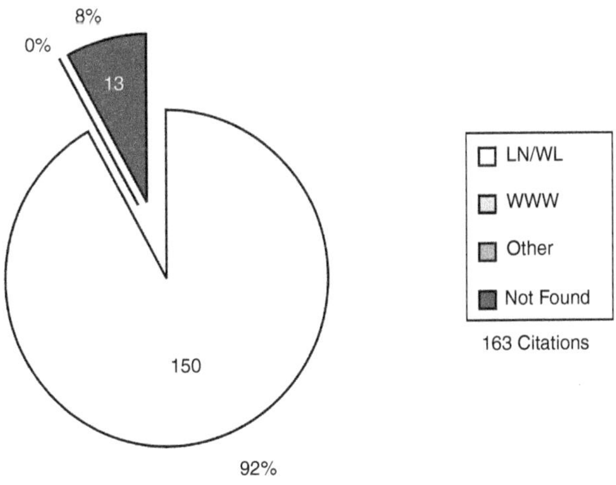

- *Legal Periodicals Pre-1990:* Older legal periodicals were much more difficult to locate online. Of 107 total, Westlaw and LEXIS had only 26 (24%). None of the remaining 81 resources cited could be located on another database or the World Wide Web.[2]

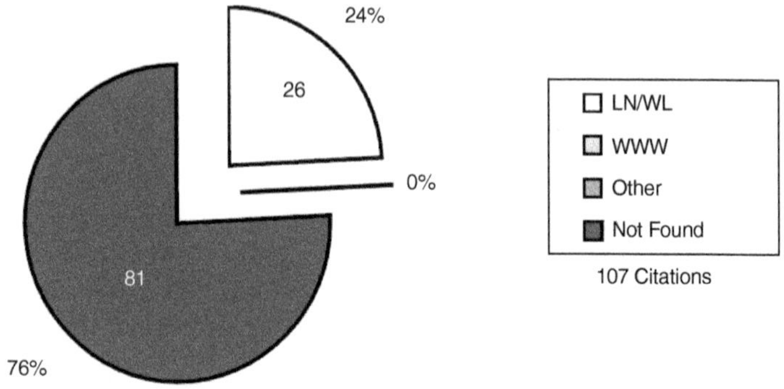

- *Non-Legal Periodicals 1990-Present:* Full-text versions of roughly two-thirds (67%) of the recent non-legal periodicals were located online. In this category, 80 of the 169 citations (47%) were available on LEXIS or Westlaw, and 34 more (20%) were found on other databases, such as JSTOR.[3]

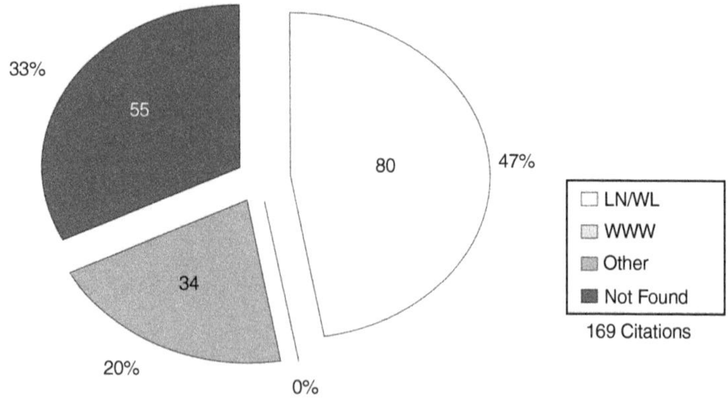

- *Non-Legal Periodicals Pre-1990:* Of the 16 citations to older non-legal periodicals, none were available on LEXIS or Westlaw. Half (8) were accessible through other databases, and half could not be found.

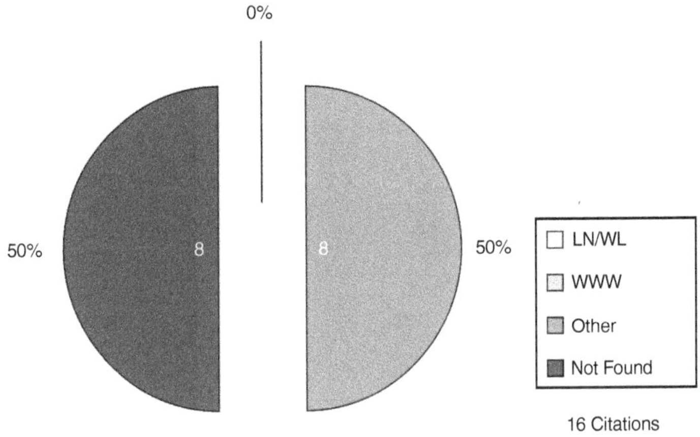

- *Books:* Books is the major category with the lowest online coverage rate. LEXIS and Westlaw contain the text of some important treatises and looseleaf services, but the vast majority of monographic works, legal or non-legal, are not reproduced online.

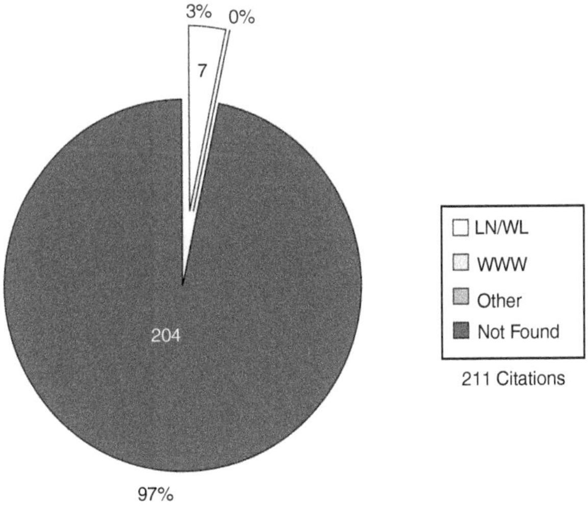

- *Reports/Working Papers:* Three of the seven articles reviewed cited frequently to various types of reports and working papers. When available online, most of these documents reside on the Internet.

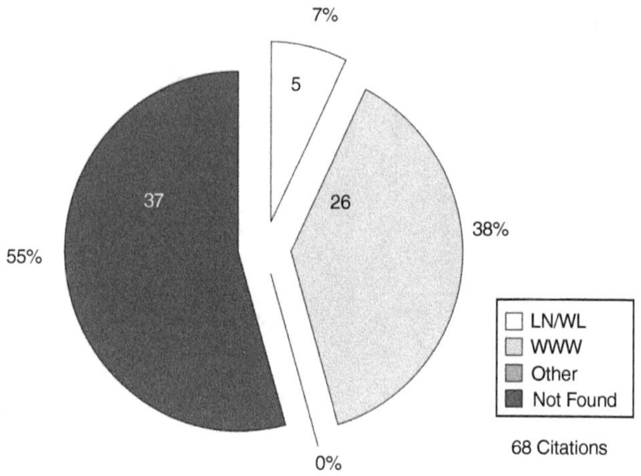

- *Federal Cases:* With 844 footnote references, federal cases were the most heavily cited category of material in the seven articles. LEXIS and Westlaw provided access to every cited case.

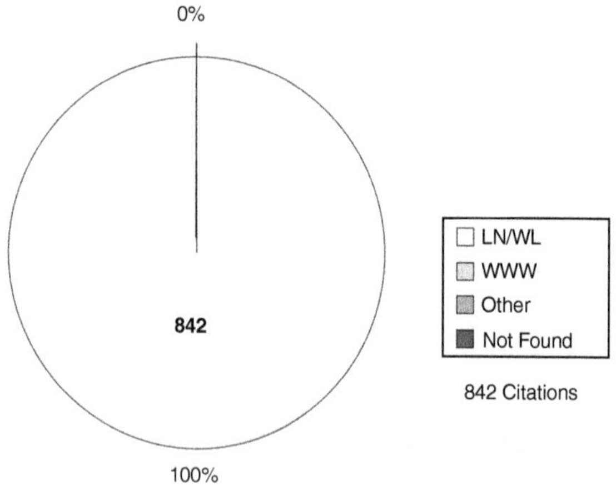

- *State Cases:* LEXIS and Westlaw provided access to each of the 214 state cases cited.

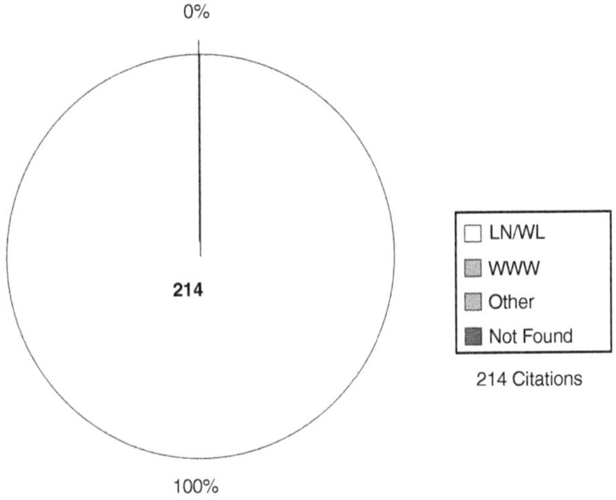

- *Federal Law:* Almost all U.S. statutory and administrative material is available on LEXIS and Westlaw. Some superseded material could not be found.

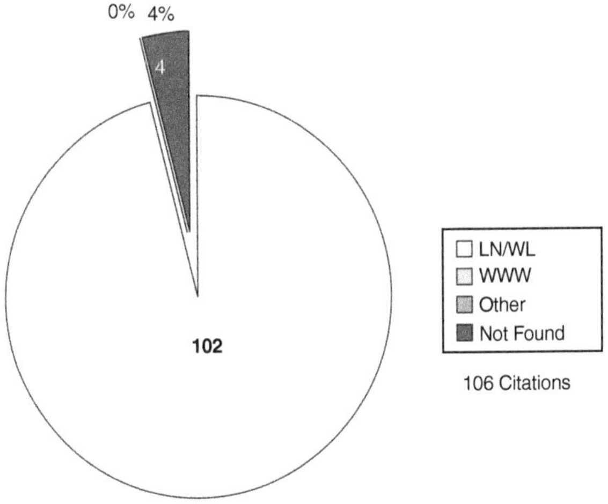

- *State Law:* The seven articles reviewed only cited to state statutory or regulatory material six times. All were found on LEXIS or Westlaw.

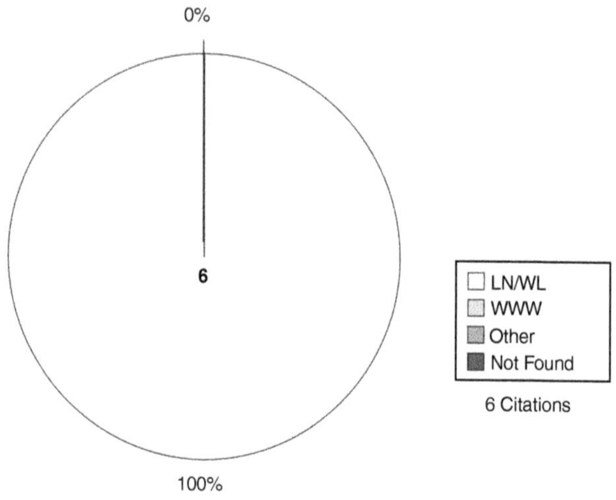

- *Uniform Laws:* Uniform Laws, Model Codes, and Restatements were cited 12 times. All 12 are available on LEXIS or Westlaw.

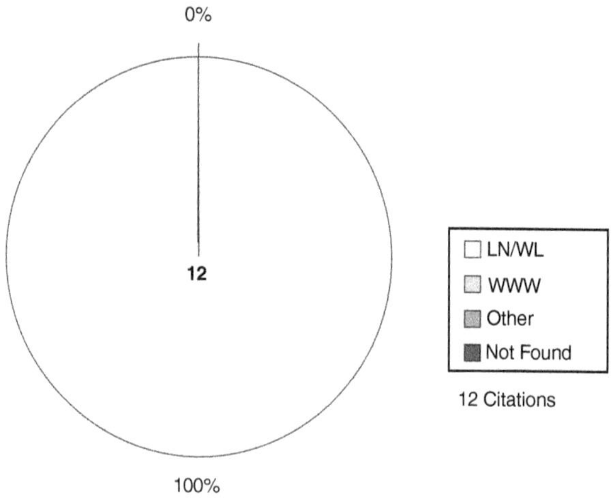

- *Foreign Law:* Nearly three quarters of the foreign legal material cited in the seven articles could not be found online. Most of the available material was on the World Wide Web rather than LEXIS or Westlaw.

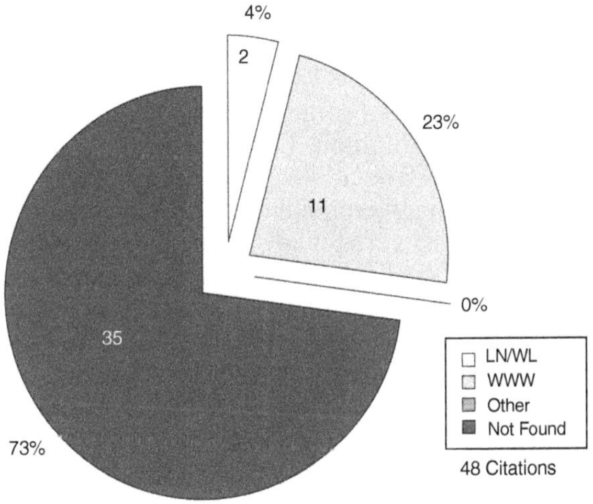

- *Court Filings/Transcripts:* Pleadings, motions, and trial transcripts were cited frequently in one article (Boese & Mcclain). None of the 20 cited items could be found online.

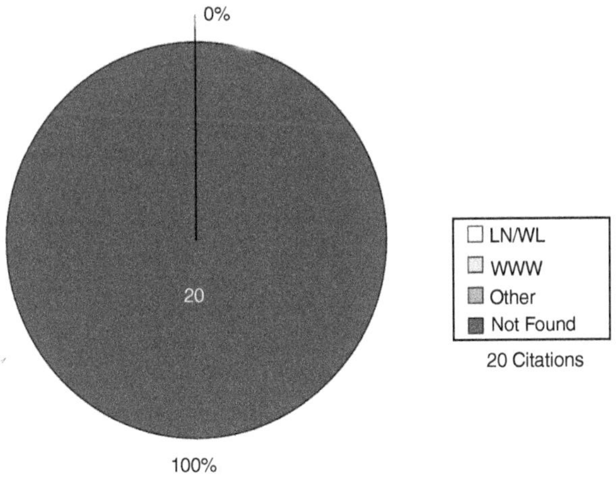

CONCLUSIONS

Online databases are rich resources for the full-text of certain types of documents cited in recent law review articles. For instance, LEXIS and Westlaw covered over 95% (1,166 out of 1,222) of citations to primary legal materials. The figure jumps to 99% (1,164 out of 1,174), when limited to United States law.

As expected, LEXIS and Westlaw are much less effective for retrieving secondary sources. Only 37% (280 out of 766) of cited legal and non-legal secondary material could be found. When combined with other databases available at Columbia University, and the Internet, the total jumps to nearly 50% (380 out of 766). The World Wide Web offered reasonably good access to government documents, working papers, and reports. Other databases covered many non-legal publications.

The fact that 77% of cited resources were found in electronic form shows how vast the universe of online fulltext materials has become. Yet it also illustrates the opportunity for improvement. Many law review articles cite to books of all kinds, yet precious few can be located outside of print.[4] In addition, LEXIS and Westlaw's coverage gets thinner as sought-after material gets older. Databases will never solve the research needs of individuals engaged in legal scholarship unless they extend their reach back in time.

Nevertheless, for a number of reasons it seems clear that the percentage of cited works available electronically in fulltext will increase. First, an enormous amount of new material is uploaded every year.[5] And as search engine technology improves, we will be better able to find the information that has been posted.[6] Second, in recent years there has been an emergence of interest in making electronic versions of significant historical documentation available. Hein-On-Line,[7], JSTOR,[8] Early English Books Online,[9] and American Memory[10] are significant examples of efforts to provide access to older works.

Third, authors tend to cite to recent publications. Of the periodicals cited in the articles examined by this study, for instance, 73% (332 out of 455) were written in the 1990s. We also know that recently released articles are much more readily available electronically. With authors increasingly referencing new publications with electronic outlets, it seems likely that the percentage of cited works available online will increase.

Finally, it's becoming clear that works get read and cited because they are available online. Students who grew up with the Internet will use available electronic resources and avoid print.[11] Right or wrong, many people believe they can find everything they need online. And as materials that are easily findable online get cited more and more often, authors will feel pressured to publish with journals that provide electronic access. Otherwise their articles may never be read.

NOTES

1. Originally, it was intended that each cited work would be searched only once, and all "id" and "supra" references would be ignored. However, problems with statutes made this unrealistic. Here is a hypothetical set of footnotes that illustrates the problem:

1. 42 U.S.C. § 1015 (1994).
2. Id. § 1015(g).
3. Id. § 1015(b)-(h).
4. Id. §§ 1014-1018.

The last footnote covers the first three, and the first footnote covers the second and third. So it was unclear how many discrete sources would result from this list. Rather than create an arbitrary rule for dealing with such situations, it made more sense to count each citation once, even if that source had been cited before.

2. Note that these results were tabulated before Hein-On-Line became available at Columbia University. At this writing, Hein-On-Line offers scanned images of over 150 legal journals beginning with their earliest issues, and will include 3.5 million pages by the end of 2001. See *http://heinonline.org/HeinDocs/Overview.htm.*

3. The results here depend on the databases to which Columbia University subscribed at the time the study was undertaken. More of these materials may be on OCLS FirstSearch or Ebsco, for instance, but those are not available on campus. The results are still valid in the sense that few people will have access to every full text database.

4. It remains to be seen whether E-Books will make a significant change in this regard. *See generally* Lucia Snowhill, E-Books and Their Future in Academic Libraries: An Overview, D-Lib Mag. (July/Aug. 2001), at *http://www.dlib.org/dlib/july01/snowhill/07snowhill.html*; Mick O'Leary, *Ebook Scenarios*, Online, at 62 (Jan./Feb. 2001).

5. See Michael K. Bergman, The Deep Web: Surfacing Hidden Value (2001), available at *http://www.brightplanet.com/deepcontent/tutorials/DeepWeb/deepwebwhitepaper.pdf*. Bergman measured the accessibility of "deep Web" sources, which feature searchable databases responsive to direct requests. The study concluded that the "deep Web is the largest growing category of new information on the internet."

6. See id.

7. *http://heinonline.org/.*

8. *http://www.jstor.org/.* JSTOR is a searchable archive of over 250 prominent journals in various fields. Every article is presented in PDF format, and therefore retains the authority that comes with original pagination.

9. *http://wwwlib.umi.com/eebo.* Early English Books Online features images of over 125,000 books published before 1700.

10. *http://memory.loc.gov/ammem/.* American Memory is a significant piece of the Library of Congress' National Digital Library Program, an effort to make electronically available materials important in American history. One small subset of American Memory is A Century of Lawmaking, *http://memory.loc.gov/ammem/amlaw/ lawhome.html*, which contains scanned images of Congressional documents from 1774-1873.

11. See Philip M. Davis & Suzanne A. Cohen, The Effect of the Web on Undergraduate Citation Behavior 1996-1999, 52 JASIS 309, 311 (2001) (finding that as Web use among students increased, the proportion of bibliography citations to books decreased from 30% to 19%).

Strategic Planning for Distance Learning in Legal Education: Initial Thoughts on a Role for Libraries

Richard A. Danner

SUMMARY. Distance learning technologies will be used increasingly by law schools both to enhance learning within their existing residential programs and to reach new audiences. For law librarians, the questions involved in serving distance learners are a subset of the questions about the future of the law library that arise from changes in the legal information environment. This article discusses current distance learning alternatives for law schools, and the impacts of distance learning and other technological innovations on the future role of the academic law library in legal education. *[Article copies available for a fee from The Haworth Document Delivery Service: 1-800-HAWORTH. E-mail address: <getinfo@haworthpressinc.com> Website: <http://www.HaworthPress.com>]*

KEYWORDS. Distance learning, law school curriculum, legal education

---

Richard A. Danner is Senior Associate Dean for Information Technology and Research Professor of Law, Duke University School of Law.

This article is based on a paper prepared for the conference: "Not a Box but a Window: Law Libraries and Legal Education in a Virtual World," University of Toronto, February 23, 2001. A video archive and links to papers presented at the conference are maintained at <http://www.law-lib.utoronto.ca/conferences/future/index.htm#8> (last visited December 1, 2001).

[Haworth co-indexing entry note]: "Strategic Planning for Distance Learning in Legal Education: Initial Thoughts on a Role for Libraries." Danner, Richard A. Co-published simultaneously in *Legal Reference Services Quarterly* (The Haworth Information Press, an imprint of The Haworth Press, Inc.) Vol. 21, No. 2/3, 2002, pp. 69-85; and: *Law Library Collection Development in the Digital Age* (ed: Michael Chiorazzi, and Gordon Russell) The Haworth Information Press, an imprint of The Haworth Press, Inc., 2002, pp. 69-85. Single or multiple copies of this article are available for a fee from The Haworth Document Delivery Service [1-800-HAWORTH, 9:00 a.m. - 5:00 p.m. (EST). E-mail address: getinfo@haworthpressinc.com].

> The next big killer application for the Internet is going to be education. Education over the Internet is going to be so big it is going to make e-mail usage look like a rounding error.
>
> –*John T. Chambers, CEO, Cisco Systems*[1]

> Law school is a product. . . . The question is not 'Will we see virtual law schools? [but] when will we see virtual law schools.'
>
> –*A. Michael Froomkin*
> *Professor of Law, University of Miami*[2]

The 2001 downturn in the United States economy resulted in numerous reports of failures among the high-profile information technology companies that had only so recently been credited with creating what many called a "New Economy" based in the work of "brain toilers," rather than in traditional service and manufacturing industries.[3] Included among the casualties were many e-learning companies involved in development and promotion of distance education programs, including companies focused on the apparently limitless potential of the business education market.[4] Yet, despite the reported setbacks in online business education, established business schools have continued to develop their own online programs and to work with for-profit distance learning companies, while prominent universities have continued to develop their own profit-seeking distance learning spin-offs. The potential impact of the Internet on the delivery of degrees and other products in higher and professional education has remained a major topic of discussion for educators, foundations, technology entrepreneurs, and business gurus alike. For many analysts, the higher and continuing education markets continue to be valued in numbers high enough to attract the attention of venture capitalists and other investors.[5]

The environment for distance learning in law differs from the less regulated (and less restricted) world of business education. For legal education in the United States, distance learning's potential for growth and development depends in large part on the regulations and practices of the American Bar Association and other agencies that monitor legal education. While encouraging U.S. law schools to invest in information technology, the ABA's 1997 distance education guidelines[6] have fostered experimentation with some forms of distance learning, but have limited experimentation with others.

This article examines some of the distance learning opportunities available to those law schools willing and able to commit the resources needed to explore the possibilities, as well as some of their implications for law school libraries. The discussion is based in part on ongoing discussions about these matters at my own institution.

EDUCATIONAL TECHNOLOGY AT DUKE LAW

Duke Law School's current student body is about 680. Seventy-five or so of our students are international lawyers enrolled in either a one year LL.M. program or an advanced doctoral program; the rest are studying for the J.D. Duke is noted for its interdisciplinary and international programs, as well as for its long-standing commitment to a strong information technology infrastructure. The law library, which has played a leadership role in the Law School's technology initiatives,[7] has over 565,000 volumes, placing it among the largest, though not the very largest, of American law libraries. Because of the investments in infrastructure and support, a number of members of the law faculty at Duke have become interested in developing and using new technologies to enhance instruction and learning in the residential program.

Since 1990, Duke has made significant investments in networking the Law School building and making networked resources widely available to all members of the community. Our students are required to own portable computers and we have installed network connections in our classrooms, throughout the library, and in all faculty and staff offices. Wireless networks are used in parts of the building where the costs of wired network retrofitting are prohibitive. The Law School has placed a high priority on developing its web site as a means for disseminating information about the School, communicating with external constituencies, publishing scholarship, and sharing information within the Law School community. Significantly for the School's educational mission, the site features a rich curriculum section focusing on course support, which includes information about all courses, instructors, and schedules; access to course home pages; information about prerequisites and courses of study; biographical and bibliographical information for the faculty; and other expanded "bulletin-type" information for students.

A major mid-nineties building addition focused on new faculty and administrative offices, library improvements, and better spaces for public events. Since then, the Law School has made substantial investments in upgrading teaching and learning technologies in its classrooms and courtroom. All regularly-used classrooms and seminar rooms are now equipped with video/data projectors, computers connected to the Law

School network and the Internet, and audio and video players. Duke Law instructors control all teaching technologies electronically through touch pads installed in custom-built teaching consoles. All classrooms provide power outlets for student computers and nearly all have network connections at each student seat. Since 2000, the Law School has constructed new mid- and large-sized classrooms, a courtroom, and seminar rooms with built-in taping, video conferencing, Webcasting and other distance learning capabilities managed from a central control room.

As capabilities have grown, Duke faculty members have gradually incorporated a variety of teaching technologies into their courses and have used network technologies to promote opportunities for learning outside the classroom. Each course has an e-mail discussion list through which faculty can respond to student questions and provoke discussion outside of class. Most instructors use locally-designed and supported course home pages on the Law School Web site for posting (and easily updating) course syllabi, assignments, and other materials, and to support chat rooms and other discussion forums beyond the e-mail discussion lists. Increasingly, faculty are seeking to expand their use of the course pages to provide links to Web materials for students to explore outside of class or to use in the classroom. A number of faculty are supported in these efforts by Technology Teaching Assistants, a corps of technology-savvy law students available to help faculty develop new uses of technology for their teaching. Since fall 2001, the school's efforts to promote productive uses of technology in its educational programs are coordinated by a director of educational technologies, working in conjunction with the computing services department and the law library.

To date, some highlights of faculty uses of technology for teaching and learning include: Professor John Weistart's project to develop a full set of video-based Contracts course materials with Duke Professor H. Jefferson Powell and Professor Girardeau Spann of the Georgetown Law Center;[8] Professor David Lange's incorporation of student-produced video assignments into his courses on intellectual property and entertainment law;[9] Professors Jonathan Wiener and Thomas Metzloff's innovative uses of commercial course support software to bring faculty from other schools and outside attorneys into Web-based discussions with students in their mass torts classes; Professor Michael Byers's use of video conferencing in his International Dispute Settlement Seminar to bring in guests from the Cambridge University law faculty; and Professor Metzloff's work with faculty colleagues to explore the potential uses of PowerPoint in the classroom. In spring 2001, Professor Metzloff taught his course in Distinctive Aspects of American Law to law students at Tsinghua University in Beijing using Webcasting and live video conferencing to supplement video and text materials offered through the Law School Web site.

In the course of their experimentation, the faculty have found that many teaching technologies help them think in new ways about the boundaries between learning within the classroom and learning that occurs outside class. Many of the increasingly common applications of technology in the residential J.D. program (video conferencing, online discussion groups, etc.) can be used effectively both in residential programs and in distance learning environments. As a result, the Duke law faculty are becoming increasingly experienced and comfortable with distance learning applications in the course of their regular teaching, and the distinctions between residential and distance learning technologies are increasingly blurred for both faculty and students.

CURRENT AND FUTURE CAPABILITIES: NEW MARKETS?

The networked information technology environments of higher education, business, and the professions provide the infrastructure for delivering education and training faster and with greater possibilities for individualized learning and interaction between instructor and learners than was possible in the past. Distance learning can no longer be thought about simply in terms of correspondence courses, videotapes, or public television programming. To develop effective institutional distance learning strategies in a rich technological environment, it is necessary to analyze new opportunities along a number of dimensions: the specific technologies to be employed (e.g., synchronous or asynchronous); desired levels of interactivity (e.g., video conferencing or Webcasting); potential audiences (e.g., degree-seeking students or adult learners); pedagogical approaches (e.g., lecture, discussion, self-study, etc.); costs of development; and potential for income.

As a result, the successful pursuit of distance learning initiatives at any institution will require the articulation of a rationale for making the investments necessary for the program to be successful. What learners will be served? For most law schools, there are at least three possible rationales for entering into distance learning programs: (1) to improve the J.D. curriculum; (2) to expand access to programs for alumni and other natural constituencies of the law school; and (3) to capitalize on emerging market opportunities.

Distance Learning in the J.D. Curriculum

While current ABA regulations restrict applications of certain kinds of distance learning, the ABA does encourage experimentation within a set of temporary guidelines issued by the Consultant on Legal Education in 1997.[10] As a result, faculty at a growing number of law schools have engaged in distance teaching experiments, or have at least debated the implications of distance learning for the education of law students.[11] To date, many of these experiments have relied on available ISDN video conferencing technologies to create shared classrooms at two or more law schools with either a single instructor or instructors participating at each site. In addition to creating a space for real-time teaching and discussion, courses employing video conferencing can be supplemented with shared Web pages, e-mail discussions and some of the more sophisticated features of commercial courseware packages (chat rooms, document sharing and other web capabilities designed to facilitate collaborative work).

To test the effectiveness of low-cost approaches to distance learning in law, Professor Peter Martin at the Cornell Law School has experimented both with real-time Internet video conferencing,[12] and with asynchronous courses using a wide range of Web-based instructional technologies. Professor Martin's most recent efforts are described in "A Report on the LII's Two Multi-Law School Courses Conducted via the Internet in 2000-2001," prepared for the ABA Consultant on Legal Education.[13]

The equipment and infrastructure needed to employ ISDN video conferencing and Web-based technologies in distance courses should be available on most university campuses, if not in law school buildings themselves. Duke Law has used video conferencing in experiments with other North American law schools, to develop joint courses with Cambridge University through its Public Law Program, and as one component of a spring 2001 project to offer the law school's "Distinctive Aspects of the American Legal System" course at Tsinghua University in Beijing. Video conferencing has been used successfully to extend the reach of conferences sponsored by Duke's Global Capital Markets Center and other programs.[14] Success in these efforts, domestic and international, requires investments at each end in planning, good support structures, and educating faculty to understand the ways in which teaching remote students differs from normal classroom teaching.

Most ideas for distance learning courses (or components of courses) offered on a law school-to-law school basis using video conferencing or other synchronous technologies fall within the ABA's current temporary distance education guidelines, without requiring prior approval by the ABA's Consultant on Legal Education.[15] New distance learning standards proposed in December 2001 further encourage the use of synchronous video technologies.[16] As the ability to offer high quality video improves with the implementation of Internet 2,[17] there is little doubt that law faculty will make increasing uses of collaborative distance learning technologies to co-teach or otherwise enhance courses in the J.D. and LL.M. programs, or that law schools will offer courses taught by faculty in remote locations. Within the near future, many faculty will think no more of using these technologies to enhance their teaching than their predecessors did of using chalk boards and overhead transparencies.

Distance Programs for Alumni and Others

Successful experiments and greater familiarity with distance learning applications in the J.D. curriculum will provide experience for faculty and encourage law schools to explore developing specialized distance learning programs for domestic and international alumni, and other natural constituencies of the law school. Local conferences and other programming can be developed into distance learning vehicles using video conferencing (or Webcasting), Web-based chat and other discussion capabilities, and delivery of conference materials. Programs can also be created specifically for alumni (e.g., a series of Webcast programs featuring law faculty members discussing contemporary legal issues) or other audiences. Duke has pursued several beneficial distance learning activities using its own resources, without the assistance of external partners. Since the construction of two distance learning classrooms in 2000 and 2001, the School has successfully Webcast major lectures and conferences sponsored by its Public Law and Intellectual Property programs. In November 2000, Duke Law Webcast a faculty panel discussion on the Supreme Court's review of the U.S. presidential election to Law School alumni as an experiment in "continuing education on a moment's notice."[18] Typically, lectures and conferences are Webcast live, then are edited and post-produced into archival versions that remain accessible through the Law School Web site.[19]

Such targeted programs do not necessarily require the high investment in content development or sophisticated delivery systems of the commercial distance learning initiatives discussed in the following section of this article. Without committing the resources needed for commercial product development, law schools can offer occasional distance programming using the same sorts of delivery technologies that will be used increasingly by faculty in the J.D. program. Such efforts will promote a school's public service and educational missions, and enhance ties with national and international alumni. Like the uses of distance learning in the residential J.D. program, many of these activities will become commonplace as the technology continues to improve and becomes more accessible. Any potential for significant earnings, however, will be limited unless a law school wishes to expand its markets, and work with outside partners capable of the substantial investments needed to develop and maintain the technologies required to support sophisticated (and constantly changing) delivery technologies.

Distance Programs in New Markets

Within higher education, business schools have been quicker than law schools to explore the commercial possibilities of distance learning programs. At Duke, the Law School has closely monitored the Fuqua School of Business's global distance learning programs to determine how Fuqua's models and experiences could benefit the Law School's own thinking about distance learning. Fuqua's M.B.A.-Global Executive program[20] and other distance-based executive education programs have served to create new markets for the educational offerings of the Fuqua School. Fuqua's programs emphasize the importance of face-to-face classroom interaction. Students gather together periodically in Durham or elsewhere, but do much of their work remotely from locations in the U.S. and abroad. A number of business schools have developed similar distance degree and executive education programs. Although the programs differ in the emphasis they place on face-to-face meetings, all necessarily rely extensively on Web-based tools to facilitate communications between students and their instructors and other students.

Potential earnings in the online M.B.A. and executive education markets early on attracted the interest of for-profit e-learning companies. The most prominent of these companies has probably been UNext.com, which offers courses under the name Cardean University.[21] UNext's university partners include Carnegie-Mellon University, the University of Chicago Graduate School of Business, the Columbia University Business School, the London School of Economics and Political Science, and Stanford University. Typically, faculty members at the partner schools develop courses for the UNext curriculum and the partner schools hope to receive a share of profits from the company.[22]

Because the initial and ongoing development costs for delivering course content in a competitive market are so high, it is unlikely that existing educational institutions will be successful in reaching new markets without engaging in the kinds of partnerships offered by companies like UNext, or by building their own for-profit subsidiaries. Some universities (e.g., Temple, Columbia, NYU, and Cornell) have developed their own distance learning entities;[23] others have worked in concert with like-minded schools to develop their own delivery platforms and establish distance learning brands.[24] In developing its programs, Duke's Fuqua School contracted with Pensare.com, a UNext competitor, to support some of its offerings, and later established its own for-profit distance learning entity, Duke Corporate Education, which operates independently from the Fuqua School.[25]

Distance learning markets for law comparable to those for business education are yet to be developed. In general, law schools are only beginning to consider the possibilities seriously. Unlike established business schools and for-profit entities, which can offer M.B.A. degrees to students studying individually in distance learning programs, law schools are limited by the ABA in their abilities to grant credit toward the J.D. degree for distance learning courses. At present, there are no law schools approved by the ABA that provide a J.D. degree via distance learning or correspondence study. In the immediate future, therefore, most law school interest in creating new markets for educational offerings is likely to focus on advanced degree programs or some form of continuing education.

Not all law schools have the technological infrastructure and other resources necessary to consider distance learning initiatives aimed at developing new markets and new educational products. In addition, law school missions differ. Some law schools have primary missions centered on their home states or regions, which may create opportunities to serve their natural constituencies while foreclosing or limiting pursuit of broader initiatives and wider markets. Yet, many law schools do have potential markets both in domestic continuing education programs, and for domestic and international LL.M. degrees, as well as the potential to develop products in these areas based on known strengths of the law school's faculty, specialized centers and programs, and international visibility.

Whether or not a law school chooses to develop aggressive institutional strategies in distance learning, individual faculty members will see increasing opportunities to provide course content through external vehicles. The possibilities for individual faculty agreements with commercial enterprises have contributed to some universities' interests in developing their own for-profit ventures.[26] In law, faculty members with expertise in subjects adaptable to the M.B.A./executive education market are most likely to have immediate opportunities to develop courses or provide initial content for online courses developed by companies like UNext and its competitors.[27] There will also be opportunities in continuing legal education[28] and with new online law schools, such as Kaplan, Inc.'s Concord University School of Law.[29]

Much of Concord University School of Law's initial publicity centered on the course ownership questions raised at Harvard Law School by Professor Arthur Miller's relationship with the School. (If nothing else, the potential for future commercial partnerships will provide a forum for law faculty to examine questions of intellectual property rights and ownership of courses and course materials.) But, Concord's program has gained significant national attention apart from the questions raised by its affiliation with a celebrity law professor.[30] In addition, some established law schools are themselves showing interest in distance learning programs. St. Thomas University Law School offers an LL.M. degree in international taxation.[31] The Open Education programs of the Harvard Law School's Berkman Center for Law & Society offer a variety of computer-mediated seminars on the Internet and the law, with CLE credit available.[32] Boston University School of Law offers an internationally-oriented distance course on legislative drafting.[33]

Some law schools will be better positioned than others to pursue initiatives aimed at marketing educational products to national and international audiences. Some will gain strategically within their universities by pursuing entrepreneurial, expansive distance learning programs to raise the school's profile and attract outside investment to support core programs. Success in new markets will depend upon determining what kinds of partnerships are most appropriate for the school, what kinds of distance learning products the school should offer, what audiences it can reach, and how quickly it should act.

FIRST ISSUES FOR THE LAW LIBRARY

There is little doubt that distance learning technologies will be used increasingly by law schools to enhance learning within their residential programs, to improve communication and maintain contacts with alumni, and to promote the activities of centers and programs showcasing the law school's strengths and specialties, even if a school does not develop a broader, more expansive, distance learning strategy.

Regardless of which route a law school takes toward distance learning, a number of logistical and support issues will need to be resolved, not least how to provide library services to remote learners.[34] For law librarians, the questions involved in serving distance learners are a subset of the questions about the future of the law library that arise from changes in the legal information environment.

I have written elsewhere about approaching questions about the future of the law library from the perspective taken by David W. Lewis in the journal *Information Technology and Libraries.*[35] In his article, Lewis discusses two key questions: "What are libraries?" and "What are libraries for?" Lewis comes quickly to the point that, while libraries have traditionally concentrated on "gathering, organizing, preserving, and using *things*" (emphasis added) in local collections, information seekers in a networked information environment will have less need for the things ("books and serials and their derivatives") that libraries have traditionally collected.[36] In a distance learning environment, both the information seekers and the information they seek will be dispersed, and there could be even less value attached to local collections than when a library's primary mission is supporting only residential programs.

Lewis predicts that, instead of purchasing artifacts and storing information locally, educational institutions and other organizations will use site licenses or similar devices to obtain rights to access information. Libraries, of course, already purchase site licenses to access digital content locally, so using the library to provide access to licensed information for distance learning programs is an easy extension of traditional library services. Indeed, among the selling points for the St. Thomas distance international tax LL.M. program are Internet access to a number of general and tax specific legal databases and e-mail reference service for the LL.M. students.[37]

The ABA's Temporary Distance Education Guidelines stress the importance of having "a library or information resource center of significant size" available at the locale where a distance education program is received, but they also note that post-J.D. programs "may be considered differently from regular J.D. programs."[38] The ABA's acquiescence in the St. Thomas LL.M. degree, in effect accepts the proposition that remote access to databases and e-mail reference is sufficient library support for a highly specialized advanced distance learning program in international tax.

If library support of this sort is suitable for an online LL.M. degree, one must ask why would it not be just as suitable for other kinds of distance learning programs in legal education, including programs designed to offer the basic juris doctor degree? If a program met other accreditation requirements, if course materials were supplied to students in print or electronic formats, and if background and research materials were made available through accessible databases over the Internet, why would distance students, including J.D. students, need to have a readily available "library or information resource center of significant size?" What else is it that the library provides the learner beyond local access to information? Why do any law students need a readily available library if the information they need is available in digitized form via any networked computer? As David Lewis would put the question: "What are libraries for?"

The beginnings of an answer might be found in the ABA distance learning materials themselves. The Temporary Guidelines start from the principle that professional education in law "involves more than the mere delivery of information or simply learning facts, history or even logic," and that the "law school experience involves interaction with faculty not only in the classroom, but also in other places and at other times. Students also learn from each other by inquiry and challenge, review and study groups."[39] Interpretation 306-3 of the December 2001 proposed distance education standards emphasizes the benefits of "being part of a law school community and the learning and socialization into the legal profession that occurs outside, as well as inside, the classroom."[40] Because of the high value placed on these kinds of experiences in American legal education, law schools will struggle with the difficulties of replicating them in the distance learning environment.

To date, the St. Thomas LL.M. program and the J.D. program of Concord Law School are the primary examples of distance learning programs in law that focus on geographically dispersed students and rely extensively on asynchronous communication to solve the problems posed by distance and separation. St. Thomas's descriptive materials note the course's reliance on "[a]synchronous threaded chat room discussions and the ability to e-mail faculty and fellow students with course questions and comments on assignments and case studies."[41] Concord's program emphasizes the use of online dialogues led by professors, designed to provide students with greater feedback than they would receive in a traditional law school classroom. According to at least one Concord professor, the result of this (and the other components of Concord's efforts to reconstruct the law school classroom for distance learning) can be a greater sense of community feeling and class personality than in the traditional place-based law school classroom.[42]

It is too early to know whether these specific approaches to online education will be able to replicate, let alone improve upon, the experiences of law students enrolled in residential degree programs. It is unlikely, though, that any distance learning program in law will be successful unless it provides not just the means to access information or for asynchronous dialogue among students and faculty, but the means for developing a sense of community among all the participants engaged in the study of the law. This is one of the primary roles of the residential law school. As a result, establishing, developing, and maintaining a sense of community and all that it entails will be major challenges for the success of distance-based learning initiatives in law.

In residential legal education programs, the law library is a large factor in successful community building. As Peter Lyman has pointed out, the traditional library is not only a collection, but "a shared intellectual resource and site for a community."[43] Lyman asks whether the virtual communities created in distance education and by digital libraries and networks can "be designed to facilitate the moral values of community, such as trust, reciprocity, and loyalty." In responding to the challenges of supporting distance learning initiatives, librarians must be careful not to concentrate too much on what they can do to facilitate access to information and too little on the role that the library has traditionally played in developing and nurturing a sense of community within the law school. The primary challenges for law librarians will be found in the need to replicate this long-standing, but sometimes under-appreciated, role in the virtual law school. Law libraries do more for their institutions than provide access to information. They are also important sources of community building and sustenance.

NOTES

1. *Quoted in* Thomas L. Friedman, *Foreign Affairs: Next, It's E-ducation*, N.Y. Times, Nov. 17, 1999, at A29.

2. *Quoted in* Wendy R. Liebowitz, *Law Professors Told to Expect Competition from Virtual Learning*, Chron. Higher Educ., Jan. 21, 2000, at A45.

3. For an early exposition on "brain toiling," see Rector, Holy Trinity Church v. U.S., 143 U.S. 457, 464 (1892).

4. *See* Katherine S. Mangan, *Expectations Evaporate for Online MBA Programs*, Chron. Higher Ed., Oct. 5, 2001, at A31. *See also* Sarah Carr, *Is Anyone Making Money on Distance Education?*, Chron. Higher Ed., Feb. 16, 2001.

5. *See* Thomas Kostigen, *Higher Education: Education Stocks Graduate to New Levels This Year*, CBS MarketWatch, Oct 2, 2001, *at* http://cbs.marketwatch.com/news/story.asp?guid={23C7354E-736D-4347-BD73-EBBF6BC22C44}&siteid=mktw&archive=truereg. *See generally* Peter Drucker, *Putting More Now Into Knowledge*, Forbes, May 15, 2000, at 84.

6. For the current "temporary guidelines," see Memorandum from James P. White, Consultant on Legal Education to the American Bar Association, to Deans of ABA Approved Law Schools (May 6, 1997) (hereinafter Temporary Guidelines), *available at* http://www.abanet.org/legaled/distanceeducation/distance.html#MEMORANDUM D9697-59. For proposed revisions to the ABA Standards regarding distance education, see Memorandum from John A. Sebert, Consultant on Legal Education and Rudolph C. Hasl, Chair, Standards Review Committee, to Deans of ABA-Approved Law Schools (Dec. 10, 2001) (hereinafter Proposed Standards), *available at* http://www.abanet.org/legaled/standards/proposed.html.

7. The Duke Law Library's role in these developments is described in *Law Library Determines Digital Direction*, Syllabus, May 2001, at 34.

8. The materials were first used, in place of a standard casebook, in first year Contracts courses at Duke and Georgetown during the spring 2001 semester.

9. *See*, *Next Stop, Court TV*, Syllabus, Aug. 2001, at 45. Students use the facilities of a new media laboratory to edit and produce videos to fulfill course requirements in lieu of written research products. The Law School employs a full-time media production coordinator to support these projects and other video initiatives.

10. *See* Temporary Guidelines, supra note 7.

11. *See, e.g.*, Henry H. Perritt, *The Internet is Changing the Face of American Law Schools*, 33 Ind. L.Rev. 253 (1999); Harry J. Haynsworth, *Temporary Distance Learning Guidelines Provide Opportunities for Flexibility and Innovation*, 34 Ind. L.Rev 47 (2000); David A. Thomas, *American Legal Education: Moving from the Classroom Without Paper to Instruction Without the Classroom?*, 2001 JILT, no. 1, *at* sec. 5. http://elj.warwick.ac.uk/jilt/01-1/thomas.html; Robert H. Woods, *'Order in the Virtual Law Classroom . . . Order in the Virtual Law Classroom'–A Closer Look at American Law Schools in Cyberspace: Constructing Multiple Instruction Strategies for Effective Internet-based Legal Education*, 2001 JILT, no. 3, *at* http://elj.warwick.ac.uk/jilt/01-3/woods.html.

12. Professor Martin's initial courses are discussed in Peter W. Martin, Distance Learning–The LII's Experience and Future Plans (December 1999), *at* http://www.law.cornell.edu/background/distance/liidistance.htm.

13. *See* Memorandum from: Peter W. Martin to John A. Sebert, ABA Consultant on Legal Education (October 23, 2001), *available at* http://www.law.cornell.edu/background/distance/2001_abareport.htm.

14. Video conferencing has also been used on an experimental basis by the career services office in the student interviewing process.

15. *See* Temporary Guidelines, supra note 7; Haynesworth, supra note 12, at 48.

16. *See* Proposed Standards, supra note 7.

17. At present, the transmission quality of Internet video-conferencing is generally low compared to ISDN-based video conferencing, but will improve, at least on an institution-to-institution basis, with the full deployment of Internet 2. For background on Internet 2, see Florence Olsen, *Internet2 Effort Aims to Build Digital-Video Network for Higher Education*, Chron. Higher Educ., April 21, 2000, at A49.

18. Jennifer Chorpening, *Duke Professors Host Election Discussion on Web*, The [Durham, N.C.] Herald-Sun, November 30, 2000, at A13. The use of Webcasting to offer faculty perspectives on national events was used again on October 2, 2001 for a live Webcast of a faculty panel on "National Security and Civil Liberties: How to Strike the Balance?," one in a series of public forums at Duke University on issues surrounding the Sept. 11 terrorist attacks.

19. Archived versions of Duke Law Webcasts are available at http://www.law.duke.edu/webcast/ (last visited December 1, 2001). Video proceedings of the Conference on the Public Domain (November 9-11, 2001) can be viewed (and conference papers downloaded) at http://www.law.duke.edu/pd/.

20. The Global Executive program is described at http://www.fuqua.duke.edu/admin/gemba/index.html (last visited December 1, 2001).

21. The programs are described at http://www.unext.com/ (last visited December 1, 2001). UNext's beginnings as part of financier Michael Milken's Knowledge Universe are chronicled in Stephen P. Pizzo, *Master of the Knowledge Universe*, Forbes, September 10, 2001, at 64.

22. In late 2001, UNext was reported both to be reducing its workforce and attempting to restructure its agreements with its academic partners. *See* Katherine S. Mangan, *UNext Lays Off 135 Employees, Citing Need to Spend Conservatively*, Chron. Higher Educ. Distance Education (Sept. 13, 2001), *at* http://chronicle.com/free/2001/09/2001091301u.htm; Goldie Blumenstyk, *UNext Seeks to Restructure Its Relationships With Universities,* Chron. Higher Educ. Distance Education (Aug. 7, 2001), *at* http://chronicle.com/free/2001/08/2001080701u.htm. Questions about sales and profitability were raised earlier in the year. *See* Sarah Carr, *Rich in Cash and Prestige, UNext Struggles in Its Search for Sales.* Chron. Higher Educ., May 4, 2001, at A33.

23. For an early introduction to the for-profit subsidiaries under development at several U.S. universities and the reactions of faculty members, see Sarah Carr, *Faculty Members Are Wary of Distance-Education Ventures*, Chron. Higher Educ., June 9, 2000, at A41. 2001 did not prove to be a good year for some of these initiatives. Temple and NYU reportedly shut down their distance learning subsidiaries. *See* Goldie Blumenstyk, *Temple U. Shuts Down For-Profit Distance-Education Company*, Chron. Higher Educ., July 20, 2001, at A29; Scott Carlson & Dan Carnevale, *Debating the Demise of NYUonline: Did the venture go under because of the changing economy or bad decisions?* Chron. Higher Educ., Dec. 14, 2001, at A31. Columbia's Fathom project went through changes in organization and approach. *See* Scott Carlson, *For-Profit Web Venture Shifts Gears, Hoping to Find a Way to Make a Profit*, Chron. Higher Educ., Feb. 9, 2001, at A33. On the other hand, in November, Cornell began offering courses

through its eCornell subsidiary. *See* Michael Arnone, *Cornell's Distance Education Arm Readies New Program, and Hopes for Profits*, Chron. Higher Educ., Nov. 2, 2001, at A48.

24. Perhaps the most notable partnership was that created by Oxford, Princeton, Stanford and Yale under the name: Alliance for Lifelong Learning (http://www.allianceforlifelonglearning.org/). (last visited December 1, 2001). In November, Princeton announced its withdrawal from the Alliance in order to focus on other educational technology priorities. Michael Arnone, *Princeton University Pulls Out of High-Profile Distance Learning Alliance*. Chron. Higher Educ., Nov. 23, 2001, at A29.

25. *See* "Duke's Fuqua School of Business Forms Private Company; First to Provide Global Top-to-Bottom Executive Education." (June 30, 2000), *at* http://www.fuqua.duke.edu/admin/extaff/news/customexec.htm. The programs are described at http://www.dukece.com/ (last visited December 1, 2001).

Pensare.com did not survive the downturn in the economy and filed for bankruptcy in June 2001. Goldie Blumenstyk, *Online-Course Company Files for Bankruptcy*, Chron. Higher Educ., June 15, 2001, at A32. In November 2001, Duke Corporate Education itself cut its workforce and scaled back its revenue projections, citing the September 11 terrorist attacks and business executives' reluctance to travel as creating difficulties for programs that incorporate large segments of face to face meeting time. Katherine S. Mangan, *Duke's For-Profit Executive-Education Program Cuts Employees to Avoid a Deficit*, Chron. Higher Educ.: Today's News, Nov. 14, 2001, *at* http://chronicle.com/daily/2001/11/2001111405n.htm.

26. Carr, *supra* note 24.

27. In July 2001, Cardean University announced plans to offer law-related courses on contracts, workplace rules, intellectual property, and other topics of importance to corporations and their employees. *See* "Cardean University to Offer Law Related Courses Developed in Consultation with Leading Scholars" (July 23, 2001), *at* http://www.unext.com/UNext_news/news_release_article461.htm.

28. Harvard Law School Professor Arthur Miller is listed as Director of the Committee on Educational Content and Compliance for Celesq.com's CLE programs, offered through Celesq's AttorneysED Center. The list is available at http://www.celesq.com/index.asp (last visited December 1, 2001). *See also* Kate Marquess, *See CLE on Your Home PC*, ABA J., July 2001, at 2001.

29. A number of faculty with affiliations at U.S. law schools are listed as "supplementary lecturers" on the Concord University Law School Web site. *See* (http://www.concord.kaplan.edu/info/custom/concord/index.asp?source=600019) (last visited December 1, 2001). Concord's initial programs are thoroughly described and discussed in Robert E. Oliphant, *Will Internet Driven Concord University Law School Revolutionize Traditional Law School Teaching?*, 27 William Mitchell L.Rev. 841 (2000).

30. *See e.g.*, Kristine Ellis, *A Model Class*, Training Mag., December 2000, *available at* http://www.trainingsupersite.com/publications/ (last visited December 1, 2001). Jack R. Goetz, *Interactivity Remains the Key to Successful Online Learning* (2000), *at* http://jurist.law.pitt.edu/lessons/lesnov00.htm.

31. The St. Thomas program is described at http://www.stu.edu/tax/master_law_degree.htm (last visited December 1, 2001). The development of the St Thomas program is discussed in William H. Brynes, *A Review of the Development of an Internet Delivered LL.M Program in the United States*, 2001 JILT, no. 3, *at* http://elj.warwick.ac.uk/jilt/01-3/brynes.html.

32. Current programs, some of which combine residential with distance segments are listed at http://cyber.law.harvard.edu/online/. (last visited December 1, 2001).

33. The current program is described at http://www.bu.edu/law/lawdrafting/distance.html (last visited December 1, 2001).

34. There is already a sizable and growing literature about the library's role in support of distance learning initiatives. *See e.g.,* Ann Walsh Lang, *Is Your Library Ready for Distance Education?*, AALL Spectrum, May 2000, at 12.

35. *See* Richard A. Danner, *What are Law Libraries For?*, 37 Law Libr. 211 (1999), *discussing* David W. Lewis, *What if Libraries Are Artifact-Bound Institutions?*, 18 Info. Tech. & Libr. 191 (1998).

36. Lewis, *supra* note 36, at 191.

37. *See* St. Thomas University Graduate Program in International Taxation. About the Program, *at* http://www.stu.edu/tax/about_the_program.htm (hereinafter St. Thomas program) (last visited December 1, 2001).

38. Temporary Guidelines, *supra* note 7. The December 2001 proposed standards for distance education do not explicitly mention libraries or information centers, but proposed Interpretation 306-5 states that "Law schools shall have the technological capacity, staff, information resources, and facilities required to provide the support needed for instructors and students involved in distance education at the school." Proposed Standards, *supra,* note 7.

39. Temporary Guidelines, *supra* note 7.

40. Proposed Standards, *supra* note 7.

41. St. Thomas program, *supra* note 38.

42. Ellis, *supra* note 31.

43. Peter Lyman, *Digital Documents and the Future of the Academic Community*, in Richard Ekman & Richard E. Quandt, eds., Technology and Scholarly Communication 366, 377 (1999).

Web Mirror Sites: Creating the Research Library of the Future, and More . . .

Claire M. Germain

SUMMARY. Libraries can play a key role in ensuring permanent access to primary legal information, both domestic and international. Web mirror sites present a particularly efficient and cost-effective way to collect, disseminate, preserve, and ensure accessibility to information far into the future. Through partnerships with the issuing governments and organizations, databases of official information can be loaded on a local server, updated directly from the issuing site, and captured at regular intervals to get a snapshot of the status of legal instruments as of a certain date. The result is similar to adding the various editions of a print book. The Cornell Law Library has recently made freely available two Web mirror sites for researchers and the public. These are the ILO (International Labour Organization) and the ICJ (International Court of Justice) mirror sites. The Law Library is archiving these sites every six months, thereby providing access to previous versions of a treaty article, or other information that was superseded, or amended. The many additional advantages of creating these partnerships with domestic and international institutions are discussed, as well as the process used to create the mirror sites, and maintaining them. The article ends with a proposal for collaboration among libraries to create

---

Claire M. Germain is Edward Cornell Law Librarian and Professor of Law, Cornell Law School, Ithaca, NY (E-mail: cmg13@cornell.edu).

This article is an expanded version of a paper delivered at the Faculty of Law, University of Toronto, Conference on "Not a Box but a Window: Law Libraries and Legal Education in a Virtual World." Saturday, February 24, 2001.

[Haworth co-indexing entry note]: "Web Mirror Sites: Creating the Research Library of the Future, and More . . ." Germain, Claire M. Co-published simultaneously in *Legal Reference Services Quarterly* (The Haworth Information Press, an imprint of The Haworth Press, Inc.) Vol. 21, No. 2/3, 2002, pp. 87-104; and: *Law Library Collection Development in the Digital Age* (ed: Michael Chiorazzi, and Gordon Russell) The Haworth Information Press, an imprint of The Haworth Press, Inc., 2002, pp. 87-104. Single or multiple copies of this article are available for a fee from The Haworth Document Delivery Service [1-800-HAWORTH, 9:00 a.m. - 5:00 p.m. (EST). E-mail address: getinfo@haworthpressinc.com].

the research library of the future. The preservation of digital law is a critical issue because information is disappearing. Libraries have a role to play because it is part of their fundamental mission to preserve information for future researchers. *[Article copies available for a fee from The Haworth Document Delivery Service: 1-800-HAWORTH. E-mail address: <getinfo@haworthpressinc.com> Website: <http://www.HaworthPress.com>]*

KEYWORDS. Electronic archives, digital law, preservation, Web sites, Web mirror sites

INTRODUCTION

Is the Nation's digital record in danger of being lost? The issue of permanent access to digital information is very much at the forefront of societal concerns. This past year, a New York Times article, "Saving the Nation's Digital Legacy," recounted a report of the National Science Foundation lamenting the possible loss of digital information and lack of plan in the Library of Congress to preserve digital-born documents.[1] This article explores the concerns raised by the digital medium, with a particular focus on legal information, and access to primary legal information, the "official" word of the law.[2] It presents the model of Web mirror sites as a possible solution toward ensuring long-term access to digital law, and describes the many additional advantages for a library to create partnerships with domestic and international institutions, as well as the process used to create the mirror sites, and maintaining them. It also offers a proposal for collaboration among libraries worldwide to create the research library of the future.

LONG TERM ACCESS TO DIGITAL LEGAL INFORMATION

The law library community has been talking for several years now about how to ensure permanent public access to primary legal information, both U.S.–state and federal–as well as international and foreign legal information. In the United States and Canada today, and increasingly worldwide, digital versions of current decisions, bills, statutes, and regulations, issued by federal and state or provincial entities, are widely available on publicly accessible Internet Web sites. Official legal information issued by international organizations is also becoming available on the Web. This new electronic environment, which may soon replace the print equivalent, raises both technological and policy issues.

Digital Law Concerns

Fragility

A first issue is the rapid obsolescence of the digital medium, because of the limited life-expectancy of software and hardware. The medium itself, e.g., magnetic tape, may degrade within a decade. This means that the information needs to be migrated and "refreshed."[3] Richard Wiggins summarizes some of the technical ways to prevent death of digital data as follows:

- Preserving the software used to view and edit digital content
- Refresh, that is, copy to a fresh copy in the same medium and format
- Migrate: copy and translate to a new format to avoid obsolescence
- Emulate: provide software tools that emulate essential applications or operating environments
- Encapsulate: store not only the text, images, audio and video, but also the necessary information to interprete the contents.[4]

Current modes of preserving digital data include offline storage, zip drives, tapes, and optical storage devices, such as CD, DVD RAM, and DVD ROM.

Authenticity and Integrity

Another issue with the digital medium is the difficulty of ascertaining the authenticity and integrity of a digital file, which can be altered easily. There are currently no standards for the production and authentication of digital documents. One has to trust the issuing organization. Much work has been undertaken to resolve these issues in ways such as using digital signatures, time mapping, and marking the images. Several groups are working in these technological areas, and some courts are doing pilot projects toward developing standards of production and of authentication.[5] The results of existing and future research and development into electronic records preservation may change the requirements for electronic preservation systems.

The American Library Association, Government Documents Round Table (ALA Godort), has appointed an Ad Hoc Committee on Digitization of Government Information, which is producing a useful clearinghouse of information sources. Different groups are charged to identify best practices in digitization, including principles of identifying projects, standards, technologies, methodology, cataloging, and authentication issues, and to create a recommended bibliography.[6]

Current Information Widely Available

The steadily expanding legal information available over the Internet comes from governmental and private sources, non-profit and commercial, and is directed toward the public and legal professionals.[7] In the United States, because of the American principle that citizens should have free access to government information, federal and state governmental Web sites provide legal information in the public domain, without being subject to copyright, and many official texts and documents are now available on the Internet. Universities and non-profit organizations also provide access to primary legal information, as well as commercial databases which have blossomed, with much value-added information in the form of editorial enhancements. LEXIS and WESTLAW are getting stronger, benefitting from increased mergers and consolidation in the legal publishing industry.

However, with digital information, researchers only get a right of access to the data, and no ownership of the legal information, or control over the data, unless it is downloaded on a server or stored on a CD. Moreover, the information is sometimes available only for a short time and then disappears from the site. The long-term access to digital legal information is a matter of great concern.[8]

Disappearing Web Contents

One major concern, of special focus in this article, is the risk of losing the content of the disappearing Web sites. Web site contents change for a variety of reasons, including revision of contents (the new replaces the old, which disappears, such as old versions of codes, or treaty articles), reorganization, death of a sponsor, lack of interest of a publisher, etc., in addition to technical problems, such as media format obsolescence (e.g., data on a 5 1/2 floppy disk), content format obsolescence (old version of wordperfect, unreadable on a new system), or disaster, when the data are not backed up.[9] In the political sphere, a change of government will lead to dramatic consequences. When President George Bush took office as President on January 20, 2001, the entire Clinton White House Web site at *www.whitehouse.gov*, as well as the companion searchable document archive *www.pub.whitehouse.gov*, were removed and replaced with a skeleton site for the new administration.[10] It took a special effort of the National Archives to find the various renditions of the Clinton White House Web site and archive them at *clinton.nara.gov.* NARA also asked other federal agencies to take measures to preserve their own Web sites, but many agencies had trouble complying.[11] Legal information sources, such as state legislative proposals and bills, are often only kept during a particular legislative session.[12] Previous versions of amended, or repealed provisions of code articles in statutory compilations are removed and no longer to be found, as Web sites only contain current information. These documents, however, are essential for researchers to find if they are doing research on a particular case relying on an old code provision, or for historical research, since law is based on historical materials, not only currently applicable provisions. Decisions of courts are often on the Web for information purposes only, which means that researchers cannot rely on finding the official, "citeable" version of the decision on the court Web site in the same reliable way that a researcher could find a decision in a print official court report.

There is currently no U.S. national policy to create digital archives of official governmental information, at the federal or state level, in spite of the mandate of the U.S. Government Printing Office for all depository publications to become electronic and be distributed in digital format, including such items as the *U.S. Code*, *Congressional Record*, *Federal Register*, *Code of Federal Regulations* (C. F. R), and others. The U.S. government has taken steps in that direction, but it remains to be seen how these measures will be implemented over the long term, depending on budgeting issues. The U.S. National Commission on Libraries and Information Science (NCUS) and National Archives and Records Administration (NARA) have also produced studies.

U.S. Federal Depository Library Program

The U.S. government has issued a plan, in the form of the Federal Depository Library Program Electronic Collection (FDLP/EC) Archive.[13] To assure permanent public access to electronic U.S. Government information, the FDLP is operating an archive of publications that are identified, described, and pointed to as part of the FDLP/EC, and which are not part of the FDLP in any other form nor guaranteed to be permanently available by their issuing agency or entity. Once a publication is no longer available on a particular agency or entity Web site, researchers will be directed automatically to the Electronic Archive. FDLP is also working on partnerships with agencies to ensure long term availability of their information.

NCLIS Study

The U.S. National Commission on Libraries and Information Science (NCLIS) has recently completed an extensive assessment of public information dissemination policies and practices at the request of U.S. Senators John McClain and Joe Lieberman. The report recommends introducing new legislation, "the Public Information Resources Reform Act of 2001," that would declare that public information has the rank of a national strategic asset, and provide for a new agency that would coordinate all agencies, and also have a budget line item in the President's budget, including a preservation and permanent access component. The NCLIS studies and ongoing activities are conveniently published on its Web site at *www.nclis.gov.*

NARA Strategic Plan

The National Archives and Records Administration (NARA) has come out with a detailed revised Strategic Plan.[14] Strategic Goal Three states, "all records will be preserved in an appropriate environment for use as long as needed." NARA's goal is to preserve and make accessible 60% of its electronic holdings by 2002, and 97% by 2007, regardless of their original format. It is planning to enter into research and development partnerships with the National Science Foundation, the San Diego Supercomputer Center, and others to discover new ways to look at preserving and providing access to electronic records within a comprehensive and stable architecture that will be infrastructure independent, scalable, modular, and extensible. The implementation of the pilot Electronic Records Archive is planned for Fiscal Year 2004.

WEB MIRROR SITES AS A POSSIBLE SOLUTION

Web Mirror Sites present a new way to disseminate and preserve digital legal information, and also offer a security backup for issuing agencies, an increasingly important factor in the new cyberspace world prone to computer hacking. Web mirror sites present a particularly efficient and cost-effective way to collect and ensure accessibility to information far into the future. Through partnerships with the issuing governments and organizations, databases of official information can be loaded on a local server, updated directly from the issuing site, and captured at regular intervals to get a snapshot of the status of legal instruments as of a certain date. The result is similar to adding the various editions of a print book.

International Court of Justice and International Labor Organization Mirror Sites

The Cornell Law Library has recently made available at no cost two Web mirror sites for researchers and the public. These are the ILO (International Labour Organization) and the ICJ (International Court of Justice) mirror sites. To get access to the mirror sites, as well as to additional and background information produced by the Law Library, go to *http//www.lawschool.cornell.edu/library* and click on "International Labor" or "International Court of Justice." The Law Library is archiving these sites every six months, thereby providing access to previous versions of a treaty article, or other information that was superseded or amended.

These mirror sites have been developed with several goals in mind, which can be adapted by other universities and organizations. Some of these goals are particularly relevant to solve some digital law concerns. Others go beyond in the direction of the library extending itself and helping in the academic world. The goals are:

- To increase reliable access and response time for persons living in the Americas and, thereby, assist in the dissemination of important information resources for research, study, and other uses. For example, researchers in Latin America had trouble logging on to the ILO Web site in Geneva, Switzerland, and the response time from the Cornell server in Ithaca, NY, is much better. The ICJ Webmaster in The Hague, the Netherlands, is very pleased to redirect users to the

Ithaca server as well, when important decisions come out and create much traffic on their Web site.

- To assure faculty, students, and staff that these sources can be used with a high degree of reliability (not dependent on functionality of communication systems outside of a particular university) for research and instructional purposes on campus and/or for distance learning purposes.
- To permit the yearly capture and retention of the information found at these Web sites on CDs or other electronic storage media, thereby providing long-term access and archiving necessary for researchers and decision-makers.
- To serve as a secure backup location for these international organizations.
- To create cost-efficient alternatives to legal research. Mirror sites are cost-efficient, from a library perspective. There are no binding, acquisitions, postage, cataloging, shelving, etc., costs. What does take place is a solution to the modern citation problem in which a researcher cites a publication residing on a Web site giving the name of the page (or best guess), URL, and the date found. If your library is the mirror site for that agency, you will have the URL saved to be viewed and used in the form for the approximate date. Since Web sites are different from print formats, this can be a significant research advantage since one has not only the publication but the look and feel of the site when used by the original researcher.
- To establish partnerships with these most distinguished international organizations, permitting the development of new courses, scholarly exchanges, faculty visits, research sabbaticals, and student internships.
- To provide sets of information useful for legal as well as multidisciplinary and interdisciplinary research, study, and instruction valuable to the entire campus and, thereby, serve as a catalyst for cooperative research. In addition, these tangible academic assets can be leveraged for grant applications and government support involving a variety of departments and schools.
- To provide a focus for producing supplemental research and background information sources on the issues that are of concern to these international organizations. These are to be developed by faculty, librarians, and students to enhance the intellectual experience associated with the use of the Web sites by international experts, researchers, and the public at large.

Creating and Running a Web Mirror Site

Web mirror sites can be created at a minimal cost. For less than $10,000, including hardware, software, and staff time, a library can acquire long term access to huge collections of primary and secondary legal information hosted on local servers. The following describes the financial and staff resources involved, as well as the cooperation with the original issuing site. Most libraries and academic institutions have servers that are already running. The mirror site can be leveraged as a resource by sharing space, or buying equipment jointly with another unit in the library or law school, or other parent institution. Many software programs, which will prove useful in developing a mirror site, are available for free. Examples include Apache's server software,[15] Netscape's Web browser and mirroring software such as "wget"[16] and "webmin."[17]

These free mirroring software programs allow the original issuing site staff to update, coordinate, and synchronize the contents of the original and the mirror site remotely and automatically. It is usually done at convenient times when there is less traffic, e.g., at night.

Other issues to consider when running a mirror site may involve the choice of search engines, e.g., local or not, peculiar to the machine, etc. We now have a local search facility and use the Alkaline Unix search engine, Vestris, Switzerland, which works very well locally.[18]

The local computer administrator, with the appropriate permissions, can give an account to the original issuing staff. The latter staff can do a lot of the day-to-day administration remotely. For instance, the ILO staff has installed a new search engine and new mirroring software remotely from Geneva, Switzerland. Another original issuing site installed Netscape, instead of the Apache software. It is estimated that it takes a few hours per month of the mirror host site staff to handle ongoing operational details. It is also important to note that the issuing organization will want to maintain control and the integrity of the database, therefore not "dropping" the work on the mirror site, but working on the site remotely.

Web mirror sites offer a way to partner with other units beyond the library. In our setting, the Library has partnered with two law faculty members, who run an important Web site on judicial statistics and empirical studies on jury verdicts and other social indicators, and were interested in access to a larger computer.[19]

Current Projects to Archive Open-Access Web Sites

Several projects are currently underway to experiment in archiving open-access Web sites, that is, information in the public domain, and not subject to copyright, even though these issues are very complicated.

Cornell-Library of Congress Minerva Web Preservation Project

The Cornell University project with the Library of Congress is designed to preserve open-access materials from the WWW. The effort, led by William Arms, Professor of Computer Science at Cornell University, in collaboration with the Library of Congress, includes a study of the technical and policy issues, the development of a long-term plan and coordination of prototypes, with the aim to move rapidly into production in these areas. The project encourages future research and development by the library and computing communities.[20]

According to William Arms, approaches for collecting open access materials from the Web can be divided into two categories, depending on the degree of automation: (1) bulk collecting, a largely automated process, is an economic way to collect very large amounts of material; and, (2) selective collecting is managed by librarians who select, index and organize materials for collection and preservation. Both approaches rely heavily on automatic processes to download, store and preserve materials from the Internet.

The Minerva Project selected Web sites, such as the White House, and the Al Gore and George Bush Election Campaign Web sites,[21] and snapshots of these sites were downloaded using the HTTrack mirroring program. The snapshots were inspected for errors, anomalies, etc. Catalog records were created using OCLC's CORC software and loaded into Library of Congress's ILS system. A trial Web site was developed to evaluate user access. This allowed users to view each version of each Web site as it was downloaded. The site also allowed users to search the ILS, or lists of URLs, titles and subject headings, with links to the collection of Web sites. Discussions were held with the Copyright Office on legal issues.[22]

Internet Archives

The Internet Archive,[23] working with Alexa Internet, has created the *Wayback Machine*, which makes it possible to surf pages stored in the Internet Archive's Web archive. The tax-exempt organization aims to rescue public online data and provide researchers free and permanent access to public materials.[24]

National Library of Australia Pandora Project

The National Library of Australia Pandora Project archives sites at the time they are cataloged. The National Library of Australia, under the auspices of its Pandora Project, has issued guidelines on the archiving and cataloging of Web sites. The guidelines are published in a report entitled *Guidelines for the Selection of Online Australian Publications Intended for Preservation by the National Library of Australia.* The selection criteria include a preference toward materials that have Australian content, choices when multiple versions are available, authority and research value, and certain topical issues.[25]

A Proposal for Collaboration

Current Digital Preservation Efforts in Law Library Community

The Cornell Law Library efforts are consistent with other projects undertaken in the U.S.A. and Canada. In the U.S., the AALL (American Association of Law Libraries) formed the Special Task Force on Authentication and Preservation of Digital Information to look at the issues of long-term access to electronic information. The Task Force met in Williamsburg, Virginia in December 1999, with the following goals:

- to develop a statement describing the issues and concerns of the law library community;
- to provide examples of best practices by courts and legislatures;
- to make recommendations and communicate with other organizations dealing with legal information, such as the ABA, the National Conference of State Court Administrators, the National Association of Court Management, and the National Center for State Courts, as well as library groups such as the RLG/Digital Library Federation Task Force formed in 1999 on Policy and Practice for Long-term Retention of Digital Materials.

A program at the July 2001 AALL meeting in Minneapolis, Minn., "Saving the World's Digital Law: Learning by Doing," explored initiatives and efforts that have already made a difference in addressing long term access to digital legal information. The work of the Special Task

Force is now being continued by a Special Committee on the Future of Law Libraries in the Digital Age, appointed by then AALL President Bob Oakley in March 2001, and co-chaired by Rita Reusch, University of Utah Law Library, and Gail Warren, Virginia State Law Library.

The Proposal for Consortial Activities

Web mirror sites present a great opportunity for law libraries to be a vital part of the intellectual life of their organizations, and they demonstrate one of the most efficient and cost-effective ways of collecting and disseminating information. Mirror sites are also great ways to experiment and provide backup databases of legal information, and they offer the potential for possible consortial activities among law libraries throughout the world. In that scheme, each participating library would become responsible for archiving and making publicly available a portion of the corpus of official primary legal information, and rely on others for other parts. The scheme would extend access to that information far into the future. In the United States, the AALL and the Law Library of Congress could play a vital role in this venture by coordinating efforts with the major stakeholders, and coordinating state-by-state plans with volunteers from each state. Each partner would buy servers and download a portion of the corpus of legal information. For instance, Cornell could keep the New York Court of Appeals decisions (currently produced by the Legal Information Institute at Cornell), the documents of the International Labor Organization (currently running from a mirror site set up at Cornell; includes treaties and national labor laws from foreign countries), and the decisions of the International Court of Justice (running from a mirror site at Cornell). Cornell would make these documents available to other libraries. It would rely on partner libraries for access to other materials.

This collaborative plan would ensure that libraries successfully continue their leading role of preserving and making information available to present and future generations of scholars. What is at stake is the transmission of official documents, "the word of the law," to future generations. Web mirror sites fit into the goal to make sure that in a paperless world there will be a permanent record of the law in its many forms and the document will be authentic. This Web mirror site proposal would be an addition to other preservation measures taken by courts, legislatures, and publishers. This would spread the burden; provide redundancy and efficiency; and create an especially good way to preserve reliable and neutral access to official legal information far into the future, independent of commercial publishers who often only provide access, but not ownership of the materials. It would offer the neutrality for which libraries have always been admired.

WHY SHOULD LIBRARIES BE INVOLVED

There have been some good discussions about whose responsibility it is to preserve digital information for the future. The issuing agency seems to be the right place, especially if it is an official governmental Web site. However, there is much interest and usefulness in having a "neutral" site, such as a library Web site, which will insure the integrity of the database of information in the same way that libraries have insured access to official versions of governmental texts in the print world with the various editions of state and federal codes and volumes of court decisions that cannot be tampered with. Libraries should be involved because it fits into their fundamental mission: to preserve and make information available to present and future generations of scholars.

Your comments and feedback on this proposal are encouraged. Please send them to *cmg13@cornell.edu.*

NOTES

1. Katie Hafner, "Saving the Nation's Digital Legacy," *New York Times*, Thursday, July 27, 2000 at G1.

2. Primary legal information sources or authorities are classified in legal research textbooks as "authorized statements of the law by governmental institutions." (See Jacobstein, Mersky, and Dunn, Fundamentals of Legal Research, 7th ed., at 2, 1998). They include court decisions, legislation, court rules, and the rules, regulations, and opinions of administrative agencies. Secondary sources or authorities are everything else, that is, commentaries on the law in the form of treatises, law review articles, encyclopedias, indexes and digests.

3. Several authors have written on these issues. Jeff Rothenberg was one of the first and most eloquent writers, articulating the main technological issues in "Ensuring the Longevity of Digital Documents," 272 *Scientific American* 24-29 (1995). The article was expanded in *Avoiding Technological Quicksand. Finding a Viable Technical Foundation for Digital Preservation*, (January 1998) available at *http//www.clir.org/pubs/reports/rothenberg/contents.html*. Richard Wiggins provides a good summary of the issues in "Digital Preservation Paradox & Promise," *Library Journal Netconnect* 12-15 (Spring 2001), available at *http//www.libraryjournal.com/digital_preservation.asp*. *See also* Abby Smith, *Why Digitize?* Council on Library and Information Resources,

1999. Introduction also available at *http://www.clir.org/pubs/reports/pub80-smith/pub80.html*.

4. Richard Wiggins, *see supra* note 3 at 14.

5. The Oklahoma courts are often cited as an example of best practices. *See www.oscn.net*.

6. *American Library Association Government Documents Round Table Ad Hoc Committee on Digitization of Government Information, WORKGROUP 3 Resource Bibliography*. Available at *http//sunsite.berkeley.edu/GODORT/dgi/group3bibliography.html*.

7. For an analysis of the contents and the quality of legal information on the Internet, with a special focus on the United States, its impact on legal research and access to legal information, *see* Claire M. Germain, "Contents of Legal Information on the Internet: U.S. Perspectives," 27 International Journal of Legal Information 289-306 (1999), also available at *http//www.lawschool.cornell.edu/library/Faculty_Services/facbib/legalinf.html* [1998].

8. Claire M. Germain, "Digital Legal Information: Here Today, Gone Tomorrow?" *Syllabus (ABA)* 17 (Spring 1998); Claire M. Germain, "Digital Legal Information: Ensuring Access to the 'Official' Word of the Law," 26 *Cornell Law Forum* 11-14 (July 1999).

9. *See* Richard Wiggins, *supra* note 3 at 13.

10. *Id.* at 12.

11. *Id.*

12. *See http//assembly.state.ny.us/*. New York House and Senate bills are only available for the current term. Even commercial online services, such as Lexis and Westlaw, only make the current bills available. Both systems only make the current federal and state court rules available, as well as the federal local court rules.

13. U.S. Government Printing Office, Federal Depository Program, The Federal Depository Library Program Electronic Collection (FDLP/EC) Archive, available at *http//www.access.gpo.gov/su_docs/fdlp/ec/ecarc.html*.

14. *www.nara.gov*.

15. *http://www.apache.org*.

16. *http://www.gnu.org/software/wget/wget.html*.

17. *http://www.webmin.com/*.

18. *http://alkaline.vestris.com/*.

19. *http://teddy.law.cornell.edu:8090/questata.htm* by Professors Ted Eisenberg and Kevin Clermont.

20. William Y. Arms, Web Preservation Project Interim Report, January 15, 2001. *www.cs.cornell.edu/wya/LC-web. Collecting and Preserving the Web: The Minerva Prototype*, by William Y. Arms, Roger Adkins, Cassy Ammen, and Allene Hayes. RLG DigiNews, 5(2), April 2001. *http//www.rlg.org/preserv/diginews/diginews5-2.html#feature1*.

21. *http//www.whitehouse.gov/*; *http//www.algore2000.com/*; *http//www.georgewbush.com/*.

22. *See* note 19, William Arms' *Interim report*, 2001.

23. *www.archive.org*.

24. *See* a good review by Kathy Biehl, "The Internet Archives: Preserving the History of Web Pages, LLRX, Nov. 1, 2001, available at *www.llrx.com/columns/webcritic12.htm*.

25. *http://pandora.nla.gov.au/selectionguidelines.html*.

REFERENCES

American Library Association Government Documents Round Table Ad Hoc Committee on Digitization of Government Information, Clearinghouse of Government Documents Digital Projects, 2002. Available at http//sunsite.berkeley.edu/GODORT/dgi/.

American Library Association Government Documents Round Table Ad Hoc Committee on Digitization of Government Information, WORKGROUP 3 Resource Bibliography. Available at http//sunsite.berkeley.edu/GODORT/dgi/group3bibliography.html.

Arms, William Y., Roger Adkins, Cassy Ammen, and Allene Hayes. *Collecting and Preserving the Web: The Minerva Prototype.* RLG DigiNews, 5(2), April 2001. http//www.rlg.org/preserv/diginews/diginews5-2.html#feature1.

Clearinghouse of Government Documents Digital Projects. *American Library Association Government Documents Round Table Ad Hoc Committee on Digitization of Government Information,* 2002. Available at http//www.gl.iit.edu/services/ref/diggovclearinghouse.htm.

Arvidson, Allan, Krister Persson and Johan Mannerheim. *The Kulturarw3 Project–The Royal Swedish Web Archiw3e–An Example of "Complete" Collection of Web Pages.* 66th IFLA Council and General Conference, Jerusalem, Israel, 13-18 August 2000. http//www.ifla.org/IV/ifla66/papers/154-157e.htm.

Assessment of Formats and Standards for the Creation, Dissemination, and Permanent Accessibility of Electronic Government Information Products. Marjory S. Blumenthal and Alan S. Inouye. Computer Science and Telecommunications Board, National Research Council. NCLIS, July 1997 Draft Report. www.nclis.gov/info/gpo1.html. See also later reports on Web site.

Good summary of current issues. Discusses some strategies and models currently explored, as well as specific initiatives from libraries and professional associations.

Building Digital Collections. Technological Information about American Memory Collections. Library of Congress. Available at http//memory.loc.gov/ammem/techdocs/digcols.html.

Commission on Preservation and Access (website). http//www.clir.org/programs/cpa/cpa.html.

Framework for the Preservation of and Permanent Public Access to USDA Digital Publications. Paul Uhlir, Project Consultant, National Academy of Sciences, National Research Council, Nov. 1997.

Hartmann, C.N. "Storage of Electronic Files of Federal Agencies that have Ceased Operationia Partnership for Permanent Access," 17 *Government Information Quarterly* 299 (2000).

HTTrack, the Web Mirror Utility. http//httrack.free.fr/.

The Internet Archive. *Building an Internet Library, 1996-.* http//www.archive.org/.

ImterPARES PROJECT, http://www.interpares.org/.

The InterPARES Project is a major international research initiative in which archival scholars, computer engineering scholars, national archival institutions and private industry representatives are collaborating to develop the theoretical and methodological knowledge required for the permanent preservation of authentic records created in electronic systems. The InterPARES Project is based in the School of Library, Archival and Information Studies at the University of British Columbia.

Issues and Innovations in Preserving Digital Information. American Research Libraries, 1998. http//www.arl.org/transform/pdi/index.html.

McClure, Charles R. and J. Timothy Sprehe. *Analysis and Development of Model Quality Guidelines for Electronic Records Management on State and Federal Websites Final Report January 1998.* Available at http//istweb.syr.edu/~mcclure/nhprc/nhprc_title.html.

National Archives and Record Administration. *Electronic Records Archives Program.* Available at http//www.nara.gov/era/index.html.

National Commission on Libraries and Information Sciences (NCLIS) (2001). *Comprehensive Assessment of Public Information Dissemination*, July-Dec. 2000. Available at http//www.nclis.gov/govt/assess/assess.html.

National Library of Australia. *Pandora Archive Preserving and Accessing Networked Documentary Resources of Australia, 1996-.* http//pandora.nla.gov.au/pandora/.

National Preservation Program for Agricultural Literature. Nancy Gwinn, Assistant Director, Collections Management, Smithsonian Institution Libraries. May, 16, 1993.

The Official Version. A National Summit To Solve the Problems of Authenticating, Preserving and Citing Legal Information in Digital Form, November 20-22, 1997, Sheraton Hotel, Toronto.

Proceedings of Canada Summit on Digital Legal Information Issues. A shorter version of the print document is available at http//www.callacbd.ca/summit/index.html.

National Research Council. *A Digital Strategy for the Library of Congress.* National Academy Press, 2000. http//www.nap.edu/books/0309071445/html/.

National Research Council. *The Digital Dilemma, Intellectual Property in the Information Age.* National Academy Press, 2000. http//www.nap.edu/html/digital_dilemma/.

OCLC. *Cooperative Online Resource Catalog.* http//www.oclc.org/oclc/corc/.

OCLC Office of Research. *Web Characterization Project.* http//wcp.oclc.org/main.htm.

Preserving Digital Information. Final Report of the Task Force on Archiving of Digital Information Recommendations. Commissioned by the Commission on Preservation and Access and Research Libraries Group, 1996. Available at http//www.rlg.org/ArchTF/.

Ready Access to Essential Evidence The Strategic Plan of the National Archives and Records Administration, 1997-2007. Revised 2000 http//www.nara.gov/nara/vision/nara2000.html#3.3.

Rothenberg, Jeff. *Avoiding Technological Quicksand. Finding a Viable Technical Foundation for Digital Preservation*, January 1998. Available at http//www.clir.org/pubs/reports/rothenberg/contents.html.

Expanded version of his article "Ensuring the Longevity of Digital Documents" that appeared in 272 *Scientific American* 24-29 (1995).

Ross, Seamus. *Changing Trains at Wigan: Digital Preservation and the Future of Scholarship.* London: National Preservation Office, 2000.

Standards for Digital Information Interchange. A Resources Page. http//ahds.ac.uk/resource/standards.html and *Digital Preservation.* ahds.ac.uk/resource/preserve.html.

These two publication of the UK Arts & Humanities Data Service (AHDS) provide useful references and links to organizations and digital library initiatives in the US and the United Kingdom.

Staying Digital. Recommendations on Preserving New Jersey Government Information in the Digital Age, Adopted by the Documents Association of New Jersey, (June 1, 2001). Available at http//andromeda.rutgers.edu/~govdocs/stayingdigital.pdf.

A Strategic Policy Framework for Creating and Preserving Digital Collections. ahds.ac.uk/manage/framework.htm.

Final report of a study undertaken by the AHDS Executive on behalf of the Digital Archiving Working Party of the UK's JISC, British Library, and National Preservation Office (July 1998).

Thibodeau, Kenneth. "Building the Archives of the Future Advances in Preserving Electronic Records at the National Archives and Records Administration," 7 *D-Lib Magazine* (Feb. 2001), available at http//www.dlib.org/dlib/february01/thibodeau/02thibodeau.html.

U.S. Office of Management and Budget. *Management of Federal Information Resources.* 1996 (Circular A-130), available at http//www.whitehouse.gov/omb/circulars/a130/a130.html.

U.S. Government Printing Office. Federal Depository Program. *The Federal Depository Library Program Electronic Collection (FDLP/EC) Archive.* Available at http//www.access.gpo.gov/su_docs/fdlp/ec/ecarc.html.

U.S. Government Printing Office. Superintendent of Documents. Library Programs Service. *Managing the FDLP Electronic CollectionA Policy and Planning Document,* October 1, 1998. Available at http//www.access.gpo.gov/su_docs/fdlp/pubs/ecplan.html.

Wiggins, Richard. "Digital Preservation Paradox & Promise," *Library Journal Netconnect* 12-15 (Spring 2001). Available at http//www.libraryjournal.com/digital_preservation.asp.

ORGANIZATIONS

American Research Libraries (ARL). www.arl.org/.

Comprises 121 large North American research institutions, both in the U.S. and Canada. ARL at 21 Dupont Circle, Suite 800, Washington, DC 20036, voice 202-296-2296. Fax 202-872-0884; arlhq@arl.org. Executive Director: Duane E. Webster.

Coalition for Networked Information (CNI). www.cni.org.

CNI is an organization to advance the transformative promise of networked information technology for the advancement of scholarly communication and the enrichment of intellectual productivity. Founded in 1990 by the Association of Research Libraries, Educom, and CAUSE. CNI is supported by the members of an institutional Task Force representing higher education, publishing, network and telecommunications, information technology, and libraries and library organizations.

Digital Library Federation (DLF). www.clir.org.

Founded in 1995 to establish the conditions for creating, maintaining, expanding, and preserving a distributed collection of digital materials accessible to scholars, students, and a wider public. The Federation is a leadership organization operating under the umbrella of the Council on Library and Information Resources. It is composed of participants who manage and operate digital libraries. A consortium of fifteen of the U.S.'s largest libraries and archives cooperating to ensure access to digitized materials. The site provides links to member organizations with a range of digital library access and preservation projects. Contact Donald J. Waters, Director, Digital Library Federation, Council on Library and Information Resources, 205 Church Street, Third Floor, New Haven, CT 06510-1805. Phone: 1-203-498-6076; Fax: 1-203-498-6078; Email: dwaters@clir.org.

NARA National Archives and Records Administration. Center for Electronic Records. http//www.nara.gov/nara/electronic/.

Research Libraries Group (RLG). www.rlg.org.
Contact Ricky Erway, Member Services Officer, Digital Initiatives, RLG, 650-691-2228, bl.rle@rlg.org.

U.S. National Commission on Libraries and Information Science. www.nclis.gov. Independent agency within the executive branch, created in 1970, to advise the U.S. president on national policy issues relating to libraries and informational needs of the country. 1110 Vermont Avenue, N.W. Suite 820, Washington, DC 20005-3522. Telephone 202-606-9200; Fax 202-606-9203. Jeanne Hurley Simon, Chairperson; jhsimon@siu.edu. Robert S. Willard, Executive Director; rw_nclis@inet.ed.gov.

Legal Scholarship and Digital Publishing: Has Anything Changed in the Way We Do Legal Research?

E. Dana Neacsu

SUMMARY. Scholarship, including legal scholarship, depends on the reliability of sources used so that subsequent scholars can build upon the work. Reliability is here defined as including accurate access to sources that reproduce faithfully the original source. Legal scholarship depends on the existence and reliability of accessible materials to verify the accuracy and validity of the ideas advanced in the source. The growth of digital publishing,[1] which includes both distributing information directly in electronic format and the conversion of paper materials into electronic format, threatens the established reliability of source materials. The current legal literature has failed to address this issue; the author's examination of 20 law review articles, all containing at least four citations to the Internet, found that 12 of the 20 contained an online source which could

---

E. Dana Neacsu (Facultatea de Drept, Bucharest, Diploma de Drept, Faculte de Droit et des Etudes Politiques, Caen, France, DEA, Harvard Law School, LLM, and CUNY, MLS) is Reference Librarian, Arthur W. Diamond Law Library, Columbia Law School and a New York attorney.

The author would like to thank CUNY Professor Colleen Cool, Jody Armstrong, and Kent McKeever for their invaluable assistance.

This article was first presented as a paper at the conference, "Not a Box but a Window: Law Libraries and Legal Education in a Virtual World," held at Bora Laskin Law Library, Faculty of Law, University of Toronto, on Feb. 22-24, 2001. A draft of the oral presentation can be viewed at <http://www.law-lib.utoronto.ca/conferences/future/archives.htm>.

[Haworth co-indexing entry note]: "Legal Scholarship and Digital Publishing: Has Anything Changed in the Way We Do Legal Research?" Neacsu, E. Dana. Co-published simultaneously in *Legal Reference Services Quarterly* (The Haworth Information Press, an imprint of The Haworth Press, Inc.) Vol. 21, No. 2/3, 2002, pp. 105-122; and: *Law Library Collection Development in the Digital Age* (ed: Michael Chiorazzi, and Gordon Russell) The Haworth Information Press, an imprint of The Haworth Press, Inc., 2002, pp. 105-122. Single or multiple copies of this article are available for a fee from The Haworth Document Delivery Service [1-800-HAWORTH, 9:00 a.m. - 5:00 p.m. (EST). E-mail address: getinfo@haworthpressinc.com].

no longer be accessed within a year of the online source's publication. The author suggests that librarians and scholars be aware of the risk digital publishing presents to future research. *[Article copies available for a fee from The Haworth Document Delivery Service: 1-800-HAWORTH. E-mail address: <getinfo@haworthpressinc.com> Website: <http://www.HaworthPress.com>*

KEYWORDS. Online legal research, digital publishing, source authority, legal scholarship

INTRODUCTION

Reliability: Essential Attribute of Scholarship

Scholars have engaged in the enterprise of scholarship for centuries, even millennia. The Oxford English Dictionary defines scholarship as the "attainment of scholars,"[2] and as "the sphere of polite learning."[3] Other definitions present it as the "pursuit of knowledge,"[4] and as the activity that brings "wisdom to the nations."[5] For example, Decartes' Method[6] explains how knowledge is built on past knowledge that is clearly and distinctly perceived as true.[7] Thus, more than the transitory process of study, the production of new knowledge and the continuing search for truth cannot be done, at least not in the Western tradition, without reference to past knowledge.

As scholarship promotes "the development, representation, and utilization of knowledge,"[8] it obviously requires accretion and derivation, which enable later scholars to build on earlier results of scholarship. The scholarly development of Greek philosophy, for example, was possible because Aristotle, and his contemporaries, as well as all those who came later, had access to Plato's *Republic*, and they had access to the same text regardless of the edition used. Additionally, whenever Plato's *Republic* is cited today as a source in a footnote, scholars and lay persons assume that it is the same one they already read. Scholarship thus requires access to the product of earlier study. It also requires some assurance that what is accessed faithfully reproduces the original.

Irrespective of how variously it is defined from age to age and discipline to discipline, scholarship thus relies on "a base of expertise, a 'scholarly knowing' that needs to and can be identified, made public and evaluated."[9] This accurate access (emphasizing both access and accuracy) to sources is defined here as reliability.[10] Reliability, in this sense, ensures that both lay persons and other scholars might share the same product.[11] Reliability, as one of the prerequisites of Western scholarship allows acknowledgement of the sources used in a scholarly product,[12] and, by way of consequence, assurance of access to their faithful reproductions.

Reliability: Essential Attribute of Legal Scholarship

As the pursuit of legal knowledge, legal scholarship[13] is no different from other disciplines. Legal scholarship bears the same essential attributes as any other type of scholarship, including reliability. In legal literature, the importance of reliability has assured access to and accuracy of the content is exemplified by the notorious footnoting culture within law review articles.[14] As is commonly known, legal scholarship relies on the existence and reliability of accessible materials as the means of verification of the accuracy and validity of the ideas advanced within a legal text. There are thus at least two possibly overlapping features of scholarship that directly apply to the form and content of footnotes, all of which are impacted by the advent of digital publishing–the dual needs for access and accuracy, which, to repeat, is defined here as reliability.

STATEMENT OF PURPOSE

In addition to reliability defined as assured access and accuracy of the content, this paper discusses the impact on legal scholarship of digitization (which will include electronic publishing) in relation to the same requirement of reliability. While there is a vast array of legal and non-legal literature addressing the role of scholarship, its content, or its authorship, there is no single source discussing reliability–as used here–as an essential aspect of legal scholarship.[15] This paper argues that reliability is an essential attribute of legal scholarship because, as is true of all scholarship, it requires accurate access to the products of earlier study. It further argues that digital publishing as defined here,[16] at least potentially, may have a direct impact upon legal scholarship, and as shown below, there are reasons to worry. There are several reasons why digital publishing inherently places reliability at risk. First, self-publishing, much-celebrated[17] but often unexamined, raises the risk that non-institutional sources may not have the stability over time to assure reliable access nor the internal regulation to assure that different versions are always so identified like different editions, translations, etc. Second, the electronic transmission inherent to digital publishing, as shown herein, raises technical risks to both access and accuracy. Third, because digital publishing is itself a technological innovation, it raises the problem inherent to all innovation–that of changing standards and formats, increasing the risk of future problems of access and perhaps of accuracy as well.[18]

REVIEW OF RELATED LITERATURE

Legal Scholarship: Generalities

Whether viewed narrowly as simply the work product of law professors in addition to their classroom duties,[19] or more broadly as "that scholarship that seeks to inform and guide practitioners, legislators, other policymakers, and judges,"[20] legal scholarship is merely a discipline specific form of scholarship. Thus, it requires the same degree of reliability, in terms of accurate access to any body of work, so that it, too, can serve as a source of "wisdom." Nevertheless, works on legal scholarship seem to ignore this aspect of the very nature of scholarship, instead focusing on the professional or social role[21] of such scholarship, its content,[22] or issues of authorship.[23]

For example, in 1998, Mary Beth Beazley and Linda H. Edwards produced a comprehensive bibliography of law review articles on legal scholarship, "The Process and the Product: A Bibliography of Scholarship about Legal Scholarship."[24] Although it contains articles divided into five categories, none of these categories seem to focus on scholarship's reliability, as defined here as assurance that the public or later scholars have access to tamper-free content including its cited sources.

For example, Beazley and Edwards' first two categories focus on the needs of new members of academia. The very titles of the categories–"How and Why To Do Scholarship," and "The Broader Value of Scholarship"–purport to supply the rationale for the very idea of legal scholarship and its mechanics. There are twenty-seven articles mentioned under the first category and fifty-eight in the second.[25] However, the "how" and "why" are not related to the broader significance of scholarship within the realm of human knowledge. Instead, as is the question of its value, they are devoted to its significance to the professional and social lives of these academics.

The next three categories examine what constitutes legal scholarship in terms of format (whether or not they are published in law reviews, which law reviews in particular with regard to the well-known hierarchy of law review prestige, and the procedures by which various reviews select articles for publication[26]), topicality, and authorship. The third category "Comments on Scholarship in General," contains 103 articles; the fourth category, "Comments on Emerging Forms of Scholarship," contains eighty-eight; and the final category, "Critiques of the Publication and Editorial Process" contains sixty articles. In sum, there is a great deal of material devoted to the professional significance of legal scholarship, but there is very little, if any, relating it to the enterprise of scholarship generally–or, more particularly, to its function and nature within the Western tradition. Since 1998, the same lack of attention to scholarship's overall nature, especially the central requirement of reliability, accurately characterizes the literature in this pervasively electronic age. Authors are more concerned about dissemination–in the sense of immediate, though not necessarily long-range, access to information[27]–than reliability, which means assuring accurate and continuing access to the same body of work.

Legal Scholarship: Digital Publishing

For the purpose of this article, digital publishing includes electronic publishing (defined herein as the distribution of information directly in electronic format[28]) as well as digitization (the conversion of paper materials into electronic format[29]). Although digitization is often viewed in terms of archiving and electronic publishing in terms of accessing in formation, both are electronic means of disseminating information. Generally, law review articles that discuss electronic publishing seem to ignore its threat to reliability, in terms of assuring accurate access to the same body of work.[30]

For example, Michael Geist, in "Changing the Face of Legal Scholarship,"[31] noted that the "Internet is [. . .] having a significant impact on the dissemination of legal scholarship." Indeed, alternative electronic dissemination of legal journals affects their accessibility as a "democratiser of [. . .] knowledge,"[32] but dissemination alone does not assure reliability. Geist simply values dissemination, the immediacy of accessibility to information, not necessarily to the exclusion of, but surely without regard for, reliability.

M. Ethan Katsh raised the issue of the Internet impact on legal scholarship in nuanced ways.[33] First, he lauds digitization because "the World Wide Web provides opportunities for interactivity, for forms of argument that are hypertextual and non-linear, and for graphical representations that were often discouraged in print journals."[34]

At the same time he does not seem alarmed by the fact that publishing on the Web places information in, as even he puts it, a "form where [many] facets of print works such as fixity, uniformity, and authenticity, would be questioned,"[35] or that publishing on the Web fundamentally alters the idea that every available copy is the same as every other copy.[36] Storage or preservation issues are not mentioned. Katsh's article seems to suggest that reliability, storage, and preservation issues are of little concern. Only unbounded access to the work seems to count. Katsh's current stance seems radically and mischievously inconsistent with the views expressed in his 1989 book, *The Electronic Media and the Transformation of Law,* where he seemed concerned that "law may . . . be hurt by a process of communication that is open to doubt, is changeable and is not always subject to easy verification."[37]

James L. Hoover, Professor of Law at Columbia Law School, examines the electronic age and its impact on legal scholarship and legal libraries. In his view, law libraries would become more concept than place. Although he does not raise the issue of digitization's potential negative impact on scholarship's public accessibility, as defined here, he clearly understands the value of such reliable access.

His discussion of optical imaging,[38] as a way of storing and preserving scholarly products through this new age, recognizes the importance of this role of the law library, by capturing the exact image, let alone its digitized content, in reproducible form. As an aside, law libraries, by their very nature, ensure continuous public accessibility to the works listed in their catalogs. It seems inescapable and certainly logical that law libraries will become one of, if not the only, important custodians of electronic collections, assumedly fulfilling the same demands of accessibility, storage, and preservation as they do today in print or microform collections. Thus, it is appropriate to question whether the literature in this field is overly concerned with promoting the advantages of instant electronic dissemination, to the disadvantage and possible exclusion of questions regarding whether stored information is safe from alteration and inaccuracy. This concern is magnified when one considers the immediate cost of greater dissemination–the risk to reliability created by the much ballyhooed advent of self-publication.

WHAT IS DIGITAL PUBLISHING'S IMPACT ON LEGAL SCHOLARSHIP?

Digitization and Its Impact: General Aspects

Whether through digital publishing or electronic archiving, legal scholarship is under siege. While electronic publishing may be viewed as electro-publishing in opposition to in-print publishing, and digitization as electro-archiving in-print collections,[39] legal scholarship products can be found in both. Digital data repositories contain digital libraries, CD-ROMs, and digital form databases, including LEXIS/NEXIS and Westlaw. Virtually all digital sources are accessed via the Internet, which usually means through the World Wide Web. Amongst legal digital databases, LEXIS and Westlaw are the major players, as they contain electronic versions of law reviews–the major repositories of legal scholarship (although, it is important to note that other sources, such as treatises and monographs, and all older works except for case reporters, are conspicuously absent from this format). Thus, it becomes obvious that digital publishing, whether in its broader or narrower senses, poses responsibilities in the area of legal scholarship because it raises such issues as assured access and accuracy. Digital information, excepting image-type documents, "by its very nature, is open to manipulation, alteration, reformatting, and erasure, because those who create and use digital information usually love consideration for the current use and nature of the information."[40]

With print versions, reliability, in the sense of assured access, and accuracy, is easily assured. Traditionally, libraries received the works of scholarship and ensured their accessibility, storage and preservation. In the legal world, apparently, common sense rules produced reliability–continuous public accessibility, archiving, and accuracy–and they have been regularly published in *The Bluebook*.[41]

Digitization and Its Impact: Concrete Examples

The Bluebook is a repository of rules that enable users of law reviews to find, and thus access cited, and by definition extant, legal scholarship; it ensures that legal scholarship possesses the kind of reliability that legal scholars demand in the sense of consistent citation equals assured access, and accuracy.[42] Its role becomes clear if we understand that "[a] uniform and common-sense citation system makes legal writing easier and helps readers to retrieve cited works with a minimum of fuss. In the computer age, free-form citation may also hamper legal research."[43]

Until the advent of LEXIS and Westlaw, *The Bluebook* did not contain any rules regarding electronic sources,[44] because legal scholarship was unquestionably limited to in-print format.[45] Nevertheless when it started including rules about sources on electronic format, the rules to those citations essentially discouraged their use. For example, the 16th edition of *The Bluebook*[46] dissuaded citations to online sources "[b]ecause of the transient nature of many Internet sources."[47] The rule tacitly acknowledged the lack of reliability of Internet sources. Allowing such extraordinary citations effectively opened the door to the acceptance of unreliable sources–a door that remains open today.

The 17th edition of *The Bluebook*[48] distinguishes between the rules of citations covering commercial electronic databases (such as LEXIS and Westlaw) and those covering the rest of the online sources (thus covering the rest of the legal digital databases). It allows citations to LEXIS, Westlaw, and Dialog, in "preference to the other [online] sources"[49] because of their "reliability and authoritativeness."[50] *The Bluebook*, while allowing for citation to "authoriatative" online resources, maintains[51] the inhibiting tone of its previous rule of giving Internet citations only as "parallel citations using the explanatory phrase 'available at,'"[52] and to the extent possible, mentioning "the traditional source."[53] At least by implication, citations lacking a traditional source are anticipated when citation to the traditional source is not possible, leaving the door opened in the 16th edition[54] still ajar.[55] Even if the rule was initially intended to discourage the use of less reliable forms, one of its unintended consequences has been to encourage or accept citation to electronic media of suspect reliability.

For example, of the first twenty of 535 results to a query which searched the LEXIS/NEXIS Academic Universe[56] for law review articles published within the last six months and that cited at least four documents published on the Web,[57] twelve articles, or 60% of those first twenty, cited at least one online source which had become publicly inaccessible when accessed within a year from their publication, modification or last contact by a user. Those online sources, as shown in the Appendix, varied from federal and local governmental sites to self-published ones. By allowing for citations to purely digitally published sources, then, *The Bluebook*, if only in what appears today to be extraordinary circumstances, has offered encouragement, however unintended, to those who would abandon traditional assurances of reliability. Although the LEXIS and Westlaw legal databases have become more and more reliable in terms of comprehensive accessibility,[58] and seem to have passed the threshold *The Bluebook* imposes, no one can say that they offer the same reliability and access as the print version. Users understand that what they access on LEXIS, for example, may be the same only for as long as Reed Elsevier, Mead Data Central's[59] successor[60]–the company that gives us LEXIS–has access to it. For example, after libraries gave up subscriptions to in-print French legal documents such as the French Official Journal, relying on LEXIS, LEXIS lost or abandoned its subscription to such French documents in the summer of 1999. Or, as another example of the fragility of digital collections, in November 1999, at the request of the University of Denver,[61] both LEXIS and Westlaw removed from their collections Wines' "The Critical Need for Law Reform to Regulate the Abusive Practices of Transnational Corporations: The Illustrative Case of Boise Cascade Corporation in Mexico's Costa Grande and Elsewhere."[62] Thus, currently, the article is only available through libraries' in-print collections. Furthermore, LEXIS and WESTLAW coverage, as shown here, is constantly changing, even if its central role as a reliable electronic repository of case law seems–so far–unvarying.

CONCLUSIONS

Law review articles about digital publishing and legal scholarship seem to celebrate and emphasize the greater distribution and range of sources since the advent of the Internet without concern for the effects digital publishing may have on scholarship's reliability. However, seemingly by definition, digital publishing brings either constant alterations to the content of online sources (see the "last modified" mention for every online source) or a short lifespan for far too many of those sources.[63]

As mentioned before, attempting a random sample of URLs,[64] twelve cited works cited in the first twenty articles of recent law journals were no longer available.[65] If these authors were truly faithful to *The Bluebook*, and these failed citations are only supplementary, then these failures are not fatal to the enterprise of legal scholarship. (This ignores, however, the continuing threat that arises from the possibility of exceptional rules.) To the extent, however, that the directions of *The Bluebook* do not absolutely compel citations to some alternative in-print source, the advent of digitization or electronic publishing has, at the very least, introduced a higher degree of risk to the entire enterprise.

Then, the looming question concerns what digital publishing offers in terms of legal scholarship when more and more research is done online and more sources seems to be stored online. To the extent digital libraries are controlled by law schools,[66] law school libraries,[67] governmental organizations,[68] non-governmental institutions,[69] companies whose business is to perform or assist online research,[70] and other similar institutions,[71] the access, preservation, and storage issues, although inevitably affected by the agendas of those controlling entities, seem relatively secure.

Without those guarantees and absent any regulation (public or private) of the reliability of digital publishing, in terms of assured access and accuracy, the Internet may offer very little other than a starting research point to legal scholarship. Scholars and librarians cannot forget that digital publishing may indeed be more like a window than a strongbox for research, offering greater transparency and access but also greater fragility because of its transient nature.

History reminds us that the Library of Alexandria was burnt to the ground and that too many Eastern European libraries have been destroyed in local wars. It would be unfortunate if, through the apparently benevolent means of novel technical innovation, public accessibility to legal scholarship was limited.

NOTES

1. The term "digital publishing" is used to embrace two more conventional concepts: digitization, often limited to mean the conversion of printed to electronic content, and electronic publishing which embraces and frequently emphasizes the creation, storage, and transmission of digitized content. See, Amiran, Eyal. Electronic Time and the Serials Revolution, The Yale Journal of Criticism 10.2 (1997): 445-454.

2. OED, Vol. XIV (2nd edition), at 630.

3. Id.

4. A. Cornelius Benjamin. "The Ethics of Scholarship: A Discussion of Problems That Arise in Its Application." *Journal of Higher Education*, Vol. 31, No. 9. (Dec., 1960): 471-480, at 472.

5. Howard Mumford Jones. "The Scholar and the World: Scholarship as Ritual, Contest, and Civil Independence." *Journal of Higher Education*, Vol. 50, No. 4. (Jul.-Aug., 1979): 429-438, at 438.

6. René Decartes. *Discourse on Method and Related Writings* (Penguin Classics).

7. W. H. Walsh. "Knowledge in Its Social Setting." *Mind, New Series*, Vol. 80, No. 319. (Jul., 1971): 321-336.

8. Michael Paulsen and Kenneth A. Feldman. "Toward a Reconceptualization of Scholarship: a Human Action System." *Journal of Higher Education*. Vol. 66, No. 6 (Nov.-Dec. 1995): 15-40, at 16.

9. Id.

10. I thus use the term "reliability" throughout this piece to include accurate access to sources that reproduce faithfully the original source.

11. The tragedy of the library of Alexandria was not a physical one, but a trauma to the very nature of scholarship, for it fatally interfered with the ability of scholars to engage in their enterprise, the very essence of which is access to the stored product of earlier ages. The Library of Alexandria, built in the ancient Egyptian metropolis by the Ptolemies, in the fourth century BC, functioned as the world's first university, a great library, and a publishing house. When it burned down, its 700,000 of listed and classified manuscripts were destroyed. See Jon Thiem. "The Great Library of Alexandria Burnt: Towards the History of a Symbol." *Journal of the History of Ideas*, Vol. 40, No. 4. (Oct.-Dec., 1979): 507-526.

12. Benjamin. "The Ethics of Scholarship . . . ," supra, at 480. Michael Paulsen and Kenneth A. Feldman. "Toward a Reconceptualization . . . ," supra note. See also Anthony Grafton. "The Death of the Footnote (Report on an Exaggeration). *The Wilson Quarterly*. Vol. 21, No. 1 (Winter 1997): 72-78, at 73. ("The story of the footnote in fact began long before Ranke, or the 19th century, dawned. Even in the ancient world, when most historians saw their genre as one that depended on oral reports from participants in the events they described, some found it necessary to cite official documents, such as treaties. Josephus, the historian of the Jews, and Eusebius, the historian of the early Christian church, produced elaborate compilations of earlier sources.")

13. See Mary Beth Beazley and Linda H. Edwards. "The Process and the Product: A Bibliography of Scholarship About Legal Scholarship." *Mercer Law Review*. Vol. 49 (Spring, 1998): 741-70, for an extensive bibliography on legal scholarship arranged by four subject categories: (1) "How and Why To Do Scholarship," (2) "The Broader Value of Scholarship," (3) "Comments on Scholarship in General," (4) "the development of emerging forms of scholarship, including interdisciplinary scholarship, clinical scholarship, and empirical scholarship," and (5) a "critique of the publication process," including articles about the more recent explorations of the implications of electronic publishing.

14. See Philip M. Davis and Suzanne A. Cohen. "The Effect of the Web on Undergraduate Citation Behavior 1996-1999." *Journal of the American Society for Information Science* (2000) (to appear) ("In the world of academic scholarship, references form a link to original works, give credit to original ideas, and form a network of connections to related documents."). See also Grant H. Morris. "The Shortest Article in Law Review History: A Brief Response to Professor Jensen." 50 *Journal of Legal Education* (June, 2000): 310, the entire text of which is reproduced here:

> Not so! [FN1].
>
> [FN1] I write this footnote only because at least one footnote is, or at least should be, mandatory for a law review article. I note that although the title to my article is longer than Professor Jensen's, see Erik M. Jensen, The Shortest Article in Law Review History, 50 J.Legal Educ. 156 (2000), the text is shorter (by one word), and there are fewer footnotes (by one footnote). If I had so desired, I could have shortened the text by merely proclaiming, "Wrong!" However, I did not assert that my article was the shortest, only that Professor Jensen's was not.

(emphasis added). See also Erik M. Jensen, The Shortest Article in Law Review History, 50 *Journal of Legal Education* (2000): 156.

15. On reliable accessibility as a technical issue in the general context of electronic publishing, see Martin Kramer. "The Politics and Processes of Scholarship," *Change*, Vol. 40, No. 4 (July-August 1996): 61. ("Plainly, some of these issues are purely technical, and technicians are the right people to resolve them–issues such as assuring the integrity and permanence of a tamper-proof archival record and authoritatively documenting claims of first publication.")

16. See, supra, fn. 1.

17. See, e.g., Bernard, J. Hibbits. "The LHR Electronic Resource Page: Changing Our Minds: Legal History Meets the World Wide Web." Law and History Review. Vol. 17 (Summer, 1999): 385-87. Bernard, J. Hibbits. "Last Writes? Re-Assessing the Law in the Age of Cyberspace." New York University Law Review. Vol. 71 (June,

1996): 615-88, and Hoover, James, L. "Legal Scholarship and the Electronic Revolution." Law Library Journal. Vol. 83. (Fall, 1991): 643-651.

18. One can view all innovations in writing as technical developments which have, on occasion, raised the risk of reliability. Were it not for this risk, the Rosetta stone would not have resisted decoding so well, nor would we face the continuing problem of attempting to understand the writings of the Hittites, the Mayans, and others. We do not know whether future generations will view what we think of as the height of modernity as nothing more than another form of undecipherable hieroglyphics.

19. Marin Roger Scordato. "The Dualist Model of Legal Teaching and Scholarship." *American University Law Review.* Vol. 40. (Fall, 1990): 367-417.

20. Harry T. Edwards. "Another 'Postscript' to 'The Growing Disjunction Between Legal Education and the Legal Profession.' " Washington *Law Review* Vol. 69 (July, 1994): 561-572, at 571.

21. Kozinski, Alex. "The Relevance of Legal Scholarship to the Judiciary and Community: Address Who Gives A Hoot About Legal Scholarship?" *Houston Law Review.* Vol. 37 (2000): 295-319.

22. Many articles have been written on evaluating scholarship. See, e.g., Edward L. Rubin. "On Beyond Truth: A theory for Evaluating Legal Scholarship." *California Law Review.* Vol. 80 (July, 1992): 889-963.

23. Paul W. Kahn. *The Cultural Study of Law. Reconstructing Legal Scholarship.* at 129. Chicago: The University of Chicago Press, 1999. (decrying "legal scholarship made by legal practitioners").

24. *Mercer Law Review.* Vol. 49 (Spring, 1980): 741-70.

25. Of course, this author admits that there is a margin of error in her count, but it does not seem significant to the outcome.

26. See, e.g., William C. Whitford. "The Need for and Exclusive Submission Policy for Law Review Articles." *Wisconsin Law Review.* (January/February, 1994): 231-33.

27. In this sense the literature seems thrilled–to a fault–at the prospects of self-publication (the ultimate in access of a sort) without considering the greater risk implicit to such institutionally free information regimes. See, e.g., Bernard, J. Hibbits. "The LHR Electronic Resource Page: Changing Our Minds: Legal History Meets the World Wide Web." Law and History Review. Vol. 17 (Summer, 1999): 385-87. Bernard, J. Hibbits. "Last Writes? Re-Assessing the Law in the Age of Cyberspace." New York University Law Review. Vol. 71 (June, 1996): 615-88.

28. Martin Kramer. "The Politics and Processes of Scholarship."(book reviews) *Change.* Vol. 28 no. 4 (July-August 1996): 61-63, 61.

> [W]e can think of electronic publishing as occurring whenever a reader receives material to be read or examined from a computer, whether or not it has existed or will ever exist as print on paper. This broadest definition would, of course, include many kinds of materials of interest or concern to society as a whole but not especially of interest to scholars, such as an Internet edition of The New York Times or a piece of digital pornography. It would also include materials transmitted via computer merely out of convenience, such as a facsimile or scanned version of a paper document housed at a remote library.

29. These definitions owe their brief and concise nature to Kent McKeever, director of Arthur W. Diamond Library.

30. Of course, there are many other scholarly products concerned about the accurate accessibility to electronically published works. See Kramer. "The Politics and Pro-

cesses of Scholarship," *Change*, Vol. 40, No. 4 (July-August 1996): 61. ("However much electronic publishing there is now, how much there will be in the future, and how we choose to define it, there has to be concern when the presentation and accessibility of scholarly products change so drastically.")

31. *Law and Technology* (September 21, 1998), accessed at http://lsprod.mtcibs.com/lawtech/archive/199803.htm on October 18, 2000, at 4:02 p.m.

32. Simon Schama. "People's history Digital archives are a huge step forward in the democratization of historical knowledge." *The Guardian* (Nov 13, 1999): 24.

33. "Law Reviews and the Migration to Cyberspace." *Akron Law Review*. Vol. 29 (Winter, 1996) 115-120.

34. Id. at 119.

35. Id.

36. Id. Bernard J. Hibbits, professor at the University of Pittsburgh School of Law, shares the same enthusiasm. See Bernard, J. Hibbits. "The LHR Electronic Resource Page: Changing Our Minds: Legal History Meets the World Wide Web." *Law and History Review*. Vol. 17 (Summer, 1999): 385-87, and Bernard, J. Hibbits. "Last Writes? Re-Assessing the Law in the Age of Cyberspace." *New York University Law Review*. Vol. 71 (June, 1996): 615-88.

37. In Ethan Katsh, *The Electronic Media and the Transformation of Law,* at 94.

38. Hoover, James, L. "Legal Scholarship and the Electronic Revolution." *Law Library Journal*. Vol. 83. (Fall, 1991): 643-651, 647.

39. Middleton, Michael. *Library Digitisation Project Management.* Availability: Web site: http://educate.lib.chalmers.se/IATUL/proceedcontents/chanpap/middleto.html, accessed on October 20, 2000, at 5:57 p.m. ("Digital libraries are defined in many ways. A common understanding is that they are data repositories that are being newly created in digital form in databases, on Web sites, or from file servers in a variety of combined text and image formats.")

40. Peter Mazikana. "The Challenges of Archiving Digital Information." *International Information and Library Review*. Vol. 29 (1997): 307-317, at 313.

41. *The Bluebook. A Uniform System of Citation*. Cambridge: The Harvard Law Review Association.

42. James W. Paulsen. "Book Review: An Uninformed System of Citation." *Harvard Law Review*. Vol. 105 (May, 1992): 1780-1794, at 1786-87.

43. Id. at 1793-94. I use "in-print" to include all other forms of tangible works.

44. Nazareth A. M. Pantaloni III. "Legal Databases, Legal Epistemology, and the legal Order." *Law Library Journal*. Vol. 86 (Fall, 1994): 679-706, at 695. (discussing the 13th edition of *The Bluebook*.)

45. Id. at 1786-87.

46. *The Bluebook. A Uniform System of Citation*. Cambridge: The Harvard Law Review Association, 1996.

47. Id. Rule 17.3.3. at 124.

48. *The Bluebook. A Uniform System of Citation*. Cambridge: The Harvard Law Review Association, 2000.

49. Id. Rule 18.1 at 130.

50. Id.

51. Rule 18.2.1 at 133.

52. Id.

53. Id.

54. *The Bluebook. A Uniform System of Citation*. Cambridge: The Harvard Law Review Association, 1996: Rule 17.3.3. at 124.

> Because of the transient nature of many Internet sources, citation to Internet sources is discouraged unless the materials are unavailable in printed form or are difficult to obtain in their original form. When citing to materials found on the Internet, provide the name of the author (if any), the title or top-level heading of the material being cited, and the Uniform Resource Locator (URL). The Uniform resource locator is the electronic address of the information and should be given in angled brackets. For electronic journals and publications, the actual date of publication should be given. Otherwise, provide the most recent modification date of the source preceded by the term "last modified" or the date of access preceded by the term "visited" of the modification date is unavailable [. . .].

55. *The Bluebook. A Uniform System of Citation*. Cambridge: The Harvard Law Review Association, 2000: Rule 18.2.1 at 132-33.

> This rule requires the use and citation of traditional printed sources, except when the information is not available in a printed source, or if the traditional source is obscure or hard to find and when the citation to an Internet source will substantially improve access to the same information contained in the traditional source. In the latter case, to the extent possible, the traditional source should be used and cited. In such cases, the Internet source may be given as a parallel citation using the explanatory phrase *"available at"* no explanatory phrase should be included when the author accesses only the Internet source [. . .]. For material found exclusively on the Internet, such as on-line journals, the explanatory phrase *"at"* should be used. The principles of Internet citation (other than the requirement of citing source actually used or accessed by the author) are intended to be flexible guidelines applied in light of the nature of the information being cited, the state of the Internet as it develops over time, the standards or requirements applicable to the citing work, and the uses to which the citing work are to be put [. . .].

56. Electronic Presentation: Lexis-Nexis, a division of Reed-Elsevier Inc.

57. The query dated November 10, 2000 looked for law review articles published within the last six months and which contained references to more than one electronic source. Thus, the query was limited to articles that mentioned the term "www" at least four times: "www. w/25 www. and www. and www."

58. See, e.g., Nazareth A. M. Pantaloni III. "Legal Databases, Legal Epistemology, and the legal Order." supra.

59. See *West Publishing Co. v. Mead Data Central, Inc.* 799 F.2d 1219 (8th Cir. 1986).

60. In 1994 Reed Elsevier paid $1.5 billion for Mead Data Central, parent of the Lexis-Nexis online legal information service. See John J. Oslund. "West Publishing looks at options, including sale; Eagan firm hires investment bankers to help find 'financial strength to succeed.' " *Star Tribune* (August 30, 1995): 1D.

61. Peter Monaghan. "A Journal Article Is Expunged and its Authors Cry Foul." *Chronicle of Higher Education*. (December 8, 2000): 14.

62. *Denver Journal of International Law and Policy*. Vol. 26 (1998): 453-515.

63. For example, when attempting to access the Uniform Resource Locator (URL) for a source cited in note 256 of Christina N. Gifford's "The Sonny Bono Copyright Term Extension Act," Dennis S. Karjala's Challenge to Constitutionality ("last modi-

fied Nov. 13, 1999") <http://www.public.asu.edu/dkarjala/constitutionality.html>, the result achieved is a "not found" error.

64. The search was limited to law review articles containing citations that included "www" in their URL.

65. See the Appendix.

66. See Hastings College of Law's digital library on Center for Gender and Refugee Studies at http://www.uchastings.edu/cgrs/.

67. See Bora Laskin Law Library's digital library on *Women Human Rights' Resources* at http://www.law-lib.utoronto.ca/Diana/.

68. See the Library of Congress' legislative information database at http://thomas.loc.gov/.

69. See the United Nations' digital library at http://www.un.org/.

70. See LEXIS at http://www.lexis.com/ and Westlaw at http://www.westlaw.com/.

71. See JSTOR, at http://www.jstor.org.

BIBLIOGRAPHY

Amiran, Eyal, Electronic Time and the Serials Revolution. *The Yale Journal of Criticism* 10.2 (1997): 445-454.

Benjamin, A. Cornelius. "The Ethics of Scholarship: A Discussion of Problems That Arise in Its Application." *Journal of Higher Education*, Vol. 31, No. 9. (Dec. 1960): 471-480.

The Bluebook. A Uniform System of Citation. Cambridge: The Harvard Law Review Association, 2000.

Davis, Philip M. and Suzanne A. Cohen. "The Effect of the Web on Undergraduate Citation Behavior 1996-1999." *Journal of the American Society for Information Science* (2000).

Decartes, Rene. *Discourse on Method and Related Writings* (Penguin Classics).

Faerber, Charles, N. "Book Versus Byte: The Prospects And Desirability of a Paperless Society." *The John Marhall Journal of Computer & Information Law* Vol. 17 (Spring, 1999): 797-829.

Grafton, Anthony. "The Death of the Footnote (Report on an Exaggeration)." *The Wilson Quarterly*. Vol. 21, No. 1 (Winter 1997): 72-78.

Haigh, Richard. "What Shall I Wear to the Computer Revolution? Some Thoughts on Electronic Researching in Law." *Law Library Journal*. Vol. 89 (1997): 245-264.

Hibbits, Bernard, J. "The LHR Electronic Resource Page: Changing Our Minds: Legal History Meets the World Wide Web." *Law and History Review*. Vol. 17 (Summer, 1999): 385-87.

Hibbits, Bernard, J. "Last Writes? Re-Assessing the Law in the Age of Cyberspace." *New York University Law Review*. Vol. 71 (June, 1996): 615-88.

Hoover, James, L. "Legal Scholarship and the Electronic Revolution." *Law Library Journal*. Vol. 83. (Fall, 1991): 643-651.

Jensen, Erik M. The Shortest Article in Law Review History, 50 *Journal of Legal Education* (2000): 156.

Jones, Howard Mumford. "The Scholar and the World: Scholarship as Ritual, Contest, and Civil Independence." *Journal of Higher Education*, Vol. 50, No. 4. (Jul.-Aug., 1979): 429-438.

Kozinski, Alex. "The Relevance of Legal Scholarship to the Judiciary and Community: Address Who Gives A Hoot About Legal Scholarship." *Houston Law Review*. Vol. 37 (2000): 295-319.

Kramer, Martin. "The Politics and Processes of Scholarship." (book reviews) *Change*. Vol. 28 no. 4 (July-August 1996): 61-63.

Mazikana, Peter. "The Challenges of Archiving Digital Information." *International Information and Library Review*. Vol. 29 (1997): 307-317.

Martin, Peter, W. "How New Information Technologies Will Change the Way Law Professors Do and Distribute Scholarship." *Law Library Journal*. Vol. 83 (Fall, 1991): 633-41.

Middleton, Michael. *Library Digitisation Project Management*. Availability: Web site: http://educate.lib.chalmers.se/IATUL/proceedcontents/chanpap/middleto.html, accessed on October 20, 2000, at 5:57 p.m.

Morris, Grant H. "The Shortest Article in Law Review History: A Brief Response to Professor Jensen." 50 *Journal of Legal Education* (June, 2000): 310.

Pantaloni, Nazareth A. M. III. "Legal Databases, Legal Epistemology, and the Legal Order." *Law Library Journal*. Vol. 86 (Fall, 1994): 679-706.

Paulsen, James W. "Book Review: An Uninformed System of Citation." *Harvard Law Review*. Vol. 105 (May, 1992): 1780-1794.

Paulsen, Michael and Kenneth A. Feldman. "Toward a Reconceptualization of Scholarship: A Human Action System." *Journal of Higher Education*. Vol. 66, No. 6 (Nov.-Dec. 1995): 15-40.

Rier, David, A. "The Future of Legal Scholarship and Scholarly Communication: Publication in the Age of Cyberspace." *Akron Law Review*. Vol. 30 (Winter, 1996): 183-213.

Rubin, Edward L. "On Beyond Truth: A Theory for Evaluating Legal Scholarship." *California Law Review*. Vol. 80 (July, 1992): 889-963.

Scordato, Marin Roger. "The Dualist Model Of Legal Teaching And Scholarship." *The American University Law Review*. Vol. 40 (Fall, 1990): 367-417.

Stefancic, Jean & Delgado, Richard. "Outsider Jurisprudence and the Electronic Revolution: Will Technology Help or Hinder the Cause of Law Reform." *Ohio State Law Journal*. Vol. 52 (Summer, 1991): 847-58.

Thiem, Jon. "The Great Library of Alexandria Burnt: Towards the History of a Symbol." *Journal of the History of Ideas*, Vol. 40, No. 4. (Oct.-Dec., 1979): 507-526.

Walsh, W. H. "Knowledge in Its Social Setting." *Mind, New Series*, Vol. 80, No. 319. (Jul., 1971): 321-336.

APPENDIX

1. Gostin, Lawrence O. and James G. Hodge, Jr. "The Public Health Improvement Process in Alaska: Toward a Model Public Health Law." Alaska Law Review. Vol. 17 (June, 2000): 77-125. (The Web page of *Alaska Department of Environmental Conservation–Division of Air and Water Quality*, <http://www.state.ak.us/local/akpages/ENV.CONSERV/dawq/dec <uscore>dawq.htm> accessible on Apr. 14, 2000,[1] but not on November 10, 2000.)

2. Silberlight, Adam. "WWW. How to Be a Master of Your Domain.com: A Look at the Assignment of Internet Domain Names under Federal Trademark Law, Federal Case Law and Beyond." Albany Law Journal of Science & Technology. Vol. 10 (2000): 229-280. (The Web page of *Network Solutions* <http://www.networksolutions.com/legal/disclaimer. html> accessible on Aug. 1, 2000,[2] but not on November 10, 2000.)

3. Faust, Susan M. "Baby Girl or Baby Boy? Now You Can Choose: A Look at New Biology and No Law." Albany Law Journal of Science & Technology. Vol. 10 (2000): 281-303. (The Web page of Bryan S. Jick's *Gender Selection–The Latest Techniques for Choosing the Sex of Your Child* <http://www.parenthoodweb.com/articles/ phw839.htm> accessible on Feb. 25, 2000,[3] but not on November 10, 2000.)

4. John S. Goldkamp, "The Drug Court Response: Issues and Implications for Justice Change." Albany Law Review. Vol. 63 (2000): 923-961. (The Web pages of *The Center for Court Innovation, a public/private partnership that works to develop innovative court programs* at <http://www. community courts. org/resource/homecci.htm> and of *The plan of the Midtown Community Court*, at <http://www.courtinnovation.org/demo01mcc. html> both accessible on April 4, 2000,[4] but not on November 10, 2000.)

5. Karen Swenson. "School Finance Reform Litigation: Why Are Some State Supreme Courts Activist and Others Restrained?" Albany Law Review. Vol. 63 (2000): 1147-1182. (The Web page of the U.S. Census Bureau's *Census of Governments* <http://www.census.gov/ ftp/pub/econ/ www/go0100.html> accessible on March 26, 2000,[5] but not on the census cite on November 10, 2000.)

6. Michael West. "High Court Study: Arrested Development: An Analysis of the Oregon Supreme Court's Free Speech Jurisprudence in the Post-Linde Years." Albany Law Review. Vol. 63 (2000): 1237-1295. (The Web page of *Oregon Blue Book: Voting and Voter Registration* <http://www.sos.state. or.us/BlueBook/1999%202000/state/elections/elections 27.htm> accessible on Apr. 20, 2000,[6] but not on November 10, 2000.)

7. Mark Smith, Janice Buckingham, Conni Gibson, and Jason Dubchak. "Recent Legislative and Regulatory Developments of Interest to Oil and Gas Lawyers Alberta Law Review." Vol 38 (June, 2000): 170-257. (The Web page of the Government of Alberta's *Code of Practice for the Temporary Diversion of Water for Hydrostatic Testing of Pipelines*, <http://www.gov.ab.ca/qp/ ascii/codes/divers.tex> last modified in October, 1999,[7] and inaccessible on November 10, 2000.)\

8. Samuel M. Stricklin and Alexander P. Okuliar. "Characterization of Healthcare Receivables: Are Post-Petition Healthcare Receivables Subject to Pre-Petition Liens as 'Proceeds' or 'Rents' under the Bankruptcy Code, or are They Excluded as After-Acquired Property?" American Bankruptcy Institute Law Review. Vol. 8 (Spring, 2000): 47-76. (The Web page of the Department

of Health and Human Services's *National Health Expenditures Projections 1998-2000* <http://www.hcfa.gov/stats/NHE-Proj/ proj1998/hilites.htm>, last modified Jan. 10, 2000,[8] and inaccessible on November 10, 2000.)

9. Lucien J. Dhooge. "The Wrong Way to Mandalay: The Massachusetts Selective Purchasing Act and the Constitution." American Business Law Journal. Vol. 37 (Spring, 2000): 387-484. (The Web page of Central Intelligence Agency's *The World Factbook* 3 (1997) <http://www.odci.gov/ cia/publications/ factbook/bm.html> accessible on November 3, 1998,[9] but not on November 10, 2000.)

10. Barbara Crutchfield George and Kathleen A. Lacey and Jutta Birmele. "The 1998 OECD Convention: An Impetus for Worldwide Changes in Attitudes Toward Corruption in Business Transactions." American Business Law Journal. Vol. 37 (Spring, 2000): 485-525. (The Web page of the *Convention on Combating Bribery of Foreign Public Officials in International Business Transactions, Dec. 17, 1997, 37 I. L. M. 8* <http://www.oecd.org./daf/ cmis/bribery/20nov23.htm>,[10] not accessible on November 10, 2000.)

11. George J. Siedel. "Commentary: Six Forces and the Legal Environment of Business: The Relative Value of Business Law among Business School Core Courses." American Business Law Journal. Vol. 37 (Summer, 2000): 717-742. (The Web page containing the *French Law of May 19, 1998 on Liability for Defective Products* <http://www.faccparisfrance. com/them/5leg120 .htm>, accessible on July 29, 1999,[11] but not on November 10, 2000.)

12. Gary Eisenberg. "Foreign Corrupt Practices Act." American Criminal Law Review. Vol. 37 (Spring, 2000): 595-615. (The Web page of the U.S. Department of Justice's *Foreign Corrupt Practices Act Review Procedure Releases* <http://www.usdoj.gov/criinal/fraud/fcpa/r8501.html>, accessible on October 10, 1999,[12] but not on November 10, 2000.)

NOTES

1. "The Public Health Improvement . . . ," note 143, at 125.
2. "WWW. How to Be a Master of Your Domain.com: . . . ," note 93, at 280.
3. "Baby Girl or Baby Boy? . . .," note 7, at 303.
4. "The Drug Court Response . . . ," note 6, at 961.
5. "School Finance Reform Litigation . . . ," note 72, at 1182.
6. "High Court Study . . . ," note 1, at 1295.
7. "Recent Legislative and Regulatory Developments . . . ," note 71, at 257.
8. "Characterization of Healthcare . . . ," note 1, at 76.
9. "The Wrong Way to Mandalay . . . ," note 39, at 484.
10. "The 1998 OECD Convention . . . ," note 1, at 525.
11. "Commentary: Six Forces and the Legal Environment . . . ," note 7, at 742.
12. "Foreign Corrupt Practices Act." note 72, at 615.

Trust v. Antitrust: Consolidation in the Legal Publishing Industry

John Dethman

SUMMARY. The legal publishing industry in the United States went through a period of rapid consolidation during the last decade of the 20th century. Almost all United States publishers are now owned by foreign conglomerates that have a vast presence in the *information* business. The consequences of this change and consolidation of ownership has had far-reaching effects; some are already known, but some are certainly unknown at this time. In looking at the phenomenon, this article tries to give some historical perspective on legal publishing, examines the conglomerates as *businesses* (a "top down" approach), considers important legislation concerning databases, and wonders at the effects all this concentrated change may have on law libraries and the patrons they serve. *[Article copies available for a fee from The Haworth Document Delivery Service: 1-800-HAWORTH. E-mail address: <getinfo@haworthpressinc.com> Website: <http://www.HaworthPress.com> © 2002 by The Haworth Press, Inc. All rights reserved.]*

KEYWORDS. Legal publishing industry, antitrust law, legal information industry, publishing mergers

INTRODUCTION

Professor Robert C. Berring, the Librarian of Boalt Hall, the University of California Law School, in his 1995 California Law Review arti-

---

John Dethman is Access Services/Reference Librarian, University of Missouri-Columbia School of Law.

[Haworth co-indexing entry note]: "Trust v. Antitrust: Consolidation in the Legal Publishing Industry." Dethman, John. Co-published simultaneously in *Legal Reference Services Quarterly* (The Haworth Information Press, an imprint of The Haworth Press, Inc.) Vol. 21, No. 2/3, 2002, pp. 123-151; and: *Law Library Collection Development in the Digital Age* (ed: Michael Chiorazzi, and Gordon Russell) The Haworth Information Press, an imprint of The Haworth Press, Inc., 2002, pp. 123-151. Single or multiple copies of this article are available for a fee from The Haworth Document Delivery Service [1-800-HAWORTH, 9:00 a.m. - 5:00 p.m. (EST). E-mail address: getinfo@haworthpressinc.com].

cle, *On not throwing out the baby: the future of legal information*, bases his discussion on the premise "that the United States has the world's best legal information system."[1] I agree. And I think that it is likely to remain the best. The question I raise is whether the United States' legal information system can sustain that stature given the changes wrought in the legal publishing industry this past decade. Note that Professor Berring's article was published in March 1995, 15 months prior to West Publishing Company's acquisition by the Canadian publishing conglomerate The Thomson Corporation (see below).

The history of legal publishing in the United States mirrors that of the publishing industry as a whole. In the beginning there were many publishers, mostly local, who catered to their particular market. There were many reasons for this including the difficulties of transportation and communication. As the nation spread across the continent the numbers grew. But, as transportation and communication improved, it became possible for publishers to serve markets far removed from their home office. Consolidation was inevitable and continues. Multimedia conglomerates dominate information delivery and publishing. The breadth and reach of the new AOL-Time Warner company is staggering. Its market capitalization is over $100 billion–at this time it is not active in the legal publishing industry.[2]

Legal publishing in the United States is now centered in three foreign conglomerates–The Thomson Corporation (Canadian), Reed Elsevier (Anglo-Dutch) and Wolters Kluwer (Dutch). All together it is estimated that they control 90% of the legal publishing business in the United States. Thirty-two years ago, when the American Bar Association issued its *Recommended Law Books*, 3% was under foreign ownership.[3]

This article is divided into 9 sections: Section 1, *History as Legal Documents* explores how legal documents have existed since the beginning of the written word and have "recorded" the history of their times; Section 2, *The Fast and Furious '90s–Unprecedented Consolidation by Foreign Invasion* considers in short order a pivotal decade in the international consolidation of legal publishing; Section 3, *Who are these Players–the Conglomerates Behind the Imprints?* examines who the new legal publishers are; Section 4 questions *Who's Left?*; Section 5 glances at *The Canadian Experience*; Section 6 observes *Antitrust–the United States' Perspective*; Section 7 ponders the emerging problem of *Database Protection* and how government may respond to concerns of both owners and users and to international concerns; Section 8 looks at *The Bottom Line*; and Section 9 wonders about *The Big Picture*.

SECTION 1: HISTORY AS LEGAL DOCUMENTS

The oldest evidence for a legal code: tablets from the ancient archives of the city of Ebla (now at Tell Mardikh, Syria) date to about 2400 B.C. The best-known ancient code is the Babylonian Code of Hammurabi, circa 1750 B.C., a collection of legal decisions carved on a stone stela. No one knows who the publisher was–it was likely an "official" reporter.[4] There have also been clay tablets discovered that may contain terms of ancient commercial contracts.[5]

The Romans were great lawgivers. The writings of Cicero and others have inspired many lawyers over the centuries. Justinian ordered his jurists to excerpt the best and most reliable sections of earlier Roman texts and to assemble them under appropriate headings in a massive *Digest.* To this was added the *Institutes*, a textbook for students and one of the most influential law books of all time. Finally, he commissioned the *Codex*, a collection of all Imperial statutes. Together they formed what became know as *Corpus Juris*, a familiar name for today's lawyers in a slightly different context.[6]

Medieval law took much from the Romans. This is not surprising with the Catholic Church's important position in the temporal world and its critical place in maintaining learning and preserving knowledge, particularly in its monasteries. Much of the foundation of modern jurisprudence can be traced to England's Henry II, who sent out his judges to give the justice of the king rather than justice of the local lord. These judges returned to London to discuss their decisions so that there could be uniformity in the application of law, a *common law*, and the beginning of the concept of *stare decisis.* Henry's reign also saw what is likely the first legal practitioner's book, *Glanvill*, written in Latin circa 1189. It first appeared in manuscript, of course, but, since the printing press, there have been editions made every century.[7] This was followed fifty years later by *Bracton*, perhaps the first book on Anglo-American legal theory.[8]

But all this history of law is through documents that were in manuscript at best. They were not generally available. This began to change in the 15th Century with the advent of the printing press. The first legal publishers were printers.[9]

The earliest abridgement of English law–summaries of cases under broad topic headings allowing for actual use of the concept of precedent–was published in 1490.[10] Rastell's Dictionary–the first English law dictionary–appeared in 1527, but still in Latin.[11] Christopher St. Germain's *Doctor and Student* was the first major law book published in English in 1530.[12] Publication of English law in English accelerated with Coke's *Reports* in 1600[13] and Blackstone's famous *Commentaries on the Law of England* in 1765.[14]

In the "colonies" the first laws were printed by Mathew Day in 1648–*The Lauues and Libertyes of Massachusets.*[15] Early printers found a ready market for such books as *The Office and Authority of the Justice of the Peace* published by George Webb in 1736.[16] But perhaps the most important early legal publishing triumph was the American edition of Blackstone's *Commentaries* in 1771 by Robert Bell, who had also published Thomas Paine's *Common Sense.*[17]

After the American Revolution the legal publishing business sought to distance itself from its English heritage. Swift's 1795 *A System of the Laws of Connecticut*, the first American legal treatise, acknowledged its debt to England by citing 125 English authorities to only four from the new United States of America.[18] Thirty years later, his *Digest of the Laws of Connecticut* relied more, but not completely, on American law.[19] James Kent's *Commentaries on American Law* in 1826, derived like Blackstone's from university lectures, completed the separation.[20] Following on its heels were Justice Story's *Commentaries* published between 1832 and 1845.[21]

But the true flowering of American legal publishing as a business begins with the law reports, their digests and related annotated statutes, beginning with Kirby's *Reports of Cases Adjudged in the Superior Court of the State of Connecticut, from the year 1785, to May 1788 in 1789.*[22] The first official reporter was George Gaines, whose *New York Term Reports of Cases Argued and Determined in the Supreme Court of that State* for 1803-1805 was published in 1804-1806.[23] The U.S. Supreme Court had an official reporter prior to the states' efforts. The most famous of these were Wheaton, 1816-1827, and Peters, 1828-1842, who were on the opposite sides of the first copyright decision by the Court at 33 U.S. 591 (1835).

In the later half of the 19th century two entrepreneurs changed the legal publishing landscape. In 1876, a twenty-four year old John B. West began what would quickly evolve into the North-Western Reporter and, within 10 years, the National Reporter System, which was intended to publish all appellate cases.[24] Two years earlier, Frank Shepard began to painstakingly review Illinois Supreme Court decisions to determine what cases were cited therein and provide that information for attorneys.[25] Today this process of checking citations is often known as "shepardizing."

Congress has always provided that the laws it passed were to be published. The *Statutes at Large* were printed by what would be Little

Brown beginning in 1846.[26] The Government Printing Office took over this duty in 1874 when the *Revised Statutes* were also published for the first time.[27] Finally, the United States Code replaced previous compilations in 1926.[28] At the state level, New York's *Revised Statutes* in 1829 set the standard that other states were quick to follow.[29] Both West Publishing Company and Lawyers Co-op Publishing Company published annotated United States Codes and various state codes when that trend established itself latter in the 19th century. West's USCA was the first to use "pocket parts" for supplementation.[30]

The Federal Register appeared in 1936 in response to the burgeoning growth of administrative law.[31] This led to the increased popularity of loose-leaf services, begun in the tax area in 1913, to keep up with this constantly changing environment.[32]

Law publishing in the United States has always been an intensely practical business that prospered by serving its market, attorneys and judges. The need for help in efficiently finding the law led to numerous treatises, dictionaries, encyclopedias and other finding aids from many publishers. The West Digest system and Shepard's citation system are perhaps the best known of these finding aids.

Perhaps as a harbinger of things to come, later in the 20th century, many states gave up their official reporters for West's National Reporter System. Legal publishing had become a big business. West Publishing Company was reputedly one of the largest closely held businesses in the United States. It had acquired numerous other publishing companies, including the venerable Foundation Press.

The publishing landscape was changing in another way. In the early '70s, Mead Data, operating out of Dayton, Ohio, launched its clunky Lexis dial-up, computerized legal research service. Screens were small and modems slow–when text finally appeared, it "crawled" across the screen. But in time, bigger screens, faster modems and, most of all, the Internet, made online legal research essential to legal practice and the business really began to hum.

SECTION 2: THE FAST AND FURIOUS '90s– UNPRECEDENTED CONSOLIDATION BY FOREIGN INVASION[33]

In 1990, Reed International PLC (United Kingdom) purchased Martindale-Hubble and the principal listing of United States lawyers was in foreign hands. By 1994, Read International had created a joint venture with Elsevier NV (Netherlands) called Reed Elsevier that purchased Lexis-Nexis and took control of the (then) leading online legal research service. It continued its expansion by acquiring Mathew Bender and Shepard's. These purchases cost over $3 billion.

Wolters Kluwer, a Dutch conglomerate, arrived in 1994 with its purchase of Prentice Hall Law and Business, Commerce Clearing House (CCH) in 1995 and Little Brown & Company in 1996. These purchases exceeded $2 billion.[34]

Importantly, a proposed merger of Reed Elsevier and Wolters Kluwer fell apart in 1998. This was apparently due to antitrust concerns raised by the new European Union.[35] At least one observer of recent antitrust history and legal publishing has expressed surprise at this turnabout due to the failure of either the EU or the U.S. antitrust authorities to derail the Thomson-West union (see below).[36]

The Thomson Corporation, a Canadian conglomerate, crossed the border to purchase Bancroft-Whitney, Lawyers Co-op, Research Institute of America, Clark-Boardman, and, finally, in the largest purchase in this amazing period, acquired West for over $3 billion.[37] In one year, 1996, Thomson became the major player in United States legal publishing.

It is significant that these three foreign corporations are *conglomerates* primarily in the information businesses. They have great presence outside of legal publishing. Their impact is felt in many kindred fields, notably STM (science, technical and medical) and academic publishing and online databases.

SECTION 3: WHO ARE THESE PLAYERS– THE CONGLOMERATES BEHIND THE IMPRINTS?

The Thomson Corporation[38]

Roy Thomson founded The Thomson Corporation when he purchased his first newspaper in Timmins, Ontario in 1934.[39] Over the next 20 years he acquired the largest group of newspapers in Canada, including the *Toronto Globe and Mail*, one of the country's national dailies. But by then he had moved to the United Kingdom and began to establish a media empire, earning a hereditary title and becoming Lord Thomson of Fleet.[40] His newspapers included the famous *Times of London* and the *Sunday Times*. His fortunes increased with the discovery of oil under the North Sea. He entered the book publishing business in 1964 with Thomson Publishing.[41] He was succeeded at his death in 1976 by his son, Kenneth, as the 2nd Lord Thomson of Fleet. (Kenneth Thomson controls 73% of Thomson and is the richest man in

Canada.)[42] During the next decade the business began to shift its emphasis. It began selling off its media enterprises in the United Kingdom, including the Times Newspapers in 1981. Its first foray in legal publishing began in 1987 with the purchase of Sweet & Maxwell in the United Kingdom, Carswell in Canada, and The Law Book Company in Australia.[43] In 1989, it acquired Lawyers Co-op and RIA.[44] In 1994 it entered the database business with the purchase of Information Access Company, a U.S. provider of broad-based reference and database services.[45] But it lost the bidding battle for Lexis-Nexis.[46] (By this time, it had divested itself of all its United Kingdom newspapers and has or will divest itself of all its North American newspapers except the *Toronto Globe and Mail* in which it retains an interest through its 20% ownership in a joint venture with BCE, the Canadian telephone company, called Bell Globemedia.)[47]

The loss of Lexis-Nexis may have been a blessing in disguise for in 1995 West Publishing Company put itself on the market.[48] Despite some significant antitrust concerns (see Section 6 below), Thomson purchased West in 1996 for almost $3.5 billion. In one fell swoop, Thomson became the largest legal publisher in the U.S. No longer a newspaper and media holding company, Thomson has restructured itself into an information services company.[49] In 2000, it purchased Dialog, Carson Group, and Primark, all information/database companies. In 2001, it acquired a competitor, FindLaw, a no fee Internet legal information reference site.

Thomson's legal publishing business is part of its Thomson Legal & Regulatory division. Within that division are many of its U.S. assets, the West Group, Thomson Tax & Accounting and Dialog (touted as "The world's largest commercial online information collection–with more than 6 billion pages of text and 3 million images, all of which can be searched in seconds").[50] The West Group includes West Publishing Company (including some former Warren Gorham & Lamont titles), Westlaw, Bancroft-Whitney, Clark Boardman Callaghan, Foundation Press, Lawyers Co-op and other imprints. Thomson Tax & Accounting includes RIA and Warren Gorham & Lamont. Findlaw has found itself in the West Group.[51]

Although Thomson Legal & Regulatory is the largest of the Thomson divisions, others include Thomson Financial (First Call), Thomson Scientific & Health Care (Institute for Scientific Information, better known as ISI), and Thomson Learning, which has received certain Harcourt General assets as part of Reed Elsevier's acquisition of that corporation[52] (see below) and includes the Gale Group, provider of LegalTrac, an online legal periodicals finding tool.[53]

The Thomson Corporation is a big company–36,000 employees and $5.9 billion in revenues in 2000.[54] It is listed as TOC on the Toronto Stock Exchange. It has generally outperformed the market having more than doubled since its acquisition of West in 1996.[55]

Reed Elsevier[56]

Albert E. Reed & Company was founded as a newsprint manufacturer in 1894. Over the years it expanded into pulp and paper mills, packaging material and building materials. It entered the international publishing arena in the 1970s with the acquisition of International Publishing, Mirror Group Newspapers and Cahners. In the 1980s it disposed of all its non-publishing assets and focused on publishing. During this period its purchases included Octopus Publishing, the second largest book publisher in the United Kingdom, and Martindale-Hubble, the long-time provider of U.S. lawyer biographies.[57]

Elsevier NV began in 1880 when Jacobus George Robbers started a publishing company in Rotterdam. He took the name Elsevier from a 16th century Dutch family of booksellers and printers. His first runs were literary classics and an encyclopedia, *Winkler Prins*. By the 1990s it was a leading publisher in the scientific, business and professional areas.[58]

Reed Elsevier was formed in 1993 by a joint venture of Reed International PLC and Elsevier NV that combined their operating businesses, each retaining a 50% ownership of the resulting corporation. It was agreed that neither of these companies would undertake any other significant activities apart from managing the new corporation.[59] The corporate strategy was to concentrate on the development of its core businesses and to acquire new businesses based on the following five criteria:

1. English language publishing,
2. High margin professional publishing rather than the more volatile consumer markets,
3. Increasing its capability to publish electronically,
4. Acquire market leaders only, and
5. Provide high value-added and must-have information.[60]

The first major purchase of this new entity, Lexis-Nexis in 1994, clearly met the criteria. This continued with the purchase of Tolley Publishing, a United Kingdom publisher of legal and tax information in 1996.[61] In 1997, its momentum was slowed with the announcement of a merger with Wolters Kluwer (discussed below). When this deal was abandoned in 1998, it returned to the U.S. legal publishing market to acquire Shepard's (it was already a 50% owner) and Matthew Bender.[62] This was an important strategic move notwithstanding the high cost of these purchases. Matthew Bender's strong analytical content was needed to compete with Thomson's stable of treatises and services. By acquiring the portion of Shepard's it did not own, it was able to bring it "in-house" and make it an exclusive service of Lexis-Nexis.[63] (This move forced Westlaw to develop its KeyCite feature–ah, the benefits of competition.)

Reed Elsevier is organized into four core segments: Science and Medical, Legal, Business and Education.[64] In Science and Medical, it is a global leader garnering an estimated 25% of the market, particularly in higher education. Its portfolio of over 1,200 journals includes the British *The Lancet*, one of the world's most respected medical journals.[65] It has made a commitment to online publishing. Its ScienceDirect database had posted over 1 million articles by early 2000. It has the highest profit margin among the segments.[66] Its Business segment is the largest B2B (business-to-business) information provider in the world.[67] It provided almost 50% of all revenues in 1999 with 1/2 of that coming from the U.S.[68] Lexis-Nexis provides over 60% of the Legal segment's revenue.[69] It also owns Butterworths, the United Kingdom's leading legal publisher. Its educational and professional publishing was formerly part of its legal segment, but it is now, like Thomson Learning, a separate unit.[70]

In the late '90s, contemporaneous with its failure to consummate its merger with Wolters Kluwer, Reed Elsevier had severe management problems.[71] It was without a CEO for almost a year. With that position filled by Crispin Davis in 1999, things began to change.[72] Cahners, an essential part of its Business segment, suffered a total management overhaul.[73] In Legal, Andrew Prozes came over from West, where he had been COO of Westlaw, with a clear mandate to regain market share lost to his former employer.[74]

The stock markets were not kind to the Reed Elsevier owners during the period of management turmoil following the failure of the Wolters Kluwer merger. Their shares, RUK for Reed and ENL for Elsevier on the New York Stock Exchange, are individually traded (i.e., you cannot buy shares in Reed Elsevier) and have rebounded substantially from their lows in late 1999 and early 2000, only to fall back again and slowly rise with some effects from the events of 9/11.[75]

Wolters Kluwer[76]

In terms of sales, Wolters Kluwer is the junior member of this international information triumvirate. It was created by the merger of the Wolters Samson Group and Kluwer in 1987. It is organized similarly to Thomson and Reed Elsevier into divisions: Legal, Tax & Business, International Health & Science, and Education.[77]

The leading legal publisher in Europe, it did not have a significant U.S. presence until the mid '90s when it joined the invasion and acquired in short order Aspen Law and Business (1994), Commerce Clearing House (1995), Little Brown's legal publications (1996) and Wiley Law Publications (1997).[78] Its most significant U.S. holding, of course, is Commerce Clearing House. This leader in loose-leaf publishing was founded in 1913, the year the U.S. federal income tax began.[79] It is the market leader in almost all U.S. market segments where it has a presence.[80] Its principal publication is *The Standard Federal Tax Reporter*, possibly the finest publication of its type and the standard by which others are measured. Its recent purchase of Loislaw should add to its online penetration. Loislaw will be integrated into its Aspen unit.[81] While Commerce Clearing House already has a substantial online presence within its niches, it will be interesting to see if its products will be found on Loislaw in the future and obtain wider Internet use.

Wolters Kluwer has also recently added to its scientific database business with the purchase of SilverPlatter. It will become part of its Ovid Technologies. This purchase will more than double the size of its presence in this segment.[82]

Wolters Kluwer experienced growing pains similar to that of Reed Elsevier in a slightly later time frame.[83] In March 2000, its CEO, Caspar van Kempen, resigned after only six months on the job. Its share price fell and has not yet recovered to where it was in 1999.[84] It is traded over-the-counter as WTKWY.[85]

SECTION 4: WHO'S LEFT?

There are small legal publishers attempting to find a niche that the majors ignore or have given up due to size and/or profitability. Most notable is the Bureau of National Affairs (BNA).[86] However, 4 of the 10 publishers interviewed for Susan Yoder's 1999 article *The Rise of the Small: the Effects of Industry Consolidation on Small Legal Publishers*[87] are no longer independent. FindLaw has been purchased by West Group, CD Law and Versuslaw (minority stake) by Lexis-Nexis and LOIS by Wolters Kluwer.[88]

The major private competitor is the Bureau of National Affairs. With total sales of $280 million in 1999, West and Lexis-Nexis are each four times its size. It is a private company, owned by its employees. It began in 1926 as a newspaper, the *United States Daily*. The Bureau of National Affairs was established in 1929 to "report, interpret, and explain the increasingly complicated workings of the federal government and their far-reaching impact on the economic life of the nation." It is likely that those with this "far-reaching" ideal then could not foresee how great that impact would become. Its Daily "Reports" are required reading in many executive, legal and governmental suites. Its *Tax Management Portfolios* are unparalleled. With its ownership structure, it is likely to remain independent.

Perhaps the only real "competitor" for the Players is government. The U.S. government is a major publisher of legal materials from primary sources to simple "explanations" of complex tax provisions. All this material is available to the public and to private companies. Much of it is available online through various government portals such a GPO Access,[89] FirstGov,[90] FedWorld[91] and usgovsearch.[92] State governments are similarly engaged in self-publishing.

To a lesser extent, nonprofit organizations may offer limited competition within their areas of expertise. One of the most prominent of these is Tax Analysts, Inc., which may be accessed through its own reasonably priced subscription service.[93]

SECTION 5: THE CANADIAN EXPERIENCE

Canada's history of legal publishing has some similarities and some differences with the United States' experience, in part due to a later time frame involving settlement and the more intimate continuation of the political connection of Canada to England. Both, of course, trace their basic laws and books on the law back to England. Its earliest reports were funded by its law societies (bar associations in U.S. terms).[94] The first legal publishers did not appear until the 19th century. The precursors of the Canada Book Company can be traced back to as early as 1855. They included indigenous companies such as Carswell Company and a subsidiary of the British Butterworths (not until 1913).[95] Commerce Clearing House appeared in 1939 to bring its loose-leaf approach in the form of the Canadian Tax Reporter.[96] Canada has had a similar history of creating companies that are acquired by others. Carswell was acquired by the British Sweet & Maxwell that was in turn acquired by the Canadian The Thomson Corporation.[97] Butterworths is now part of the Read Elsevier and CCH (Canada) is in the Wolters Kluwer stable.[98] Its Canada Law Book Company stands out as a family owned company that has stood against this tide (although The Thomson Corporation is also both Canadian and 73% family owned).[99] All in all, the Canadian market is also consolidating. However, since its market is not as large as the U.S. market, will these large international legal information providers be as responsive to its needs? Perhaps the inherently jurisdictional nature of legal publishing will protect it.

SECTION 6: ANTITRUST– THE UNITED STATES PERSPECTIVE

Two major legal issues have faced legal publishing in this century–antitrust and copyright. They both have their foundation in the economies of scale inherent in publishing and both involve concerns with monopoly power, one forbidden and the other with limited sanction.

Antitrust came to the fore in The Thomson Corporation purchase of West Publishing Company in 1996 (see above). As with any large-scale merger, it had to pass muster with the Federal Trade Commission and the Department of Justice. Both of these agencies are staffed in large part by lawyers who might be likely to take a keen interest in this particular transaction.

Actually, West had come under antitrust fire shortly before The Thomson Corporation made its offer. In 1994, Attorney General Janet Reno announced that the Justice Department would explore various means by which the public could have better access to legal information.[100] There was an interest in developing a non-proprietary system of citation and a public domain database of federal and state judicial opinions. She noted the obvious:

> Currently, most electronic research is done by leasing access to privately owned systems, such as WESTLAW and LEXIS, that electronically search through databases of federal cases and other materials.

This initiative caused a firestorm of protest from West and its friends in Congress.[101] It was supported by many public interest groups, including the American Association of Law Libraries, who in a letter to the Attorney General stated, in part:

> Unlike some of the others who have written to you, we do not believe that the government should own its case law. The copyright laws of the United States clearly preclude Federal government ownership of its information. We believe that that is as it should be and applies with special force to legal information.
>
> Actually, it is a fundamental part of our belief that no one should own the law, either outright or in practical effect. Regrettably, the assertion of ownership of some parts of the published case law together with the requirements of courts and others to cite to certain privately published versions of the case law, have, in practical effect, given one publisher substantial control over the legal information market.
>
> AALL does not wish to minimize in any way the important role that the West Publishing Company has played in the publication of legal information. For over a century, West has worked to collect and make accessible the case law of the United States. For this, they deserve much credit and appropriate reward.
>
> However, West's claim of copyright in the numbering and pagination of its volumes together with the requirements of the courts and traditional legal citation manuals that pinpoint cites be provided to West products gives West near monopoly-like power and severely limits the ability of others to enter the market and compete effectively.[102]

Even these words were to no avail against the political power of nine members of the Minnesota delegation writing to President Clinton voicing objections to the plan.[103]

Thomson's political power was again evident when it made its play for West Publishing Company two years later.[104] While the Department of Justice and seven state attorney generals filed a complaint against the purchase, there was a speedy settlement on terms that could only be considered favorable to Thomson. It seems there was a "rush to judgment."[105] The major concession in the settlement was an agreement to license the so-called "star pagination" scheme of numbering pages in the National Reporter System. West had fought and won cases for years to defend their claim that these page numbers were protected by copyright. But the writing was already on the wall that their claim was about to lose. The 1991 Supreme Court decision in *Feist* overturned the judge-made law of "sweat of the brow" claims to copyright protection for compilations of facts, which now would include databases.[106] Another case would seal the coffin.[107] It is difficult to believe that the Department of Justice was not aware of this possibility and that they may have been buying a "pig in a poke."[108]

Another major acquisition has now been completed. In late 2000 Reed Elsevier and The Thomson Corporation announced that they would be acquiring pieces of Harcourt General, a major SMT and educational publisher for $4.5 billion. The deal was delayed due to regulatory issues in the European Union regarding Reed Elsevier's purchase.[109] The EU was concerned that with the Harcourt General assets Reed Elsevier would dominate the SMT market. Based on past experience, the consensus was that the transaction would be completed.[110] The U.S. did not appear to be a force in this merger, much to the dismay of the academic community.[111] Ultimately, the sale was approved.[113] While this transaction has little impact, if at all, on legal publishing, it does illustrate again that the forces at work are much larger than the concerns of lawyers and law librarians.

SECTION 7: DATABASE PROTECTION

The next big issue on the horizon is the legal status of databases. Databases pervade our lives. Our names and numbers are stored electronically in many places. Information of all types is contained in bits and bytes stored in various formats. For the general public, the principal concern seems to be privacy and security–will their personal information be kept from other's prying eyes and will that same information not be used without their consent? These are very legitimate concerns. It is likely that they may never be totally resolved.

For publishing, however, the issue is ownership. The law of copyright has long held that "facts" may not be owned, and, therefore, not protected by copyright, but that compilations of them may be protected. This was the central issue in the case of *Feist Publications, Inc. v. Rural Tel. Service Co.* as set forth in an excellent opinion by Justice O'Connor:[113]

> This case concerns the interaction of two well-established propositions. The first is that facts are not copyrightable; the other, that compilations of facts generally are. Each of these propositions possesses an impeccable pedigree. That there can be no valid

copyright in facts is universally understood. The most fundamental axiom of copyright law is that "[n]o author may copyright his ideas or the facts he narrates."

There is an undeniable tension between these two propositions.

The key to resolving the tension lies in understanding why facts are not copyrightable. The sine qua non of copyright is *originality.* To qualify for copyright protection, a work must be original to the author. Original, as the term is used in copyright, means only that the work was independently created by the author (as opposed to copied from other works), and that it possesses at least some minimal degree of creativity.

It is this bedrock principle of copyright that mandates the law's seemingly disparate treatment of facts and factual compilations. "No one may claim originality as to facts." This is because facts do not owe their origin to an act of authorship. The distinction is one between creation and discovery: the first person to find and report a particular fact has not created the fact; he or she has merely discovered its existence.

Factual compilations, on the other hand, may possess the requisite originality. The compilation author typically chooses which facts to include, in what order to place them, and how to arrange the collected data so that they may be used effectively by readers. These choices as to selection and arrangement, so long as they are made independently by the compiler and entail a minimal degree of creativity, are sufficiently original that Congress may protect such compilations through the copyright laws.

This protection is subject to an important limitation. The mere fact that a work is copyrighted does not mean that every element of the work may be protected. Originality remains the sine qua non of copyright; accordingly, copyright protection may extend only to those components of a work that are original to the author. Thus, if the compilation author clothes facts with an original collocation of words, he or she may be able to claim a copyright in this written expression. Others may copy the underlying facts from the publication, but not the precise words used to present them. Where the compilation author adds no written expression, but rather lets the facts speak for themselves, the expressive element is more elusive. The only conceivable expression is the manner in which the compiler has selected and arranged the facts. Thus, if the selection and arrangement are original, these elements of the work are eligi-

> ble for copyright protection. No matter how original the format, however, the facts themselves do not become original through association.
>
> It may seem unfair that much of the fruit of the compiler's labor may be used by others without compensation. As Justice Brennan has correctly observed, however, this is not "some unforeseen byproduct of a statutory scheme." It is, rather, "the essence of copyright," and a constitutional requirement. The primary objective of copyright is not to reward the labor of authors, but "[t]o promote the Progress of Science and useful Arts." To this end, copyright assures authors the right to their original expression, but encourages others to build freely upon the ideas and information conveyed by a work. This principle, known as the idea/expression or fact/expression dichotomy, applies to all works of authorship. As applied to a factual compilation, assuming the absence of original written expression, only the compiler's selection and arrangement may be protected; the raw facts may be copied at will. This result is neither unfair nor unfortunate. It is the means by which copyright advances the progress of science and art.
>
> This, then, resolves the doctrinal tension: Copyright treats facts and factual compilations in a wholly consistent manner. Facts, whether alone or as part of a compilation, are not original, and, therefore, may not be copyrighted. A factual compilation is eligible for copyright if it features an original selection or arrangement of facts, but the copyright is limited to the particular selection or arrangement. In no event may copyright extend to the facts themselves.

This is the "law" that Mathew Bender used to break the Thomson West Group's stranglehold on the use of its "star pagination," the page numbering system for its National Reporter System,[114] and this is the stumbling block database owners find in their road that has sent them scurrying to Congress for help. To date, the Congressional battle has had no real results. Two House Committees of the current 107th Congress, which have taken different approaches in the past that have led to stalemate, announced that they plan to work together "to do our level best to make it work."[115] However, the tragic events of September 11, 2001 precluded any action until at least 2002.[116]

In the 106th Congress two competing approaches were put forth. They were H.R. 354 and H.R. 1858. It is likely that one of these approaches, or a compromise, will prevail. The implications for lawyers, law libraries and legal publishing are great, but they are only small players in this international production.

H.R. 354 was introduced into the 106th Congress as the Collections of Information Antipiracy Act.[117] (Who would support piracy?) This bill had the support of major owners of databases including the two leading owners of legal databases, Reed Elsevier and The Thomson Corporation.[118] Against it were a Who's Who of academic and public organizations, including the American Association of Law Libraries.[119]

H.R. 1858 was introduced in the 106th Congress as the Consumer and Investor Access to Information Act of 1999.[120] ("Access" certainly seems like a good idea.) Essentially, those that oppose H.R. 354 (above) supported this alternative and vice versa.[121]

As might be imagined, based on who was supporting one approach or the other, there are significant differences between the two bills. Below is a synopsis of the facts in the case of *H.R. 354 v. H.R. 1858*:

What Is Protected?

H.R. 354–Collection of Information: information that has been collected and has been organized for the purpose of bringing discrete items of information together in one place or through one source so that users may access them. Information: facts, data, works of authorship or any other tangible material capable of being gathered and organized in a systematic way. There is an exception for "narrative literary prose," but, therefore, effectively includes any nonfiction work.

H.R. 1858–Database: a collection of discrete items of information that have been collected and organized in a single place, or in such a way as to be accessible through a single source, through the investment of substantial monetary or other resources for the purpose of providing access to those discrete items of information by users of the database. Information: facts, data, or other tangible material capable of being collected or organized in a systematic way, with the exception of works of authorship. This exception should effectively exclude all copyrighted works.

Prohibitions!

H.R. 354–(1) Making, or extracting to make available, all or a substantial part of a collection of information, causing harm to the primary or related market for the product of another party. (2) Extraction of a substantial part of a collection of information so as to cause material harm to the primary market.

H.R. 1858–Prohibition against distribution of duplicates: sale or distribution to the public of a database that is the duplicate of a database collected by another in competition with that original database. The first obvious difference is the threshold level at which the amount of information triggers the proposed statute: all or a substantial part of versus duplicates. Note also the difference in competition.

H.R. 354 would prevent competition in a related market (actually it is worse; primary market includes those in which it may reasonably expect to sell its collection of information). This would effectively prevent anyone from taking the "facts" from one (or more) database(s) and finding a way to sell them to a market so far untapped by the original. Should the fact that the owner of a "collection of information" has not found a way to tap a new market prevent someone else that opportunity? More importantly from the point of view of public policy, should this new (related?) market be prevented from having this information because the first did not choose to, or did not know how to, provide it? This problem may be particularly acute if the reason to not have access to a collection of information is economic. This is not the diffusion of knowledge on which so much progress, particularly in this *information age*, has been based to the benefit of all.

Exclusions

H.R. 354–Collections of information maintained by or for a government, including educational institutions; computer programs (leaving this to the software licenses of adhesion?); internet transfer information.

H.R. 1858–Government databases; computer programs; internet transfer information; nonprotectable subject matter: individual ideas, facts, procedures, systems, methods of operation, concepts, principles or discoveries. Nonprotectable subject matter, what a difference!

Permitted Actions (Differences)

H.R. 354–Individual items of information or insubstantial portions of a compilation (but repeated use not permitted); verification of information obtained by other means, if it does not harm the primary market; nonprofit educational, scientific or research purposes that do not materially harm the primary market.

H.R. 1858–Scientific, educational or research purposes, if not a consistent pattern engaged in for the purpose of direct commercial competition.

If this portion were all that was considered, it might seem that H.R. 354 was the more permissive. However, since it starts off the more restrictive, that is an illusion. At the risk of oversimplification, H.R. 354 would prevent any use of a substantial part of the information obtained from a "collection of information" that would harm its business. H.R. 1858 would prevent use of "duplicates" only if that were its purpose, i.e., "direct commercial competition."

Reasonable Use

H.R. 354–Similar to that allowed by copyright;[122] genealogical information for nonprofit religious purposes. (Do you think the sponsors of this legislation knew that it would have to go through Senator Hatch of Utah, which is the home of one of the world's great collections of information on genealogy?)

H.R. 1858–It has no provision and none is needed. Its purpose is to prevent harmful duplication of databases, not their use.

Enforcement

H.R. 354–Creates a misappropriation cause of action in the U.S. District Court under Title 17 of the United States Code (the copyright title). It also provides for criminal penalties.

H.R. 1858–Gives the Federal Trade Commission jurisdiction to enforce its provisions, a violation of which shall be treated as an unfair or deceptive practice.

This is a huge difference, at least to lawyers. On one hand (H.R. 354) you have a new private cause of action in federal court with the usual problems of *economic estoppel* and harassment. On the other (H.R. 1858) you have enforcement power placed with the FTC, which may not have the resources to perform that function.[123] To the owners, a private cause of action is the hammer they want. Users rightly fear such a hammer.

Effective Dates

H.R. 354–Provides a 15-year term of protection with collections of information created up to 15 years prior to passage also included.

H.R. 1858–Provides no specific term.

Some fear that the dynamic nature of collections of information would effectively provide perpetual protection under the H.R. 354 approach.

There is also an important international dimension to the issue. The European Community has issued what is known as the Database Directive.[124] By its terms, it will not include under its protections databases from other countries that do not provide at least as much protection. This factor is claimed as a principal impetus for H.R. 354 and a reason to choose it over H.R. 1858. The term of art used in the Database Directive is *sui generis:* of its own kind or class; unique or peculiar.[125] It is this protection that is provided in the Database Directive and in H.R 354. Though not as strong as full copyright, *sui generis* protection provides "for the maker of a database which shows that there has been qualitatively and/or quantitatively a substantial investment in either the obtaining, verification or presentation of the contents to prevent extraction and/or re-utilization of the whole or of a substantial part, evaluated qualitatively and/or quantitatively, of the contents of the database."[126] In the Database Directive, this protection lasts 15 years. This, of course, is the general term of protection of H.R. 354. Opponents of H.R. 354 point out that whether or not they consider the Database Directive an incorrect method of resolving a perceived problem, a subsidiary operating in the EC would provide protection for all its brethren.[127] For the three principal legal publishers in the United States (The Thomson Corporation, Reed Elsevier, and Wolters Kluwer), this should be a minimal problem. They all have European operations and two are EC corporations. It may be interesting to note that Mr. Henry Horbaczewski, Senior Vice President and General Counsel for Reed Elsevier, Inc., in his testimony before the Subcommittee on Telecommunications, Trade, and Consumer Protection of the Committee on Commerce in 1999 against H.R. 1858 (and in support of

H.R. 354), claimed that use of this provision would be "at the expense of U.S. jobs and tax revenues."[128]

These proposed statutes are indicative of where the law may be going. It is ironic that H.R. 354 may have prevented Lexis from copying cases from the Westlaw database (collection of information). Now, Reed Elsevier is testifying before Congress to prevent similar action by others.

For law librarians and academic users of information, H.R. 354 would virtually insure that there would be no new players in the collection of information/database market. No one could economically recreate the information contained in Westlaw or Lexis or the Web of Science, just to name three. That is exactly what the current database owners want. They have collected it; if someone else wants to use the factual information contained therein to transform it into a new and different database, they should pay the first generation collectors for the chance to become second-generation collectors. It does not matter to them whether the information is public domain or owned by another under copyright. It is clearly the "sweat of the brow" revisited.

SECTION 8: THE BOTTOM LINE

Much of the concern in the law library community regarding the consolidation in the legal publishing business centers on two issues. One is fairly obvious and immediate: cost. The other may have even more importance on the level of public policy: sovereignty and the public's access to the law under which it lives.

Cost

Costs are notoriously difficult to compare. It is gospel in the law library community that the consolidation of legal publishing into two or three conglomerates has increased the costs of acquisition beyond what is reasonable and, certainly, beyond what the economy had experienced.[129] The publishers, of course, respond that the users, including libraries, are getting much more "added value" that more than justifies cost increases. It seems likely that they are both right from time to time and work to work. It is likely that cost escalation will continue. These conglomerates have paid and will continue to pay high prices for acquisitions as they seek economies of scale and market share. Academic law librarians must remember that practicing lawyers are the market. They are notoriously unconcerned with the cost of their research tools. Publishers say that they provide "need to know" information. If you drive a cab, you must buy gas. If you want to practice law, you must have up-to-date, reliable information. No one has accused the publishers of failing to provide that. As long as they do, they can charge what the "practicing lawyer" market will pay. And that market will set the pricing. Witness the "secrecy" policy now common in online contracts. The publishers are very price conscious, but, understandably, do not want to lose revenue by being played off against the price paid by another lawyer. Yet, neither do they want to lose market share and it does not cost them much to add another customer.

An aspect of cost is the additional processing expenses associated with the upheaval caused by consolidation. Titles have migrated from one imprint to another, often from one "family" to another, the latter often in response to antitrust concerns. Library staff has often had a difficult time figuring out where to find the continuations or updates of documents in their collections. This may work itself out over time from both the library side and the publisher side. A more difficult, but related, question is whether publisher responsiveness which librarians have relied upon in the past, but feel now is lacking, will return.[130] These customers feel that there has been an increase in turnover of publisher staff that has negatively impacted service.[131] As noted above, Reed Elsevier hired the COO of Westlaw to revamp Lexis.

An interesting situation exists with law school libraries and their legal research needs. They must provide access to online legal research tools as well as the traditional print resources. Both Lexis and Westlaw reputably provide access at rates that would shock a practicing lawyer. It may be questioned why they charge law schools at all. They must reach the thousands of lawyers-to-be while they are in school. Lexis has fallen behind Westlaw in this regard and has indicated that it intends to catch up.[132] Could law schools somehow combine their market power both as consumers and the essential future market for the online services? In many ways, the publishers need the law schools more than the law schools need the publishers. But, individually, the law schools cannot succeed. Remember Benjamin Franklin.[133]

Sovereignty

When the North American continent was rediscovered by Europe, Britain was a dominant country. The British colonies and, later, the United States took much of their initial law and law books from that source.[134] Over time an indigenous publishing industry went with the country to the Pacific Ocean. It adapted to what was necessary for a new country far larger than Britain. Men like West and Shepard were an important part of the growth of American law. The rise and fall of various publishing companies that contributed to this growth was common. Many were family owned and failed after a few generations. This is not an unusual trend in many industries. But all of those legal publishers were American and part of the "process." Their stakes and their interests were part of the fabric of the law and of the country. But time passes. Globalization is upon us. American industry and culture and, yes, law has, for better or for worse, for the last 57 years or so, permeated the world. We have championed free trade with limited restrictions on investment in the United States. These restrictions have generally been in areas that were thought essential to national security–the military industrial complex, utilities, and finance. As even those restrictions have waned and the world, especially Europe, has amalgamated, foreign investment has become a fact of life. This is no less true in the publishing industry, the legal publishing industry in particular. Now this is the way the world is. The control of the United States legal publishing business is in foreign hands. That seems unlikely to change. The question to be asked, if anyone cares, is whether the world's only superpower can afford to allow the literature of the rule of law, the foundation of the country, to be controlled abroad. Apparently, this is not considered, and has never been considered, a national security issue. Perhaps it should be.

SECTION 9: THE BIG PICTURE

Where have all the publishers gone, gone overseas every one? However, the imprints are still here. It is unlikely that many of the jobs involved will leave the United States, even if control is in foreign lands. Law is a local institution, a jurisdictional business. Publishers must, therefore, respond to local needs. But the intimacy and familiarity that was the early legal publishing business is gone. Perhaps it would have disappeared without a foreign invasion. The overall decisions of the conglomerates that control legal publishing in the United States will not be based on what is good for the country, the legal system, lawyers or law libraries. Their decisions will be made based on what they think is in their financial best interest. Perhaps it has always been so–but it doesn't seem that way, or, at least, not quite so much.

It's a small world. In many ways, the United States made it so. People have called this the "information age." That may be true–certainly better than the "nuclear age," or "the computer age." But, perhaps, the most important aspect of this explosion of information and its availability via computer and otherwise is the fact that it has shrunk the globe. The Internet is only the most recent edition of this phenomenon. For legal publishing, the most important aspect of this is the rise in the importance of computer assisted legal research. It is difficult to see how attorneys can successfully, or ethically, represent their clients without utilizing this wonderful tool. But the size of the databases, most of which may not be protected by copyright,[135] militates against any new entrants into this essential market. This is notwithstanding the "benefits" of *Feist*.[136] Whatever the outcome of the Congressional battle over databases, this will be true. Neither approach would allow wholesale copying of the current private legal databases to allow competition. Only the Federal government has the clout to change this result. It is unlikely to act.

Is nothing to be done–assuming anything should be done–to offset the concentration of power in three foreign information conglomerates? The only thing that can offset such power is power. When market concentration is so great and the consumer so fragmented, there is little hope for change. But can these free spirit lawyers (a picture many would chuckle at) and longhaired academics somehow combine to offset such power? It does not seem likely. Probably.

The United States has, and will continue to have, the best legal information system in the world. It will continue to improve provided there is sufficient competition to drive the publishers of the information to continue to upgrade both content and delivery.

NOTES

1. Robert C. Berring, *On not throwing out the baby: planning the future of legal information,* 83 Cal. L. Rev. 615, 618 (March 1995).

2. AOL's Market News on February 26, 2002, *www.aol.com.*

3. Julius J. Marke & Richard Sloane, *Legal Research and Law Library Management*, 46A-1-2 (2001 ed., originally published 1990).

4. Legal code, *Encyclopedia Britannica, http://www.britannica.com/eb/article?eu=48509*, printed November 22, 2001.

5. *http://www.metmuseum.org/toah/ho/03/waa/ho_66.245.5b.htm*
6. Daniel R. Coquillette, *The Anglo-American Legal Heritage*, 4-5 (1999).
7. Ibid. at 61.
8. Ibid. at 61-62.
9. Thomas A. Woxland & Patti J. Ogden, LANDMARKS IN AMERICAN LEGAL PUBISHING: An Exhibit Catalog, p. 1 (1990).
10. Ibid. at 8.
11. Ibid. at 10.
12. Supra. Note 8 at 187-188.
13. Supra. Note 11 at 11.
14. Ibid. at 18.
15. Ibid. at 16.
16. Ibid. at 17.
17. Ibid. at 18.
18. Ibid. at 22.
19. Ibid. at 22.
20. Ibid. at 23.
21. Ibid. at 25.
22. Ibid. at 30.
23. Ibid. at 32.
24. Ibid. at 38.
25. Ibid. at 43.
26. Ibid. at 67.
27. Ibid. at 68.
28. Ibid. at 69.
29. Ibid. at 66.
30. Ibid. at 69.
31. Ibid. at 45.
32. Ibid. at 70.
33. For a more complete review of this period see Kendall F. Svengalis, *The Legal Information Buyer's Information Guide and Reference Manual*, 4-15 (2000). To keep up to date on the ownership relationships in the legal publishing business, log on to *http://www.aallnet.org/committee/criv/resources/tools/list/, A Legal Publisher's List* of the Committee on Relations with Information Vendors (CRIV) of AALL (formerly a collaborative effort maintained by Rob Richards, Technical Services Librarian, University of Colorado Law Library).
34. Supra. Note 33 Svengalis, pp. 8, 13.
35. William M. Hannay, *The Publishing Merger That Failed: Reed Elsevier and Wolters Kluwer*, 26 The Acquisitions Librarian 173 (2001).
36. Ibid. Svengalis at 10; Dan Roberts et al., Reed Elsevier: A Strategic Review, by securities analysts for Charterhouse Securities, dated July 2000, p17; and Susan M. Yoder, *The Political Economy of Legal Information: TheNewLandscape,* 17 Legal Ref. Services Q. 59, 61 (1999).
37. Supra. Note 3 at 46A-3.
38. *http://www.thomson.com/*
39. Ibid. at About Us, History.
40. Ibid.
41. Ibid.

42. Frank L. Harte et al., The Thompson Corp., a report by securities analysts of Rabo SecuritiesNV, dated March 20, 2001, p.12.
43. Supra. Note 40.
44. Ibid.
45. Ibid.
46. Supra. Note 35, Svengalis at 6.
47. Elie Cassorla, Canadian Transformers, The Internet Analyst Individual Investor Edition–International Scene–Issue #62, June 1, 2000 at *http://www.multexinvestor.com/*, printed April 6, 2001.
48. Supra. Note 45.
49. Andre Horan & Drew McReynolds, The Thomson Corporation, a report by securities analysts for RBC Dominion Securities, dated December 22, 2000, p. 1.
50. *http://www.thomson.com/Businesses/Legal.html* as of November 26, 2001.
51. *http://www.westgroup.com/aboutus/history.asp*
52. Thomson Learning press releases:
October 27, 2000, The Thomson Corporation to Acquire Select Harcourt Business Units from Reed Elsevier, and February 21,2001, The Thomson Corporation Acquisition of Select Harcourt Businesses Delayed, archived at *http://www.thomsonlearning.com/press/default.asp*.
53. Ibid.
54. CBS MarketWatch, *http://cbs.marketwatch.com/news/*, on February 26, 2002.
55. Ibid.
56. *http://www.r-e.com/*
57. Ibid. at About Us, Company History.
58. Ibid.
59. Company Data Report, Reed International Plc (United Kingdom), History, p. 2 of 6 on *http://www.fisonline.com*, printed April 24, 2001.
60. Supra. Note 35 Roberts, at 12.
61. Supra. Note 57.
62. Ibid.
63. Supra. Note 57 at 13-14.
64. Supra. Note 53, About Us.
65. Supra. Note 57 at 36.
66. Supra. Note 48 at 42.
67. Supra. Note 59 at 39.
68. Ibid.
69. Ibid. and at 40.
70. Supra. Note 63.
71. Supra. Note 68 at 32.
72. Ibid.
73. Ibid.
74. Ibid.
75. aol.com Market News Center, Select a Chart for RUK and ENL in November 22, 2001.
76. *http://www.wolters-kluwer.com/*
77. Ibid.
78. Supra. Note 47 at 6.
79. Supra. Note 32.
80. Dan Roberts et al., Wolters Kluwer, a report by the securities analysts for Commerzbank Securities, dated April 10, 2001, at 7.

81. Supra. Note 75, News Release, Wolters Kluwer concludes tender offer for Loislaw.com, dated January 31, 2001.

82. Ibid. News Release, Wolters Kluwer acquires Silver Platter, dated April, 2001.

83. Supra. Note 79 at 6.

84. CBS MarketWatch, *http://cbs.marketwatch.com/news/*, on February 28, 2002.

85. *http://www.hoovers.com/*, Wolters Kluwer "capsule," printed April 8, 2001.

86. *http://www.bna.com/*

87. Supra. Note 35 for citation.

88. Supra. Note 33.

89. *http://www.access.gpo.gov/su_docs?index.html*

90. *http://www.firstgov.gov/*

91. *http://www.fedworld.gov/*

92. *http://usgovsearch.northernlight.com/*

93. *http://www.tax.org/*

94. Vivienne K. Denton, *Canadian Law Publishers: A Look at the Development of the Legal Publishing Industry in Canada,* in Martha L. Foote, ed., Law Reporting and Legal Publishing in Canada: A History, CALL/ACBD Occasional Paper No. 2 (1997) at 17.

95. Ibid. at 24, 26.

96. Ibid. at 29.

97. Ibid. at 26.

98. Ibid. at 29, 31.

99. Lisa Moran, *The Legal Publishing Industry in Canada,* 2000: *Challenges and Opportunities,* 25 Canadian Law Libraries 153 (Autumn 2000).

100. Department of Justice, Press Release, Justice Department Seeks to Improve Public Access to Court Rulings, dated September 2, 1994 at *http://www.usdoj.gov/opa/pr/Pre_96/September94/501.txt.html*, printed April 28, 2001.

101. Supra. Note 98. Doug Obey and Albert Eisele, West: A Study in Special Interest Lobying, The Hill–the Capital Newspaper, Washington, D.C. Vol. 2, No.8. Wednesday, February 22, 1995, p. 1, *http://www.hyperlaw.com/hill3.htm*; West Launches PR Blitz Against Public Domain cites and database, *http://www.cni.org/Hforums/roundtable/1994-04/0044.html*, all printed April 28, 2001.

102. AALL on DOJ Legal Procurement, Letter from Robert Oakley for the AALL to Attorney General Reno, *http://lists.essential.org/1995/info-policy-notes/msg00087.html*, printed February 28, 2002.

103. Why West Is Fighting Hard, The Hill–the Capital Newspaper, Washington, D.C. Vol. 2, No.8. Wednesday, February 22, 1995, p. 1, *http://www.hyperlaw.com/hill3.htm,* printed April 27, 2001.

104. Moving Money Through State Capitals, All Politics, CNN/TIME at *http://www.cnn.com/ALLPOLITICS/1997/04/11/jackson/*, printed April 28, 2001.

105. See AALL and Publisher Relations: An Open Statement to the Membership, from Frank Houdek, President, dated March 17, 1997 at *http://www.aallnet.org/board/houdek_statement.asp*, and another thoughtful letter on behalf of the AALL by Mr. Oakley to the Department of Justice, dated July 29, 1996, referred to therein at *http://www.ll.georgetown.edu/aallwash/lt072996.html*; and a similar letter from James P. Love of the Consumer Project on Technology at *http://www.cptech.org/legalinfo/thomwest1.txt*, all of which were printed on April 28, 2001.

106. *Feist Publications. Inc. v. Rural Tel. Service Co.*, 499 U.S. 340 (1991).
107. *Matthew Bender & Co. v. West Publ. Co.*, 158 F.3d 693 (2nd Cir 1998). West's petition for a writ of certiorari was denied by a unanimous Supreme Court at 522 U.S. 3732 (1999).
108. Supra. Note 45 Svengalis at 7.
109. Supra. Note 51.
110. Supra. Note 54 at 7.
111. David Malakoff, *Librarians Seek to Block Merger of Scientific Publishing Giants,* 290 Science Magazine 910-911 (November 3, 2000).
112. *http://production.investis.com/ReedElsevierPlc/pressreleases/2001-0713/?version=1*
113. Supra. Note 105 at 344-360, heavily edited, with apologies, citations omitted and emphasis freely added.
114. Supra. Note 106. And see Note 101, the last paragraph of Mr. Oakley's letter.
115. American Association of Libraries, Database Protection Legislation, Current Status at *http://www.ala.org/washoff/database.html.*
116. *http://www.newsbytes.com/news/01/170742.html*
117. From Thomas at *http://thomas.loc.gov/*, printed April 9, 2001.
118. The Consumer and Investor Access to Information Act of 1999: Hearing of H.R. 1858 Before the Subcommittee on Telecommunications, Trade, and Consumer Protection of the Comm. on Commerce, 106th Cong. 34-40 (1999) (statement of Testimony of Henry Horbaczewski, Senior Vice President and General Counsel for Reed Elsevier, Inc. on behalf of the Coalition Against Database Piracy, which includes The Thomson Corporation).
119. Letter of Nils Hasselmo to Rep. Neil Abercrombie on behalf of the Joint Education/Library/Scientific Associations at *http://arl.cni.org/info/letters/abercrombie.html*, printed April 29, 2001 and Database Data Mission Statement at *http://www.databasedata.org/Statement/statement.html*, printed April 29, 2001.
120. From Thomas at *http://thomas.loc.gov/*, printed April 29, 2001.
121. Ibid. and Supra. Note 115.
122. 17 U.S.C. §107 (2001).
123. The Consumer and Investor Access to Information Act of 1999: Hearing of H.R. 1858 Before the Subcommittee on Telecommunications, Trade, and Consumer Protection of the Comm. on Commerce, 106th Cong. 78-88 (1999) (Prepared Statement of the Federal Trade Commission).
124. Directive 96/9/EC OF THE EUPOPEAN PARLIAMENT AND OF THE COUNCIL of 11, March 1996 on the legal protection of databases at *http://europa.eu.int/ISPO/infosoc/legreg/docs/969ec.html.*
125. Black's Law Dictionary 1448 (7th ed. 1999).
126. Supra. Note 21, Chapter III, Article 7.
127. Intellectual Property Protection for Noncreative Databases, Congressional Research Service, Report for Congress 98-902, updated September 15, 1999 at *http://cnie.org/NLE/CRSreports/Science/st-54.cfm,* printed April 30, 2001.
128. Supra. Note 115 at 39, note 10.
129. Supra. Note 107, Svengalis at 13-14; supra. Note 36 at 46A-7-8.
130. Linda Will, *Diary of a Mad Cybrarian*, 18 Legal Information Alert 1 (February 1999).
131. Supra. Note 107 Sevengalis at 13.

132. Supra. Note 70 at 34-35.

133. "We must all hang together, or assuredly we shall all hang separately." At the signing of the Declaration of Independence, July 4, 1776. *http://www.bartlebv.com/100/245.21.html*, printed 4/30/01.

134. See Section 1 above.

135. See Section 7 above.

136. Supra. Note 111.

Access versus Ownership: A Changing Model of Intellectual Property

Scott Matheson

SUMMARY. This paper discusses changes in the ownership models of intellectual property and how they are shifting the way libraries provide information. The author argues that the main change in intellectual property is the way that owners distribute information, not in the sense of new media, but in the sense of new legal constructs governing distribution. The article discusses the impact on libraries of a move toward viewing information as a service that must be licensed, not bought. The potential effects of protecting intellectual property with contract law instead of copyright and property law are detailed. *[Article copies available for a fee from The Haworth Document Delivery Service: 1-800-HAWORTH. E-mail address: <getinfo@haworthpressinc.com> Website: <http://www.HaworthPress.com> © 2002 by The Haworth Press, Inc. All rights reserved.]*

KEYWORDS. Copyright law, legal publishing industry, legal information industry, database licensing, contract law, intellectual property

INTRODUCTION

There is no there there.

–Gertrude Stein, *Everybody's Autobiography,* 1937.

Scott Matheson is Reference Librarian, Yale Law School Library.

This article was prepared for the course Current Issues in Law Librarianship, Professor Penny Hazelton, May 2001.

[Haworth co-indexing entry note]: "Access versus Ownership: A Changing Model of Intellectual Property." Matheson, Scott. Co-published simultaneously in *Legal Reference Services Quarterly* (The Haworth Information Press, an imprint of The Haworth Press, Inc.) Vol. 21, No. 2/3, 2002, pp. 153-176; and: *Law Library Collection Development in the Digital Age* (ed: Michael Chiorazzi, and Gordon Russell) The Haworth Information Press, an imprint of The Haworth Press, Inc., 2002, pp. 153-176. Single or multiple copies of this article are available for a fee from The Haworth Document Delivery Service [1-800-HAWORTH, 9:00 a.m. - 5:00 p.m. (EST). E-mail address: getinfo@haworthpressinc.com].

Thirty years ago, a researcher wishing to find a journal article on his topic would have pulled down a multi-volume index, searched through several subject headings and written down some citations. He might have consulted the card catalog to determine if the library had the journals available and then checked the shelves. If the volumes were not checked out or in use by another patron, he could read the articles and scribble some notes onto a legal pad or a stack of index cards.

Fifteen years ago, our lucky researcher could have approached a computer terminal, selected from among a few databases (sometimes by choosing which dedicated terminal to use, sometimes by choosing from a menu or rack of CD-ROMs) and constructed a rudimentary search. Unless he was a sophisticated and well-funded researcher, he likely did not have access to a system as comprehensive as DIALOG or LEXIS-NEXIS. After finding his citations, he could have selected the ones he was interested in and printed the citations or abstracts. Arguably a step up from scribbling on scraps of paper, but in any case, he still had to go track down the items he wished to read, either in print, microform or maybe on a CD-ROM of page images. A major change from the way things had worked for the past eighty years, right? Not really, just a different way of accessing the library's holdings.

Today, our intrepid researcher approaches most any computer anywhere and selects from a variety of publicly and privately produced databases. Some may require that he prove his affiliation with some library somewhere that has purchased a license for the database. After finding his citations or other data, as likely as not he will be able to instantly view the full text or chart or image or video on the same screen. Perhaps a step forward, perhaps not, but a significant change from the first two scenarios.

The location of the researcher, while it may make the biggest difference to the patron and the library's public services staff, is not the most fundamental change. In fact, the enormity of the fundamental change is transparent to most users; not as jarring as the transition from card catalogs to online catalogs; not heralded from the rooftops as the "next big thing" like the Internet was. In fact, some people who know about the change don't want anyone else to find out.

The information our present-day researcher found and used was *not* in the library. The library didn't own it. It could disappear from the library's collection in two minutes, tomorrow or in two years.

Most patrons realize that *they* don't have to be at the library–they know that they can phone or login or surf to access library resources. What they don't realize is that the journals, newspapers, even books and audio-visual materials don't have to be at the library either. The legal framework that allows libraries to instantly provide their patrons with materials that are not physically present in the library often means that the library does not own the information in any traditional sense. The library may have access to the information for as long as it can afford to pay licensing fees to the information owner and for as long as it abides by its license agreement. If it could no longer afford to pay or if it (or one of its patrons) violates a term of the license agreement[1] the library could lose access to the information.

Just as Ms. Stein lost her childhood home when she found no "there," some libraries are in danger of losing their information, leaving their patrons with no "there."

THE FUNDAMENTAL CHANGE

> The public good fully coincides in both cases [patent and copyright] with the claims of individuals.
>
> –James Madison, *Federalist 43,* 1788.

Libraries have traditionally been repositories of information. As information has changed, libraries have adapted. The scroll racks from Alexandria would hardly be of much use in a present day public library. Similarly, Alexander's librarians would not have known what to do with an online catalog. Formats for storing information change and libraries adapt; the addition of periodicals, recordings and motion pictures to library collections did not represent as big a change as today's addition of DVDs and electronic databases. However, format is not the fundamental change.

Libraries have been adapting to format changes for thousands of years; from scroll to codex to periodical to microform to audio-visual to computer disc to networked database, libraries have accommodated the changes. The fundamental change libraries face today is in the concept of ownership of a collection. Today's librarians might quibble with Alexander's collection development practices, but there was no denying that the scrolls at Alexandria or any early library were owned by that library. Until relatively recently, in fact, books were kept under lock and key, or literally chained to the shelves. Today we have tattle tape. There is no doubt that under all the "property of" stamps, date due stickers, barcodes and spine labels, the books belong to the library. What makes the new formats so different is not the way that they transmit, store and retrieve information; it is the way that they are sold, or more properly, not sold at all.

Most patrons probably don't think about who owns the information in the books because, in a sense, it belongs to everyone. Anyone wanting the information can buy a copy of the book that contains it. The information is used but not consumed. Because a book can be borrowed, used and returned, a book can be read by a great number of patrons, and all can get the information out of the book without damaging the information. In this sense, information is a public good. It can be used by all and not diminished.

Why would anyone give information to the world? Historically, information was preserved for religious reasons and by those in power who needed to keep official records or track their property.[2] Today, some information is produced purely for the public good or in the course of the public's business (e.g., government research and documents), but much is produced for private gain. As Mr. Madison points out, the public good should be coincident to the private gain. This is the underlying balance in the copyright law.

The economic system of U.S. society is based on the notion of property.[3] To make information fit into this structure, the Framers established a system that "secured for limited times to authors and inventors the exclusive right to their respective writings and discoveries."[4] In exchange for making their work public and eventually giving it up altogether, authors were granted a monopoly for period of time to exploit the work. By transforming certain kinds of information into property, the Framers created something the legal system was better equipped to handle. During the monopoly period, which has varied in length over the years, authors have the full force of the legal system to defend their property. The courts will protect them if someone tries to take their intellectual property just as if someone attempted to take their real property.

The value of this intellectual property is significant.[5] As the value of the intellectual property has increased, the desire to retain and protect it increases as well. With very valuable properties (even those of questionable artistic merit), the desire for continued exploitation can be a strong political motivator. Imagine a world with a public-domain Mickey Mouse, *Gone With the Wind*, or "Happy Birthday to You." The principles underlying the system originally aimed to reward the sharing of creativity, learning and expression, not to create legally protected golden-geese.

Mr. Madison's statement that the public good fully coincides . . . with the claims of individuals assumes that there is an underlying balance in the system. For the public good and the claims of individuals to be equally served, the period of protection must be long enough to induce creators to create and short enough to allow the public to make use of the works once they are known. The length of copyright protection has ballooned in the past 200 years while patent terms have hardly changed at all (see Table 1). The dramatic expansion of the period of copyright from 1789 through 1998 makes one question whether a balance has ever been reached or maintained.

Balanced or not, the system has created a great many works.[6] It has also created a framework of rules and customs that have become part of our cultural way of life. Doctrines like first sale[7] and fair use[8] have almost become internalized in information consumers. Authors, publishers, libraries and their patrons are all at least familiar with the system, even if not entirely pleased or compliant with its provisions. Adding electronically delivered information to existing formats does not require changing the copyright system.

Notwithstanding the increased duration of copyright protection, some authors have decided that the copyright system is no longer a satisfactory way to distribute their work. To find a new way to exploit information, they return to the concept of property. Landlords know that they often get a better return on investment by renting or leasing a property rather than selling the property. Today's information owners (infolords?) realized that they could get a better return on their investment by leasing information rather than selling it and have begun to opt-out of the (arguably) carefully balanced copyright system. By licensing information instead of selling it, the owners create a system that doesn't depend on new ideas. The new system only depends on a continuing need for information that already exists.

Some suggest that this transition from selling to licensing is driven by technological necessity. While technology might have created new questions for publishers about how to best exploit their intellectual property, it did not dictate a shift to a licensing model. Technology merely made the shift possible. It was, and sometimes still is, possible to purchase outright a database or other electronically stored information. Record companies, for a premium, sell digital copies of their intellectual property–the digital "phonorecord" or compact disc.[9] Purchasers of CDs have the same first sale and fair use rights as if they had purchased a clunky old-fashioned analog compact cassette.[10] Though the new formats make copying easier and faster,

TABLE 1. Copyright and Patent Terms Compared

Year (statute)	Copyright Term (years) (non-corporate author)	Patent Term (years) (utility patent)
1790 (c. 7, 1 Stat. 109 (Pat.), c. 15, 1 Stat. 124 (Copyright)	28 (14 + 14)	14
1831 (c. 16, 4 Stat. 436)	42 (28 + 14)	
1836 (c. 357, 5 Stat. 117)		21 (14 + 7 in some cases)
1861 (c. 88, 12 Stat. 246)		17
1909 (c. 320, 35 Stat. 1075)	56 (28 + 28)	
1976 (Pub.L. 94-553, 90 Stat. 2541)	Life of the author plus 50	
1994 (35 U.S.C. § 154)		20 years from application
1998 (17 U.S.C. § 302)	Life plus 70	

they don't eliminate the protection granted by copyright law. If information owners are unhappy with users who steal their information in the digital age, they can take them to court, just as they would have in the age of analog media. Owners can take infringers to court for longer periods and for greater sanctions than ever before. Even criminal sanctions are available.[11] The shift from analog to digital distribution does not dictate a shift from selling to licensing.

Once publishers realized that they were not in the printing business, but in the information distribution business, they began to see their role differently. By using virtual tools to deliver their product, publishers reduce their long-term production costs, provide more value to their customers, charge more for the same information, and most importantly, create a continuous, unending income stream to make their shareholders happy.

Some information consumers, who may soon be in the majority,[12] prefer electronic information. It is easily searchable and re-purposed for use in briefs and memos without all that pesky typing. Other consumers can be convinced that electronic information is actually cheaper than print because, in the short-term, it is.

Researchers may realize that "computer research is expensive" but what they likely don't realize is that when they pay to see a copy of a case or statute, even if they print it out (which might cost more than simply looking at it), their co-workers will pay again when they look at the same statute or case. Once an institution owns the Federal Reporter or the United States Code Annotated, the institution's employees, indeed anyone the librarian wants to allow access to, can read all the cases, as many times as he wants, without the institution paying more.

From the distributors' point of view the new distribution model allows them to "double-dip"–that is charge over and over again for the same information, for as long as the customer wants to continue to access the information. Information consumers may not perceive this until they want to stop paying for the information and realize they have nothing once the contract is terminated.[13] In the old model, they would have retained ownership of the copies they had purchased. Once a library has paid for its books, it would take more than an annoyed publisher to take them away.

The other side of the argument, and it is persuasive enough to make the licensing models viable, is that print libraries are expensive as well. There are ongoing subscription costs as well as labor and space costs that can be quite high, especially for important but infrequently used materials.

These tensions are at the root of the debate over access and ownership. Electronic information is easy and fast and cool; tangible information is big and expensive and slow. However, electronic information is ephemeral and can't be owned, tangible information is reliable and once purchased, (somewhat) permanent.

HOW COPYRIGHT WORKS

> To qualify for copyright protection, a work must be original to the author . . . Original . . . means only that the work was independently created by the author . . . *and* that it possesses at least some minimal degree of creativity.
>
> –Associate Justice Sandra O'Connor
> writing for a unanimous court in
> *Feist Publications Inc. v. Rural Telephone Service Co.*,
> 499 U.S. 340 (1991)

The copyright model in the United States is not static, although the ultimate goal of copyright remains the same: to advance the progress of science and the useful arts. In an effort to optimize both creation and public access, the model has changed over the years. Both legislative and judicial changes have been made in response to the tensions between the goal of public access to information and the need to provide an incentive for authors to create new works. As exceptions to meet the public access goal have been grafted into the system (e.g., fair use), the reaction seems to have been to increase the duration that authors can exploit the remaining rights in their works. In addition to tweaking the duration and exceptions to copyright, changes have been made in the scope of subject matter that is protected by copyright.

The term of copyright has expanded over the years. This grants authors a longer monopoly on their works. This increases the incentive to create. Theoretically, it also increases the production of creative works, although this is not necessarily the case with legal information.[14] As the term has increased, so have the defenses to infringement. Fair use as a concept developed over the past 150 years in the case law.[15] It was not codified until the 1976 act–at the same time the term was extended.

Exceptions developed in the common law as well as in statute. The library exemption was added in 1976.[16] This exception recognizes that libraries and archives have a unique role to play in the preservation and dissemination of information. The provision allows qualified libraries and archives to make full copies of certain works to ensure preservation and continued access. Of course, the section also balances the rights of information owners; the exception does not apply if the owner is still "actively exploiting" the work, i.e, if the library or archive can simply purchase another copy from the information owner or her publisher. The library exception serves the public's right to access information that has been protected by copyright, even though the owner has abandoned it. The copyright balance is maintained by protecting the author as long as he is exploiting the work, while ensuring that libraries can prevent the work from being lost.

While the amount of information published may increase, and the amount of creative work may, at the margins, increase, the cost of creating intellectual property has not increased significantly. Yes, there is inflation in the cost of library materials, but most researchers do not pay directly for the library materials they use. The most significant cost to write a book or article remains the cost of the human capital it takes to produce such a work. So if the cost of gathering information and creating new works is not increasing significantly, and the period of protection for those who own the information gets longer and longer, the system may have reached the point of diminishing returns (for the public). If increasing the length of copyright protection beyond a certain point only serves to make publishers richer, not to make society richer, the term length should not be extended.

As libraries adapted to new formats for information, so too has U.S. copyright law. The original 1789 act protected only books, maps and charts. Protection was extended to prints in 1802. Music (1831), motion pictures (1912), choreographic (1976) and architectural works (1990) were added to the list of protected works as time went by.[17]

Technology has provided information consumers with the ability to easily fix (record) or copy information that they have never been able to copy before. In fact, the information had been difficult and extremely expensive even for the copyright owners to fix. In the late 1970s, consumers could easily make copies of television broadcasts and replay them at any time. The courts responded by applying a fair use test and reiterating the rule, just as they had when the photocopier made it cheap and easy to copy written materials.[18]

Just as the fundamental change in libraries didn't come from the computer or the telephone, the fundamental change in copyright didn't come from the photocopier or the VCR. The revolution in copyright turns out not to be in the area of copyright law at all. Information owners are abandoning the centuries-old view that information is property and are migrating to the view that providing information is a service. People who provide services generally do so as part of a contract. The emerging non-copyright scheme is based on this new view of information as a service governed by contract law.

HOW THE NON-COPYRIGHT SCHEME WORKS

> You are granted a nonexclusive, nontransferable, limited license to access and use for research purposes the Online Services and Materials from time to time made available to you.
>
> –General Terms and Conditions for Use of the Lexis-Nexis® Services, § 1.1 (1996) (Lexis Agreement)

> West hereby grants Subscriber a non-exclusive, non-transferable, limited license to access WESTLAW.
>
> –Westlaw Subscriber Agreement, § 1(a) (2001) (Westlaw Agreement)

When information providers distribute non-print information today, they usually do it pursuant to a license agreement and often with electronic protection measures of some sort, e.g., passwords or encryption. The underlying material may be subject to copyright protection as well, but the license agreement usually sets much tighter restrictions on the use of the information than the copyright law would alone. For instance, copyright law might allow a student to photocopy a few pages from an encyclopedia for a research project. However, if the library subscribes to an electronic version of the same encyclopedia the license could preclude *any* duplication of the electronic information. This distinction has nothing to do with the format of the information, it has to do with the ownership of the information. In the second case, the library doesn't own the information, it only licenses access to it. Because there has been no "first sale," the library must use the information only as allowed by the terms of its license. The license may grant access to the information wherever they are in the world. The library and its patrons reap one of the chief benefits of digitized information–easy accessibility (a good thing). But, the library's license might also dictate that the patrons cannot print or email any portion of information (a bad thing). Patrons would be back to the pre-photocopier research model, scribbling notes onto index cards and legal pads.

When a copyright owner's rights are violated by an infringer, he can sue to enjoin further copying, have the copies already made destroyed, recover monetary damages and perhaps even have the infringer jailed. The alleged infringer must prove that his use of the material is not an infringement or falls within an exception. When a user violates a license agreement, the information owner can resort to self-help–that is, the owner can stop providing the service because the contract has been breached.[19]

This may not seem like such a big deal, but it fundamentally alters the tenuous balance that has been set up in the copyright law. The licensing schemes do not serve to further the public interest goals of copyright. They serve only to increase the information owners' control over information. Increased control from licensing schema, combined with increased control from horizontal and vertical integration, allows the information owners to set terms, conditions and prices almost unilaterally. As the balance of power shifts from consumer to supplier, consumers will be paying far more for far more restrictive licenses.

Few libraries are forced to accept these licensing schema yet. Many products can still be purchased in a physical sense and the first sale doctrine usually applies to these copies. But some products, citators, for instance, are more useful in electronic format and require entering into a license agreement with an information service provider. Libraries that depend on very current and constantly updated information, and have the budgets to pay for it, are the libraries that will find themselves with no choice of format (or distribution model) when it comes to obtaining the information they need. The two most obvious kinds of special libraries that this will, and is already beginning to impact, are biomedical and law libraries. These industries demand the most current information, but also a depth of historical information, and they can afford to pay for it. Or, more precisely, as the information vendors have discovered, they can't afford *not* to pay for it.

Laws are beginning to reflect the change in the approach of information vendors. The Digital Millennium Copyright Act (DMCA),[20] makes it a criminal offense to circumvent an electronic security system that protects an information product. This provision is referred to as "anti-circumvention." The DMCA prohibition is absolute and does not inquire into the motives of the person circumventing the protection scheme.[21] The act punishes the circumvention of the technological protection measures, not the use or theft of the underlying information. Thus even fair use of the protected material, which would be legal under the copyright law, is made criminal because of the circumvention. The Act provides for the Register of Copyrights to promulgate regulations that provide some narrow exceptions to this rule.[22] The Commerce Committee concerned that the act could eliminate longstanding principles of fair use and be used to develop a "pay-per-use society"[23] included this provision in the law. Many in the library and information community are unhappy with the resulting regulations.[24] Under the current regulations, the only works excluded from the DMCA's anti-circumvention rule are lists of Internet sites contained in filtering software and literary works that fail to permit access because of damage, malfunction or obsolescence.

An application software innovation, the "shrinkwrap" license is making its way into the more general information environment as more and more information is distributed via the Internet. The "shrinkwrap" license, so called because it was originally inside of a shrinkwrapped box (sometimes visible, sometimes not), is the ultimate contract of adhesion. The manufacturer of a piece of software licenses the software using these contracts, which generally state that once the shrinkwrap is opened, the user is bound by the license agreement.[25] Now, as software distribution moves away from shrinkwrapped boxes on store shelves, manufacturers are creating "click-through" licenses. These licenses work in much the same way that shrinkwrap licenses do, except the license is visible as part of the software download or installation process.

If the license is displayed during the download process (the most user-friendly alternative), the user sees the full text of the license and must agree to it before being granted access to download the software. After downloading the software from a Web or FTP site, the user runs a program that installs the software on his computer. If the click-through license is displayed during installation (as is often the case with software distributed in physical media), the license text is displayed in an on-screen window during the installation process. The user must agree in order to complete the software installation.

Some courts have upheld the validity of shrinkwrap licenses,[26] but some commentators, citing basic contract law principles, criticize the practice of using shrinkwrap licenses while acknowledging that they can be binding in some circumstances.[27] Librarians and users must be aware of the existence of these licenses and be made aware of their terms in order to comply with them. In the best case, the librarian would read the license prior to installing the software or information product and determine if he wished to bind his institution and his patrons to that license. Unfortunately, because these types of licenses are contracts of adhesion, most librarians are faced with a choice of accepting the terms or not using the product at all.[28]

Another new legal construct that affects some users is the Uniform Computer Information Transactions Act (UCITA to its friends).[29] This is a model law that two states have passed[30] and three have explicitly rejected, at least temporarily.[31] It is similar in structure to the Uniform Commercial Code and was originally conceived as an amendment to the UCC. It is important for all users of computers or information to know about this proposed law because it can affect users even in states where it has not been passed. If a user agrees to a license that contains a choice of law clause specifying the law of a state where UCITA has passed, that user could be subject to the UCITA rules. UCITA codifies the validity of shrinkwrap licenses, it allows unilateral changes in terms, severely limits the liability of software producers and among other things, allows software manufacturers to impose almost limitless restrictions on the use and transfer of the software.[32] There are benefits as well, including a uniform standard (at least in those states which adopt the law) and some areas of the law that are currently murky are made more clear.[33]

A full discussion of the impacts of UCITA is outside the scope of this paper, but it is a prime example of an attempt to clarify the law and create tools to deal with ownership and protection of information. As the concepts of digital delivery of information and licensing of information mature, more legal tools are sure to emerge.

As each of these new legal tools emerge, librarians and information consumers should be sure that they are well informed about the implications of the tools for libraries and individual consumers. The more information consumers know about how information is delivered to them and understand the legal framework in which they function, the better off all information users and creators will be. If users know about the limits that are put on their use of information and understand the full scope of the license or ownership interest they do have, they will be better able to respect the rights of information producers. Everyone will be better served by a more informed user and creator population.

CHAOS AND CONTROL

> *Flan:* What makes it exceptional is that Kandinsky painted on either side of the canvas in two radically different styles; one wild and vivid, the other somber and geometric . . . We flip it around for variety.
>
> *Ouisa:* Chaos, control. Chaos, control . . .

–Flan and Ouisa Kitteridge
discussing a two sided painting by Wassily Kandinsky
in John Guare's play, *Six Degrees of Separation*

Differences in the character of the information provided by licensed online systems may help account for publisher's desire for more control over the information. The thinking goes something like this: "Once the information is digital, it could go anywhere and be copied over and over again. The first time I release my information in digital form may be the last time anyone ever offers to pay me for it. I had better get as much money as possible for it *and* try to make sure it doesn't get copied." The same impulse that drives users to print out a copy of a Web page or print a copy of a case they know is online controls the publisher's thinking. There is something fundamentally difficult about controlling things we can't see, like electronic bits and bytes once the computer is turned off.

Because the user can control the pieces of paper that the information is printed on, he prints out the case or the Web page, even if he will not need it again. The familiarity of holding the information in his hand is what is required, even if it is easier and faster to store the information on the computer. Similarly, publishers need to feel that they have control over their information, but it is psychologically difficult to assert control over a bunch of invisible ones and zeros. In order to feel a greater sense of control over the information, publishers create license agreements that put them firmly in control not only of the information, but also the contractually defined vendor-purchaser relationship.

Ironically, from a user's point of view, and a larger, societal point of view, the information is far more secure on the publisher's servers and Web sites than it ever was in a book. When books were all copied by hand, they were enormously valuable. They were kept literally under lock and key. Even as printing became more widespread, some libraries still kept their books locked up or chained to the shelves. In today's American free public libraries, not to mention bookstores, books are left unattended on the shelves. Even extraordinarily valuable books are relatively insecure when compared with electronic information.[34] Tattle tags notwithstanding, anyone who wants a copy of a book has several options apart from purchasing it, not the least of which are taking the physical object (stealing from the library) or photocopying (could not the effect of photocopying be the motivation for publishers–they have seen the rampant copying of information through copying?) the portion he is interested in, up to and including the entire book (perhaps stealing from the publisher and/or author). Digital information stored behind a password is more secure than analog information sitting on the shelf for the public to read. By keeping the information on their computer systems, publishers actually have more control over their information than they do by printing it and putting in bookstores.

While there will always be thieves and miscreants, it is foolish to suggest that more people will break the law simply because the information is digital. Photocopiers, and for that matter bookstore cafés, have made it just as easy to steal analog information as it is to steal digital information. On the contrary, the ease of getting just exactly what one wants, in any format, should make consumers less likely to steal and more willing to pay. Digital formats simply make this sort of selective purchasing easier. The economies being equal, if a user doesn't have to purchase (and store and maintain) an entire set of books simply to use a few articles or cases once in a while, why would he?[35]

Another aspect of digital information delivery that delights users and gives publishers pause is that once a work is in electronic form, there is no limit to the number of people who can use it at the same time. In a print world, if a book is off the shelf, there is no hope of discovering what wonders it may hold. In a digital world, every user of the library can look at the same book at the same time. This makes users happy because they don't have to wait for someone to return the book they are interested in before they can read it. This makes publishers nervous because it limits their ability to profit from exceedingly popular, high-demand works. To avoid this, publishers license a limited number of simultaneous users. They may do this by limiting the number of simultaneous logins, or, in the case of a file held by the library itself, by a token passing scheme.[36] The token passing scheme allows the publisher to give the library a file that can only be used by one person at a time (just like a book). The file is encrypted and the library has one key for every copy of the file that it purchased (just like a book). When a user requests the file, the library sends it, along with the key. After a designated time period, the key "expires" and makes its way back to the library, which can then lend it out again (just like a book).[37]

Information providers are reluctant to make their information available digitally because copies of digital works are indistinguishable from the original. This, the providers claim, would allow digital thieves, unlike video pirates who copy analog recordings, to make identical, high quality copies of their information. Technology will once again catch up. Token passing software, digital watermarks and other copy-limiting schema, will allow information owners to limit copying. These technologies, in reality, will only serve to keep the law-abiding from breaking the law. Determined thieves will almost always find a way around copy-protection technology.[38] The legal structures are now being put in place to make the technological solutions legally enforceable. The Digital Millennium Copyright Act, with its anti-circumvention rule is one such tool. The Uniform Computer Information Transactions Act is another.

Perhaps the most troubling development for librarians does not relate to publisher's efforts to protect their rights, but responding to the age-old library question: do we have that book? As books become available digitally, they can be cataloged in much the same way the rest of the library collection is. Journals, while more complicated, fall into much the same boat. Many vendors provide or sell MARC records for electronic holdings, but this is only half of a solution. Once a library can keep track of the databases it has access to and the contents of each database, it must also track the rights it has in each. For libraries that serve different classes of patrons, this can be a complicated question.[39] If publishers and librarians have trouble knowing what they have and what their rights are in each item, how can patrons be expected to understand? Most people know that copying computer software or a CD to give to a friend is illegal, even if they do it anyway. There is likely a class of information consumer who, although they respect the property rights (and criminal sanctions) set out by copyright law, may not have an equal respect for contract law (especially a contract they had no part in negotiating and may not even know about). When the biggest class of information users, otherwise law-abiding, author-respecting people, are unsure of what the scope of their rights are, they may inadvertently trespass on the rights of an author or publisher.[40]

IMPLICATIONS FOR LIBRARIES AND USERS

The implications of the access versus ownership question on libraries are staggering. The faster, better, cheaper, more accessible access arguments seem to be an easy out, but they cannot be considered alone without some consideration of permanence, certainty, and fixed costs of paper-based storage. The enticing opportunity to provide access to a huge collection that the library could never physically hold is tempting, but it must be balanced against the need for a collection that is stable and accessible to all (in a public library, at least). While the prospect of providing users with access from home or work or vacation is appealing, it must be balanced against the prospect of losing your entire collection because one user violates a license agreement.

Of course, these are extreme examples of the impacts some decisions could have, but in lieu of losing an entire collection, would losing all the books from one publisher be any less devastating to a patron's ability to effectively use a research collection? A research library that loses all of its Nolo Press titles would probably continue to function. On the other hand, if it lost all of its American Law Institute titles, there could be serious problems. Similarly, if a court library lost its annotated code, or a county law library lost all access to Nolo Press titles or form books, it would be a serious problem. And in the law library context, imagine being cut off from *all* West Group or Lexis Publishing titles. What if CCH would no longer sell anything to your tax firm library?

With the increased access that electronic, licensed titles bring to patrons, comes the risk that the title could disappear from the collection without warning. Electronic access, licensed or purchased, also brings with it the added burden of printing out each item the user wants to have a copy of. This may not be a problem if users are in the habit of photocopying each case or statute anyway, but then again, it is much easier to click "print" than it is to stand at the copier and copy each page. Electronic resources can provide an opportunity to create less paper, thereby saving money, but a librarian should not count on this being the case, at least not without substantial user training.

Having large numbers of electronic resources licensed for users can free researchers to do more reading and synthesis. It can help them spend more time using the information than finding it. But it can also be limiting. If the only place users look for information is in the computer, they may miss the perfect source that is sitting on the shelf. Depending on the type of library and collection, most of the titles may be available online. It is more likely, however, that the majority of titles in the collection are owned outright and sitting on the shelf, and further, many of these titles are not available online, even with an unlimited budget.[41]

Electronic materials owned by the library create preservation issues. The media used to store electronic information is not even as stable as paper. Luckily, if a library licenses electronic material instead of buying it, preservation is a non-issue . . . for the library. Someone has to make sure that the information will still be available in years to come. This should not be a problem for popular sets that get lots of use, but a service provider can choose to stop providing a service that is not well used or is no longer kept current.[42] While popular resources will likely continue to be available online somewhere, the library may lose access to those materials that are not commercially viable because information providers choose to stop producing the material.[43]

The lack of certainty created by this one-sided licensing distribution model should be disconcerting to librarians making decisions to retain an item only in digital form. The distributor can control exactly what the library and its patrons can and cannot do with the information provided. In the past, copyright law controlled the use of information, and it was basically the same for everything in the library. Now, services that contain identical data may come with different restrictions. For instance, the daily newspapers in Seattle are available on Lexis-Nexis, Westlaw, or UMI's Proquest. Westlaw's and Lexis-Nexis' lengthy, complex licenses provide roughly the same limited rights to users. For example, both companies' licenses dictate that the information may only be used for research purposes. Proquest's license is much more conscise:

> This service contains copyrighted material of Bell & Howell Information and Learning Company and its licensors, which retain sole ownership of these materials. You may create printouts of materials retrieved through the service via on-line printing, off-line printing, facsimile, electronic mail, or from printers operated by Bell &

> Howell Information and Learning. All reproductions and distribution of such printouts and all downloading and electronic storage of materials retrieved through the service is subject to the Copyright Act of 1976, title 17 U.S.C.

The choice between the three services allows users to access the *identical* information subject to three different sets of restrictions. If a user read all three license agreements, and wished to take advantage of his fair use rights, he would use Proquest to access the information, even if he prefers the Westlaw or Lexis-Nexis search engines. In fact, he could conduct his searches using the Westlaw or Lexis-Nexis search engines and, after finding the desired article, simply retrieve it from Proquest and completely escape the restrictions of the Westlaw or Lexis-Nexis license.

These choices highlight the potential loss of the fair use or library exception or first sale doctrine rights when decisions are made to license information *rather than to purchase it*. If the information is only licensed to users, they must ensure that their license allows them to retain the rights granted by congress under the copyright act.

A library may also need to protect its right to a day in court or even its right to plead its case. If a copyright owner wishes to recover actual or statutory damages, gain injunctive relief or seek to have a willful infringer thrown in jail, he must go to court. However, if a publisher who licenses his information includes an arbitration clause in the contract, the consumer who has a grievance with the publisher won't even be able to sue on the license contract in court. Additionally, the licensor can include no-notice immediate termination clauses in the license agreement. The licensee will be entirely without service while the judicial or arbitral action is pending. By adopting a licensing model, the publishers have shifted the burden of proof from themselves to the licensor.

Speaking of burden shifting, the adoption of a licensing scheme changes the fiscal burden of the library. The cost burden of providing licensed online access does not end with the purchase of the license. The library must somehow provide users access to the digital treasure trove. The library must figure the cost of computer workstations, network connectivity and printing hardware and supplies into the budget. These costs must be considered as ongoing costs because of obsolescence: bookshelves don't become obsolete, computers do. Computers must be replaced as they age, and while they are functioning, someone will have to tend to their care and feeding. This may not mean the library has to hire another staff member; it could. It will certainly mean more work for existing staff.

The cost of hiring computer technicians can be quite high, but on the other hand, bookbinders and catalogers are also very expensive. Similarly, computer servers and network connections are expensive, but space for storing bookshelves can be very expensive indeed, depending on the location of the library. When bookshelves fill up, the collection must be weeded or the library must physically expand, move volumes to off-site storage or convert some holdings to microform. When a server drive fills up, new 80 gigabyte hard drives are available for less than $200. Want to add another volume of Premise CD? CD-ROM drives are $50.

Finally, let's consider the impact of licensing on interlibrary loan. Technologies like Ariel (a system for sending high-quality page images over the Internet), online holdings and borrow-lend systems make traditional ILL faster, more efficient and more practical. However, because licenses generally only cover the users affiliated with the licensing institution, licensed content cannot generally be shared with users at other libraries via interlibrary loan.[44] A collection based largely on licensed material would not allow the library to participate very effectively in interlibrary lending arrangements. Many books can be sent, even via express mail, and many articles can be faxed, even long-distance, for the cost of a license agreement. As part of the negotiation of a license, librarians should inquire into the vendor's position on the sharing of information in the database via interlibrary loan. These considerations should weigh in a librarian's decision to enter into a license agreement.

CONCLUSION

> Ironically, we who work in public libraries, we who treasure books and revere the people who write them, have for all the most virtuous reasons, helped to instill in the American public the notion that the fruits of the intellect should be accessible to all citizens regardless of their ability to pay . . . We have championed the establishment of publicly supported institutions that make books and periodicals available, even for home use often, because this educates and culturally uplifts society.
>
> –Carol D. Billings,
> in a presentation on "Copyright in the New Millennium"
> at the American Association of Law Librarians Annual Meeting,
> July 2000

Because librarians know that information is both expensive and valuable, they should strive to be aware of the bounds of the license agreements that they sign. In order to make a wise and informed decision on whether to purchase an item in print or license its electronic equivalent, librarians must know exactly what it is they are acquiring. Librarians must use their understanding of copyright law as it relates to print materials to determine whether to lease digital information. Armed with a basic understanding of how copyright worked when the entire collection was in print, the librarian is poised to conquer the license agreement. A careful examination of the agreement, and discussions with the vendor and the library's counsel will allow the purchasing librarian to understand the rights granted by the license. Then, and only then, can he move on to consider the costs involved with each option. After considering the costs and benefits of each option, the librarian can balance the users' desires for instant, full-text access and the library's need to provide information to future patrons.

Once a license is purchased, the librarian should endeavor to educate patrons about the bounds of their rights to use the information. Vendors can help by making license agreements readily available, and as concise as possible. Users should be taught that there are different rights to use different works in different ways and informed about the cost to provide the information. Though most users would not like to see a bill for the services a library provides, some private libraries do just that. While public libraries have no place billing patrons who return their materials, they should let the patrons know the costs involved with providing the information they have used.

Often libraries are information producers themselves. A librarian knowledgeable about licensing agreements might find such contracts a useful tool to help offset the cost of the library's publishing efforts. Other libraries can benefit from the information and the producing library can recover part of the cost of production.

Licensing electronic information is not all bad; purchasing physical copies of information is not all good. Each has good and bad points, and a conscientious librarian will explore the pluses and the minuses of each model before committing to one. The models are not mutually exclusive. A library may decide that its patrons are best served by having both electronic access and print access to one work. Similarly, if only one format can be purchased the library may decide either that the need for archival copies of the work militate against licensing the electronic version or that the need for current, accessible information outweighs the benefits of print.

Understanding the new distribution models of information, librarians position themselves to ensure that whether patrons visit the library in person or on the Web, there is always a "there there."

NOTES

1. One example of a license term found in "General Terms and Conditions for Use of the LEXIS-NEXIS® Services" section 1.1(a) grants users "The right to electronically display Materials retrieved from the Online Services to no more than one person at a time . . . " The same license also provides "The provider of the Online Services may suspend or discontinue providing the Online Services to you without notice . . . if you fail to comply with any of your obligations hereunder" in section 5.2. Let's all think about that the next time we're teaching students online research skills and using a video projector. "Fair Use," you might protest. "No," comes the reply from Reed-Elsevier, "that only applies in copyright law. This is contract law. No more Lexis-Nexis for your institution." http://www.lexis-nexis.com/terms/general/ (last viewed March 3, 2002).

2. Harris, Michael H., *History of Libraries in the Western World, 4th ed.*, Lanham, Md.: Scarecrow Press, (1995) at 7.

3. Beard, Charles A., *An Economic Interpretation of the Constitution of the United States*, New York: Macmillan (1925).

4. U.S. Const. art. I § 8.

5. "Arts, Entertainment and Recreation" gross receipts in 1997 were over $85 billion, the class of businesses grouped under the heading "Information" had receipts of over $623 billion. Much of the income from these sectors of the economy is derived from the exploitation of intellectual property. U.S. Census Bureau, 1997 Economic Census. Non-government GDP in 1997 was $7.4 trillion, so these two sectors represent about 10% of the whole economy. U.S. Bureau of Economic Analysis, http://www.bea.doc.gov/bea/dn/nipaweb/ (last visited March 4, 2002).

6. From 1790-2000, over 29 millions copyrights were registered. Annual Report of the Register of Copyrights 2000.

7. The first-sale doctrine provides that once a copy of a work is sold, the owner may do with it as she pleases. This is the rule that allows libraries to lend books and music lovers to sell their used CDs. The rule is set out in 17 U.S.C. § 109. Compare with 17 U.S.C. § 117(b), restricting the lending of computer programs.

8. The concept of fair use, which allows for incidental use of copyrighted materials for, e.g., education and criticism, was judicially created in *Folsom v. Marsh*, 9 F. Cas. 342 (1841) and eventually codified at 17 U.S.C. § 107 as part of the 1976 act.

9. The copyright statute prefers the general, if archaic-sounding, term. One can, however, accept that a compact disc is indeed a phonorecord because it contains a record of sound.

10. But see note 38, infra.

11. *See* 17 U.S.C. § 506(a), 18 U.S.C. § 2319.

12. *Hardy, I. Trotter,* Why legal research training is so bad: a response to Howland and Lewis. (response to Joan S. Howland and Nancy J. Lewis, 40 Journal of Legal Education 381, 1990), 41 Journal of Legal Education, 221 (1991).

13. The service contract can be unilaterally terminated upon material breach, without advance notice by the provider in the case of Lexis-Nexis or Westlaw. Even if there is no breach, either service provider can cut off a customer for any reason with less than a month's notice.

14. The amount of primary legal information remains relatively static and in any case is not influenced by changes to the copyright system. There are not significantly more cases filed or statutes passed from one year to another. The increase in copyright protection may have resulted in more of the existing information being published, but not in more information being created. *See, e.g., Judicial Business of the United States Courts*, pp. 12, 48.

15. *See, e.g., Folsom v. Marsh*, 9 F. Cas. 342 (1841) *Sheldon v. Metro-Goldwyn Pictures Corporation*, 81 F.2d 49 (2nd Cir. 1936); *Edward Thompson Co. v. American Law Book Co.*, 122 F. 922, (2nd Cir. 1903); *Mead v. West Pub. Co.,* 80 F. 380 (Minn. 1896); *Lawrence v. Dana*, 15 F.Cas. 26 (Mass. 1869).

16. Pub.L. 94-553, title I, § 10, Oct. 19, 1976, 90 Stat. 2546 codified at 17 U.S.C. 108 (1994 and Supp. V).

17. United States Copyright Office, *Circular 1a: United States Copyright Office: a Brief History and Overview* (1996), *at* http://www.loc.gov/copyright/docs/circla.html.

18. See the line of cases represented by *Sony Corp. of America v. Universal Studios, Inc.*, 464 U.S. 417 (1984).

19. *See* Lexis-Nexis Agreement, Appendix 1 § 5.2 "...The provider of the Online Services may suspend or discontinue providing the Online Services to you without notice and pursue any other remedy legally available to it if you fail to comply with any of your obligations hereunder.", and Westlaw Agreement, Appendix 2 § 12(i) "West may terminate this Agreement immediately upon giving written notice of termination to Subscriber if Subscriber commits a material breach of any obligation to West under any other agreement between the parties[.]"

20. Pub. L. 105-304 October 28, 1998.

21. 17 U.S.C. 2101 (2001).

22. 37 C.F.R. Part 201 (2000).

23. H. Rep. 105-551, pt. 2, at 26 (1998).

24. Letter from Assistant Secretary of Commerce for Communications and Information, conveying the views of the National Telecommunications and Information Administration (September 29, 2000) available at http://www.loc.gov/copyright/1201/commerce.pdf, last viewed March 4, 2002.

25. More recent (and fair) licenses do not deem removal of the shrinkwrap acceptance, instead becoming effective upon the consumer's installation or use of the software.

26. *ProCD, Inc. v. Zeidenberg,* 86 F.3d 1447 (7th Cir. 1996); *M.A. Mortensen Co., Inc. v. Timberline Software Corp.*, 998 P.2d 305 (Wash. 2000); *but see Klocek v. Gateway, Inc.,* 104 F.Supp.2d 1332 (D.Kan., 2000).

27. *The Validation of Shrink-Wrap and Click-Wrap Licenses By Virginia's Uniform Computer Information Transactions Act,* 7 Rich. J.L. & Tech. 27, 37 (2001*); Why Article 2 Cannot Apply to Software Transactions*, 38 Duq. L. Rev. 459 (2000); Restatement (Second) Contracts § 19 (1979).

28. If librarians band together and form large consortia, or are part of a very large institution, some vendors who use this type of license might be willing to modify it. For a large enough customer, a vendor may make exceptions. If concessions from the licensor can not be obtained, the library is faced with a very hard choice indeed: agree to be

bound by an unfavorable license (that may or may not meet the library's needs) or forego the information product altogether.

29. The text of UCITA as adapted and adopted by Maryland and Virginia are linked from the American Library Association's web site at http://www.ala.org/washoff/ucita/news.html. The draft that was approved by the National Council of Commissioners on Uniform State Laws is available at http://www.law.upenn.edu/bll/ulc/ucita/citam99.htm. Amendments were proposed by NCCUSL in December of 2001.

30. Maryland and Virginia, as of this writing.

31. Iowa, West Virginia and North Carolina.

32. See www.4cite.org

33. See www.ucitaonline.com

34. *See* Harvey, Miles *The Island of Lost Maps: a True Story of Cartographic Crime*, New York, Random House, 2000.

35. Witness Napster: a clearer example of industry not meeting the needs of consumers has never been had. Consumers wanted single songs, not entire albums and they wanted them instantly. Digital technology made it possible to deliver exactly what consumers wanted when they wanted it. By all accounts, some consumers would have paid for the privilege of buying exactly what they wanted. *See* http://www.cnn.com/2001/TECH/internet/02/21/napster.reax/ and http://www.cnn.com/2001/WORLD/europe/01/29/napster.charges/index.html.

36. For a description of digital property rights management technology, see http://www.sciam.com/0397issue/0397stefikbox1.html.

37. This type of lock-and-key system is just the sort of thing the DMCA is designed to protect. Computers and computer hackers are very adept at breaking codes. Now publishers don't have to worry so much about creating "unbreakable" codes, they can just call the police and have the offending codebreaker arrested. Commentators refer to this as "preventing an arms race" in encryption technology. The assumption is that such an arms race is not economically productive.

38. See Harmon, Amy, CD Technology stops copies, but it starts controversy, C1 New York Times, March 1, 2002 at C8, noting that software makers could easily allow users to copy "protected" CDs, but will not do so for fear of prosecution under the DMCA.

39. For examples of attempts to organize this information in several ways, see http://www.lib.washington.edu/types/databases/ and http://www.library.yale.edu/databases/ (visited March 4, 2002).

40. It took this author about half an hour to *find* the Lexis-Nexis and Westlaw agreements. Reading (and understanding) them would likely take users even longer. And these are general agreements; a specific user might have additional terms to comply with or even entirely different terms. Some databases, though they are more and more the exception rather than the rule, do not even provide copies of their licenses online, e.g., CDlaw at www.cdlaw.com.

41. Hazelton, Penny A., How Much of Your Print Collection is Really on Westlaw or LEXIS-NEXIS?, 18(1) Legal Ref. Services Q. 3 (1999).

42. See Lexis-Nexis Agreement. "2.4 Materials and features may be added to or withdrawn from the Online Services and the Online Services otherwise changed without notice."

43. Granted, this could happen to a print source as well, but in that case, the library would still hold the last instance of the print resource. If the only holdings are online, the library would be left with nothing when the online source is discontinued.

44. ". . . [Y]ou are prohibited from downloading, storing, reproducing, transmitting, displaying, copying, distributing, or using Materials retrieved from the Online Services" Lexis-Nexis Agreement, § 1.3, 2.1, "Subscriber may not copy, download, store, publish, transmit, transfer, sell or otherwise use the Data, or any portion of the Data, in any form or by any means..." Westlaw Agreement, § 1(b) (In fairness, West does allow some fair use claims but not §108 interlibrary loans, Lexis seems to allow some rights under "applicable copyright law" but these are limited by database.).

BIBLIOGRAPHY

Administrative Office of the United States Courts, *Judicial Business of the United States Courts: Report of the Director* (2000).

Patricia Brennan, *Timeline: A History of Copyright in the U.S.* (1998), *at* http://arl.cni.org/info/frn/copy/timeline.html.

Andy Ruff, *Knowledge Commodities: an Exploration into Digital Copyrights* (2001), *at* http://www2.iastate.edu/~ruffguy/ps487x/history.html.

United States Copyright Office, *Circular 1a: United States Copyright Office: a Brief History and Overview* (1996), *at* http://www.loc.gov/copyright/docs/circla.html.

Verner Warren Clapp, Copyright Committee of the Association of Research Libraries, *Copyright: a Librarian's View* (1968).

Committee for a Study on Promoting Access to Scientific and Technical Data for the Public Interest, Commission on Physical Sciences, Mathematics, and Applications, National Research Council, *A Question of Balance: Private Rights and the Public Interest in Scientific and Technical Databases* (1999).

Jon O. Newman, *New Lyrics for an Old Melody: the Idea/Expression Dichotomy in the Computer Age* (1999).

Marci A. Hamilton, *The Historical and Philosophical Underpinnings of the Copyright Clause* (2000).

Copyright and Fair Use: the Great Image Debate (Robert A. Baron, ed., 1997).

Barry Torno, *Ownership of Copyright in Canada* (1981).

Audio tape: Gateways to Leadership: American Association of Law Libraries 93rd Annual Meeting (July 15-20, 2000) (available from Mobiltape, Valencia, CA).

National Commission on New Technological Uses of Copyrighted Works, *Final Report of the National Commission on New Technological Uses of Copyrighted Works* (1979).

A Law Library in the New Century: The Creation of the University of St. Thomas Law Library

Edmund P. Edmonds
Margaret Maes Axtmann

SUMMARY. The authors of this article were charged with the creation of a new academic law library at St. Thomas School of Law. They were able to create a collection development plan from scratch. Their decision process provides insights into the current state of law book and electronic publishing and the constraints of going to a totally digital environment.

KEYWORDS. Law schools, collection development, law library creation

INTRODUCTION

Only a small group of law librarians are offered the opportunity during their career to participate in the establishment of a new law school library. The authors of this article eagerly embraced this challenge in 2000 when the University of St. Thomas decided to reopen its School of Law.[1] It is a rare treat to create a new enterprise and to enjoy the chance

Edmund P. Edmonds is Director of the Law Library and Professor of Law, University of St. Thomas School of Law, Minneapolis, MN.

Margaret Maes Axtmann is Associate Director for Information Resources, University of St. Thomas Law Library, Minneapolis, MN.

[Haworth co-indexing entry note]: "A Law Library in the New Century: The Creation of the University of St. Thomas Law Library." Edmonds, Edmund, P., and Margaret Maes Axtmann. Co-published simultaneously in *Legal Reference Services Quarterly* (The Haworth Information Press, an imprint of The Haworth Press, Inc.) Vol. 21, No. 2/3, 2002, pp. 177-188; and: *Law Library Collection Development in the Digital Age* (ed: Michael Chiorazzi, and Gordon Russell) The Haworth Information Press, an imprint of The Haworth Press, Inc., 2002, pp. 177-188. Single or multiple copies of this article are available for a fee from The Haworth Document Delivery Service [1-800-HAWORTH, 9:00 a.m. - 5:00 p.m. (EST). E-mail address: getinfo@haworthpressinc.com].

to address the staggering number of essential questions necessary to develop a new library.

In this article, the authors detail the planning and the implementation of a system of delivering legal information to first, the students, faculty, and staff of this new law school, and second, to all other users including university students, faculty and staff, and other patrons. The authors also offer a plan for the continuing development of the collection beyond the first year.

THE STARTING POINT

A significant factor in the development of any new law library is an understanding of the reasons surrounding the creation of the new host law school. The best chance for generating a sustained cohesive effort during the initial years exists with the establishment of a clear mission statement at the beginning. A thorough understanding of the rationale of the founders should help guide the decision-making process of the librarians and become the starting point for strategic planning. Although it might be difficult to spend precious time on recording decisions or discussing the process and activities about the new enterprise, the dedication of time to writing should be a high priority. It is important to document the origins of decisions that are made, what options were considered, and the reasons behind various choices. Furthermore, it is helpful to have written statements because the process of writing produces clarity of thinking and self-discipline.

The University of St. Thomas School of Law was created as part of a faith-based[2] diocesan[3] Catholic university. The mission is focused on making that tradition and heritage central to the formation of lawyers. The law school is also critically interested in establishing a robust and intensive mentoring program.[4] The curriculum is being developed within this context. As is true at most law schools, the first year curriculum is viewed as the chance to build a foundation for future years of study and work as a lawyer. This process of producing individuals with rigorous analytic skill equipped with the tools of precise and effective communication is a goal shared with all law schools.

The first year curriculum focuses on traditional core courses taken by most students at American law schools: civil procedure, constitutional law, contracts, criminal law, lawyering skills, property and torts. One distinctive feature is the immersion aspect that makes lawyering skills the only continuation course taught in both semesters. Students take only three substantive courses per semester, courses meet four or five days per week, and every course is completed within a single semester.

The initial planning and development naturally formed around the desire to support these courses.

BASIC PRINCIPLES

The early planning process after the hiring of Ed Edmonds as Director of the Law Library included the development of a vision statement and a plan for staffing. The traditional concept of collection development was titled information resources to emphasize the dynamic forces in legal information during the past decade. Because of the continuing development of new formats for the delivery of legal information, the focal point of our effort is the balancing of traditional print and microform resources with electronic access. One of the earliest decisions made was that access and ownership would have equal consideration in the building of the information resources that would be made available to the user community. This allows the staff to accept the intellectual challenge of reconsidering every underlying premise about the delivery of information and the nature of the sources of that information.

Furthermore, decisions should be made in the context of other information centers within the community. We are fortunate to have strong academic and special libraries in the Twin Cities area, and we recognize in particular the strengths of other public and private law libraries. Our goal is not to duplicate existing collections but rather to develop a collection that will complement and enhance the holdings of other libraries. The local law library community has a strong tradition of formal and informal cooperation, and we are pleased to have the opportunity to share our resources.

Another significant desire is to create a library that is truly a central feature in the educational mission of the institution. This requirement is also mandated by the Standards for Approval of Law Schools promulgated by the Section of Legal Education and Admissions to the Bar of the American Bar Association Standard 601(a).[5] Although promotional literature in catalogs and on Web sites trumpets this goal, hard work is necessary to ensure that this becomes reality. The recent interest in technology within legal education and the knowledge of law library staffs in this area have created a stronger relationship between law libraries and their parent law schools.

STAFFING ISSUES

The foundation for building a successful new law school library begins with staffing. The plan adopted for the University of St. Thomas was to move aggressively to hire a senior staff of seasoned law librarians. The underlying rationale for the plan was to assemble a group with the depth of knowledge and experience that would enable them to take advantage of the opportunities that creating a new law library offers.

After much thought and consultation with a number of law librarians throughout the country, Ed Edmonds created a four-person senior management team. This senior management team is structured to work in a collaborative mode to plan all aspects of the new library. The members of that team include the director and three associate directors. The titles of the positions of the associate directors are information resources, public services, and technical services.

The hiring of an associate director for information resources acknowledges the priority given to building the information resources of the library. This is a crucial factor in reaching the goals of supporting the scholarly and curricular needs of the primary users. In addition to the balancing of traditional print and microform resources with electronic access, a primary feature of this activity is developing a strong treatise collection. Nearly all American academic law libraries have the core primary and major secondary sources, but historically the distinguishing factor in an analysis of the strengths of Anglo-American law collections has been the depth of the treatise collection. The development of such a treatise collection will be labor intensive because it ultimately requires a title by title decision-making process.

The associate director for public services is responsible for the delivery of reference and access services, including direct support to the lawyering skills curriculum. The decision to be an active force in the lawyering skills program is based upon the philosophical argument that the library must occupy a formal place in the first year curriculum. Without the opportunity to teach research skills to first year students, the law library staff runs the great risk of being disconnected from the most important aspect of the library's role in the institution. This decision heightened the need for someone with teaching acumen and the ability to motivate and direct the rest of the public services staff.

The associate director for technical services is responsible for all aspects of organizing the resources that the library wishes to present to its users. Because UST is interested in using the integrated automated library system as a platform for providing access to all information resources, whether they are owned, leased, or freely available through the Internet, it was essential to hire an experienced individual to head this area.

INFORMATION RESOURCES

As has been noted, we chose a collection development model that fits our mission and our curriculum. We discarded previously held assumptions about how to develop a law school library collection and decided to focus first on evaluating content and second on choosing the most appropriate format for the type of information. With this approach we recognize that there can be strong counter arguments for each collection decision that is made. The decision-making process also included an analysis of the Standards for Approval of Law Schools of the American Bar Association Section of Legal Education and Admissions to the Bar. Compliance with the standards is critical to gaining accreditation.

One critical decision concerns the purchase of annotated state codes.[6] The cost of annual upkeep for all fifty state codes is approximately $55,000 per year.[7] Because these codes are readily available on LexisNexis and Westlaw, it is wise to ask whether the library users need all fifty state codes in print format. More precisely and for the sake of arguing from a geographical perspective, does a law school in Minnesota need to acquire the *Alaska Statutes* or the *Maine Revised Statutes Annotated*? In this case we made the decision to purchase all state codes in print, in part because of the ABA standard, but more importantly because they are fundamental resources around which to build a core collection. The projected cost over time is justified by the relative ease of use of the printed codes over the online versions. Current legislation and status information is widely available on state legislative Web sites or commercial databases, however, so we have elected not to subscribe to legislative update services.

Another significant decision concerned case law. Because of the importance of case law in Anglo-American jurisprudence and the heavy reliance on case analysis in legal education, we opted to add all of the National Reporter System beyond the first series in hard copy. Despite the substantial availability of case law in digital form, this collection, together with federal and state statutory material, constitutes the core of a strong law library. We acquired nearly ninety percent of this material in good used condition from a variety of sources. We also decided not to add any duplicate sets of the National Reporter System because of its electronic availability.

In making these two fundamental decisions, we elected not to pursue a more aggressive position of relying exclusively on electronic access for these primary sources. This decision was guided by the developing nature of our lawyering skills program, by an analysis of the Standards for Approval of Law Schools, and by the availability of the used reporters. However, the overriding reason was the belief that these materials ought to be available to our users in print format because they are fundamental to legal research.

Beyond these two basic decisions, how does one start to build a law school library collection? For the last several years, with the downsizing trend in other types of law libraries, we have seen an increase of materials available for little or no cost. At UST we were fortunate to have some of our core collection donated by law firms and court libraries, including full runs of reporters and periodicals. Many other donated items, such as digests, encyclopedias and looseleaf services, were discarded because the cost of bringing these sets up to date was more expensive than the cost of acquiring new complete sets. We continue to receive regular inquiries about potential donations. Although we are very selective in our responses to these offers, we acknowledge the positive impact of gifts on our collection development.

After evaluating and selecting the donated material, we turned our attention to establishing relationships with the legal publishers and vendors who could supply major primary and secondary works. These companies included William S. Hein & Co., Inc., Congressional Information Service (now LexisNexis Academic & Library Solutions), Primary Source Microfilm, LexisNexis, and West Group. In all cases we asked for proposals based on our specific collection goals and our desire to select print, microform and electronic resources according to content and usability.

The Law Library decided to lease access to both LexisNexis and Westlaw from the inception. We did this for a number of reasons. First, although both databases are substantially similar, there are differences. For instance, access to *Shepard's Citations* is available now only on LexisNexis. The availability of Key Cite on Westlaw provides a different citation service. The two services together provide more comprehensive coverage of one of the most critical components of legal research, determining the value of authority and locating more recent sources.

The coverage available from the two different news services also differs. Access to articles from *The New York Times* is substantially greater on LexisNexis. But a word of caution is in order. The United States Supreme Court in *United States v. Tasini*[8] held that copyright ownership of the electronic reproduction of the work of freelance authors resides with the original author absent a contract covering the issue of the transfer of electronic rights. In response to this decision, *The New York*

Times has removed 100,000 articles from its electronic databases.[9] Although 15,000 articles were restored after the *Times* reached agreements with the writers, the results of the Supreme Court decision underscore the concerns of reliance upon electronic access. Materials leased from an electronic provider can disappear for any number of reasons. A library that owns a capital asset, a book or a piece of microfiche, can always provide access to that item as long as it remains in a useable state.

Second, the Library wants to provide access to both systems for our students because it is crucial to our mission to graduate students with strong practical skills. To accomplish this goal, it is essential to train students to use both databases effectively. To further this goal, the library staff is committed to providing all of the initial training on the use of both systems. During our first year, two members of the library staff presented two and one-half hours of classroom instruction supplemented with a fifty minute session in a computer lab for each of the two systems.

Third, faculty have established preferences for one of the two systems. A decision to offer only one of the two would create undue frustration for some of our faculty. Beyond research, faculty use Westlaw's TWEN and LexisNexis's Web Courses powered by Blackboard to support curricular offerings.

Fourth, a cost-benefit analysis would favor the addition of both LexisNexis and Westlaw. Because both databases provide access to a tremendous number of documents, the cost per accessible document is low. Adding LexisNexis and Westlaw precludes the need to purchase certain materials, e.g., session laws for all fifty states, administrative codes, attorneys general opinions, specialized case reporters, form books and other practice materials, newspapers, and certain digest sets. This eliminates the need to spend money on hard copy for those materials and to cover the transactional cost in staff time to file, shelve, or check in the material.

Before deciding to purchase certain materials in micoforms, the Law Library investigated equipment options. We decided to purchase two Minolta MS 6000 machines and attach them to two Dell computers and to the UST backbone. This equipment uses scanning software to produce digitized documents and laser quality printing. The recent improvement of equipment for access to microform-housed information is an important contributing factor in the decision to rely on microforms for certain components of the collection. Although we acquired a significant microform collection, we decided not to purchase certain major sets often found at established academic law libraries such as state session laws, attorneys general opinions, and bar journals.

We also made some early decisions in partnership with our lawyering skills faculty. We were able to meet with the director of the lawyering skills program several months before the start of classes to discuss the planned approach to teaching legal research and writing. Out of these conversations came an understanding that we would acquire both print and electronic resources to complement the instructional program, even though a great deal of the information being taught in the program is available electronically. The current program at St. Thomas teaches research skills with an emphasis on print resources during the majority of the first semester. This instruction is supplemented with limited access passwords to LexisNexis and Westlaw. Late in the first semester, the limitations are removed. Many programs are moving through a transitional stage where instruction is based upon the nature and type of authority rather than the format that embodies that information. If our program develops in this nature, we may be able to withdraw some print versions or drop certain subscriptions.

The following list completes the initial set of decisions made long before the entering class arrived:

- Our donations included the first series of the National Reporter System in ultrafiche and a substantial amount of the second series in print. To complete the collection, we purchased pre-NRS state reports in microfiche. We also purchased the volumes necessary to bring all sets up to date and entered continuing subscriptions.
- After discussions with the lawyering skills program director, we decided to acquire all three versions of United States Supreme Court decisions in print in spite of the duplication among the three print sets and with other print and electronic resources. There are enough variations in the editorial features of the sets to make each version important for research purposes.
- We made a similar decision to acquire the *United States Statutes at Large* and all three versions of the United States Code. Various citation guides require citing to the official edition, and each annotated edition has different strengths. We have found that this redundancy also helps when a large number of students are working on legal research assignments and need access to the same materials.
- In consultation with the director of the lawyering skills program, we selected a list of states for which we would acquire supplemen-

tary material in print, including Shepards, encyclopedias, digests, and practice sets. In addition to Minnesota, we chose states from the Midwestern geographic area. We also chose highly populated states that have an impact on legal development in the United States, either through legislative activity or through a high volume of judicial decisions. The availability of strong practice-oriented materials was a further influence on our selection of states.

- On the other hand we made a conscious decision to minimize the purchase of retrospective state session laws, limiting our collection to the laws of Minnesota and Wisconsin. Unless significant research interest develops in this area, the UST Law Library will rely on interlibrary loan for access to this information.
- With a few exceptions, we acquired bound periodicals from 1980-present in print and earlier volumes in microform. This decision was based on a belief that articles older than 20-25 years are used less often, and we are comfortable that microform will satisfy the limited demand. We looked ahead to the planning of a new library and decided that we did not want to devote precious stack space to little used bound volumes. We also subscribed to Hein-On-Line as an added resource and one that provides complete coverage of many major law review titles. We acquired the retrospective volumes of the *Index to Legal Periodicals and Books (ILP)*, and we licensed the electronic versions of both *ILP* and *LegalTrac*.
- We deferred a decision on purchasing the CIS microfiche library until we know more about the extent to which our faculty's research will require older Congressional documents. Although we have not licensed Congressional Universe yet, we plan to do so as soon as we resolve some institutional IP address issues. The future development of Congressional Universe and other electronic products will also affect our decision regarding the microfiche library.
- We purchased the 19th and 20th Century Legal Treatises sets from Primary Source Microfilm as a foundation for the strong treatise collection we plan to build. The low cost per volume made this a highly cost-effective acquisition. Although we might duplicate classic older treatises in print, we can concentrate most of our retrospective print purchases on later materials from the 20th century.
- We acquired a variety of other major microform products, including federal administrative agency decisions, the complete set of *American Legal Manuscripts from the Harvard Law School Library*, the *United States Supreme Court Records & Briefs*, *A.A.L.S. Law*

Books Recommended for Libraries, the *English Reports*, and the *United Nations Treaty Series*.

FUTURE DEVELOPMENT

The establishment of a plan for the development of information resources requires a comprehensive understanding of the mission and goals of the institution, the needs of faculty and students within the context of the curriculum, and the scholarly needs of the faculty and student population that grows from interaction with the curriculum.

Most of our first-year faculty were not available for face-to-face conversations until a month before the start of classes. Our immediate emphasis was on acquiring materials needed to support the first-year curriculum, including copies of all the required texts for the reserve collection as well as other basic texts, hornbooks, nutshells, multi-volume sets, and legislative histories that would supplement the required readings. The Associate Director for Information Resources then met individually with faculty to discuss their scholarly and research needs as well as any additional resources desired for their classes.

Decisions regarding format for the foundation of the collection resulted in a familiar emphasis on print resources. During the next phase of development, we will be working aggressively with our faculty to evaluate and select electronic resources instead of print for materials such as looseleaf services and current awareness newsletters. This is an optimal time to make different choices than one might make in an established library, because the wide array of electronic resources available today makes it possible to choose electronic instead of print rather than in addition to print. We will be able to take advantage of the fact that many legal publishers, including CCH, BNA and RIA, now are offering academic pricing packages for core electronic resources.

The Associate Director for Information Resources also talked with used book dealers who specialize in law titles, and we purchased a large collection of treatises on the Supreme Court. We will continue to use this method to acquire some of the retrospective treatise materials, but we will also purchase available reprints from a variety of publishers.

We made a decision to not seek membership in the Federal Depository Library Program for two reasons. First, the cost of the personnel needed to satisfy the reporting requirements of the Government Printing Office outweighs the value of the publications available in traditional formats. Second, while primary sources have been available for many years on Westlaw and Lexis, the recent explosion of primary and secondary electronic information available at no cost from government providers will make it possible to choose free electronic access for a wide range of secondary resources that once would have been easier to acquire through the depository program.

IMPACT ON DEVELOPING THE NEW BUILDING

The decisions concerning information resources have significant relationship to the development of the plans for the temporary law library and the new law library slated to be opened in 2003. To facilitate access to electronic resources, the temporary facility currently in use has over one hundred fully wired locations for access to the University's information infrastructure. The new facility will most likely be a mixture of hard-wired and wireless connections. To a great extent the law library will be hard-wired because of our concern about the bandwidth of wireless networks.

Because modern law libraries are not just warehouses for the storage of information, plans for the new building include efforts to recognize the collaborative context of research. Therefore, planning has emphasized a large number of group study rooms and group works areas, which will account for nearly thirty percent of the total library seating.

CONCLUSION

The UST Law Library has gathered a veteran group of skilled librarians to tackle the challenges of creating a system for the delivery of information resources in the midst of the most dynamic period for legal research and legal resources in over a hundred years. Because of dramatic recent changes, we have created an information resources plan after testing and challenging all of the basic premises of collection development learned during our twenty-five years of professional library experience. The challenge is exhilarating and demanding. The focus has been the creation of a solid foundation with an emphasis during 2001 on the first year curriculum. During the next phase of development, we will turn to the establishment of a collection that will support the needs of our faculty and second and third year students. During the next three to five years, the UST Law Library will focus its collection development activities in two complementary areas: acquisition of a significant print treatise collection and aggressive pursuit of electronic resources for all other materials.

NOTES

1. The University of St. Thomas organized its original law school in April 1923 and operated until 1933. Joseph P. Connors, Journey Toward Fulfillment 204, 275; Bulletin of the College of St. Thomas, Catalog Number 1932-33 With Announcements for 1993-34 (March 1933-vol. XLVIII, number 1).

2. The UST Law mission is "to integrate faith and reason in the search for truth through a focus on morality and social justice."

3. The University of St. Thomas is located within the Archdiocese of Saint Paul and Minneapolis. See http://insideust.stthomas.edu/universityinfo/mission.cfm.

4. A detailed discussion of the mentoring program is available at: http://www.stthomas.edu/lawschool/rw/rw_mp.htm.

5. The text of Standard 601 is as follows:

> (a) A law school shall maintain a law library that is an active and responsive force in the educational life of the law school. A law library's effective support of the school's teaching, research and service programs requires a direct, continuing, and informed relationship with the faculty, students, and administration of the law school.

6. Interpretation 606-6: "A law library core collection shall include the following: . . .

> (2) all federal codes and session laws, and at least one current annotated code for each state . . ."
>
> Interpretation 606-7: "The format of the core materials depends on the needs of the library and its clientele."

Standards for Approval of Law Schools of the American Bar Association Section of Legal Education and Admissions to the Bar.

7. Information taken from the fund accounting system at Loyola University New Orleans.

8. 533 U.S. 483 (2001).

9. Scott Carlson, *Once-Trustworthy Newspaper Databases Have Become Unreliable and Frustrating*, Chron. of Higher Educ., Jan. 25, 2002.

Electronic Journals in the Academic Law Library–Law Reviews and Beyond

Marguerite Most

SUMMARY. This article is an introduction to electronic journals in the academic law library and to the questions librarians face and must respond to as they provide timely access to legal scholarship in an increasingly electronic environment. Such factors as licensing, use statistics, reference linking, user education, and the preservation of digital formats are considered.

Although law reviews are the main form of scholarly communication in law and are comparatively inexpensive, law faculty and students look beyond traditional law journals in their research, and law librarians buy journals beyond student-edited law reviews. The author considers how spiraling subscription costs and changing publication patterns in other disciplines have led to a "serials crisis," and how that "serials crisis" has led to a "scholarly communication crisis." In addition, new technology allows the rapid dissemination of information and in some disciplines has led to changes in electronic publishing, such as articles with navigational features, and to alternatives to the traditional journal format, such as preprint servers. She goes

---

Marguerite Most is Collection Development Librarian, Boston College Law Library.

The author thanks Sharon O'Connor of Boston College Law Library, Richard Danner of the Duke University School of Law Library, and Blair Kauffman of the Yale Law School, Lillian Goldman Library, for their thoughtful comments and encouragement, and Brian Haley of Boston College Law Library for his research assistance.

[Haworth co-indexing entry note]: "Electronic Journals in the Academic Law Library–Law Reviews and Beyond." Most, Marguerite. Co-published simultaneously in *Legal Reference Services Quarterly* (The Haworth Information Press, an imprint of The Haworth Press, Inc.) Vol. 21, No. 4, 2002, pp. 189-258; and: *Law Library Collection Development in the Digital Age* (ed: Michael Chiorazzi, and Gordon Russell) The Haworth Information Press, an imprint of The Haworth Press, Inc., 2002, pp. 189-258. Single or multiple copies of this article are available for a fee from The Haworth Document Delivery Service [1-800-HAWORTH, 9:00 a.m. - 5:00 p.m. (EST). E-mail address: getinfo@haworthpressinc.com].

on to ask if the scholarly communication crisis and the responses to it in other disciplines have implications for legal scholarship and for the future of journals in the academic law library. *[Article copies available for a fee from The Haworth Document Delivery Service: 1-800-HAWORTH. E-mail address: <getinfo@haworthpressinc.com> Website: <http://www.HaworthPress.com>*

KEYWORDS. Electronic journals, legal periodicals, law reviews, scholarly communication

Web to weave, and corn to grind,
Things are in the saddle, And ride mankind.

–Ralph Waldo Emerson

INTRODUCTION

Electronic journals offer users timely access to information and flexible delivery options, and present libraries and librarians with many new challenges. These challenges include: heightened user expectations for full-text delivery of articles any time and from anywhere; increased complexity in the supply chain and new subscription models; questions about copyright and licensing and about the changing nature of ownership and archiving; and changing staffing needs as new staff are involved in the collection development and user education loops.

The first electronic law reviews were published in 1994. These specialty journals focused on law and technology, and with their volume and issue numbers, they looked much like the print law reviews after which they were modeled. In 1996 Professor Bernard Hibbitts published an article online arguing that the law review as we know it is on the verge of obsolescence and calling for self-publishing by legal scholars.[1] In 2001 an Advisory Group to the Association of American Law Schools presented a report in which they recommended that the AALS support separate projects of Hein Publishing Company and JSTOR to provide electronic access to law journals.[2] Later that same year, a coalition of library organizations, one of which includes three academic law libraries, issued *Declaring Independence: A Guide to Creating Community-Controlled Science Journals. Declaring Independence* (a Web site and pamphlet) is one of several resources for scientists interested in re-establishing publishing control over their scholarship.[3]

E-print servers of pre-print articles and post-print articles; mergers in the publishing industry and price increases that far exceed the cost of living; consortia deals with aggregators for huge packages of journal titles; volatile titles and formats–all contribute to a serials environment of rapid and often bewildering change, and to what librarians in other subject fields call a "serials crisis" and scholars in other fields call "a scholarly communication crisis." As Pamela Bluh points out in the introduction to a series of essays published by the American Library Association, librarians working with electronic serials today are participating in an evolutionary, even revolutionary cycle.[4]

In some ways, academic law librarians have had an easy time. Over twenty years ago Westlaw and Lexis began offering faculty and law students "free" access to the full text of law reviews, bar journals, and other interdisciplinary and subject-specialized legal periodicals through their law schools' institutional contracts.[5] In the meantime, print subscriptions to American law reviews have remained a relatively low-priced bargain.[6] Law faculty and students have paper copies of law reviews on the library shelves, and the more recent of these–from about 1980 on, are duplicated in Lexis and Westlaw. We have been able to have our cake and eat it, too.

On the other hand, we are somewhat isolated in this special library environment. What science and medical, and even social science and humanities librarians, call a revolution is happening all around us. And today's first-year students are part of this revolution. They enter law school accustomed to searching the Internet and to finding what they need online in an electronic environment, and they are upping the ante on us.

This article begins with a look at how and why the journals revolution began, including a look beyond law and law reviews at how our colleagues in the "main" library are dealing with electronic serials, and how scholars in other disciplines are taking advantage of the Internet to explore new kinds of publishing opportunities. The second part is a kind of snapshot of electronic journals today and focuses on the more mundane questions facing librarians who work with journals every day. The article ends with some speculations about electronic journals in tomorrow's academic law library. Does what is happening elsewhere on the campus have implications for law libraries and for legal periodicals? This article suggests that it does.

I. WHAT "SERIALS CRISIS"? WHAT "SCHOLARLY COMMUNICATION CRISIS"?

Ten Years Ago– A Very Short History of Scholarly Electronic Journal Publishing

In 1991 when Ann Okerson spoke to an OCLC Users Council meeting about electronic journals, paper journals completely dominated the scholarly scene; two institutional preprint services were in development; and OCLC was just beginning development work with the AAAS (American Association for the Advancement of Science) as an electronic publisher of scientific articles.[7]

In 1991 when the Association of Research Libraries began tracking electronic publications, 110 electronic journals and newsletters were listed in the *Directory of Electronic Journals, Newsletters and Academic Discussion Lists*.[8] These early electronic journals were available as CD-ROMs, or were available through FTP sites, or were sent by email using listserv software.

By 1997, the *Directory* listed over 3,400 journal and newsletter titles. This significant increase in titles in part reflected the entry of large, commercial publishers into the market as the Internet became the preferred method of distribution.[9] The year 1997 has been identified as the year when the market in electronic journals exploded. It seemed that every publisher announced new products at the ALA midwinter meeting. The most widely used format was the Portable Document Format, .pdf, which was considered by many to be a transitional stage until publishers adopted a searchable format.[10] In 2000, 3,915 electronic journals were listed in the *Directory*.[11]

Today, as Okerson predicted in 1991, computer equipment and user sophistication are pervasive, although not ubiquitous. Parallel electronic and paper journals are available for many serious academic journals. The big five of academic publishers–Academic, Elsevier, Kluwer, Springer and Wiley–now have all their major STM (scientific, technical and medical) journals online. Second-tier publishers, including the large academic presses like Oxford and Cambridge, are not far behind.[12] Both Oxford University Press and Kluwer Law International offer some legal journals in both print and electronic forms, and Oxford offers an email table of contents service.[13] Librarians are dealing with contract law and licenses, as well as with subscriptions. And several academic libraries have issued strategic plans that call for eliminating print subscriptions if online versions are available.

Electronic Journals–The Dream

"The new generation of library user expects information to appear on a screen as a result of a search that involves no more than half a dozen clicks on the mouse, with a final click on the mouse to produce a print copy."[14]

The benefits of electronic journals and the electronic environment are well-documented. Electronic journals are available 24 hours a day from the user's desktop, and can be read by more than one person at a time. Journals are often available electronically long before a print copy arrives in the mail. Electronic articles can be searched by words and phrases, and copied and pasted. Articles can be downloaded, rather than photocopied. Articles can be enhanced with graphics, audio and video features. While reading one article, the user can click on a link and go to other articles cited in a footnote, or to the text of the court case or statute or treaty referred to by the author.

Scholars can publish longer articles with extensive sidebars; these sidebars can be made available in full-text; and the article can be "published" as soon as it is written–no more waiting for the colleague down the hall to meet his deadline before the journal goes to press. And for the library–accurate usage statistics can help with collection development decisions–no gobbling up of shelf space, no claiming of missing issues, no bindery costs, and the prospect of savings in operating costs by eliminating the need to handle paper copies of journals that can be accessed electronically.

Goodbye to missing volumes and interlibrary loan and inconvenient library hours. Hello to a "seamless Web" of information available 24 hours a day. That, of course, is the future. Reality is a bit more sobering. But maybe not too far behind.

What Is Driving the Push to Electronic Journals?

Not long ago, librarians were leading the way. Today, users, especially students, are pushing librarians. They want and expect full-text access to journals from the desk top. And if they can't find what they want through the library, user surveys and statistical usage counts show them turning directly to Internet search engines such as Yahoo and HotBot and Google.

Pricing trends associated with publisher mergers are another factor and are often cited as a major explanation for the continuing journal price increases in many academic fields. Price increases have led to subscription cancellations by libraries, and to frustrated scholars, especially in the sciences, who find themselves without the resources they need for their research and writing. These scientists often serve as free referees for commercial scholarly journals. Several years ago they began questioning why they should provide free refereeing to journals produced by publishers that are perceived as price gouging their libraries. And so began the movement to return scientific publishing to scientists, a movement that uses technology to publish electronic alternatives to print journals.[15] This is the scholarly communication movement, a movement that arises precisely from a crisis in scholarly communication.

Electronic resources are sometimes seen as the answer to the library's space problem. "But it will all be online. Why do you need so much space for books?"[16] Few law librarians today advocate an all-electronic law library and few, if any, law libraries are discarding print law reviews and replacing them with electronic copies. Digitalization projects do, however, offer potential opportunities to economize or reorganize stack space. Libraries have the option of moving print journals out of "prime real estate," and arguably, reducing the need to build new shelf space. Certainly this move to toss print journals and rely on electronic access is happening in the law firm library.[17]

For some libraries, the savings may, in fact, have the potential to be significant. For example, the capital costs associated with housing the backfiles of journals in JSTOR (assuming full runs and 7,000 volumes, the number available in JSTOR in 2001) have been estimated to be roughly $175,000. These costs will increase over time as content is added.[18]

Impact of Electronic Serials on Library Users–and Vice Versa

Study after study shows users choose electronic data over paper. At Washington State University, faculty are "happy as can be" to dial into a university subscription from their offices, and "students will stand in line for the terminal rather than walk up one flight of stairs to get the paper copy."[19] (Query whether the student even knows a paper copy is available? But, this is a topic for others to explore.)

At Drexel, faculty and students "embraced the new technology almost universally." Factors contributing to this include: a highly computer literate faculty and student body; programmatic emphases in areas where publishers have emphasized electronic journals; a high speed ubiquitous network; dissatisfaction with the print journal collection; and a strong distance learning program.[20]

In a recent study of use patterns at the biomedical library of the University of Southern California, researchers compared accessing patterns for identical journals available both electronically and in print. Their findings: 28,000 electronic viewings of full-text articles compared to 1,800 uses of the corresponding print volumes; and just over 20% of titles accounted for nearly 60% of use in both formats. This later finding was unexpected since the ease of electronic access is generally thought to expand the range of titles that users can and do access.[21]

A 1999-2000 study at Texas A&M looking at use statistics, with usage defined as a request for the journal through the library's Web site, revealed that remote use of titles from off-campus was higher than in-house library use.[22]

The OhioLink executive director reported usage data showing over half the articles selected came from journals not held by the member library. In each institution, users were accessing a much wider array of journals than those held by the library in print.[23]

In *What if What We Know Isn't True?* David Kohl, University Librarian at the University of Cincinnati, which is an OhioLink library, reported more use of non-selected journals (aggregator deals) than of articles from journals selected by collection development librarians. His conclusion: "access trumps selection."[24] Taken a step further, these figures imply that libraries should focus more on increasing access through better indexing tools, and less on selecting titles. How budgets are spent to increase access is more important than increasing numbers of titles.

Users are accustomed to finding information when they use a standard search engine to search the Web. They expect a result, and it will be increasingly important for libraries to meet that expectation with the resources they can make available. Or the user will turn elsewhere. One writer suggests that while the quality of the information is important, users are likely to be more tolerant of poor quality than of no information, providing too much information will be more acceptable than providing too little.[25]

A February 2000 survey of how scientists in one field retrieved publications found "a clear trend for young researchers to go around subscription barriers (both paper and electronic) and rely almost exclusively on what they can find free or on the Internet, which often includes working versions posted on the homepages of the authors."[26]

At Georgetown University Law Library, photocopying, circulation and shelving statistics show noticeable changes in use patterns over a recent ten-year period, and suggested to the authors that student use of the print collection had decreased dramatically. Shelving statistics for the most current bound journals, those from 1980 to the present, dropped by 61% over the five years from 1993-94 to 1998-99.[27] Shelving statistics at other law libraries also suggest that fewer printed volumes are being used.[28] Although they are careful to point out that there is no way to directly link these declines to electronic resources, the authors of the Georgetown study speculate that students "seem to have embraced almost totally the instant gratification and 'fast and flexible' characteristics of most digital products."[29]

The "Serials Crisis"–Measuring Journal Costs

In subject fields other than law, the rise in numbers of electronic journals has often been accompanied by spiraling subscription costs. A concrete, although extreme, example illustrates the problem. In 1985 an annual library subscription to the *Journal of Comparative Neurology* cost $1,920. The institutional subscription price in 2000 was $15,000.[30] For a longer-term look at serial prices, see a 1986 report Ann Okerson prepared for the Association of Research Libraries in which she detailed the history of serial prices and in which she noted that there is "nothing new under the sun."[31] In a 1927 report to the Association of American Universities, Cornell University complained of the increasing volume of publications and rapidly rising prices. Between 1910 and 1925 a Cornell list of 633 periodical subscriptions increased in price by 182 percent.[32]

The serial crisis would be less relevant to law libraries, if the journals used in scholarship and research were limited to law-school law reviews, where large price increases have not been a problem. However, legal scholarship and research, and the needs of courts and practicing lawyers, often extend into other fields such as the environmental sciences, medicine and economics. Academic law libraries buy journals from many other publishers; often these are commercial publishers concerned first with the bottom line.

In an interesting first-hand account, Professor Robert Berring described what he found when he looked at several Supreme Court decisions published in volume 175 of *United States Reports* (1899). He noted that a century ago the Court relied on, and cited, earlier court reports, relevant statutes, and little else.[33] In 1899 the *Brandeis Brief*, which legitimized the use of social science and statistics by the Court, had not yet been written.[34] *Brown v. Board of Education*, with its reliance on nonlegal authority, would not be decided for another half century.[35] Today it is common for the Court to consider nonlegal information in its deliberations. In a recent analysis of citations to nonlegal information by courts, including the United States Supreme Court, a dramatic increase in citations to nonlegal information is explained by a decrease in the cost of access to such information (newspapers, nonlegal scholarly journals, popular magazines, etc.) compared to the cost of access to traditional information (cases, statutes, etc.).[36]

Twenty years ago law firm librarians provided answers to legal questions. Today they are asked for information on "everything from business and economic trends to alternatives for cold storage facilities."[37] Globalization of law, and law practices that reach across borders, are broadening the research needs of practicing lawyers. Law schools today offer courses outside the traditional law school curriculum–law and economics, law and medicine, law and society. The increased focus on foreign and international law, and in areas tangential to law, place added demands on the library. Law librarians have responded by collecting journals in other disciplines to supplement the traditional law collection. Journals from other jurisdictions and in tangential subject areas are where law librarians are seeing hefty price increases. For example, subscriptions to two commercially published titles chosen at random show annual increases well beyond the increases allotted for serials in most library budgets. A subscription to *The British Journal of Criminology* went up approximately 10% each of the past three years and now costs $232.00; a subscription to *International Tax Journal* went up approximately 15% each of the past three years and now costs $305.00.

The library literature today is replete with articles about spiraling journal prices. But in 1986 when physics Professor Henry Barschall published his study of rising costs in physics, philosophy and mathematics journals, the crisis was of minor concern except to serial librarians.[38] Barschall concluded that "all the publishers whose journals have low average costs per character or low rations of cost to impact are scientific societies or associations, while the publishers whose journals have high costs per character or high rations of cost to impact are commercial firms."[39] Gordon and Breach, one of the commercial publishers whose titles were cited in the Barschall article as among the least cost effective, sued, alleging "illegal comparative advertising" of the not-for-profit journals, and threatening additional litigation to challenge adverse commentary about its journals.[40]

Professor Barschall's "Wisconsin data" (updated) is available and has been used by librarians at other schools in conversations with faculty about identifying potential journal cancellations.[41] Law titles are not included. Barschall's study focused on a high-priced field, and later studies have identified a "profile" of expensive journals that routinely post extraordinarily high rates of price increase. The title is typically in the science-technical-medical (STM) area. For a sense of how periodical prices have skyrocketed over the last few years, see the *Library Journal 2000 Periodicals Price Survey.*[42]

As with law reviews, the STM journals are the primary vehicle for the communication of scholarly information in their fields. American law reviews, which are viewed as educational activities for students and are supported by non-profit law schools, remain reasonably priced. In the STM fields, by comparison, the publisher is likely to be a for-profit company as opposed to a not-for-profit society or association.[43] A comparison of prices in law, where the average journal subscription in 1996 was $110.83 and in 2000 was $145.41, with prices in other subjects suggests why the push for change is coming from other disciplines. In the year 2000, libraries paid on average $1,879.71 for physics subscriptions; $1781.58 for chemistry subscriptions; and $996.45 for biology subscriptions. "Scholarly communication is now big business."[44] Perhaps law librarians should consider themselves fortunate in facing only a 30% price increase over the past five years. Certainly the unique publishing character of American law reviews is one reason prices have remained relatively reasonable.

For a sense of the economics of scholarly journals as they have affected libraries since 1990, see the *Newsletter on Serials Pricing Issues.*[45] Topics include journal pricing projections, library cancellation projects, journal publisher and subscription agent efforts to reduce costs, electronic publishing ventures that may impact pricing, and good news such as price reductions.

The Impact of Publishers' Mergers

In an article in which they report on the increased number of nonlegal citations by the courts, Professors Frederick Schauer and Virginia Wise provide two explanations. The first is what they call the economic integration of the legal publishing industry.[46] Legal publishers have been bought up by publishing conglomerates that publish far beyond the legal domain. West is now owned by Thomson; Lexis-Nexis is part of Reed-Elsevier, as are Michie, Shepard's Citations and Butterworths. Little Brown belongs to Kluwer. These publishing industries have an interest in expanding access to their nonlegal resources, as can be seen in the large numbers of nonlegal databases and journals on both Lexis-Nexis and Westlaw.

However, librarians who write and talk about mergers in the publishing world are likely to focus on money, not on changes in citation patterns. Particularly with journals, where rising costs have been most dramatic and have been draining other parts of the materials budget, they are likely to express amazement, if not horror, at what the dollar figures say. For example, for fiscal year '97-'98, the returns on equity of two commercial publishers of scholarly journals were 37.5% (Wolters Kluwer) and 33.7% (Reed Elsevier). The median return on equity for periodical publishers was 19.3% during the same year. These margins are matched only in luxury areas such as fine jewelry, yachts, and expensive cars.[47] The year 1997-98 was not an anomaly. Between 1986 and 1996, the consumer price index increased 44 percent. Over that same ten years, the cost of monographs increased by 62 percent. The cost of health care increased 84 percent. And scholarly journals increased 148 percent–three times more than the rate of inflation and almost twice the rate of growth in health care costs.[48] To see more, look at *The Cornell Journal Price Study*, and the tables in *Competition in Scholarly Publishing? What Publisher Profits Reveal*.[49]

In reporting on his study of the impact of mergers in the commercial publishing world, Professor Mark J. McCabe opened his article with a mention of the proposed (and failed) merger in 1998 of Reed Elsevier and Wolters Kluwer.[50] Although the proposed Elsevier/Kluwer merger failed in 1998, more rumors surfaced (but were dismissed) in early 2002. Nevertheless, mergers have continued, especially in the STM publishing world, and in law.[51] McCabe argued that commercial publisher mergers are directly correlated to journal price rises.[52] He attributed this to a market in which demand for journals is relatively inelastic. Journal titles compete with one another over an entire field, rather than across a narrow subfield. Libraries do not subscribe only to the best value, but instead buy across a broad field of study. Policy implications include his suggestion that the Department of Justice permit libraries to form a national buying consortium to counter the market power of the publishers. As an aside, McCabe noted that even the controversial merger of Thomson/West in the legal publishing field resulted in few meaningful divestitures.[53]

The bottom line in McCabe's summary, based primarily on data collected on the STM titles, is that publishers have a strong incentive to increase prices faster than library budgets grow. Inflationary trends are not limited to the commercial publishers. In the biomedical field he found that nonprofits have also raised prices. Nor are inflationary trends limited to STM titles. Some social science journals are posting annual increases even greater than those in STM areas.[54]

In a message posted to Liblicense in January 2002, listserv members are referred to a recent news article, *Bad Economy is Good News for Large Information Companies*. According to this article, companies such as Reed Elsevier, Thomson and Wolters Kluwer are out to replace niche competitors through one-stop shopping for information services and are focusing product development on unifying separate products under a common user interface–and at the same time, "scooping up" smaller companies.[55]

Electronic Journals and Hidden Costs

Most articles about library costs and electronic journals have focused on subscription costs. However, a library's operational costs–receiving, processing, shelving and bindery–may far exceed the subscription costs. Carol Hansen Montgomery has written about these related costs in an article describing the Drexel Library experience, following a decision to shift a large part of their print journal collection to electronic access. A change in staff workload was the most immediate impact, but space, equipment and supplies were all affected. More specifically, the operational costs for a library to provide access to electronic journals include costs associated with selection, acquisitions and cataloguing, and new costs associated with license negotiating and bibliographic instruction for users. Montgomery noted that these new costs often require staff with higher skills levels.[56]

From the publisher's perspective, the company is asked to provide new features, such as statistics and archiving, both of which libraries handle in-house for paper journals. In addition, publishers have costs associated with hardware, software and the conversion of paper journals to electronic, often with added features, such as site-searching mechanisms that are not available in the paper copy. Then there are marketing and technical support staff costs. In a recent article reporting on an ALA Midwinter 2001 presentation on journal costs, the author noted that publishers privately report initial increases in staffing can cost 40% or more and that publishers were raising print subscriptions up to 50% to recoup these costs.[57]

The Impact of the "Serials Crisis" on Library Collections

Since 1986, the average annual increase in the serial unit cost for an ARL library was 8.8%, amounting to a total serial unit cost increase of 226%.[58] In 1999-2000, ARL libraries spent almost three times as much on serials as they did in 1986. Yet the number of titles acquired was 7% fewer. Over the same time period, monograph acquisitions fell 17% overall as librarians shifted funds to cover rising serial costs.[59]

According to another source, the average North American research library has cut journal acquisitions by more than 6% since 1986. A straight-line projection of these figures suggests that by 2015 the average academic research library will have had to cancel another 17% of its journals and cut back in other areas, just to keep up with inflating prices. Another projection, based on a somewhat less favorable economy, predicts a subscription reduction of 45% for the average research library.[60]

The "Law Review Crisis"

Is the day coming when paper law reviews are a thing of the past and all law reviews are published online? Will self-publishing by legal scholars replace the law review as the primary outlet for legal scholarship? The "serials crisis" that has generated so much discussion and action in other fields, particularly in the sciences, seems at first glance to have passed over and around the discipline of law. Certainly the spiraling serials costs that fueled the movement in the sciences have not been of much concern in law. However, the law review is the major vehicle of scholarly communication in law, and legal scholars have long lamented the law review process. Today new technological advances are providing opportunities for self-publishing and archiving that may challenge the law review as an institution.

The debate over student-edited law reviews first surfaced over 50 years ago. In *Goodbye to Law Reviews*, published in 1936, Professor Fred Rodell identified two things wrong with legal writing. One is its style. The other is its content.[61] Law professors criticize law review articles for archaic language; verbose and unwieldy sentences; articles that run on and on for many pages with a plethora of footnotes. They criticize the law review system as slow and error-prone. They criticize law review staff as heavy-handed, youthful editors who are incompetent to judge academic contributions in increasingly complex fields, and who too often rely on secondary criteria such as reputation of the author's institution in selecting articles for publication.[62]

Amid this ongoing debate, the law review has not only survived, but has flourished. The number of law reviews is huge compared to the number of scholarly journals in other disciplines. Professor Lawrence M. Friedman has pointed out that economists talk about the "big five" and that there are many more academic economists than there are law professors; but there are many, many more prestigious law reviews.[63]

Sixty years after Rodell published his article, Professor Bernard Hibbitts self-published on the Internet an article predicting the end of the law review as we know it and calling for a move to self-publishing by legal scholars.[64] Hibbitts argued that although Westlaw and Lexis provide new ways of delivering and accessing legal scholarship in their online law reviews and legal periodicals, both services leave the law review system intact and are dependent on the existing publication schedules of the law schools. He argued that Internet technology allows and should encourage legal scholars to move from traditional law review publication, with its well-publicized problems, towards a self-publishing system in which electronically-posted articles would be centrally archived and made available for post-hoc open peer review.[65] Self-publishing has the potential for encouraging scholarly dialogue by expediting the publication process and by making scholars directly and immediately accountable to one another.[66]

Hibbitts also presented the same economic argument for faculty self-publishing in law that is advanced today in other disciplines. Law schools can save money. If the practice of self-publishing becomes generalized, schools will no longer have to spend money subsidizing their own law reviews, and then buy subscriptions to the law reviews of other schools.[67]

Responses to Hibbitts came from critics concerned about the perils of self-publishing, and from critics who see value in the law review as an institution. The concerns about self-publishing focus on permanence and archiving issues, and on difficulties with access if articles are scattered hither and yon on faculty Web pages. One writer cautioned against allowing authors to update their writings. Self-publishing and the capacity to update an article mean the potential for no final product, and courts would be reluctant to use precedent based on such articles.[68] In addition, "without the permanence of paper copies, legal scholarship will become fragile knowledge, dependent on the willingness of authors to be associated with their previously held opinions."[69]

Those who advocate the advantages of the law review over faculty self-publishing adduce many reasons. Student editors move along the editing process; law reviews have pedagogical relevance–student editors develop their research and writing skills, and time management skills; and the editors ensure that the author's citations are accurate. And new to the list: brand-name recognition of the law review can ease the transition from print to electronic form, and help ease faculty tenure concerns about publishing in "off-brand" electronic publications.[70]

Some of the same criticisms directed at the style and content of the law review have been offered as reasons the print law review is more convenient and will survive. William Manz pointed out that law review articles are complex and require close reading, and that navigating through a 90 or 100 page article online is more difficult than reading the same article on the printed page. He added that libraries have little financial reason to eliminate hard copy in favor of free electronic versions of law reviews and have shown little inclination to cancel their paper subscriptions in favor of online-only versions. He reminds us that the availability of law reviews on Lexis-Nexis and Westlaw has had little impact on print subscriptions.[71] And, since law libraries are the primary buyers of law reviews, he sees little to deter the law review from publishing its articles on the Internet, and much to gain in the way of broader dissemination.[72]

In *Yesterday Once More: Skeptics, Scribes and the Demise of Law Reviews*, Professor Hibbitts responded to his critics.[73] Today's early proponents of legal self-publishing are the early commercial publishers and their early academic supporters. Today's skeptics are the medieval scholars and scribes of the fifteenth and sixteenth centuries who believed that commercial publishers threatened to undermine the substantive quality of scholarship by enabling material that was not pre-approved by the traditional (generally religious or aristocratic) authorities to be widely marketed. As a first step towards the transition to electronic, self-published legal scholarship, Hibbitts proposed that law schools post new scholarship on the Web, and put online a complete run of back issues of the school's law reviews.[74] In an article in which he asserts that the Internet is profoundly changing American law schools, Professor Henry H. Perritt, Jr. endorses this proposal as a way to further the dissemination of legal scholarship, one of the main purposes of law reviews. He calls it "irrelevant" if Web publishing decreases paper sales.[75]

Discussions about the move from print to electronic law reviews tend to focus on the economy and convenience of the print law review. Most law reviews are published by non-profit law schools. The economic incentives driving the move to electronic journals and self-publishing in other disciplines, where the scholarly literature is often commercially published, are not a factor in the law review market. Law review and state bar journal subscriptions typically run from twenty-five to fifty dollars. (Subscriptions to foreign law journals and to journals published by commercial publishers have not remained so reasonable, however.) Academic law libraries are unlikely to respond to budget pressures by cutting law review subscriptions; instead, librarians are more likely to cut looseleaf services and practice materials with their expensive and frequent supplementation. With its student editors and law school support, the law review is a bargain.

Nevertheless, there are signs that the scholarly communications initiatives and changing patterns in the electronic publication of scholarly information, most notably in the sciences, are being followed with interest in the legal community. The following paragraphs are a brief introduction to these initiatives and publication patterns.

Scholarly Communication Initiatives

Defined simply, scholarly communication is how researchers and scholars send out into the world the knowledge they create. Within this definition, the concept extends beyond formal journals, which have served this purpose over the past four hundred years, and today includes such informal communication such as pre-print and post-print articles, telephone and email messages, in-house memoranda and listservs.[76]

More than 50 years ago Vannevar Bush recognized that "our methods of transmitting and reviewing the results of research are generations old and by now are totally inadequate for their purpose."[77] Writing in 1990, Stevan Harlan described the future as a world in which "scholarly skywriting" goes well beyond the electronic journal and encompasses the prepublication phrase of scholarship. His scholarly communication included the stages in which ideas are brainstormed informally with colleagues, are presented more formally in seminars and at conferences, and are distributed still more widely in the form of pre-prints.[78]

At the same time the new technology of the Internet was allowing rapid communication through email and listservs, and the early electronic journals were rolling off the presses, the "serials crisis" began to hit home hard. Alarmed at a situation where access to the scholarly literature had become increasingly expensive, and where libraries were canceling journal subscriptions and diverting money from other parts of library budgets to pay for remaining titles, scholars, researchers and librarians began to respond through a variety of initiatives. One of these initiatives, the Open Archives Initiative (OAI) can be traced to a physics e-print server at Los Alamos National Laboratory, which began operating in 1991.[79] As physicists began sending their work to this server, the implications for debundling the article from the journal as the only means for communicating scholarly information became clear.[80] Project Muse, JSTOR (for journal storage), SPARC (The Scholarly Publishing and Academic Resources Coalition) and HighWire Press are examples of other initiatives.[81] These initiatives focus primarily on cooperative ventures among libraries. Project Muse and JSTOR are creating digital collections of scholarly journals to address preservation and storage concerns. SPARC is an alliance of research institutions, organizations and libraries that encourages competition in the scientific scholarly communication markets. HighWire Press is an electronic publishing venture in the sciences and medicine, which began in 1995 with the online production of the *Journal of Biological Chemistry*, a peer-review journal.[82] For an extended discussion of what is driving these new initiatives, see *Returning Scientific Publishing to Scientists*.[83]

For librarians who are interested in spreading the word, the Create Change Web site is a good place to begin. Create Change is co-sponsored by the Association of Research Libraries, the Association of College and Research Libraries and SPARC. Its aim, simply put, is to help scholars regain control of the scholarly communication system. To this end, Create Change has developed a site that includes links to resources such as position papers, and a PowerPoint show for librarians who are asked to speak about the crisis with faculty audiences. The site also includes an overview of the crisis and how it happened, including a damning indictment of the commercial publishing industry.[84]

The goals of the scholarly journal include widespread and timely dissemination, the assurance of scholarly integrity, and recognition and reward.[85] The law review is also seen as an educational experience for student writers and editors. The traditional print journal has served for more than 300 years as an expedient way in which to accomplish these fundamental goals. But what we are witnessing today is a fundamental shift in mindset at a time when technology provides a way to move beyond the journal format and when the "serials crisis" has resulted in a situation where frustrated scholars, unable to access the research they need, are searching for alternative publishing choices.

Although the scholarly communication crisis was fueled in other disciplines by the "serials crisis," developments in technology make possible the ways scholars and researchers are responding to the crisis. Do these technological advances in electronic publishing have the potential to transform scholarly communication in law? Professor Richard A. Danner suggests that they do. While he is careful to point out that the journal addresses different needs in different disciplines, he sees collaborative efforts now underway that offer law schools a way into Web-based publishing of legal literature, "thereby providing not only an alternative to print journals but the potential for creating an accessible and open space for legal scholarship."[86] He bases his suppositions partly on the long-standing shortcomings of the law review system, discussed briefly above, and in numerous heavily-footnoted articles in the legal literature.

Danner sees additional indications of this interest in alternative publishing forums such as faculty pre-print and post-print postings of articles to law school Web sites and JURIST, and in the popularity of the LSN (Legal Scholarship Network), which corresponds to e-print servers in other fields.[87] The JURIST Web site includes links to calls for papers, working papers and online legal journals, as well as a range of links useful to law professors.[88] LSN, which began in 1997, is a division of SSRN (Social Science Research Network). The site includes abstracts of working and forthcoming papers and full text papers in pdf format. There are also links to what SSRN calls "fee-based partner publications" and there are "advertising opportunities for companies seeking to market their products." The *Delaware Journal of Corporate Law* in full text and the *Virginia Law Review* in full text, are examples of "fee-based partner publications"; these journals charge ten dollars and five dollars, respectively, for downloading a paper. Educational institutions that wish to post announcements are charged three hundred dollars for the first page and one hundred dollars for each additional page. Individual subscriptions are available, but most law schools have purchased a site license to LSN.[89]

II. MANAGING JOURNALS TODAY AND TOMORROW

Ten short years ago almost all journals were in paper. Titles were ordered and missing issues were claimed directly from the publisher, or perhaps through an agent. The journals were cataloged, issues were received and processed, and eventually loose issues were gathered into bound volumes that made their way to the library stacks. The library owned the journals, and subject to fair use and the copyright law, could photocopy an article to fill an interlibrary loan request, or place an issue on faculty reserve, or lend the volume to any user with borrowing privileges. All these processes are still ongoing. But, librarians who are involved in the day-to-day managing of electronic journals are also facing other complicated and different issues.

Selecting and Acquiring Electronic Journals

What is an electronic journal? The researchers who compiled the *Directory of Scholarly Electronic Journals and Academic Discussion Lists* struggled with how to define the electronic journal and eventually settled on the definition of a periodical from *The ALA Glossary of Library and Information Science (ALA, 1983)*:[90]

> Periodical: A serial appearing or intended to appear indefinitely at regular intervals, generally more frequently than annually, each issue of which is numbered or dated consecutively and normally contains separate articles, stories, or other writings. Newspapers disseminating general news, and the proceedings, papers, or other publications of corporate bodies primarily related to their meetings, are not included in this term.

Variations of the electronic journal include those that are clones of their paper counterparts, often scanned images of the print and delivered as a PDF file; those that are electronic only, created for the electronic medium; hybrids that combine features of their paper versions, but also include other functions such as hypertext linking. There are digitized copies of print journals and there are pre-print archives. Some electronic journals turn out to be only "teasers," not electronic journals, but such variations as sample issue only, current issue only, selected articles, abridged and excerpted articles.[91] This is as true in the law as in other disciplines.

The Web is now the de facto standard for the delivery of electronic journals. The most common formats for the delivery of journal pages over the Internet are HTML and PDF. HTML is an IETF (Internet Engineering Task Force) standard and because it is platform-independent, it can be read on any computer with a browser. HTML pages are transmitted quickly as ASCII text and can be indexed and searched easily. PDF (Portable Document Format), which is viewed using the free Adobe Acrobat reader, preserves the look and integrity of the page, but transmission is much slower. The main attraction of PDF for electronic journals is that it delivers pages that look exactly like the printed page. For law review authors, who are required by the *Bluebook* to cite to the print copy, and for the cite checkers who follow behind them, this is important.[92] Some publishers offer subscribers both a searchable digital format and PDF.[93]

How do we decide what journals to buy? And do we go with print journals or electronic journals or both? In November 2001 the American Association of Law Libraries (AALL) sponsored a Professional Development workshop, *New Perspectives on Law Library Acquisitions and Collection Development.*[94] Several speakers discussed the purpose and content of a written collection development policy. The policy serves as a guide for the selection and retention of materials and in the law library it often addresses intensity of collection levels by subject matter and jurisdiction. For a brief discussion by a law librarian of the importance of the written collection development statement, see *Every Library Is Special and So Is Its Collection Development Policy.*[95]

The genre statement, a new form of collection policy, is being used in some libraries to deal with the shift from paper to digital publishing. A genre statement supplements the general collection development policy statement by addressing the format of material collected, not the subject. The statement describes the process of evaluating and selecting a format, be it full text, bibliographic files or data files. The statement also provides a way to recognize and systematize the work of other divisions in the library in providing access to electronic resources.[96] Guidelines that might be included are content, pricing, use and functionality, duplication and substitution, and licensing. For example, content addresses questions such as updating, currency, and consistency with paper issues; access asks about validation methods, simultaneous users, remote access, etc.[97]

The Boston University Law Library *Electronic Resources Selection Policy* and the University of Minnesota Law Library's *Collection Development Policy for Electronic Resources* are examples of law library genre-type statements.[98] In a message to the lawlibdir-l listserv, one academic law library director posted a proposed "e-journal policy" in which the library would provide journal subscriptions in one format only, with defined exceptions. Preference would be given to electronic formats for new titles, subject to defined exceptions.[99] A site maintained by Rob Richards at the University of Colorado Law Library, for the Acquisitions Committee, Technical Services Special Interest Section of the AALL, provides links to the policies of several law libraries. The site also links to a bibliography of models, to standards, and to guides for creating law library collection development policies.[100]

Electronic journals are available directly from the publisher, over the Internet, through abstracting and indexing services, and from aggregators. Among the essays coming out of the ALCTS Electronic Serials Institutes is one by George Machovec, associate director of the Colorado Alliance for Research Libraries. Machovec presents a short, but comprehensive overview of the management and technical issues librarians face when selecting and integrating electronic resources into the collection, discusses the importance of partnerships for buying power, and cautions libraries to avoid duplicative efforts by staying informed about developments in the marketplace and in the wider library community.[101]

Since academic libraries often buy electronic journals in large packages, another part of the job for the collection development librarian or team is deciding which packages to buy from which vendors. Northwestern University's Electronic Collection Committee charged a Working Group with reviewing aggregators and publishers of electronic journals, and the providers of software to manage the journals. The process the Group used, as well as evaluation criteria and questions that were asked of each vendor, are useful for anyone engaged in this process.[102] The Group ultimately recommended that Northwestern continue to buy individual journals, rather than use aggregators where duplication of titles was common. They suggested that library money would be better spent acquiring services that offer a more seamless integration of indexes and journals through links from library databases to journal articles.[103] The reasons behind their recommendation are worth reading.

Which payment plan do we want? Within the commercial market, a library may encounter a variety of pricing choices for electronic journals. Although so many choices can initially be confusing, in some ways, the best bargains in town these days are scholarly journals. HighWire Press provides over one-fifth of its more than 200 journals for free. PubMed Central provides free access to biomedical journals linked to the free Medline indexing. Project Muse offers unlimited simultaneous use for subscribing libraries. Science Direct, in response to customer requests, will allow customers to purchase subsets of Elsevier journals rather than all or nothing.[104]

FTE counts are popular because an academic library has an easily identifiable and countable user population. Full-time equivalency is generally counted as 15 credit hours, making it easy to include part-time students within a uniform counting system. Pricing based on the number of concurrent users permitted is another common practice, although it is used less often with journals than with other kinds of databases products. Obviously usage statistics are important when a library is monitoring costs under this kind of plan. IP class is a less-common pricing choice. This method, which is sometimes offered along with other measures such as FTE, involves charging by the number of class C or B Internet Protocol (IP) domains.

Some variation of print plus fee is another common choice. Sometimes publishers tie the price of the electronic version of the journal to its print equivalent. Sometimes the publisher offers online access at no added cost if the print subscription is continued. Sometimes what begins as electronic access at no added cost becomes an additional fee a year or two down the road. And sometimes electronic access is available for a surcharge, usually a percentage of the print cost alone. Within this print plus fee model are additional variations. For example, when a consortium buys access to the full database of Academic Press titles based on a surcharge to the print subscriptions at the time of the deal, members, even those without the print subscriptions, get access to all titles.[105] Tying electronic access to a print subscription can be problematic if the electronic version has added features, which is often the case, or if the print version disappears at some point. Electronic access on its own may be charged as a percentage of the print cost, or the same as the print cost, or the print cost plus a surcharge.

User-based pricing has historically been the most popular pricing model because charges are based on real use. This may involve counting numbers of articles viewed, or number of searches, or counting by connect time. However, user-based pricing is difficult to budget for, and in a variation on this model, the library might buy a set number of sessions or searches or minutes. Recently aggregators and publishers have begun offering pay-per-view (PPV) options when demand by the library is light, or perhaps, to allow the library to shift costs to the user. Another recent trend is for publishers to offer different pricing models such as restricted access for one user at no additional cost, and broader access for a fee.[106]

HighWire Press out of Stanford University was one of the first publishers to offer major scholarly journals through a PPV arrangement. Many commercial publishers now offer the choice. All it takes is a Visa or MasterCard. What the user is actually buying is access to the article. Access can last for several days to a week or more. Another choice is a site pass that allows access to all articles in a journal for a specified time for a higher fee. Charges average about ten dollars per article, but sometimes are much higher.[107]

Bundling refers to several kinds of pricing models. A publisher (or an aggregator) may include in an electronic package or a subject-based subpackage, titles the library would not otherwise buy, or may tie the purchase of electronic access to the continued purchase of paper copies. From the library's perspective, bundling can provide access to a broader range of titles, insures against unexpectedly large bills, and means easier budgeting. But, in a counter move directed against the "all or nothing" site licensing available from some large publishers, the California State library system sent out a request for a proposal for a customized database of journals selected by Cal State. The resulting contract, although it included only about 500 of the almost 1,300 titles on the librarians' list, moved responsibility for selecting titles back to the librarians.[108]

In a November 2001 message posted to the Liblicense listserv, the director of BioMed Central announced another concept in electronic journal publishing–charging authors a "processing fee" of $500.00 to have their articles published in this peer-reviewed online journal.[109] Access for users will remain free. A recent article in *The Chronicle of Higher Education* suggested that some professors sympathetic to the company's goal object to the fees.[110] Within two weeks after instituting its new pricing scheme, BioMed introduced an institutional pricing scheme.[111] The future of this publisher will be interesting to watch.

Responding to the library market, Elsevier Science recently announced E-Choice, an electronic-only subscription for its ScienceDirect package that allows libraries to add on paper copies, but does not tie the print and electronic together. A library can pay a base amount for an electronic subscription, then add on 25 percent of the paper-subscription price for paper copies. The library community is reported to be reacting with cautious approval. "The devil's in the details," said the dean of libraries at the University of Arizona.[112]

A recent statement on electronic journal licensing issued by the International Coalition of Library Consortia (ICOLC) discusses pricing and purchasing models, explains why the Consortium endorses certain models, and is useful for librarians who want to understand the issues from the library and publishing communities perspectives. For example, ICOLC, with provisos, endorses a move from "print plus" to "electronic plus" with the electronic journal supplied for a base price, and a price for print copies added to that base price. ICOLC encourages publishers and aggregators to discontinue: the removal of content part-way through a license period; the practice of embargoing content (e.g., not allowing access to the most recent content until a stated number of months after publication); and making content available in the print versions that is not available in the electronic version. The preferred practices section covers contract negotiations, pricing, data access and archiving, system platforms, licensing terms, and user authentication.[113] For an analysis of the various routes libraries are taking, see the *Final Report of the Task Force on Journals in Aggregator Databases*.[114]

Buying in Bulk–Aggregators and Consortia

Providers of electronic journals are of two types: publishers who provide access to their own publications, and aggregators. Although some publishers sell individual electronic journal titles directly to the library or to the end user, buying journals in an aggregator package is a common practice in the academic library, either buying all of a publisher's titles from the publisher, or through an agent. In addition, there are two ways to think about buying electronic journals in bulk. The library can work directly with an aggregator or the library can buy as a member of a consortium. Either way, the library gives up the power to choose individual titles in exchange for some advantage, which is most often price.

Aggregators can be subscription agents, who provide access to journals provided by publishers; abstract and index (A&I) producers; and publishers who act as aggregators for their own and other publications. The aggregator's role is to provide the user a single access to publications from different publishers in one system with one interface. But, even while some publishers are putting their content into aggregated databases, publishers of some core academic journals are pulling content from some aggregators that they see as undermining their subscription bases by encouraging librarians to cancel print for online.[115]

Of course, law librarians have been dealing with aggregators and bundling for years. Both Westlaw and Lexis-Nexis are aggregators and act as middlemen, providing full-text access to journals in electronic format. Both companies add and delete titles at their discretion. And both companies offer the academic law library a take it or leave it deal. On the other hand, the "deal" really is a bargain basement deal. While other electronic journal collections, such as Project Muse, only provide more recent years of journals, Westlaw and Lexis-Nexis periodical databases go back to the early 1980s.[116] While other collections, such as JSTOR, provide an electronic version of all years up to about three to five years prior to the current year (the moving wall concept), Westlaw and Lexis-Nexis are relatively up-to-date.[117]

Library consortia come in many shapes and their missions vary. As Diane Klaiber, the former director of the New England Law Library Consortium (NELLCO), points out, the Canadian libraries have a national consortium, the Big 10 and the Big 12 Plus libraries each have consortium, medical libraries have a consortium, but there is no national law library consortium.[118] The main advantage for libraries in acquiring electronic journals through a consortium is that groups can get a better price. For publishers, working with a consortium can mean lower sales and administrative costs and may expand their market to smaller libraries that would otherwise not buy in. Among the benefits of a consortium listed by Klaiber in her proposal for a national law library consortium, is the advantage of collective negotiating with publishers. Library consortia give libraries the opportunity to pool resources and to buy some negotiating power as well as financial power. The NELLCO contract with Hein-On-Line is an example of a group purchase of an online journal collection. Pricing for Lexis-Nexis Academic Universe is based on a national consortia arrangement hosted by the Southeastern Library Network (SOLINET).[119] Klaiber also mentions the potential for savings in time and money when one representative acts for several libraries.[120] This time savings is especially true when it comes to license negotiations. At a recent AALL Collection Development professional workshop, one speaker estimated that she now spends over 45% of her time negotiating licenses.[121]

So what's the "Big Deal?" The "Big Deal" is a phrase coined by Ken Frazier, Director of Libraries, University of Wisconsin, who fears that big deal contracts will weaken the power of libraries to influence scholarly communication systems in the future. He sees the usual deal as a one-price, one-size fits all package in which the strongest publisher titles are bundled with the weakest titles. Although such a license offers expanded information access in the short run, Frazier urges librarians not to buy. When he writes about the big deal, Frazier writes about "enhanced loyalty." "There is no loyalty like enhanced loyalty, and nothing enhances customer loyalty quite like indispensability." Libraries that buy in to a big deal are obliged to be loyal customers because they can't cancel individual subscriptions. All they can do is cancel the subscription to the paper copy, and under the terms of the license, continue to pay for electronic access to the original journal.[122]

Other concerns have been raised about aggregator deals, especially large consortia deals. In a recent ARL report the author discussed the situation with OhioLink libraries. As a result of a big deal with Elsevier, more than half the articles they offered users in one discipline came from Elsevier, even though Elsevier did not control more than 20-25% of the core journals in the field. The author suggested this allows the publisher to manipulate use by promoting certain journals at the expense of other publishers.[123] Responses to a survey on electronic journal bundling in academic library members of the Boston Library Consortium indicated that although none of the libraries had cancelled print subscriptions to purchase an electronic package, over half anticipated making such cuts in the future, and 25% had shifted money from monograph funds to subscribe to electronic journal bundles.[124]

Signing on the Bottom Line

Whether electronic resources are purchased directly from the publisher, or through an aggregator, entering a subscription to an electronic resource means signing a license. As the introductory remarks to Yale University's Liblicense *Licensing Digital Information* Web page note: "licensing agreements often are complex, lengthy documents filled with arcane and unfamiliar terms such as indemnity, severability and force majeure."[125] Liblicense is an excellent resource for anyone involved in license negotiations. The site includes a model standard license agreement (which can be used verbatim or as a template for contract negotiating or as a checklist to evaluate terms of a license); a license vocabulary list in which terms such as indemnity, severability and force majeure are defined; links to the text of publishers' licenses; and links to resources for authors.

There is also a link to the Liblicense-l listserv archives. Messages vary. Some address everyday problems. For example, a recent posting to Liblicense informed readers of an attempt to address the common situation in which electronic journal subscriptions end on December 31, even though renewal instructions have been sent. A *Code of Good Practice* from the Association of Subscription Agents and Intermediaries calls on agents and publishers to permit access through a "grace" period of at least two months.[126] This list is often the site for lively, sometimes heated debates between librarians and publishers. It was on Liblicense that the *Nature* embargo of some content for institutional subscribers was publicly debated.[127]

For an overview of licensing, see *Principles for Licensing Electronic Resources*, which was developed by six library associations, including the American Association of Law Libraries.[128] For practical help de-mystifying licensing, see: *Strategic and Practical Considerations for Signing Electronic Delivery Agreements*, which includes a comparison of permissible uses under copyright and the conditions introduced by a license.[129] There are also links from this ARL publication to university Web sites where these issues are explained in more depth.

And for a step-by-step guide to negotiating a license, see: *A License to Kill for . . .* an article, which includes practical advice such as how broad the license definition of user can be and still be acceptable to publishers; what interlibrary loan provisions publishers are likely to accept when asked; and what steps are "reasonable" to expect librarians to take in prohibiting unauthorized users.[130] The author concludes with an appendix setting out standard licensing provisions and suggestions of changes librarians may want to negotiate.[131]

No discussion of licensing and libraries is complete without mention of intellectual property law, and of how the law is changing. According to one lawmaker: "As copyrighted works are afforded more protection, they will be encrypted in 'digital wrappers' that make them impenetrable to anyone other than those who are willing to pay the going rate. While that may sound like the American way, it is not."[132] For an apposite article with many footnotes to specific sections of the Digital Millennium Copyright Act (DMCA) and the Uniform Information Computer Transactions Act (UCITA), see Sarah Sully's essay on how changes in copyright and electronic contracts will affect libraries.[133] Sully thinks the trend in copyright law is towards expanding rights of copyright owners and what she calls increasing commodification of copyrighted works.[134]

Pay-per-view has been seen as a goal of the publishing industry for a long time and encryption technology makes such a system possible. At a conference in which he gave the keynote address, Professor Robert Oakley, Director of the Library at Georgetown University Law Center, identified encryption as "the copyright owner's trump card" because it gives the owner total control. He described encryption as an electronic envelope on which are written the conditions for opening and reading the contents. The user authorizes payment and is permitted to read the article, or if he doesn't pay up, probably with a credit card, the envelope remains sealed.[135]

Section 1201(a)(A)(1) of the DMCA states: "No person shall circumvent a technological measure that effectively controls access to a work protected under this title." Decryption is included as a measure that circumvents access, and is forbidden under the DMCA. As Sully points out, although the law contains an exception for nonprofit libraries, there is no fair use exception. In effect, an encrypted work can not be decrypted to allow use of the work, even if the use would be defensible under fair use.[136] And as Congressman Rick Boucher of Virginia recently pointed out, section 1201 "can be used to keep library patrons from copying even a paragraph from a book without making a separate payment. The only conduct that should be declared criminal is circumvention for the purpose of infringing a copyright. That approach would provide adequate protection for copyright owners without abridging the legitimate fair-use rights of consumers, libraries, educators and other users."[137] AALL's *Primer On The Digital Millennium Copyright Act: What The Digital Millennium Copyright Act and the Copyright Term Extension Act Mean for the Library Community* provides a more extensive introduction and analysis of the DMCA.[138]

The Uniform Computer Information Transactions Act, which has been enacted by several states, including Virginia, is a proposed uniform law whose purpose is to clarify rights of parties in electronic contracts. Its broad scope encompasses electronic journals and "computer information," and unless parties to a license opt out of the Act, its provisions will control in states where it is in effect. Among other things, UCITA validates terms in "shrink-wrap" and "click-on" licenses. Library concerns include how choice of law is determined, if it is not specified in a license; the validation of agreements whose terms later change; the ability of licensors to disclaim warranties, even for known defects; and the right of the licensor to engage in "self-help" (that is, to remotely turn off data).[139] The AALL Washington Affairs Office has issued several documents about the act including *A Quick Look at the Uniform Computer Information Transactions Act (UCITA)*, a primer that spells out library and consumer concerns.[140] A statement released by AFFECT in January 2002 responding to proposed amendments to UCITA is available on the AALL Washington Affairs Office Web page.[141]

Counting the Journals and Measuring Their Use

> Law libraries lie somewhere between being warehouses for books and centers for access to information, and the ABA statistics must somehow reflect this reality.[142] Libraries are approaching the time, perhaps not too distant, when the balance of our budgets will tip from hardcopy collections to leased digital information–when we pay more for access to databases and online resources than we do for putting books and journals on the shelves.[143]

These two quotations, the first from a 1992 article by Professor Laura Gasaway in which she reviews the history of academic law library statistics, and the second, written in 2001 about collection development in the Internet age by a librarian in the chemistry library at the University of Texas at Austin, reflect a problem shared by all academic libraries, universities and accrediting bodies today. How do we evaluate our libraries when the volumes on the shelves and the titles in the catalog reflect only a small portion of what we make accessible to our users? How do we define and measure academic library performance in the digital age? How do we measure the right things in the right ways?

For law libraries, the difficulties of counting legal periodicals have only increased since Professor Gasaway's article was published, and are of more than theoretical concern. In the autumn each year, academic law libraries are asked to respond to a questionnaire from the American Bar Association; several of the questions address serial volume and title count. The ABA 2001 Questionnaire defines serial subscription as:

> A serial subscription is any serial title, regardless of format, for which the library maintains an active record for continuous receipt. Gift subscriptions, free subscriptions, and any complimentary subscriptions are included in the serial subscription count. Package plans are treated as follows: unless titles received on the plan are cataloged individually, the package plan is counted as one subscription. Do not count as serial subscriptions titles accessed via on-line databases (Lexis-Nexis, Westlaw/Dialog, Internet) unless the individual title within that database is a separately cataloged record in the library's catalog.

The few librarians who responded to a February 2002 inquiry on the LAW-ACQ listserv seemed to agree that Hein-On-Line is like Lexis-Nexis and Westlaw, and its titles should not be counted unless they are individually cataloged. The general consensus was that Web sites added to the 856 field are not titles for ABA counting.[144] An earlier inquiry to LAW-ACQ in April, 2001 yielded similar results; the library posting the question decided to add as new titles only those resources that are cataloged separately as Web sites.[145]

As members of larger library communities, many law libraries also report statistics to the Association of Research Libraries. The author of a recent article about library rankings and volume count studied ARL statistics from member libraries and concluded that ARL ranking simply reflects the relative size of university libraries. She discusses a concern of many librarians that continuing efforts to rank libraries using quantitative data may distort the allocation of resources over time, and even the quality of the collection.[146] In response to such concerns and to requests from ARL members for new ways to measure new (mostly electronic) products and services, the ARL *New Measures Initiative* was formed in 1999.[147]

If, in fact, the resource budget is shifting towards electronic titles, the more librarians know about who uses electronic journals and how much and when and from where, the better prepared they will be to make a case for increased funding, or for a switch from print to electronic journals, or for the need to increase staffing to teach users how to find resources. Usage statistics can be a valuable source for this information.

Anecdotal evidence tells us users are shifting from paper materials to electronic files. But meaningful usage statistics are not easy to come by. Several years ago the Council on Library and Information Resources commissioned a study of how and what statistics are being collected.[148] The report provides a "snapshot" of developments in the industry. In the year 2000, less than half the publishers who offered electronic journals provided usage statistics. Librarians expressed doubts about what statistics to ask for, and publishers expressed concern that librarians would use whatever statistics they received to justify canceling paper copies. But the most common concern about usage statistics voiced both by librarians and publishers was the lack of comparable data.[149]

To be comparable, data must be collected from the same platform with common hardware and shared software. What is counted–searches, abstracts, HTML pages viewed, and how–whether internal use such as demonstrations, or external use such as spider "hits," are excluded, will vary according to the software used. Even when comparable statistics are available, insufficient data about paper use makes it difficult to place what is reported about electronic journal use into a broader context. And there are other factors that come into play. Publicity and promotion of a product affect level of use; user privacy is a concern.

Although guidelines are emerging, they have not yet been widely developed. One group that has adopted guidelines is the International Coalition of Library Consortia (ICOLC).[150] ICOLC guidelines identify and define data elements that must be provided and spell out minimum requirements to be provided for each element. Data elements include number of sessions (logins), queries (searches), menu selections, and full-content units examined or downloaded.[151] The New England Law Library Consortium (NELLCO), among other organizations, has endorsed these guidelines.

Another group that is developing guidelines is the PALS Usage Statistics Working Group. The PALS Working Group is charged with developing a common Code of Practice for publishers and vendors to use to record online-use statistics. Information about the kinds of data to be collected, links to other initiatives, and reports from a vendor-based forum in June 2001 are on the PALS Web site.[152]

Accessing Library Resources

Traditionally, librarians have provided access to the library's holdings through the catalog. But today the catalog is only one of several tools. This section begins with a discussion about adding electronic resources to the catalog, and then considers other ways libraries provide access to electronic journals.

In an interesting article that includes a backward look at the catalog, as well as a call for librarians to reduce the time spent cataloging books, Sarah Thomas suggests librarians should reallocate their time to provide access to other resources, especially Internet resources. She asks: "Should the catalog encompass all items that are considered part of a library's collection, even if those items are not physically held by the library? Should it even serve as a general gateway to the entire Web?"[153] A discussion of the catalog as portal (or gateway) includes the following arguments for adding electronic resources (including free electronic journals) to the library catalog: cataloging conveys credibility through an affirmative selection by a real human being; cataloging tells the user that the resource is readily obtainable, that it possesses authenticity, and that the resource consulted today will be available in the future.[154] Proponents of the catalog believe strongly that it has enduring value and can evolve to be a useful tool. Critics do not foresee any role for the library catalog in the digital age.

Should free electronic journals be cataloged? Or only journals received by paid subscription? One record or two? Should URLs for journals in collections point to the initial page of the database? In December 2000, AALL sponsored *Cataloging Electronic Resources*, a moderated listserv discussion.[155] Although this was a widely-ranging discussion about cataloging electronic resources generally, some messages addressed cataloging electronic journals. There appeared to be consensus among academic law librarians (at least among librarians responding to the list) that access to electronic journals should be provided through the catalog. Beyond that, practices varied considerably. Some libraries cataloged only "paid subscriptions"; one library cataloged any law review available in Web format and free; another library was not adding URLs for online law reviews that duplicate their print titles. If a library has the same journal in print and online, the single record approach seemed to be preferred; duplicative records in the catalog were seen as confusing to users.[156] Libraries often provided access to electronic journals from the online catalog by adding a URL in the 856 field of the MARC record. This was especially common for titles to which the library had a paid subscription. However, maintaining access through a URL in the catalog record, or on a Web site, can be high maintenance, since some URLs change with regularity.

Several librarians identified aggregator journal databases as a major challenge. At one library where individual titles within aggregators are cataloged (Academic IDEAL was the example), the library adds an 899 field to the bibliographic record to help identify the aggregator, and to help identify a record for deletion, should the electronic subscription end.

Among the services Hein-On-Line offers libraries, is an online cataloging aid designed to assist with adding links to bibliographic records in the library's catalog. This link lets users click in the record, and go directly to the corresponding title at Hein-On-Line. The aid, which has an entry for each title in the Hein collection, includes such information as title, volume coverage, OCLC control number, and a direct URL to the title in Hein-On-Line suitable for cutting and pasting to a bibliographic record.[157]

A more recent trend may be away from the single record or "piggybacking," at least for the large academic library that buys electronic journals through packets from publishers or aggregators. Big deals such as those from Elsevier or OCLC contain large numbers of titles with coverage that is constantly changing, as titles are added or taken away. These vendors are now offering bibliographic records in MARC format, a service that allows the library to catalog all titles in the package and to have a direct maintenance link to the provider; however, the services will probably not work with piggybacked records.[158]

Two articles about cataloging electronic resources in academic law libraries have recently been published. In *Cataloging Remote Electronic Resources*, Hope Breeze explains why many librarians have questioned the advisability of cataloging resources whose availability and maintenance are controlled by external agencies such as publishers and aggregators. Her article chronicles the failure of the Westlaw and Lexis Cataloging Project at the law libraries of the University of Minnesota and the State University of New York at Buffalo. However, times have changed. Breeze sees today's Web-compatible online catalogs as a way to provide a direct gateway to the Web using hotlinks from catalog records to remote resources.[159] Breeze's article was followed by an article by Karen Selden which is "heavy on practical ideas and examples."[160] In fact, Selden's article is much more than a how-we-do-it-here article; it includes policy discussions behind the cataloging choices made at the University of Colorado Law Library.

In July 2000 OCLC put into production a service called CORC, the Cooperative Online Resource Catalog. Although not a topic of conversation on the AALL discussion list, CORC is of interest in law libraries, as it is in other libraries. CORC uses standard formats such as MARC, Dublin Core RDF and HTML and pulls information such as title, LC subject heading, and brief descriptions from Web sites. These can be enhanced and edited locally. Over 400 libraries are participating in this Web-based product that is designed to create a database of records to Web resources.[161] OCLC includes CORC records in its WorldCat database.

When an electronic title is added to the catalog, is it cataloged as a serial or as a monograph? The ALA definition of periodical calls for numbered and dated issues that appear at regular intervals. Under AACR2 a serial must be issued in successive, numbered or dated parts with the intention of being continued indefinitely.[162] AACR2 requires that seamlessly updated serial-like publications such as online magazines (and looseleaf services) be cataloged as monographs.[163] The move from the early 1990s listserv model of delivery of electronic journals as complete issues sent by email to subscribers to the delivery of electronic journals over the Internet complicates the question and the answer. Some publishers have abandoned the concept of the electronic journal and release articles as they are ready. Journals that are originally issued in issues may be rearranged alphabetically or chronologically. Titles may change and the Web site may have no indication of the earlier title. Internet publishers who add new documents as they become available can create a seamless compilation of articles without volume or issue number.

Writing for librarians who are not catalog specialists, Regina Romano Reynolds, head of the National Serials Data Program at the Library of Congress, discussed the monograph-serial dichotomy problem as it relates to electronic journals and electronic publishing, and why online magazines, which are seamlessly updated rather than divided into issues, are considered monographs under present AACR2 rules. Her essay also considered the ramifications of several serial rule-revision proposals, and discussed what is meant by "continuing resources," an umbrella category that recognizes the seriality of resources that continue over time, and that usually have no predetermined conclusion. Under the continuing resources umbrella are successively-issued serials, including series and electronic journals, and integrating resources, including most looseleaf services, databases and Web sites. What distinguishes the electronic journal from integrated resources such as looseleaf services, is that it consists of articles which are "successive parts" and that remain discrete.[164]

Metadata is "data about data" and has been described as "the sum total of what one can say about any 'information object' at any level of aggregation."[165] Metadata is the information librarians have traditionally put into catalogs, although the term is used most often to refer to information about Web resources. Library metadata include indexes, abstracts, and catalog records, as well as authority forms such as Library of Congress subject headings. Metadata can be created by a computer by pulling terms from a keyword index, for example, or by a person using catalog records. The Dublin Core Metadata Element Set (DC) is a small, simple set of metadata elements that can be used to describe and search across a wide variety of information resources on the Web.[166]

The following sentence comes from a recent article in *D-Lib*, *Keeping Dublin Core Simple* . . . "The OAI approach to metadata harvesting exemplifies the notion of metadata modularization, mandating simple Dublin Core metadata for cross-community interoperability while supporting, in parallel, community-specific metadata for 'drill-down' searching within domains." Got that? (Actually, the title refers not to a simple explanation of what Dublin Core is, but rather to the commitment of the Dublin Core Metadata Initiative to use Dublin Core elements as the basis for simple statements about resources, rather than as the foundation for more complicated descriptive clauses.)[167]

If it is kept simple, Dublin Core offers the possibility of bringing greater order to the Web by allowing simple descriptive cataloging with little human intervention. Unlike the detail found in a typical bibliographic database or library catalog, terms are "dumbed-down" to allow cross-domain searches. The use of metadata standards can ensure that different kinds of descriptive metadata can interoperate. But as Hope Breeze points out in her article on cataloging electronic resources, establishing record standards and getting Web composers and editors to use them will be a challenge.[168]

The Dublin Core Metadata Initiative is an open-access indexing system. Compared with the commercial journal index today and the hit-and-miss of Web searching, Dublin Core offers an opportunity to provide a far superior research tool. In reporting on a study of overlap and oversight (particularly with new electronic journals) of current periodical indexes, the authors maintain that open-access domain technology makes it theoretically possible to construct compatible systems that would increase access to research, while at the same time provide an alternative to the high cost of commercial indexing services.[169] Open-access standards, such as Dublin Core, which use the Open Archive Initiative, can increase the accuracy of online searches and integrate access to resources across different products, and can reach beyond the journal article to graphs and graphics, and to online discussions and other informal communications.

Providing Access to Journals–Beyond the Catalog

Librarians want catalog records in the OPAC to represent electronic journals, including journals in aggregations, but staff time and the volatility of the journals themselves are often obstacles to cataloging and maintaining these records. Database providers are constantly updating, adding, or dropping titles and other content from their products, while electronic journal publishers continuously expand or contract their title lists. Identifying which titles are included in a particular database or collection of electronic journals can be difficult. So, instead of, or in addition to a catalog record, libraries use title lists and subject lists on a Web page, some use paper guides, and some use all of these.

Does the library subscribe to the Berkeley Technology Law Journal? It's not in the catalog. I found a cite in LegalTrac that's right on point. Libraries today are paying for hundreds, even thousands of journals, not by individual title subscriptions, but instead, through publishers' databases and aggregators. Yet many library users don't know the journals are available. Users may continue to submit interlibrary loan requests for articles from journals in library-licensed databases, and in fact, the titles may not even be in the catalog. A variety of products on the market are designed to help users identify what journals are available, and to help librarians cope with the volume and volatility of electronic-journal packages and full-text databases. In addition to databases with customized lists of holdings to help users find journals, there are products to help librarians organize and manage journals.[170]

Serials Solutions is a commercial software program that takes the library's lists of databases and electronic journal collections and consolidates from them a title list of full-text journals. Overlap of titles within database collections is another problem addressed by Serial Solutions. Libraries may buy access to the same journal from several different vendors, and for different time periods. With Serials Solutions, the titles are collated alphabetically, and the list, with the journal's licensed availability dates from each vendor, can be mounted on the library Web page. By clicking on a link, the user goes to the resource itself, usually to a publisher's opening screen; but sometimes directly to the journal.[171] A subject list of electronic journals is presently in the development stage.[172]

For examples of how academic libraries organize online databases into a subject list, see the Harvard Libraries "e-resources" Web site where searches can be limited by "E-journal," and *VERA: Virtual Electronic Resources Access*, a listing of databases and electronic journals at MIT.[173]

JAKE (Jointly Administered Knowledge Environment) is open-source software that was developed at the Yale Medical School Library to help users identify journal holdings and to help librarians manage journal subscriptions; and what's more, it's free. JAKE takes lists of database content from information providers like ProQuest and manipulates and cross references the data to create a searchable source of information about titles, including electronic journals, that are indexed or available as full-text from various sources. A library can filter JAKE to display only information about the library's subscriptions, or to copy data into the library's own database.[174] Several libraries have created local search interfaces for JAKE.

With the Web estimated to be increasing by 10 million pages weekly, the task of indexing Internet resources is gargantuan. Instead of relying on the catalog to identify Web pages, users have turned to Web portals. *Traffick: the Guide to Portals and Search Engines* traces the portal's antecedent to the search engine or directory service that began to take advantage of the millions of site visits the service received daily.[175] A dot.com portal provides access to a wide range of materials using a sophisticated search engine, but it is common for the user to retrieve irrelevant and duplicate hits, and dead ends. In addition, proprietary information, such as licensed databases to which a library subscribes, will not be located at a dot.com portal. The local catalog, on the other hand, provides very detailed access to local resources, but only if they are, in fact, cataloged. Today libraries are building different versions of portals as an alternative to the dot.com portal and to the catalog. The scholars portal concept mentioned below, although not yet a reality, is seen by one university librarian as a "healthy sign" that libraries recognize the need to transform themselves.[176]

At its most basic level a portal or gateway can be defined as one-stop shopping. Today's law libraries use portals to organize resources by providing links to electronic databases and journal collections, to the library catalog, to information about the library, to services such as email reference and online ILL forms, and to links outside the library. A portal often includes subject or title lists of databases and electronic journals subscriptions, as well as links to information on the Web beyond the library's "for-pay" resources. Many academic law libraries and commercial Web sites have built portals in specific subject areas. Several have built law periodical portals with links to electronic journals.[177] Identifying which outside resources to link to often involves the collection development librarian or team, reference librarians, and technical support staff. In some libraries this is leading to a blurring of roles between traditional technical services and public services staff.

MyLibrary and similar products provide another variation on the portal.[178] The MyLibrary portal at Los Alamos, for example, lets the user select from over 3,500 electronic journals, over 200 databases, and from subject-based web links. The "owner" can set up a library, determine who has access, and populate the library. This "sharing" of resources is designed to facilitate team projects and interest groups.[179]

MetaLib is a commercial portal from ExLibris designed to consolidate access to all library resources on one search screen and to allow cross-searching of these resources in a single query. The resources can be local and remote resources, licensed databases, indexes and electronic journal collections, library catalogs and Web resources. Among the services MetaLib offers is its "e-basket" through which a user can customized a catalog of favorite resources.[180] ENCompass from Endeavor is a competing product designed, like MetaLib, as a portal that allows users to search many resources through a single interface.[181]

A somewhat different vision of the portal is conceived in the corporate world where the concept of knowledge management is the driving force. Industry today is using portal technology to bring explicit and tacit information together in a "push" framework. Libraries collect, organize and catalog explicit information when books and journals are ordered and cataloged. In academia, tacit information is the brainstorming at the faculty lunch table, or the after-class discussion between professor and student, or yet unwritten plans for future committee activities. For a description of what a scholar's portal might entail, such as library-selected sources, better search tools, and a validated set of resources, see a discussion by Jerry Campbell, Chief Information Officer and Dean of University Libraries, University of Southern California.[182] With consistent and comparable metadata for indexing, Campbell's scholar's portal is possible, and could provide a university's faculty and students convenient "vetted" access to academic resources. Consistent and comparable metadata standards are a goal promoted by libraries, but a goal which may be difficult to actually achieve. The industry approach is to retain control of which links are actually enabled. See the discussion about CrossRef below for more about what commercial publishers envision.

Reference Linking–DOIs, ISCs, PURLs, SFX, and OpenURLs

Full-text linking is a hot topic today. "Bring your questions . . . and learn how this works with the DOI through CrossRef, using SFX technology." A posting to Liblicense in early January 2002 invited ALA Midwinter attendees to learn more about full-text linking between electronic journals.[183]

Many libraries subscribe to more than one database or aggregator, each of which can contain hundreds of full-text electronic journals. The goal in reference linking is to let the user click a button from a citation in a bibliographic index, for example, or click on an abstract, and link directly to the full-text of the article without any navigating. And after reading that article, the user can then click on a citation within the article, or on a footnote and link directly to the cited article or footnote. Simple reference linking is common in self-published papers on the Web and is what happens when a user clicks on a URL. But URLs are notoriously unstable, and it is not uncommon to click on a citation and encounter a dead link.

OCLC's PURL is one answer to the dead link problem. A PURL (Persistent Uniform Resource Locator) acts like a URL. However, instead of pointing directly to a location on the Internet, a PURL points to an intermediate resolution service. This resolution service associates the PURL with the actual URL and returns that URL to the client. In Web parlance, this is a standard HTTP redirect. But PURLs are not universally adopted.[184]

The publishing industry is taking a different approach to the volatile URL problem, and is moving towards the use of DOIs (Digital Object Identifiers) (names) instead of URLs (locations) to take the user from one Web document to another.[185] Librarians are familiar with identifiers such as ISBN, ISSN, LCCN and call numbers, all of which are standard library identifiers for individual print items. Electronic journal identifiers are a bit more complicated because items are no longer physically tied together. One electronic journal article may consist of several "digital objects," such as text, graphs, links, and even paragraphs and sentences. Unlike the URL, which may point to information that is no longer at an address, the DOI is flexible and can adjust to the sale of a journal from one publisher to another, or the transfer of a journal from the server of one aggregator to the server of another.

With the DOI, the first part of the "catalog" number identifies publisher or location and can change. The second part uses metadata to identify the work and will not change. In the library world this identifying metadata is supplied by the publisher and can be a journal title or ISSN, an issue or volume number, page numbers, article names, etc. Although their use in libraries today is to link articles, a DOI can be embedded into any kind of metadata. Publishers see their use evolving to include any kind of online content.[186] There are several clearly written articles available for librarians interested in understanding DOI technology.[187] The basic concept is to permit the owner of online information to tag the information, allowing seamless linking by users, while keeping control of the information with the owner.[188]

Publishers have begun to register DOIs along with the URL of the article, in a central database managed by the International DOI Foundation (IDF).[189] Only the body that holds the rights to an article may register a DOI. When a DOI is sent to the International DOI Foundation and connected to its corresponding URL, the process is known as "resolution." As noted, the DOI is a project of the publishing industry. Fair use is not built into the system. As one intellectual property lawyer says: "When the full capabilities of DOI is [sic] attached to each and every datum available from a publisher and every form of information or content to be had online, the Web will be overlaid with the ultimate pay-as-you-go roadmap."[190] An example of how a publisher might use the DOI to promote book sales is available at the DOI-EB-Demo page. By clicking on the "serve the customer everywhere" link, the user goes to a pop-up menu with options to read an excerpt or a review, to buy the book, etc.[191]

CrossRef is a DOI system that functions as a sort of digital switchboard. The CrossRef article-linking project began in 2000 with 33 partners in the STM and social sciences. CrossRef holds no full text content, but rather acts as a "switchboard" effecting links through DOIs that are tagged to metadata about the object such as the title of the article.[192] CrossRef accepts metadata and returns a DOI. The DOI can then be used to retrieve the URL.

But DOIs are not the final answer. DOIs resolve to a single URL that in turn is associated with the DOI by the publisher. The system can be described as one DOI = one URL. But many libraries provide content through aggregation services. For a given library, the same journal may be available from several different vendors. In a worst case scenario, a user clicks on the DOI link, is prohibited from reaching an article at a publisher's site, and does not realize he has legitimate access to the article, perhaps through an aggregator. This "appropriate copy" problem can also arise when an article is available in several databases, but the user's library subscribes to only one of these databases.

More sophisticated linking models use the OpenURL to resolve the "appropriate copy" problem. The OpenURL is a proposed standard for transmitting metadata in a URL. The key concept here is standardization. OpenURLs can be used to "localize" linking, which means connecting the user to the article and connecting him to the article in a database the library provides access to. This might, for example, be the aggregator rather than the publisher.[193]

The target of the OpenURL is the user's institutional service component (ISC). An ISC describes the context of the user, that is, how that user is connected to the resource. Perhaps the user is an undergraduate student, or teaches at the law school, or works in a medical school laboratory, or walked in off the street. Each of these users will have access to some of the same, but some different electronic resources. Each of these users' context is different.

The SFX server from ExLibris, for example, reads an OpenURL as input (puts the user into context) and acts upon it. With SFX the user clicks on a citation in a database and sees a list of services. If a user finds an article in a database, but it is only available as an abstract, the user can next click on the SFX button to explore other access options. Depending on how a library enables SFX, these options might include a link to the full-text of the article through a different source; a link to an abstract; a link to the library catalog to check local holdings; a search by the author's name for other articles; or a Web search. In effect, the system creates hyperlinks directing the particular user (law student) from a particular database (LegalTrac) to information resources available to that law-student user (Westlaw and Lexis-Nexis and Hein-On-Line user's choice).

Beyond Reference Linking

MetaLib from ExLibris and ENCompass from Endeavor are another step beyond reference linking. Both products use the OpenURL protocol. These products let the user search different databases and library catalogs with one search query. In MetaLib, for example, a library can customize an opening screen by organizing resources in a subject schema, and provide the user "above the line" "SFXable" resources that can be searched with one query because they operate with the OpenURL protocol, and "below-the-line," "nonSFXable" resources that must be searched individually because they do not include OpenURLs. A number of information services can generate OpenURLs. PAIS International, ERIC, OCLC's Article First and the Gale Group's LegalTrac are OpenURL enabled and can be searched as a single MetaLib query.

Interoperability and the Bath Profile

Interoperability is a term that appears frequently in the reference linking literature. The term refers to that seamlessness of the Web that lets the user move from one citation to another without regard to where the article is. To achieve true interoperability with a seamless interface, libraries, consortia, database vendors, and integrated library system vendors must use communication standards that operate together. The Bath Profile is intended to provide these standards in the library world.

Computer systems communicate using the Z39.50 standard, a protocol for computer-to-computer information retrieval. Z39.50 makes it possible for a user in one system to search and retrieve information from other computer systems (that have also implemented Z39.50) without knowing the search syntax that is used by those other systems. Most library vendors have incorporated the standard into their cataloging and other applications. The Bath Profile identifies those Z39.50 features that are needed to support use of Z39.50 software for a range of library functions such as searching and retrieval of bibliographic records in electronic resources, library catalogs, and archives. The Profile, which defines a core subset of international Z39.50 specifications such as author, title and subject, is designed to support cross-domain communication.[194]

Current Awareness Services

"Keep Me Posted . . . But Not Too Much"[195]

Law has its share of current awareness services: free abstracts of new law review articles delivered by email from the University Law Review Project; paid email newsletters subscriptions, such as the *Employment Law Memo*; table of contents services that arrive by email, such as *Current Index to Legal Periodicals* from the University of Washington Law

Library, or that are accessible via the Web such as the Tarlton Law Library TOC list.[196]

Beyond law, the major vendors provide many different variations and many pricing choices. Electronic journal publishers often use "push technology" to send citations, sometimes with abstracts, sometimes with full text. Some publishers store a user query and run it periodically against updated databases. Some send "Tables of Contents" to handheld devices for users to browse and mark selections for full delivery at the next Web synchronization. Delivery of text can be by email, by fax, by Ariel, even by courier. Pricing models vary. Some vendors offer free searching and viewing of abstracts to anyone and full-text access to institutions with a site license. Document delivery charges often include a copyright fee set by the publisher, and a service charge, usually from ten to twenty dollars. Some vendors, such as ingenta, offer pricing options such as a blanket license or pay-as-you-go. Academic Press charges $38.00 per journal article with free electronic delivery. For an analyses of the major players in the market, see a recent column in *Information Today*.[197]

Interlibrary Loan and Document Delivery

From the publisher's point of view copyright law does not effectively protect electronic publications. From the library's point of view case law provides no guidance on fair use and interlibrary loan privileges comparable to that in the print world.[198] From the user's point of view interlibrary loan and document delivery may be going the way of the card catalog.

In a recent article about ILL in the electronic context, Janet Brennan Croft identifies the kinds of misunderstandings that can arise between publishers and a library as they discuss interlibrary loan. A publisher's representative wondered if ILL fees might be used to cover subscription costs. Publishers mistake the term "document delivery" to mean a business that sells articles for profit, while most libraries' fees cover only part of the transaction cost. In her discussion the author surveys ILL language in model licenses, and draws attention to various ILL options–supplying a paper copy of an electronic original, supplying an electronic original, and a prohibition on lending.[199] Interlibrary loan may be a service that has come and is going. Anyone who has searched the Internet lately using a standard Internet search engine to find a magazine article has run up against the pay-per-view (PPV) market. For many impatient users, PPV and a few dollars out-of-pocket may offer an attractive alternative to waiting a day or two.

Although ILL will likely become unnecessary in the long run as journals go online, it is in full force today. One study found that interlibrary borrowing among ARL libraries shot up 122.2% for the period 1989-1999 (8.3% annually).[200] The one interpretation of this increase is that scholars are depending on access from other libraries more and more. On the other hand, from the scholar's point of view, there are more and more articles out there to request as A&I services provide citations to more articles, and as more journals are published. Another study of 1998-1999 ARL libraries lending statistics showed an unexpected slowing in requests. The author discussed several possible reasons, such as decreases in titles libraries are buying, and the lack of up-to-date serial holdings since many libraries do not catalog serial titles received in packages, but no obvious explanation is identified.[201]

In an article written in the early 1990s, Pamela Bluh examined document delivery as a cost-effective alternative to buying materials or to licensing access to full-text electronic databases. In 1993, for example, the Uncover database (now part of ingenta) provided article-level access to journal articles that could be ordered individually and delivered by fax or email. Although some of the names and players have changed, and more delivery options are available today, this article is worth reading for the author's thoughtful discussion of access versus ownership, which is still an issue.[202]

Remote Access

Users want to reach electronic journals from the library and from campus offices and dorm rooms and home. Publishers want to restrict access to legitimate users who have been "authenticated."

In the academic library, publishers and aggregators of electronic journals generally define eligible users based upon the physical point of access of the user, rather than the identity of the individual, regardless of location. At different times and with different electronic journals, providing access to remote users may mean dealing with IP filtering, proxy servers, the dissemination of passwords, and other means of authentication.

IP filtering, that is, limiting access to specific IP addresses, is the usual way publishers control access, effectively shifting the burden of authentication to the subscribing library. The library may be required to identify IP addresses and the total number of computers associated with each portion of the library's network. IP filtering can be done on the server where information resides, or on another intermediate server before the user reaches the end point. For institutions using dynamic IP addressing, IP filtering can be a problem if addresses change.

If access to an electronic journal is by IP authentication, providing remote access requires a system that associates authenticated users with the library's Internet domain. The two general ways to authenticate an off-site user are by credential-based authentication and with a proxy server. Credential-based authentication means providing the user with some proof of legitimacy. Authentication might require, for example, the user's name or student identification number or a password. A proxy-server works by masking remote users with the IP address needed to access the resource. The user is authenticated by identifying the proxy server on his Web browser and then accessing that proxy server, which recognizes the Web browser as belonging to a legitimate user. Another approach to the authentication problem is the use of "referring" URLs. Here the user is authenticated on a local server and passed on to a remote system that is configured to accept the referral.[203]

A problem for law libraries can arise when access is by IP address, and the library's license limits access to the law school population, rather than to the larger university community. Hein-On-Line, the major legal publisher providing access to pre-1980 electronic law journals, allows IP authentication at the university-wide domain address level. Since it is licensed to the whole campus, Hein-On-Line gives the law library, which may usually piggyback access to nonlegal electronic journals through the "main library," an opportunity to provide something unique to the university collection.

Archiving

How can we guarantee perpetual access to what we pay for?[204] Print provides a permanence that is critical to academic libraries. Electronic formats, on the other hand, are seen as highly transient. Whether print is, in fact, as permanent as librarians like to think, is debatable. Consider this description by a law library director who consulted a volume of the *United States Reports*: "I should first note that volume 175 fell apart in my hands. Using the copy in the faculty library at Boalt Hall Law School, looking at the books on the surrounding shelves, I discovered that many of the volumes around volume 175 are also disintegrating. The literal crumbling of the books made me reflect upon how seldom such volumes are used (no one had touched these poor hulks in some time), and upon the myth of books lasting forever."[205]

Nevertheless, and rightly so, a major concern of librarians is permanent (sometimes referred to as perpetual) archival access to information; and librarians especially worry if the information is only in electronic form. Archiving takes on even greater importance as libraries consider whether they can really continue to afford duplicate copies of journals in print and online. This concern is further heightened in some disciplines as electronic copies, often containing supplemental materials not found in the paper copy, are coming to be regarded as the version of record.[206] And because most digital content is licensed, not owned, and often is hosted by the publisher, librarians are concerned about transferring archiving responsibility to publishers. As a general rule, licenses should include provisions to purchase, and not just to lease or provide temporary access. The ARL's *Principles for Licensing Electronic Resources* declares that when permanent use of a resource is licensed, the licensee should be allowed to copy data for preservation purposes, or to create a usable archival copy.[207] Even though technology is available to centralize archiving, two major concerns remain: insuring that archived digital materials remain in readable form when the technology is continuously changing–the challenge of obsolete technology; and resolving what organizations are the appropriate repositories. The most critical is the second question. What organizations should be responsible? Archiving is not cost effective for publishers. The cost to maintain the information exceeds revenue that could be generated by making it accessible.[208] Although publishers might be expected to provide archival access today, the author of a recent report to the Digital Library Federation agreed and noted a growing consensus that libraries are the appropriate agencies to serve this function for prosperity.[209]

There are other unresolved questions. Who should pay to maintain the archives? What kind of data refreshment is needed in the future when technology changes? If a library cancels an electronic journal subscription, does it still have access to older materials for which it paid during the subscription time? What if the publisher goes out of business? Kevin Guthrie examines each of these questions in an article about JSTOR and the Project Muse project. Guthrie also includes a description of how JSTOR provides layers of protection through identical copies of the database on servers in three geographic locations in two countries, and an additional copy in escrow at OCLC.[210]

Working with librarians and publishers, the Council of Library and Information Resources (CLIR) has developed a framework for electronic journal archiving.[211] Based on these guidelines the Mellon Foundation has awarded six planning grants to create and operate experimental electronic journal archives.[212] A seventh grant continues the development and testing of the LOCKSS system at Stanford University. LOCKSS is conceived of as a decentralized model composed of loosely-controlled repositories. The LOCKSS focus is on preserving links using a Web cache that continually updates links to journals to which a library subscribes.[213]

For more information about these projects, see *Preserving Scholarly E-Journals*.[214] The author, who is involved with the Mellon project at Harvard, noted that a key assumption of the Mellon Foundation initiatives is that there will be relatively few archives holding any given set of electronic journals and that institutions will be operating archives not just for their own users. This sharing of archives, of course, raises many issues. Who can access the archives? Subscribers only? When? When the journal is no longer online? After a certain date, such as one year? When a title changes hands? What is archived? Editorials? Events lists? Errata? Images, tables, etc., related to individual articles? In late 2001 the Harvard University Library released a report addressing the feasibility of archiving electronic journal articles. The study, *E-Journal Archive DTD Feasibility Study*, found that current Document Type Definitions (DTDs) do not meet archivists' long-term requirements. But a common DTD can be developed to allow successful conversion of content from a publisher's primary SGML and XML files into a common format for archival purposes.[215]

Archiving and the AALL and AALS

The AALL Strategic Plan, *Leadership Roles for the 21st Century: New Realities, Changing Role*, calls for the development of a national plan for the preservation of legal materials in all formats.[216] In March 2001 the AALS advised law school deans and library directors of the recommendations of the AALS Advisory Group on Electronic Access to Scholarship in Law Reviews.[217] A recent article about cooperative collection development in law libraries identified lack of geographic proximity as one potential barrier to a successful program.[218] But new digital and networking technologies have the long-term potential to effectively remove geographic location from access. In addition, the recent AALL and AALS focus on the digital preservation of legal scholarship and resources as a shared responsibility within the law library and law school communities, suggests that storage and maintenance functions need not be repeated at every library. In theory a single, or several, archival sites could serve the law library community.

LEDA, Legal Electronic Document Archives, a project which originated at the Harvard Law School Library and is now at the Cornell Legal Information Institute, is being designed to provide law schools with the means to hold legal scholarship on legal e-print e-servers. LEDA servers, which are being developed according to the Open Archives Initiative standards, will have the capacity for interoperability and cross-searching of servers. As in other disciplines, the scholarship is envisioned as extending beyond formal, published articles to include working papers, briefs, theses, whatever a law school might choose to store.[219]

Citation Style

The recognized source of authority for legal citations in the legal academy is *The Bluebook: A Uniform System of Citation.*[220] Rule 18 covers electronic media, including information in commercial electronic databases (rule 18.1) and on the Internet (rule 18.2). The rule requires citation to the print copy, if available, except under certain defined circumstances; and spells out when and how to cite an electronic source as a parallel cite.[221]

The *ALWD Citation Manual*, created by the Association of Legal Writing Directors, also includes rules on citation formats for electronic materials, including those on the Internet.[222] *Has the Bluebook Met Its Match? The AWLD Citation Manual*, an article by two law professors reviews this and other alternatives to the *Bluebook*, including the *Uniform Citation Guide* published by the AALL (discussed below). They conclude that the *ALWD Citation Manual* has a "better than average chance of replacing the *Bluebook*."[223]

The American Association of Law Libraries has also taken an active role in addressing problems associated with changes in publication format and has published the *Uniform Citation Guide*.[224] Its rules are designed to be format and publisher neutral. The Committee recently published draft rules for citing law reviews.[225] The rules include sequential numbering of articles within a journal issue, and paragraph numbers within the article. Rules 700 through 707 cover basic citation format for law reviews and apply to the law review defined as "a periodical publication containing lead articles on topical subjects written by legal scholars and shorter articles written by law review staff members." The rules apply to journals published by law schools, bar organizations, and commercial publishers, if they follow this model of organization.

III. LOOKING TO THE FUTURE

Librarians should be concerned about dust on library shelves and loss of visibility in a system where more and more information is accessed from off campus and where users are increasingly unwilling to use traditional print resources. That said, predicting where we are going is akin to crystal ball gazing. This section consists, therefore, of comments and references about the future set out in recent writings by librarians and educators, and some scattered thoughts gathered from these articles and from conversations with other librarians, the chit chat over coffee, what knowledge managers call "tacit information."

Access

One area where change is likely to occur rapidly is in how users access the content of electronic journals. Content is becoming more finely granularized with links to all levels: journals, issues, articles, graphs within the article. Reference linking today can direct a user's navigation to the licensed content, regardless of its hosting location. Linking to full text will soon be the rule and not the exception. In the immediate future, if not today, there will be links to interlibrary loan forms, and to electronic reserves and reading lists that a library might provide on its Web page.

Without doubt, there is too much information at too high a price for any library to buy it all and to continue policies centered on holdings within the walls of the building. A shift from a holding policy to an access policy is already here for some resources, including those huge numbers of journals libraries buy through aggregators. At least for titles that are not in great demand, the move in the electronic journals market may well be from "just in case access" with print journals on the shelf, to "just in time" journals.

At the same time, search engines on the Internet, which work primarily as an "information pull" to a specific query, are inadequate to handle an information explosion that extends well beyond licensed electronic journals. And the amount of information grows helter-skelter. A study reported in 2000 that the world produces between 1 and 2 exabytes of unique information per year, or roughly equivalent to 250 megabytes or the textual content of 250 books for every man, woman and child on earth![226] The authors conclude that the critical problem facing us (meaning those in the information professions, for they both work at the School of Information Management and Systems at the University of California at Berkeley) is "finding . . . better ways to locate, organize, filter and present information." They think this means new tools and a new profession trained in information management.[227] Can the library portal serve this function as a kind of door through which users pass to access information and services?

Electronic Journals–From Print to Electronic?

Thinking about the past can be a useful exercise when speculating about the future. Research shows that scholars regularly refer to older writings, and studies in other disciplines have found the average age of the 10 most frequently consulted articles in economics is more than 15 years; the average age of the most frequently consulted article in mathematics is more than 30 years.[228] Research in law found a significant difference between the numbers of citations to pre-1980 and post-1980 law review articles by those who wrote articles published in 1995-96. Over 70 percent of the cited articles were published after 1980.[229] While these results suggest that older print law reviews could be moved to off-site storage, or replaced by microfiche, the author cautions that older material may be used less often, but this should not be equated with its importance. He points out that researchers are loath to wait while a book is paged from off-site, or to use microfiche to read long articles.[230]

On the other hand, recent research in the use of electronic journals in other disciplines shows a marked preference for the electronic format. Remember the students at Washington State University who stand in line for a terminal rather than walk one flight up for a print journal. It is not difficult to imagine a future when today's journals with their dual formats of paper and electronic give way to electronic-only journals. Certainly that is a trend in the sciences today, and in law firms. It is another easy step from the electronic journal to the unbundling of articles and the end of the journal as we know it, with the jettisoning of volumes and issues altogether. After all, what possible reason is there today to hold up the publication of finished articles because another "issue" is not yet ready?

A conservative view of the electronic law review of the future can already be seen in the online law review mounted by some law schools today. This electronic journal more or less parallels its paper counterpart, but may include hyperlinks, and since articles can be added as they are written, the journal can be article-based, rather than issue-based. There are other approaches, however. For example, in response to concerns about quality and about even locating articles given the undisciplined nature of the Web, it is easy to envision law schools in a publishing role that would continue the law review as a vehicle for quality control and education, and at the same time open up and speed up the process of communication. One suggestion coming out of other disciplines is a multi-level Web site. The site might consist of three levels: open postings with standards of presentation and citation and a listing of the author's credentials, the postings would still be subject to formal review and acceptance by the organization; a second level could host articles that had been accepted for electronic publication; and a third level would be for a limited selection of articles deemed of particular importance, which might then be published in paper volume as well.[231]

Unlike scholarly journals in other disciplines, law reviews are not peer reviewed, and faculty dissatisfaction with the article selection process is recognized throughout the academy. In addition, the sheer number of journals suggests that "getting published" may not be as difficult for law faculty as it is for the economics or history professor whose publication outlets are more limited. These two factors may also suggest that compared with faculty in some other disciplines, law faculty are less committed to the law review in its present institutional form. Electronic publishing may be an easier sell in law than in some other disciplines. As Richard Danner observes, the popularity of LSN suggests that faculty are interested in electronic publication, and the functions of scholarly publication–quality certification, wider distribution, indexing, and archiving can be achieved in ways other than the print law review.[232]

A Random Note About Electronic Journals

In February 2002 New Scientist published an article, *The Great Giveaway*, under what is known as a general public license or "copyleft." The concept of the copyleft originated in the software industry with open source software, such as Linux. Under a copyleft, open source software can be copied, modified and distributed by anyone, so long as that person, too, releases it under copyleft. In the words of the editor, New Scientist is publishing *The Great Giveaway* under copyleft " . . . to see what happens. To my knowledge, this is the first magazine article published under copyleft."[233]

New Directions in Publishing

In their writings about the electronic publication of scholarly information, both Stevan Harnad and Richard Danner suggest that the early initiatives, with their emphasis on Web versions of existing journals, look backward rather than forward, and are not taking advantage of the potential of technology.

What Harnad identifies as the "real revolutionary dimension" of scholarly publishing on the net is "interactive publication in the form of open peer commentary on published or ongoing work."[234] This is his "scholarly skywriting." What Danner sees as important for librarians to understand is that "for active researchers there is much more involved in scholarly communication than the formal publications traditionally found in libraries."[235]

Harnad sees a shift away from today's "trade" model with authors selling words to a commercial publisher, to a collaborative model that would be subsidized by the institution with which the author is associated and which would provide broader reach with lower real costs. He sees a dividing line between non-give-away work (books, software, music, *People* magazine) and give-away work (scientific and scholarly papers). The most important distinction is that the author of give-away literature does not seek or receive royalties or fees. Instead, this author seeks "impact." He argues that authors of give-away articles should be "self-archiving." (Self-archiving is distinct from self-publishing, which is without peer review or other kinds of quality control.[236]) Harnad is the editor of *Psycoloquy*, an electronic journal sponsored by the American Psychological Association. This journal publishes "brief reports" (1,000 lines, or about 9,000 words) called target articles and shorter commentaries and responses, and offers law librarians a glimpse of what is happening in scholarly communication in other fields.[237] The site includes instructions for authors and commentators, and links to CogPrints: The Cognitive Sciences Eprint Archive and to The Open Journal Project (now closed).

Richard Danner is interested in how the "serials crisis" in other disciplines is changing serials publishing, and what this might portend for legal scholars, publishers and libraries.[238] He sees the e-print server as an alternative, or supplement to the law review as an avenue for scholarly communication. He points out that e-print posting and journal publication need not be exclusive alternatives, and there is no reason an author could not post to an e-print server and later publish a finished article in a law review. This is, in fact, what appears to be happening. The Legal Scholarship Network (LSN) is much like the e-print server in other fields. Danner cautions that LSN is a commercial venture. As scholars take advantage of its benefits, they could lose control of their work product, while libraries of their home law schools buy back scholarship their faculty have written, just as has happened in other fields.[239] Danner holds out LEDA (Legal Education Document Archive) as an alternative to both law reviews and LSN.[240] He notes that LEDA operates using the Open Archives initiative (OIA), which is designed to allow international and interdisciplinary access to works published on e-print servers, and to allow cross-server searching.[241]

Since Danner wrote his article in 2000, his observation that "for active researchers there is much more involved in scholarly communication than the formal publications traditionally found in libraries," is proving prophetic. LEDA has developed into an ongoing Web site at the Cornell Legal Information Institute, and other law libraries are adopting it for their own publishing activities.[242] See, for example, the Duke LEDA server on which is published an article that Danner describes as an original paper designed to foster debate over issues raised by the Supreme Court decision in *Bush v. Gore*. The paper is not scheduled for print publication and the authors hope the electronic format will foster debate over the issues raised.[243] Law schools are also publishing "working paper" series on their Web sites.[244]

And there are other recent developments that suggest the legal publishing world is in a state of flux. Consider *Global Jurist*, the new family of journals from bepress.com, the Berkeley Electronic Press. *Global Jurist* is a peer-reviewed journal that is intended as a forum for scholarly cyber-debate on issues of comparative law, law and economics, international law, law and development, and legal anthropology.[245]

In the final paragraphs of an article in which he explains why he favors self-archiving over legal electronic journals, Bernard Hibbitts writes about what he calls "knowledge networks."[246] The archival model shares the journal's focus on traditional scholarship–articles and published papers. Hibbitts envisions a "knowledge network" that goes well beyond traditional "publishing" as practiced by the law review. This network would carry courses and course materials, pathfinders to academic resources, records from meetings, and might coordinate academic mailing lists and other administrative tasks. He sees his JURIST project as more akin to a knowledge network than an archive, and he "suspects" that legal e-journals "represent the end of an evolutionary line."[247]

Role of the Librarian

Disintermediation was a buzz word of the 1990s as publishers discussed the possibility of a direct link between author and reader. No more publishers, no more bookstores, and no more libraries. The author of one recent article has suggested that librarians are in danger of being killed off as obsolete members of society. Users are not using their feet to visit libraries; they're using their fingers on a keyboard.[248]

If the serial literature is all going online, this suggests the need for restructuring some librarian skills and functions. In his examination of librarianship as a profession, Richard Danner suggests that "catalogers will need to organize access to a new variety of information sources, including materials that the library does not own. Reference librarians will play greater roles as information analysts, establishing profiles of individual user's information needs and providing information filters for their clients."[249] He goes on to explain that librarians in the future must be more concerned about context and point of view of the user, than about content in and of itself. The librarian's content expertise will be important as a way of establishing point of view. Librarians will identify, sift through and validate these huge numbers of separate pieces of information, and make this superabundance of content more understandable. "This ability to provide context to the client's process of information seeking will be key to the future of the information professional."[250] In his discussion of the role of the librarian, Danner notes that access technologies are the "means" to the information at the end of the search. Librarians must become involved in the tool-building. Content expertise will become less and less useful without the "deeper" technological proficiencies needed to provide access to information.[251]

At a more day-to-day level, the unbundling of articles from the journal format and the increased availability of articles in digitized formats will cause libraries to rethink serial check-in, claiming, and bindery practices. Interlibrary loan and document delivery, as practiced today, may be nearing the end, if users turn towards the new pricing models publishers are eager to provide.

In a recent message to the Liblicense listserv, Stevan Harnad suggested that librarians are still thinking in terms of incoming "collections" and that they should be thinking about distributed access rather than local acquisitions.[252] The author/institutional archives, which he envisions eventually replacing the scholarly journal collection as we know it, will require skills such as helping researchers to self-archive, maintaining the archive, and assuring its continued interoperability, upgrading and preservation. He sees librarians assuming these roles.[253] What is the long-term role of the library as primary document provider? Are libraries moving toward institutional self-archiving of scholarly work? Libraries do appear to be moving in this direction through the distribution of their rare materials and manuscript archives. And some law libraries have begun to self-archive on library servers those journals that are distributed in electronic form only.[254]

In a response to Harnad's suggestion that librarians take on digital archiving as a major responsibility, David Goodman points out that in addition to selecting, buying, processing and conserving documents, librarians help users find documents. And even more, libraries help users figure out what documents they want to find.[255] This teaching function is unlikely to go away. To the contrary, teaching is likely to become increasingly more important, as users try to navigate through the vast and chaotic array of resources available to them.

Commercialization of Libraries

"Is it a problem that our libraries are emptier and emptier of students every evening?" Stanley Katz, a name familiar to scholars in law and history, explained his concerns as he sees universities turning to for-profit alliances to pay for ambitious digital programs. "Perhaps we should call ours the era of U-Portal.com or the university as portal." He expressed concern that "technology is being permitted to change libraries. The library as a place is less important than it used to be."[256]

Along these same lines, a more concrete look at how technology and the commercial world might shape the future is presented in an analysis of a new breed of information competitors.[257] Steven J. Bell identified two types of competitors that are challenging the library's position as the campus gateway to information: competitors that are internal to the organization, such as purveyors of course management software and campus portals; and the for-profit company that sells directly to faculty and students. WebCT is an example of a course management software that offers "passive" competition to the library.[258] In his scenario, faculty use WebCT to create links to the product vendor's non-library resources, including electronic journals, and channel students away from the library's information gateway.

XanEdu markets directly to faculty. Its databases include the ProQuest databases with journal articles, dissertations and more.[259] Questia Media bills itself as the world's largest online library and markets directly to students.[260] Its library contains over 50,000 digitized titles in the social sciences and humanities, including a collection of scholarly journals. On the other hand, perhaps librarians should not fret too much, yet, about these direct marketing threats. A recent article in the Houston Chronicle reported that layoffs have reduced Questia to a skeleton crew of about 28 workers, just enough to maintain its Web site. Since launching its online research and paper-writing service, Questia has had trouble signing up subscribers. With monthly subscriptions of $19.95, the company originally planned on as many as 100,000 users in its first year, but the numbers have been far below that.[261] His survey of academic library directors led Bell, who is an academic library director, to conclude that many directors were not familiar with these kinds of commercial products. He suggested several ways directors can better respond to the new commercial atmosphere.[262]

In yet another article about the future of the academic library in the world of commerce and profit-making, William Bowen sees two intersecting forces: the revolution in technology and the associated, but separate, increase in the reliance on the market to solve problems. Bowen posits that "digitalization" and "commercialization" are inevitably linked, and together are propelling the university into a new world. He urges libraries to take a middle ground, to beware of selling out to the commercial world, but also to recognize that projects such as JSTOR offer new opportunities. JSTOR, for example, offers the potential for both a centralized storage facility (at the same time, libraries can collaborate to store hard copies of journals in inexpensive regional centers) and enhanced access to the stored journal literature.[263]

The "Delegalization of the Law"–And Where Will It All End?

Findings such as that of Professors Schauer and Wise of a significant increase in nonlegal citations by the courts, when considered alongside the OhioLink "access trumps selection" data, suggest the future of legal scholarship itself may be undergoing a transformation. They found that the quantity of nonlegal citations began to grow in the early 1990s and that most of the growth came from citations to textbooks and academic journals in subjects such as economics, political science, sociology, psychology, and medicine.[264] They speculated that the availability of nonlegal references, specifically nonlegal journals, has led to greater use of these journals and to a breakdown in the line between legal and nonlegal information–what they call "the delegalization of the law." This delegalization may be changing how we think about the law itself. Clearly it is pushing law libraries to expand access to electronic journals and to consider ways to provide access to more informal communication–beyond the traditional law review. Who can say where this will end? Another quotation from Bob Berring, who was writing about who we are and where we are going, sums it up well. "We are making it up as we go. We are building the airplane as we fly. We are information buccaneers."[265]

DISCUSSION GROUPS

SERIALST (*Serials in Libraries Discussion Forum*) focuses on the technical aspects of serials. Topics include cataloging, acquisitions, collection management, serials budgets and pricing concerns, binding, preservation, microfilm and other non print serials media, union list activities, news, and job postings. <http://www.uvm.edu/~bmaclenn/serialst.html>.

NewJour, the New Journal and Newsletter Announcement List for new serials on the Internet is an outgrowth of the ARL directory project. *NewJour* provides a place to announce new electronic journals, and to announce the availability of paper titles in electronic format. *NewJour* also maintains a listserv with announcements of new titles. <http://gort.ucsd.edu/newjour/NewJourWel.html>.

ARL-EJOURNAL is a list concerned with the management of electronic journals. Issues include archiving, pricing, licensing, indexing, linking, and more. <http://www.cni.org/Hforums/arl-ejournal/about.html>.

VPIEJ-L is a discussion list for electronic publishing issues, especially those related to scholarly electronic journals. Topics include SGML, PostScript, and other e-journal formats; as well as software and hardware considerations. <http://scholar.lib.vt.edu/ejournals/vpiej-l.html>.

DIGITAL-COPYRIGHT listserv is hosted by the Center for Intellectual Property, and is for those interested in digital copyright and other intellectual property matters in higher education. <http://www.umuc.edu/distance/odell/cip/listserv.html>.

NOTES

1. Bernard J. Hibbitts, *Last Writes? Reassessing the Law Review in the Age of Cyberspace,* 71 N.Y.U. L. Rev. 615, 638-639 (1996) <http://www.law.pitt.edu/hibbitts/lastrev.htm>.

2. Memorandum from Carl Monk, American Association of Law Schools, to Deans of Member and Fee-Paid Schools and Directors of Law Libraries, *Electronic Access to Scholarship in Law Reviews* (March 20, 2001) (copy on file with the author).

3. *"Declaring Independence"* is published by SPARC and TRLN (Triangle Research Network Libraries), which includes the law libraries at Duke University, the University of North Carolina-Chapel Hill and North Carolina Central University. The Web site provides a discussion of how to evaluate alternative publishing options, checklists, and more. <http://www.arl.org/sparc/di/>.

4. Pamela Blum, *Discovering Electronic Serials: An Introduction*, in Managing Electronic Serials: Essays Based on the ALCTS Electronic Serials Institutes 1997-1999, v, (Pamela Blum, ed., Brad Eden, series ed. for the Serials Section of the Association for Library Collections & Technical Services), American Library Association (2001). These essays provide an excellent overview of the issues in electronic serials management.

5. Law reviews have been available on Westlaw and Lexis since the 1980s, although complete coverage really only dates from the mid-1990s. Over 550 journals are available on Lexis and over 700 on Westlaw. Many of these are overlapping titles, but not all. William H. Manz, *Floating "Free" in Cyberspace: Law Reviews in the Internet Era*, 74 St. John's L. Rev. 1069, 1086 (2000).

6. American law review subscriptions currently cost between $25.00 and $50.00 annually.

7. Ann Okerson, *The Electronic Journal: What, Whence, and When?* 2 The Public-Access Computer Systems Review (1) (1991). Based on a presentation given at the OCLC Users Council Annual Meeting in February 1991, available at: <http://www.library.yale.edu/~okerson/pacs.html>.

8. *Directory of Electronic Journals, Newsletters and Academic Discussion Lists*, (Ann Okerson, ed., Association of Research Libraries 1991+). The Association of Research Libraries is a not-for-profit organization of over 120 major research libraries in North America. For information about ARL, see <http://www.arl.org/>.

9. Dru Mogge, *Seven Years of Tracking Electronic Publishing: The ARL Directory of Electronic Journals, Newsletters and Academic Discussion Lists*, originally published in 17 Library Hi Tech (1) 17 (1999). Available at <http://dsej.arl.org/dsej/2000/mogge.html>.

10. Judy Luther, *Full Text Journal Subscriptions: An Evolutionary Process*, 9 Against the Grain (3) 18, 20, 22, 24 (June 1997); available at: <http://db.arl.org/luther.html>.

11. A recent announcement on the *Directory* Web page announced that the 2000 paper version is the last to be published, and the electronic version will no longer be updated as of January 2002. <http://dsej.arl.org/info.html>.

12. Kathleen Born & Lee Van Orsdel, *Periodical Price Survey 2001: Searching for Serials Utopia*, Library Journal, 53 (April 15, 2001).

13. For Oxford Press, see their listings at <http://www3.oup.co.uk/jnls/fields/law/online.html>; for information about Kluwer go to <http://www.wkap.nl/journal/>.

14. Frederick J. Friend, *Keeping Your Head in a Revolution*, 5 JEP: The Journal of Electronic Publishing March (3) (2000) <http://www.press.umich.edu/jep/05-03/friend.html>.

15. Alison Buckholtz, *Declaring Independence: Returning Scientific Publishing to Scientists*, 7 JEP: the Journal of Electronic Publishing (1) <http://www.press.umich.edu/jep/07-01/buckholtz.html>.

16. Penny A. Hazelton, *How Much of Your Print Collection Is Really on WESTLAW or LEXIS-NEXIS?* 18 Leg. Ref. Servs. Q. 3 (1999).

17. For comments about Hein-OnLine in the law firm setting, see an article by a firm librarian in which he discussed space savings as a prime reason his firm subscribes to this electronic legal periodicals project. James W. Shelar, *Hein-On-Line*, LLRX.com (September 3, 2001) <http://www.llrx.com/features/heinonline.htm>.

18. William G. Bowen, *The Academic Library In A Digitized, Commercialized Age: Lessons From JSTOR* (January 14, 2001), based on Romanes Lecture delivered at Oxford University, October 17, 2000 <http://www.jstor.org/about/bowen.html>.

19. John Webb in Alison Buckholtz, *Electronic Genesis: The creation of E-Journals in the Sciences* originally published in ACADEME, 65. 65-68 (Sept.-Oct. 1999) and reprinted with permission <http://dsej.arl.org/dsej/2000/buckholtz.html>.

20. Carol Hansen Montgomery, *Measuring the Impact of an Electronic Journal Collection on Library Costs: A Framework and Preliminary Observations*, 6 D-Lib Magazine (10) (October 2000) <http://www.dlib.org/dlib/october00/montgomery/10montgomery.html>.

21. David H. Morse & William A. Clintworth, *Comparing Patterns of Print and Electronic Journal Use in an Academic Health Science Library* 28 Issues in Science and Technology Librarianship (Fall 2000) <http://www.library.ucsb.edu/istl//00-fall/>.

22. Suzanne D. Gyeszly, *Electronic Or Paper Journals? Budgetary, Collection Development, And User Satisfaction Questions*, 20 Collection Building (1) 5 (2001).

23. Tom Sanville, *A Method Out of the Madness: Ohiolink's Collaborative Response to the Serials Crisis, Three Years Later-Progress Report.* Paper presented at the North American Serials Interest Group Conference, University of California, San Diego (June 22-25, 2000), in Judy Luther, *White Paper on Electronic Journal Usage Statistics*, 6 JEP: the Journal of Electronic Publishing (3) (Mar. 2001) The Council on Library and Information Resources (October 2000) <http://www.press.umich.edu/jep/06-03/luther.html.>. OhioLINK (Ohio Library and Information Network) is a consortium of Ohio's college and university libraries and the state library of Ohio <http://www.ohiolink.edu/>.

24. David Kohl, Speech, *What If What We Know Isn't True?* NELINET Conference on E-Books & E-Journals, (May 21-22, 2001). (Notes on file with the author).

25. Frederick J. Friend, *Keeping Your Head in a Revolution*, 5 JEP: The Journal of Electronic Publishing (3) (Mar. 2000) <http://www.press.umich.edu/jep/05-03/friend.html>.

26. Bo-Christer Bjork & Ziga Turk, *How Scientists Retrieve Publications: An Empirical Study of How the Internet is Overtaking Paper Media*, 6 JEP: the Journal of Electronic Publishing (2) (Jun. 2000) <http//www.press.umich.edu/jep/06-02/bjork.html>. Although traditional paper journals and conference proceedings still accounted for the majority of publications respondents retrieved, downloading of free materials, retrieved "haphazardly" on the home pages of authors or their institutions was a reported choice. The main drawback to this, of course, is that the materials are not effi-

ciently indexed. Retrieval usually was a result of a citation elsewhere. In effect, the researchers were side-stepping paying for "official versions."

27. Gary J. Bravy & K. Celeste Feather, *The Impact of Electronic Access on Basic Library Services: One Academic Law Library's Experiences*, 93 L. Lib. J. 261, 266 (2001).

28. S. Blair Kauffman, Rededication Symposia: *Evolving Technology and Law Library Planning: Technology and Law Library Design*, 70 St. John's L. Rev. 163, 167-168 (1996).

29. Bravy & Feather, *supra*, n. 28 at 267.

30. Ray English & Larry Hardesty, *Shaping The Future Of Scholarly Journal Publishing*, College and Research Library News, Association of College & Research Libraries (May 2000) <http://www.ala.org/acrl/scholarlycomm.html>. Its size increased somewhat, but not enough to account for the price increase. The most significant difference is that a large commercial publisher purchased the journal in 1990. Since then, the price has gone up relentlessly.

31. Ann Okerson, *Periodical Prices: A History And Discussion, Advances in Serials Management*, 1 JAI Press 101 (Nov. 1986) <http://www.library.yale.edu/~okerson/pricing.html>.

32. *Id.*

33. Robert C. Berring, *Symposium On Law In The Twentieth Century: Legal Information And The Search For Cognitive Authority*, 88 Calif. L. Rev. 1673, 1687 (2000).

34. 208 U.S. 412 (1908).

35. 347 U.S. 412 (1954).

36. Frederick Schauer & Virginia J. Wise, *Interpreting Legal Citations: A Symposium Sponsored by the West Group: Nonlegal Information and the Delegalization of Law*, 29 J. Leg. Stud. 495 (2000).

37. Mark Estes, *Case Sensitive: Law Librarians Adapt to Net Expectations*, Library Journal 44 (Jul. 1998).

38. Henry H. Barschall, *The Cost of Physics Journals*, 39 Physics Today (12) 34, 34-36 (Dec. 1986). See also his follow-up study reported in Henry H. Barschall, *The Cost-Effectiveness of Physics Journals*, 41 Physics Today (7) 56, 56-58 (Jul. 1988); see also: Henry H. Barschall and J. R. Arrington, *Cost of Physics Journals: A Survey*, 33 Bulletin of the American Physical Society (7) 1437, 1447 (Jul./Aug. 1988).

39. Barschall, *Cost-Effectiveness of Physics Journals, supra*, n. 38 at 57.

40. For more on the law suit and a discussion of a 1998 follow-up study by the University Library, see *Measuring the Cost Effectiveness of Journals: The Wisconsin Experience* <http://www.arl.org/newsltr/205/>.

41. <http://www.library.wisc.edu/projects/glsdo/cost.html>.

42. The survey is available at <http://www.arl.org/sparc/di/appendixA.html>.

43. English & Hardesty, *supra* n. 30.

44. There is another indicator: the profit margins of commercial publishers of scholarly information are estimated to run as high as 40% per year. Sometimes they are even higher. English & Hardesty, *supra* n. 30.

45. <http://www.lib.unc.edu/prices/>.

46. Schauer & Wise, *supra* n. 36, at 511.

47. Brendan J. Wyly, *Competition in Scholarly Publishing? What Publisher Profits Reveal*, ARL Bimonthly Report 200 (Oct. 1998) <http://www.arl.org/newsltr/200/wyly.html>.

48. Association of Research Libraries, the Association of American Libraries, and the Pew Higher Education Roundtable, Institute for Research on Higher Education, Special Issue, *To Publish and Perish*, 7 Policy Perspectives (4) (Mar. 1998) <http://www.arl.org/scomm/pew/pewrept.html>.

49. The Cornell report is available at <http://www.arl.org/newsltr/205/cornell.html>.

50. Mark J. McCabe, *The Impact of Publisher Mergers on Journal Prices: A Preliminary Report*, ARL: Bimonthly Report 200 (Oct. 1998) <http://www.arl.org/newsltr/200/mccabe.html>; and *The Impact of Publisher Mergers on Journal Prices: An Update*, ARL Bimonthly Report 207 (Dec. 1999) <http://www.arl.org/newsltr/207/jrnlprices.html>. Descriptive data on nonprofit publishers in the biomedical field indicated that in 1998 the average nonprofit journal provided one and one-half times the number of papers with four times the number of citations for less than one-half the cost of commercial titles. Regardless of the explanations and implications, the two modes of publishing behaved very differently.

51. For merger activity in law publishing, see the list originally compiled by Rob Richards of the University of Colorado, *A Legal Publishers' List: Corporate Affiliations of Legal Publishers.* Maintenance has been assumed by CRIV (Committee on Relations with Information Vendors) of the American Association of Law Libraries <http://www.aallnet.org/committee/criv/resources/tools/list>.

52. McCabe, *supra* n. 50.

53. *Id.*

54. Kathleen Born & Lee Van Orsdel, *41st Annual Report Periodical Price Survey 2001: Searching for Serials Utopia*, Library Journal 53, 53-58 (Apr. 15, 2001). The data was derived from analysis of over 6,000 titles included in the three key Institute for Scientific Information (ISI) citation indexes.

55. <http://www.greenhousegrows.com/id49.htm>.

56. Montgomery, *supra* n. 20.

57. Marilyn Geller, *Serials Pricing Update–The Real Cost and Price of Ejournals*, 13 Against the Grain (2) 82, 82-84 (Jun. 2001).

58. *The Impact of Serial Costs on Library Collections.* ARL Bimonthly Report 218 (Oct. 2001) <http://www.arl.org/newsltr/218/costimpact.html>; see also, the accompanying graph: *Monograph and Serial Costs in ARL Libraries, 1986-2000.*

59. *Id.*

60. *Overview of the Issues: Scholars Under Siege: The Scholarly Communication Crisis*, Create Change, sponsored by Association of Research Libraries, Association of College and Research Libraries, and SPARC (2000) <http://www.createchange.org/librarians/issues/quick.html>.

61. Fred Rodell, *Goodbye to Law Reviews*, 23 Va. L. Rev. 38 (1936-37); see also, Fred Rodell, *Goodbye to Law Reviews–Revisited*, 48 Va. L. Rev. 279 (1962) in which he updated his critique and explained why things hadn't changed in twenty years.

62. Bernard J. Hibbits, *Last Writes? Re-Assessing the Law Review in the Age of Cyberspace*, 71 N.Y.U. L. Rev. 615, 687-888 (1996), revised from self-published online document <http://www.law.pitt.edu/hibbitts/lastrev.html>. For Hibbitts response to his critics and to his proposal for self-publishing, see Bernard J. Hibbitts, *Yesterday Once More: Skeptics, Scribes and the Demise of Law Reviews* 30 Akron Law Review 267 (Special Issue 1996) <http://www.law.pitt.edu/hibbitts/akron.htm>. For an extended review of the issues over the years, see *Last Writes?* 629-640.

63. Lawrence M. Friedman, *Law Reviews and Legal Scholarship: Some Comments*, 75 Denv. U. L. Rev. 661, 662 (1998).

64. Hibbitts, *Last Writes?, supra* n. 62.
65. Hibbitts, *Last Writes?, supra* n. 62 at 660, 685.
66. Hibbitts, *Yesterday Once More, supra* n. 62.
67. Hibbitts, *Last Writes?, supra* n. 62 at 668-669.
68. Howard A. Denemark, *The Death of the Law Reviews Has Been Predicted: What Might Be Lost When the Last Law Review Shuts Down?* 27 Seton Hall L. Rev. 1, 11-12 (1996).
69. *Id.* at 11.
70. Shawn G. Pearson, *Hype or Hypertext? A Plan for the Law Review to Move into the Twenty-First Century*, 1997 Utah L. Rev. 765, 796-798; See also, Archie Zariski, *Never Ending, Still Beginning: A Defense of Electronic Law Journals from the Perspective of the E Law Experience*, 2 First Monday (6) (Jun. 1997) <http://www.firstmonday.dk/issues/issue2_6/zariski/index.html>.
71. Manz, *supra* n. 5 at 1080.
72. *Id.* at 1070.
73. Hibbitts, *supra* n. 62.
74. Hibbitts, *supra* n. 62 at 687.
75. Henry H. Perritt, *The Law Review is Changing the Face of American Law Schools*, 33 Ind. L. Rev. 253, 258 (1999).
76. For more on the history of the journal as a means for scholarly communication, and an overview of how scholars and librarians reached a crisis situation, see Richard K. Johnson, *A Question of Access: SPARC: BioOne, and Society-Driven Electronic Publishing*, 6 D-Lib Magazine (5) (May 2000) <http://www.dlib.org/>; and also Jean-Claude Guédon, *Beyond Core Journals and Licenses: The Paths to Reform Scientific Publishing*, ARL Bimonthly Report 218 (Oct. 2001) <http://www.arl.org/newsltr/218/guedon.html>.
77. Vannevar Bush, *As We May Think*, 176 The Atlantic Monthly 101 (July 1945).
78. Stevan Harnad, *Scholarly Skywriting and the Prepublication Continuum of Scientific Inquiry*, 1 Psychological Science 342, 342-343 (1991) <http://www.cogsci.soton.ac.uk/~harnad/Papers/Harnad/harnad90.skywriting.html>.
79. E-print has been defined to refer to any paper published in an electronic archive, "pre-print" refers to papers that have not been formally published elsewhere; "post-print" refers to electronically archived versions of articles that have been published elsewhere. Richard, A. Danner, *Electronic Publication of Scholarly Information in Law: A View from the United States*, 28 Intl. J. Leg. Infor. (2000). and 465-482.
80. Jean-Claude Guédon, *supra* n. 76.
81. Project Muse provides the full text of scholarly journals, primarily in the humanities, social sciences and mathematics <http://muse.jhu.edu/>; JSTOR provides full-text journals, primarily in non-scientific subjects <http://www.jstor.org/>; SPARC is an alliance of research institutions, libraries and publishers primarily in the science, technical, and medical (STM) fields <http://www.arl.org/sparc/home/index.asp?page=0>.
82. <http://highwire.stanford.edu/>.
83. Buckholtz, *supra* n. 15.
84. To learn more, visit the Create Change Web site at <http://www.createchange.org/>.
85. Hak Joon Kim, *The Transition from Paper to Electronic Journals: Key Factors That Affect Scholars' Acceptance of Electronic Journals*, 41 The Serials Librarian (1) 31 (2001); see also Jean-Claude Guédon, *supra* n. 76.
86. Danner, *supra* n. 79 at 482.

87. Danner, *supra* n. 79.

88. JURIST: The Legal Education Network <http://jurist.law.pitt.edu/>.

89. Legal Scholarship Network <http://www.ssrn.com/lsn/>.

90. Mogge, *supra* n. 9.

91. Donnelyn Curtis, Virginia M. Scheschy & Adolofo R. Tarango, *Developing and Managing Electronic Journal Collections: A How-To-Do-It Manual for Librarians.* (Neal-Schuman Publishers 2000). This basic manual provides a good introduction to acquiring and accessing electronic journals.

92. *The Bluebook: A Uniform System of Citation* (17th ed., Columbia Law Review Association, Harvard Law Review Association, The University of Pennsylvania Law Review & the Yale Law Journal 2000). Rule 18 generally covers the citation format for law periodicals.

93. Hein-On-Line provides access both in PDF and digitally.

94. AALL Professional Development: Expanding Your Horizons, *New Perspectives on Law Library Acquisitions and Collection Development*, Washington College of Law Library, American University, November 2 and 3, 2001, Washington, DC.

95. Karen Silber, *Every Library is Special and So Is Its Collection Development Policy: A Desktop Learning Opportunity*, 4 AALL Spectrum 10 (Dec. 1999).

96. Jennifer Weintraub, *The Development and Use of a Genre Statement for Electronic Journals in the Sciences*, Issues in Science and Technology Librarianship (17) (Winter 1998) <http://www.library.ucsb.edu/istl/98-winter/article5.html>.

97. Lila A. Faulkner & Karla L. Hahn, *Selecting Electronic Publications: The Development of a Genre Statement*, Issues in Science and Technology Librarianship (Spring 2001) <http://www.library.ucsb.edu/istl/01-spring/article1.html>.

98. *Boston University Law Library Electronic Resources Selection Policy* <http://www.bu.edu/lawlibrary/tech/procedures/epolicy.htm>; and *University of Minnesota Law Library Collection Development Policy for Electronic Resources* <http://www.law.umn.edu/library/ts/EResCDPolicy.htm>.

99. lawlibdir-l is a closed listserv for academic law library directors. This message is on file with the author.

100. *Law Library Collection Development Policies: Policy Documents and Resources* Rob Richards comp., (2000) <http://www.colorado.edu/Law/lawlib/ts/aall/policies.htm>.

101. George Machovec, *Management and Technical Considerations for Acquiring and Accessing Electronic Serials* in Managing Electronic Serials, *supra* n. 4 at 67.

102. John Blosser et al., *Aggregator Services Evaluation: Not an Easy Comparison*, 41 The Serials Librarian (1) 65, 78 (2001).

103. *Id.* at 76.

104. Carol Tenopir, Gayle Baker & William Robinson, *Racing at Full Speed*, Library Journal 45, 45-58 (May 15, 2001).

105. Machovec, *supra* n. 4 at 72.

106. Geller, *supra* n. 57.

107. Larry Krumenker, *The Continuing Adventures of Scholarly Jones*, 9 Internet/Web/Online Service Information, Searcher (6) 44 (2001).

108. Lisa Guernsey, *California State U. Tries to Create a New Way to Buy On-line Journals*, The Chronicle of Higher Education (Jan. 22, 1999); Lawrence Biemiller, *New Model for Journal Subscriptions Becomes a Reality at Cal. State U.*, The Chronicle of Higher Education (July 2, 1999).

109. E-mail from Jan Velterop, to Liblicense listserv, *Re: License restrictions* (Nov. 11, 2001).

110. Jeffrey R. Young, *Publisher of Free Online Science Journals Will Charge Authors a "Processing Fee,"* (Dec. 21, 2001) <http://chronicle.com/daily/2001/12/2001122101t.htm>. The address for BioMed Central is <http://www.biomedcentral.com/>.

111. E-mail from Ann Okerson to Liblicense listserv, *More about BioMed* (Jan. 11, 2002).

112. Scott Carlson, *Elsevier Offers Electronic Only Option for Journal Subscribers*, (Jan. 22, 2002) available at: <http://chronicle.com/free/2002/01/2002012102t.htm> Chronicle Online.

113. *Statement of Current Perspective and Preferred Practices for the Selection and Purchase of Electronic Information* <http://www.library.yale.edu/consortia/statement.html>; and *Statement of Current Perspective and Preferred Practices for the Selection and Purchase of Electronic Information: Update No. 1: New Developments In E-Journal Licensing* (December 2001 update to March 1998 Statement) <http://www.library.yale.edu/consortia/2001currentpractices.htm> (accessed Jan. 21, 2002).

114. PCC Standing Committee on Automation, Task Group on Journals in Aggregator databases, *Final Report* (Jan, 2000) <www.lcweb.loc.gov/catdir/pcc/aggfinal.html> (accessed Jan. 14, 2002).

115. Born & Van Orsdel, *supra* n. 12.

116. Project Muse is a non-profit project begun in 1995 by the Johns Hopkins University Press and Eisenhower Library at Johns Hopkins University to offer the full text of scholarly journals via the Web. Holdings include journals in history, politics, economics, literature, and other humanities and social science fields. Information at: <http://muse.jhu.edu/muse.html>.

117. Legal periodicals are available on Lexis-Nexis and Westlaw from 2-4 months after the print copy is published. Hazelton, *supra* n. 16 at 10. Kevin M. Guthrie, *Challenges and Opportunities Presented by Archiving in the Electronic Era*, portal: Libraries and the Academy 1.2 (2001) 121-128 at 126 <http://muse.jhu.edu/journals/portal_libraries_and_the_academy/v001/1.2guthrie.html>.

118. Diane Klaiber, *The Time Is Now for a National Law Library Consortium*, 20 Leg. Ref. Servs. Q. (3) 3, 3-11 (2001).

119. <http://www.solinet.net/Default.htm>.

120. Klaiber, *supra* n. 118 at 5.

121. JoAnn Hounshell, *supra* n. 94.

122. Kenneth Frazier, *The Librarians' Dilemma: Contemplating the Costs of the "Big Deal,"* 7 D-Lib Magazine (3) (Mar. 2001) <http://www.dlib.org/dlib/march01/frazier/03frazier.html>.

123. *Id.*

124. Jonathan Nabe, *E-Journal Bundling and Its Impact on Academic Libraries: Some Early Results*, Issues in Science & Technology Librarianship, (30) (Spring 2001) <http://www.istl.org/istl/01-spring/article3.html>.

125. <http://www.library.yale.edu/~llicense/intro.shtml>, paragraph 3 (accessed Feb. 25, 2002).

126. E-mail from Rollo Turner to Liblicense listserv, *Code of Practice for Electronic Journal Renewals* (Dec.12, 2001).

127. The *Nature* debate, which centered on the dissemination of scientific information, has been the subject of an online forum. See <http://www.nature.com/nature/debates/e-access/introduction.html> (accessed Feb. 14, 2002).
128. <http://www.arl.org/scomm/licensing/principles.html> (accessed Feb. 20, 2002).
129. <http://www.arl.org/scomm/licensing/licbooklet.html> (accessed Feb. 20. 2002).
130. Faye A. Chadwell, *A License to Kill For*. . . in Managing Electronic Serials, *supra* n. 4 at 109.
131. Chadwell, *supra,* n. 4 at 125-128.
132. Remarks of Representative Dingell discussing the then-proposed DMCA, 144 *Cong. Rec.* H7099 (daily ed. Aug. 4, 1998), as reproduced in Sarah E. Sully, *How Intellectual Property Laws Affecting Libraries Are Changing*, in Managing Electronic Serials, *supra* n. 4 at 102.
133. *Id.*
134. *Id.* at 95.
135. Robert L. Oakley, Keynote Address at the First Library Affairs Symposium on Information Issues, *From Free Public Libraries to Pay Per View: Copyright and Access to Information in the Digital Age*, Southern Illinois University (1998), reproduced at <http://www.ll.georgetown.edu/aallwash/copyedu.html>.
136. Sully, *supra* n. 132 at 102-103.
137. Rick Boucher, *Time to rewrite the DMCA* (Jan. 29, 2002) <http://news.com.com/2010-1078-825335.html>.
138. Arnold P. Lutzker, <http://www.ll.georgetown.edu/aallwash/rep0399.html> (accessed Jan. 21, 2002).
139. Sully, *supra*, n. 132 at 95-108.
140. <http://www.ll.georgetown.edu/aallwash/UCITA2.html> (accessed Jan. 21, 2002).
141. AFFECT, Americans for Fair Electronic Commerce Transactions, is a broad-based coalition whose members include AALL <http://www.ll.georgetown.edu/aallwash/st01042002.html> (accessed Jan. 21, 2002).
142. Laura N. Gasaway, *Academic Law Library Statistics: Academic Law Library Statistics: 1876-1992*, 84 L. Lib. J. 573, 582 (1992).
143. David Flaxbart, *Collection Development in the Internet Age*, introductory remarks to special issue of Issues in Science and Technology Librarianship (30) (Spring 2001) <http://www.istl.org/istl/01-spring/intro.html>.
144. E-mail from Nancy Cowden, and various responses to LAW-ACQ *Statistical information requested* (Feb. 2, 2002) (copies on file with the author).
145. E-mail from Erica McKessy to author (Dec. 17, 2001) (copy on file with the author).
146. Johann van Reenen, *Library Budgets and Academic Library Rankings in Times of Transition*, 14 The Bottom Line: Managing Library Finances, (4), 213 (2001).
147. The ARL *New Measures* Initiative site links to several articles on this subject. <http://www.arl.org/stats/newmeas/newmeas.html> (accessed Feb. 25, 2002).
148. Judy Luther, *White Paper on Electronic Journal Usage Statistics*, 6 JED the Journal of Electronic Publishing (3) (Mar. 2001) <http://www.press.umich.edu/jep/06-03/luther.html>; copyright The Council on Library and Information Resources, (October 2000). Republished with permission.
149. *Id.*
150. ICOLC is an informal, self-organized group of over 160 library consortia <http://www.library.yale.edu/consortia/> (accessed Jan. 21, 2002).

151. *Guidelines for Statistical Measures of Usage of Web-based Information Resources* (Dec. 2001 revision of original Nov. 1998 Guidelines) at <http://www.library.yale.edu/consortia/2001webstats.htm> (accessed Jan. 21, 2002).

152. PALS, the Publishers and Libraries Solutions group of JISC, the PA, and ALPSP <http://www.usagestats.org/> (accessed Jan. 21, 2002).

153. Sarah E. Thomas, *The Catalog as Portal to the Internet*, (Final version, Dec. 2000) <http://www.loc.gov/catdir/bibcontrol/thomas_paper.html>.

154. *Id.*

155. Messages posted to the list are archived and available through the AALL Web site <http://www.aallnet.org/prodev/listser.asp> (accessed Feb. 6, 2002).

156. Karen Selden, *Linking Globally, Coping Locally: Cataloging Internet Resources at the University of Colorado Law Library*, 92 L. Lib. J. 439 (2000). For a discussion of single versus multiple records approaches, 444-446.

157. <http://washburnlaw.edu/heinonline/> (accessed Feb. 21, 2002).

158. Wayne Jones, *More Than One Record*, 41 The Serials Librarian (1) 17, 17-20 (2001).

159. Hope Breeze, *Cataloging Remote Electronic Resources*, 92 L. Lib. J. 91 (2000).

160. Selden, *supra* n.157.

161. Learn more about CORC at <http://www.oclc.org/corc/about/> (accessed Jan. 21, 2001).

162. Canadian Library Association & American Library Association, *Anglo-American Cataloguing Rules*, 8 (2d ed., 1998 rev.).

163. Regina Romano Reynolds, *Seriality and the Web*, in Managing Electronic Serials, *supra* n. 4 at 1-2.

164. Reynolds in Managing Electronic Serials, *supra* n. 4 at 4-8.

165. Anne J. Gilliland-Swetlanc, *Setting the Stage: Introduction to Metadata* <http://www.getty.edu/research/institute/standards/intrometadata/2_articles/index.html> (accessed Mar. 3, 2002).

166. <http://dublincore.org/> (accessed Mar. 3, 2002).

167. Carl Lagoze, *Keeping Dublin Core Simple: Cross-Domain Discovery or Resource Description?* 7 D-Lib Magazine (1) (Jan. 2001) <http://www.dlib.org/>; see also, Stuart L. Weibel & Traugott Koch, *The Dublin Core Metadata Initiative: Mission, Current Activities and Future Directions*, 6 D-Lib Magazine (12) (Dec. 2000) <http://www.dlib.org/>.

168. Breeze, *supra* n. 159 at 93.

169. John Willinsky & Larry Wolfson, *The Indexing of Scholarly Journals: A Tipping Point for Publishing Reform?* 7 JEP the Journal of Electronic Publishing (2) (Dec. 2001) <http://www.press.umich.edu/jep/>.

170. Nathalie Schulz, *E-Journal Databases: A Long-Term Solution?* 25 Library Collections, Acquisitions, & Technical Services 449, 449-459 (2001). This article is a discussion of various databases available to manage electronic journals.

171. Serial Solutions <http://www.serialssolutions.com/Home.asp>. See, for example, <http://www.bc.edu/libraries/resources/ejournals/a-z/s-indexb/>.

172. E-mail from Theresa Lyman to author and other members of Boston College Electronic Collections Services Committee (Feb. 1, 2002) (copy on file with the author).

173. For Harvard go to e-resources at <http://lib.harvard.edu/e-resources/subject/index.html> (accessed Mar. 3, 2002). For VERA, try a Web search for "VERA and MIT"–this address seems to change frequently.

174. Schulz, *supra* n. 170. JAKE is available at <http://jake-db.org/>.

175. <http://www.traffick.com/> (accessed Mar. 4, 2002).

176. Sarah E. Thomas, *Abundance, Attention, and Access: Of Portals and Catalogs*, ARL Bimonthly Report 212 (2000) <http://www.arl.org/newsltr/212/portal.html>.

177. Examples of law periodical portals include FindLaw's University Law Review Project, where subscribers can choose from over 30 subjects <http://www.lawreview.org/>; Hieros Gamos <http://www.hg.org/hg.html>; and *Contents Pages from Law Reviews and Other Scholarly Journals,* Tarlton Law Library, University of Texas School of Law <http://www.tarlton.law.utexas.edu/tallons/content_search.html> (accessed Mar. 3, 2002).

178. To see a MyLibrary site, visit North Carolina State University Library at <http://my.lib.ncsu.edu/>, or Cornell at <http://mylibrary.cornell.edu/> (accessed Mar. 3, 2002).

179. Los Alamos National Laboratory at <http://lib-www.lanl.gov/lww/mylibweb.htm>. See also, MyLibrary at Cornell at <http://mylibrary.cornell.edu/>.

180. <http://www.aleph.co.il/metalib/> (accessed Mar. 3, 2002).

181. <http://encompass.endinfosys.com> (accessed Mar. 3, 2002).

182. Jerry D. Campbell, *The Case for Creating a Scholars Portal to the Web: A White Paper*, ARL Bimonthly Report 211 (Aug. 2000) <http://www.arl.org/newsltr/211/portal.html>.

183. E-mail from James Mouw, University of Chicago, Head of Serials, to Liblicense *ALA Program on Linking* (Jan. 7, 2002).

184. <http://purl.oclc.org/>. (accessed Feb. 19, 2002).

185. PubMed is an example of a database with identifiers. In PubMed the identifier retrieves the index record and the index record contains a link to the full text of the article. PubMed, however, is a closed system that only works for articles in its own PubMed database <http://www.pubmedcentral.nih.gov/> (accessed Feb. 19, 2002).

186. Metadata literally is "data about data." Library metadata includes indexes, abstracts, and catalog records created according to cataloging rules and structural and content standards such as MARC, as well as authority forms such as LCSH (Library of Congress Subject Headings). An Internet resource provider might use metadata to refer to information being encoded into HTML metatags to make a Web site easier to find. Metadata can be supplied by a person, created automatically by a computer and ferreted out by a relationship to another resource, such as a hyperlink. Metadata can make it possible to search across repositories, but only if the metadata is the same or can be mapped across each site.

187. Pricilla Caplan, *Reference Linking for Journal Articles: Promise, Progress and Perils*, 1 portals Libraries and the Academy (3) 351, 351-356 (2001); Helen Atkins et al., *Reference Linking with DOIs: A Case Study*, 6 D-Lib Magazine (2) (Feb. 2000) <http://www.dlib.org/>.

188. Sully, *supra* n. 132.

189. DOI Foundation. For more information, see the Web site at <http://www.DOI.org> (accessed Feb.19, 2002).

190. Sully, *supra* n. 132 at 100.

191. <http://www.contentdirections.com/DOI-EB-Demo/mhindex.htm> (accessed Mar. 5, 2002).

192. Amy Brand, *CrossRef Turns One*, 7 D-Lib Magazine (5) (May 2001) <http://www.dlib.org/dlib/may01/brand/05brand.html> and the CrossRef Web site at <http://www.crossref.org>.

193. For more on Open URLs, see <http://www.umuc.edu/distance/odell/cip/listserv.html>. NISO, the National Information Standards Organization, a non-profit association accredited by the American National Standards Institute (ANSI), identifies, develops, maintains, and publishes Open URL standards.
194. Information about the Bath Profile is available at <http://www.nlc-bnc.ca/bath/> (accessed Feb. 20, 2002).
195. Ulla de Stricker, *Keep Me Posted . . . But Not Too Much: Challenges and Opportunities for STM Current Awareness Providers*, 10 Information Today (1) 52 (Jan. 1, 2002).
196. University Law Review Project and Tarlton TOC, *supra* n. 177. *Employment Law Memo* and its sister publication *NLRM Memo* include articles as well as summaries of decisions and recent developments <http://www.LawMemo.Com/default.htm>. SmartCLIP is a fee-based service that provides automated personalized e-mail delivery of the *Current Index to Legal Periodicals*, University of Washington Law Library <http://lib.law.washington.edu/cilp/scilp.html> (accessed Mar. 3, 2002).
197. de Stricker, *supra* n. 195.
198. J. Cox, *Model Generic Licensees: Co-operation and Competition*, 26 Serials Review (1) 3, 3-9 (2000) cited in Janet Brennan Croft, *Model Licenses And Interlibrary Loan/Document Delivery From Electronic Resources*, 29 Interlending & Document Supply Journal (4) 165 (2001).
199. Croft, *Id.* at 168.
200. Create Change, *Scholars Under Siege: The Scholarly Communication Crisis* (Aug 11, 2000) <http://www.createchange.org/librarians/issues/silent.html#WhereNow>.
201. Mary E. Jackson, *Research Library Interlibrary Lending: An Isolated Drop or the Beginning of a Trend?* ARL Bimonthly Report 211 (Aug. 2000) <http://www.arl.org/newsltr/211/ill.html>.
202. Pamela Bluh, *Striking a Balance: Document Delivery in the Nineties*, 85 L. Lib. J. 599 (1993).
203. Dennis Krieb, *You Can't Get There From Here: Issues in Remote Access to Electronic Journals for a Health Sciences Library*, Issues in Science and Technology Librarianship (Spring 1999) <http:///www.library.ucsb.edu/istl/99-spring/article3.html>.
204. Perpetual access has been defined as the ability to continue to retrieve articles from the storehouse maintained by the publisher or a designated agent. Sharon Cline McKay, *Managing Electronic Serials: An Overview* in Managing Electronic Serials, *supra* n. 4 at 64.
205. Berring, *supra* n. 33 at 1682.
206. Dale Flecker, *Preserving Scholarly e-Journals*, 7 D-Lib Magazine (9) (Sept. 2001) <www.dlib.org/dlib/september01/flecker/09flecker.html>.
207. ARL, Principle 10 <http://www.arl.org/scomm/licensing/principles.html> (accessed Feb. 20, 2002).
208. Kevin M. Guthrie, *Challenges and Opportunities Presented by Archiving in the Electronic Era*, portal: Libraries and the Academy (1.2) (Apr. 2001) <http://muse.jhu.edu/journals/portal_libraries_and_the_academy/v001/1.2guthrie.html>.
209. Timothy D. Jewell, *Selection and Presentation of Commercially Available Electronic Resources: Issues and Practices*, 24 Council of Library and Information Resources, Digital Library Federation, (2001).
210. Guthrie, *supra* n. 208.
211. <http://www.diglib.org/preserve/criteria.htm> (accessed Feb. 20, 2002).

212. Yale, Harvard and the University of Pennsylvania are working with individual private publishers on archiving the range of their e-journals; Cornell and New York Public Library are working on archiving journals in specific subject areas. MIT is working on archiving "dynamic" journals that change often. Flecker, *supra* n. 206.

213. LOCKSS: (Lots of Copies Keep Stuff Safe) is open-source software, described as the digital equivalent of the library stack, which is designed to run Web caches for journals and collect and preserve the content. For an article about LOCKSS see <http://dlib.org/dlib/june01/reich/06reich.html>. Up to date project status is available at: <http://lockss.stanford.edu/projectstatus.html> (accessed Feb. 20, 2002).

214. Fletcher, *supra* n. 208.

215. Harvard University Library, Office for Information Systems, E-Journal Archiving Project, *E-Journal Archive DTD Feasibility Study*, report prepared by Inera Inc. (Dec. 5, 2001) <http://www.diglib.org/preserve/hadtdfs.pdf>.

216. American Association of Law Libraries, Strategic Direction 4, Outcome C: Historical legal materials are preserved and accessible, c(3) AALL is to "support librarians and publishers in efforts to build consortia for preservation of historical electronic and print materials" <http://www.aallnet.org/about/strategic_plan.asp>.

217. *supra*, n. 2.

218. A. Hayes Butler, *Co-operative Collection Development Programs in Law Libraries: Barriers and Benefits*, 20 Leg. Ref. Servs. Q. (3) 13, 22-23 (2001).

219. Danner, *supra* n. 79 at 478-482.

220. *The Bluebook*, *supra* n. 92.

221. If only the Internet is accessed, provide both traditional and Internet citations with no explanatory phrase; if the print source is obscure and citation to the electronic source will substantially improve access, provide a parallel cite to the electronic source "available at," for materials available only on the Internet, such as on-line journals, use "at." The rule details how to handle dates, pin point citations, changed URLs and more.

222. Association of Legal Writing Directors and Darby Dickerson, *ALWD Citation Manual: A Professional System of Citation* (Aspen Law and Business 2000). See Rule 38.2 for general information about online formats, rule 39 for Lexis-Nexis and Westlaw, and rule 40 for Web sites.

223. Carol M. Bast & Susan Harrell, *Has the Bluebook Met Its Match? The ALWD Citation Manual*, 92 L. Lib. J. 337, 352 (2000).

224. Beginning with volume 92, *Law Library Journal* is following the rules of the *Universal Citation Guide* and the recommendations of the AALL Committee on Citation Format.

225. *Universal Citation Guide: Tentative Drafts for Law Reviews and Court Rules*, 92 L. Lib. J. 363 (2000).

226. Peter Lyman & Hal R. Varian, *How Big Is the Information Explosion?* iMP, Information Impacts Magazine (Nov. 2000) <http://www.cisp.org/imp/november_2000/11_00lyman.htm>.

227. *Id.*

228. Bowen, *supra* n. 19.

229. Richard A. Leiter, *Use of Law Reviews in Modern Legal Research: The Computer Didn't Make Me Do It?* 90 L. Lib. J. 59, 64 (1998).

230. *Id.* at 69-70.

231. *To Publish and Perish, supra* n. 48.

232. Danner, *supra* n. 79 at 477-478.

233. NewScientist.com <http://www.newscientist.com/hottopics/copyleft/copyleftart.jsp> (accessed Mar. 3, 2002).

234. *Scholarly Journals at the Crossroads: A Subversive Proposal for Electronic Publishing: An Internet Discussion about Scientific and Scholarly Journals and Their Future* (Ann Shumelda Okerson & James J. O'Donnell eds., Association of Research Libraries, 1995).

235. Danner, *supra* n. 79 at 466.

236. Stevan Harnad, *Skyreading and Skywriting for Researchers: A Post-Gutenberg Anomaly and How to Resolve It* <http://www.text-e.org/conf/index.cfm?fa=printable&ConfText_ID=7>. Harnad's extensive collection of papers on interactive publication are available on his Web site. <http://cogsci.soton.ac.uk/~harnad/intpub.html> (accessed Mar. 5, 2002).

237. <http://www.princeton.edu/~harnad/psyc.html> (accessed Mar. 5, 2002).

238. Danner, *supra* n. 79 at 467-468.

239. *Id.* at 478-480.

240. <http://leda.law.cornell.edu/leda/manual/index.htm> (accessed Mar. 5, 2002).

241. Danner, *supra* n. 79 at 481-482.

242. The Duke LEDA server is at <http://leda.law.duke.edu/leda/>. See also, the Emory LEDA at <http://els479.law.emory.edu/leda/>.

243. E-mail from Dick Danner to Teknoids listserv, *LEDA Publication Experiment* (Dec. 29, 2001).

244. See, for examples, the Working Papers site at Cornell <http://www4.law.cornell.edu/working-papers/>; the *Berkeley Law and Economics Working Paper Series* <http://www.bepress.com/blewp/>; and Boston University School of Law *Working Papers Series* <http://web.bu.edu/LAW/faculty/papers/> (accessed Mar. 5, 2002).

245. <http://www.bepress.com/gj/> (accessed Mar. 5, 2002).

246. Bernard Hibbitts, *E-Journals, Archives and Knowledge Networks: A Commentary on Archie Zariski's Defense of Electronic Law Journals*, First Monday: Peer-Reviewed Journal on the Internet (1997) <http://www.firstmonday.dk/issues/issue2_7/hibbitts/#dep5>.

247. *Id.*

248. Frederick J. Friend, *Keeping Your head in a Revolution*, 5 JEP: The Journal of Electronic Publishing (3) (Mar. 2000) <http://www.press.umich.edu/jep/05-03/friend.html>.

249. Richard A. Danner, *Redefining a Profession*, L. Lib. J. 315, 328 (1998).

250. Danner, *supra* n. 249 at 344-3.

251. Danner, *supra* n. 249 at 351.

252. E-mail from Stevan Harnad to Liblicense listserv, *Rethinking Collections and Selection in the PostGutenberg Age* (Jan. 14, 2001).

253. Stevan Harnad, *For Whom the Gate Tolls? How and Why to Free the Refereed Research Literature Online Through Author/Institution Self-Archiving, Now,* <http://www.cogsci.soton.ac.uk/%7Eharnad/Tp/resolution.htm>.

254. Conversation with Blair Kauffman, Director of the Law Library and Professor of Law, Yale University Law Library (Spring 2001).

255. E-mail from David Goodman, Princeton, to Liblicense, *Librarians*, (Feb. 16, 2002).

256. Stanley N. Katz, *Don't Mistake a Tool for a Goal*, The Chronicle of Higher Education (Jun. 15, 2001) <http://chronicle.com/weekly/v47/i40/40b00701.htm>.

257. Steven J. Bell, *Why Isn't the Library Link Linking to the Library? Academic Libraries Confront the New Competitive Marketplace*, EDU0119 Papers Presented at EDUCAUSE annual conferences, 2001 at <http://www.educause.edu/asp/doclib/abstract.asp?id=edu0119>.

258. <http://www.webct.com/> (accessed Mar. 5, 2002).

259. <http://www.mbsdirect.net/xanedu.htm>. (accessed Mar. 5, 2002).

260. <http://www.questia.com:80/Index.jsp>. (accessed Mar. 5, 2002).

261. For more information, Tom Fowler, *Questia Media Down to 28 Workers* (Jan. 21, 2002) <http://www.chron.com/cs/CDA/story.hts/headline/tech/1220472>.

262. Bell, *supra* n. 257.

263. Bowen, *supra* n. 18.

264. Schauer & Wise, *supra* n. 36 at 500.

265. Bob Berring, *Thinkable Thoughts: making it up as we go*, 4 Law Librarians in the New Millennium (1) 3 (2002).

Book Selection Services: One Law Library, Two Vendors

Maureen Garmon

SUMMARY. Book selection services are just one of the resources used by law libraries for collection development purposes. They function as a new title pre-selection service, saving collection development staff hours of time sifting through thousands of new publisher offerings to access those materials which meet their specific collection needs, resulting in far more efficient use of library staff time. They also serve as a one-stop shopping center, providing materials without the hassle of dealing with individual publishers and staff. This article is based on a yearlong study comparing just two services used by the Law Library at the James E. Rogers College of Law, University of Arizona, and examines a few specific areas of concern to that institution. It is not meant to be a comprehensive review or comparison of either service. *[Article copies available for a fee from The Haworth Document Delivery Service: 1-800-HAWORTH. E-mail address: <getinfo@haworthpressinc.com> Website: <http://www.HaworthPress.com> © 2002 by The Haworth Press, Inc. All rights reserved.]*

KEYWORDS. Hein Green Slip Service, Blackwell's book services, book selection services, approval plans, collection development

---

Maureen Garmon is Access Services Librarian at the Law Library, James E. Rogers College of Law, University of Arizona.

The author would like to thank Shaun Esposito and Renee Ferebee for their work on this project and to the representatives at W. S. Hein and Blackwell's for their helpfulness in providing information about their respective services.

[Haworth co-indexing entry note]: "Book Selection Services: One Law Library, Two Vendors." Garmon, Maureen. Co-published simultaneously in *Legal Reference Services Quarterly* (The Haworth Information Press, an imprint of The Haworth Press, Inc.) Vol. 21, No. 4, 2002, pp. 259-274; and: *Law Library Collection Development in the Digital Age* (ed: Michael Chiorazzi, and Gordon Russell) The Haworth Information Press, an imprint of The Haworth Press, Inc., 2002, pp. 259-274. Single or multiple copies of this article are available for a fee from The Haworth Document Delivery Service [1-800-HAWORTH, 9:00 a.m. - 5:00 p.m. (EST). E-mail address: getinfo@haworthpressinc.com].

BACKGROUND

This study is the end result of two events that occurred in 1998: an ABA sabbatical site inspection of the University of Arizona College of Law and the announcement of a donation pledge totaling $115 million to the college. ABA accreditation rules require that all law school libraries have collection development policies, and this donation would result in a significant increase in the library acquisition budget. The timing was right for a reexamination of the library's collection development policy and procedures.

The library's collection development policy prior to 1998 was rudimentary. Most of the acquisitions budget went to serials and continuations. Monograph purchases were selected by searching publishers' catalogs and brochures. In previous years, Rothman's Green Slip Service (now Hein's) was used, but had been discontinued as a result of budget cuts.

The Law Library also relied on the *Gauntletter* service for new commonwealth titles and reprints, and our foreign and international collection was updated through a combination of sources including the *Catalog of New Foreign and International Law Titles*[1] and individual publisher brochures and flyers.

The director immediately initiated a free new title awareness and book order subscription service through Blackwell's (Blackwell's Book Service-U.S.), and assumed the day-to-day responsibility of collection development management for the bulk of the collection. Blackwell's was chosen because it was used by the main university library, it was free, and while not exclusively a law library service, it was able to tailor its service to the unique needs of a law collection. With this new service in place, the director and the foreign and international librarian began ordering titles on a regular basis as the budget allowed.[2]

The sudden increase in the library budget (over $350,000 in just two years) also allowed for the addition of new staff. In 1998, a new position was created, a Head of Public Services, one of whose primary responsibilities was to head the library's collection development efforts. Much more attention was now being paid to the collection development process and regular examination of the collection was taking place.

By the summer of 2000, we were convinced that we could no longer rely solely on Blackwell's slips and publishers' catalogs and brochures to develop and maintain our collection. We were also certain that we were missing a lot of law-related titles under the current process. The director and head of public services initiated a subscription to Hein's Green Slip Service. Hein's was chosen based on its positive reputation among law libraries and because it is designed specifically for law library collections. The current project was then suggested as a way of determining which ordering services would be most useful to us in the long term. No other vendors were selected at the time.[3]

PROJECT GOALS

Our primary goal was to determine if the addition of the Green Slip service would provide access to a larger universe of law-related publications. We were particularly concerned that we were missing a lot of titles published by the academic presses. We also knew that our existing service was not picking up the more practice-oriented materials (e.g., bar titles). Finally, we wanted to determine if the cost of the Hein's Green Slips was justified.

THE PROCESS

Three of us were involved in the yearlong study[4]–our new head of public services, our acquisitions assistant and myself. We ordered an additional subscription to Green Slips for the period in question. This allowed us to have a complete second packet for data-gathering purposes, while ordering titles from the original set.[5] The process was as follows: the head of public services received both Green Slips and Blackwell's order packets when they arrived. He ordered titles from each service, sending the foreign and international title slips to our foreign librarian for those decisions. I was then given the complete second set of Green Slips and the "top copies" of the Blackwell's.

Our acquisitions assistant ordered titles as requested and set up corresponding order records on our online system.[6] As orders were received, she printed out the order record for each, attached it to her copy of the Green Slip/Blackwell's slip, and passed all on to me.

GATHERING THE DATA

As a newcomer to collection development, I was unfamiliar with both services and was not sure what information I should be collecting for purposes of this study. Apart from the desire to compare the two services on the basis of academic press titles, I knew that Blackwell's, a

UK-based service, was heavily used by non-law, academic research libraries, and would be particularly strong in the area of foreign and international titles, both legal and non-legal. I also figured that Hein, a U.S. provider, would offer predominantly U.S. law titles.

My first step was to determine which titles, overall, were duplicated by the two services. I gathered the Blackwell's packets together in monthly piles as I received them, and began matching them against the incoming packets of Green Slips, title by title. When I found a duplication, I verified the titles' ISBN numbers, clipped notes to both slips along with price and date offered by each service, and any reference numbers so that I could quickly retrieve the information when needed.

While I continued to check for general duplication, I also began labeling those titles that were academic press titles, making a distinction between university-affiliated academic presses, and the more purely commercial "academic" presses. I was not sure if this would prove to be a meaningful distinction but thought it important enough to track.[7] I repeated the process for private, commercial publishers, and also for "non-profit" publishers. In this last category I included government agencies, non-governmental and inter-governmental organizations, and non-profit research institutes where I could determine they were officially non-profit. All of these latter publisher types seemed to be an entirely different breed from the private commercial presses and I thought it might be worthwhile to extract them from the rest.

I created an Excel spreadsheet for these publisher comparisons, and began the process over again–this time tracking titles based on their substantive status: foreign, comparative and international law titles,[8] Anglo-American law titles, and an "other" category.[9] When I had assigned all slips to specific categories,[10] I reviewed the packets again, this time checking for duplication by category. A second spreadsheet was created to chart these comparisons.

Finally, I set up a spreadsheet to track how much of our budget was spent on titles purchased from each service, distinguishing between the amount spent on foreign and international titles as opposed to the Anglo-American collection.[11]

OVERVIEW OF THE TWO SERVICES–GENERAL COMPARISONS

Both Blackwell's and Green Slips provide libraries with a book pre-selection service, giving notice of newly published or forthcoming titles of potential interest to law libraries. Both also provide a book-purchasing service for subscribers: in addition, Blackwell's offers a book approval service, in which we chose not to participate.[12]

Blackwell's Book Services is part of the larger, UK-based Blackwell's family of companies. Its intended market is large academic research libraries and public libraries. At customer request, Blackwell's will set up an individual library profile and send notification slips for those titles whose subject areas match this pre-designed profile.[13] Our own library profile, set up in 1996, sets law as the specific subject area and, by design, selects interdisciplinary titles referencing law, such as sociology, business, psychology, etc.[14] Packets of these notification slips are sent out on a weekly basis and contain anywhere from a dozen to fifty or more titles. There is no fee paid to Blackwell's for setting up a library profile, or for the shipment of weekly packets.

Hein's Green Slip Service is also on a weekly distribution schedule, but comes in a slightly different format–3″ × 5″ slips of green paper (with a lesser number of white slips to designate items that require a service charge). Since the Green Slips cater to law library collections exclusively, there are no individual profiles as with Blackwell's–the subject matter consists of law and law-related topics, with all subscribers receiving identical weekly packets. An annual subscription to the Green Slip Service costs $685, with additional sets available for $40 each. The subscription service begins on August 1st of each year.

Green Slip Service offers roughly 3,000 titles/year for review and ordering. Included in that total are many pre-publication titles. Corrected slips may appear in subsequent packets, containing pricing, title, or other changes, as appropriate.

SPECIFICS–WHAT THE SLIPS CONTAIN

Both Blackwell's and Green Slips contain the following basic bibliographic information:

- Title/author/publisher
- Date/place of publication
- ISBN/Library of Congress call numbers and card numbers, if available[15]
- Pagination/format/volume and issue if relevant
- Subject headings–Green Slips uses LC subject headings; Blackwell's uses a proprietary thesaurus in addition to LC headings

Blackwell's also gives Dewey number, and information regarding the academic and reader levels of a title, e.g., graduate/professional, or specialist.

The Hein service also includes soft-cover pricing where relevant, and a brief abstract for some titles when available from its sources. Primary sources for these abstracts include: individual publisher Web sites, LC proof slips and cataloging in publication records, publisher's circulars and advance catalogs, and actual in-hand titles. In addition, *ABA Journal, American Book Publishing Record* and similar such standard book review publications are used by Hein book selectors.

Hein's also offers practice materials from various national, state and regional bar associations; titles published by ABA practice sections; and the publications of other professional attorney associations (e.g., NITA, ATLA). Green Slips also include the publications of the ALI, mainly the Restatements as new volumes and drafts are issued.

RESULTS

Green Slips offered a grand total of 2,857 titles over the 12-month period of the study, compared to Blackwell's 920. The two vendors duplicated a total of 291 titles.

And there were some surprises. We thought we were missing a lot of academic press titles and that our subscription to Green Slips would help fill that gap. It did, but probably not to the extent that would allow us to rely on Hein's service alone: during the year of the study, Green Slips offered 460 titles from university-affiliated academic presses compared to Blackwell's 293 (see Table 1). Duplication in this category was just over 100 titles. In other words, roughly 550 university academic press titles were not duplicated by either service. Nearly 200 Blackwell's titles and over 350 Green Slip offerings in this category would likely have been missed had we subscribed to only one or the other of these two services.

The foreign, international and comparative law category also provided some unexpected information (see Table 2). A full 42% (1,190) of Green Slips titles for the year were in this category, but only 15% of these (178 titles) were duplicated by Blackwell's. That's over 1,000 titles in the foreign/international area that were offered by Green Slips but not by Blackwell's.[16] An obvious strength of the Hein service, then, would seem to be in the whopping number of titles offered.

TABLE 1

Green Slips Titles Also Available from Blackwell's Arranged by:

Publisher Type	**Total Green Slips Titles**	**% of GS Titles by Category**	**Titles Duplicated by Blackwell's**	**% Duplication by Category**	**% Duplication Overall**
Academic Press (university affiliation)	460	16%	101	22%	4%
Commercial Academic Press	77	3%	9	13%	0%
Non-Profit/Gov't Agency/NGOs/IGOs	29	1%	1	0%	0%
All Other Private Publishers	2,291	80%	180	8%	6%
Total Offered by Green Slips Overall Duplication by Blackwell's	**2,857**	**100%**	**291**		**10%**

Blackwell's Titles Also Available from Green Slips Arranged by:

Publisher Type	**Total Blackwell's Titles**	**% of BW Totals by Category**	**Total Duplicated by Green Slips**	**% Duplication by Category**	**% Duplication Overall**
Academic Press (university affiliation)	293	32%	101	35%	11%
Commercial Academic Press	41	4%	9	22%	1%
Non-Profit/Gov't Agency/NGOs/IGOs	7	1%	1	14%	0%
All Other Private Publishers	579	63%	180	31%	20%
Total Offered by Blackwell's Overall Duplication by Green Slips	**920**	**100%**	**291**		**32%**

TABLE 2

Green Slips Titles Also Available from Blackwell's Arranged by:

Subject Area	**Total Green Slips Titles**	**% of GS Titles by Category**	**Titles Duplicated by Blackwell's**	**% Duplication by Category**	**% Duplication Overall**
Anglo-American	871	30%	96	11%	3%
Foreign/International/Comparative	1,190	42%	178	15%	6%
Other	796	28%	17	2%	1%
Total Offered by Green Slips Overall Duplication by Blackwell's	**2,857**	**100%**	**291**		**10%**

Blackwell's Titles Also Available from Green Slips Arranged by:

Subject Area	**Total Blackwell's Titles**	**% of BW Titles by Category**	**Titles Duplicated by Green Slips**	**% Duplication by Category**	**% Duplication Overall**
Anglo-American	263	29%	96	37%	10%
Foreign/International/Comparative	556	60%	178	32%	19%
Other	101	11%	17	17%	2%
Total Offered by Blackwell's Overall Duplication by Green Slips	**920**	**100%**	**291**		**32%**

As expected, Blackwell's was top-heavy with foreign and international titles: 60% of its total titles fit this category (556 titles). Thirty-two percent of these foreign and international titles were also carried by Green Slips. At 178 titles, this category represented the area of highest duplication. But again, this means that Blackwell's carried almost 400 foreign/international titles that were not picked up by the Hein service.

Anglo-American law titles (see Table 2) accounted for almost a third of the offerings of each service: 871 titles for Green Slips and 263 for Blackwell's. In the case of the Hein service, this number is considerably lower than its foreign/international offerings (30% vs. 42% for foreign).

Green Slips offered a larger proportion of interdisciplinary titles ("other" category) relative to its total offerings than did Blackwell's: 28% of all Green Slips titles were in this category vs. 11% for Blackwell's. Duplication was minimal in this category so, again, a combination of the two sources would seem the best way of ensuring the success of our collection development efforts, drawing on as comprehensive a base as possible for book-purchasing options.

Finally, since we were interested in bar-related titles, I tracked these as well. They are not broken out separately but are included in the "other" category in Table 2. Not surprisingly, Green Slips offered more of these materials–five percent of their total offerings were from bar or law professional associations, U.S. and Canadian. For Blackwell's, the total was less than one percent.

CONCLUSION

A healthy increase in our collection budget for the fiscal year in question allowed for this project to be more than simply academic: while comparing titles offered by the two services I also tracked our actual purchases. We were able to add a total of 703 titles (overwhelmingly treatises) to the neglected Anglo-American collection from just these two services, representing 53% of our total treatise purchases for the year (1,331 titles). Five Hundred and fifty-six of these were from our Hein subscription and represent the bulk of the overall increase in treatise acquisitions for the year. Seventy-three new titles were added to our foreign and international collection from these two services.[17]

While this project may have driven me forever from the ranks of aspiring collection development librarians, it has been a useful tool in helping my library to make some important collection management decisions. It has provided us with some critical data with which to begin a much-needed revision of our collection development policy. It has also highlighted the need for more than one service to adequately support our collection development efforts–the value of the Hein service merits its annual cost and we will definitely continue subscribing to both services, given their significant differences in coverage.

In fact, the differences prompt us to wonder how other services might have compared. In hindsight, it would have been useful to have included some of those into the mix, specifically Yankee Book Peddler. Further study–perhaps a comprehensive comparison of all such services would be useful for all law libraries. Any takers?

NOTES

1. This was a subscription-based, bimonthly title which ceased publication in 1998. It was used by our foreign and international librarian mainly for the purchase of international law titles.

2. The library also ordered other collection development resources such as *Legal Information Buyer's Guide & Reference Manual* by Ken Svengalis. Some budget-related cancellations were also reinstated: *Legal Looseleafs in Print* by InfoSources Pub. Other titles were continued: *Bowker's Law Books & Serials in Print.*

3. There are a number of book pre-selection services used by law libraries for collection development purposes. A query posted to law-lib elicited responses from twelve law libraries, eleven academic and one state. Most used a combination of services: Hein Green Slip Service (9); Midwest Library Services (6); Yankee Book Peddler (5); Gauntletter (4); Blackwell's Book Service (2). Other book-ordering sources were cited, but not along the lines of the above-mentioned book services (e.g., amazon.com or Lawbook Exchange). Appendix C contains contact information for these vendors.

4. Time period covered was our fiscal year July 1, 2000 through June 30, 2001.

5. For those unfamiliar with the format of these two services, Blackwell's packets consist of four copies of each title in a carbon copy format; Green Slips contain one title per individual slip of paper. See Appendix A for an illustration of each.

6. The Law Library shares use of the Innovative Interfaces system (III) with the main campus libraries at the University of Arizona.

7. In the "commercial academic press" category I put those publishers who refer to themselves as academic or university presses for marketing purposes but which have no such institutional attachment. I also added to this category academic divisions of major publishers.

8. For this category, I counted all titles in the K, JZ, KZ, or outright foreign classifications.

9. Here I included all titles that were interdisciplinary in nature, e.g., civil rights, criminology, law & philosophy, political science–basically, all call numbers that did not fit in the substantive law classifications. Also included here are information science titles, many directories, biographies and bibliographies.

10. The difficulty here lay in the fact that many of the Green Slips do not contain call numbers, since those items are often not yet published. For this information, I relied on OCLC's FirstSearch database. For those few items that did not show up on FirstSearch, I hazarded a guess as to category.

11. I had originally created a fourth spreadsheet to compare other data for the two services, such as turn-around time from order to receipt, returns due to incorrect orders shipped, and quality of customer support. However, these categories proved inappropriate or irrelevant and are not included in this report.

12. Under book approval plans, libraries receive hard copies of new titles for review, not just slips. Items not selected for inclusion are returned to the vendor.

13. Profiles can be configured in a number of ways and use more than just the subject area as criteria for selection. Information such as publisher, language, format, maximum/minimum price, time period and treatment of subject, and much else may be included.

14. See Appendix B for more information regarding the Law Library's Blackwell's approval profile.

15. Since Green Slips include many titles prior to their actual publication, this data is sometimes not available on those slips.

16. As noted above, the Hein service includes more titles on a pre-publication basis. Those same titles do not show up on Blackwell's until time of publication. Because I stopped gathering data as of June 30, subsequent Blackwell's packets, which may have contained a fair number of duplicates, were not counted.

17. Many of the acquisitions made by our foreign librarian were through brochures, not book subscription services.

APPENDIX A

CUSTOMER CODE
DOUL

BLACKWELL'S
BOOK SERVICES - US

KJE6044

Guild, Elspeth.
Immigration law in the European community / by Elspeth Guild.
(Immigration & asylum law & policy in Europe, v.2)
Kluwer Law Intl, US The Hague

341.424
01vol 2001 xv/370p

ORDER DATE
04Jun2001

PRICE USD 100.00
List price at the time of publication.

ISBN 90-411-1593-5
L.C. NO. 2001-29555
BOOK NO. R1-241661
B.N.B. NO.
INV/REF NO.

U. OF AZ. COLLEGE LAW LIB
MICHAEL CHIORA7"I
LAW

COPY 1 F
04F1

SUBJECTS: 19982035 European Community 193002 Immigration law 974208 KJE 5-7975 Regional organization

NSP'S: ACAD LEVEL: Grad text,Prof/practitioner ORIG COUNTRY OF PUB: Netherlands SERIES TYPE: 00003:NM PUB TYPE: Trade GEOG CHAR: EEC READER LEVEL: Specialist TIME CHAR: 1946-1969,1970-to date LANG BOOK: English

CUSTOMER CODE
DOUL

BLACKWELL'S
BOOK SERVICES - US

KJE6044

Guild, Elspeth.
Immigration law in the European community / by Elspeth Guild.
(Immigration & asylum law & policy in Europe, v.2)
Kluwer Law Intl, US The Hague

341.424
01vol 2001 xv/370p

ORDER DATE
04Jun2001

PRICE USD 100.00
List price at the time of publication.

ISBN 90-411-1593-5
L.C. NO. 2001-29555
BOOK NO. R1-241661
B.N.B. NO.
INV/REF NO.

U. OF AZ. COLLEGE LAW LIB
MICHAEL CHIORA7"I
LAW

COPY 3 F
04F1

SUBJECTS: 19982035 European Community 193002 Immigration law 974208 KJE 5-7975 Regional organization

NSP'S: ACAD LEVEL: Grad text,Prof/practitioner ORIG COUNTRY OF PUB: Netherlands SERIES TYPE: 00003:NM PUB TYPE: Trade GEOG CHAR: EEC READER LEVEL: Specialist TIME CHAR: 1946-1969,1970-to date LANG BOOK: English

Refer to CP 042001-247

GUILD, Elspeth.
Immigration law in the European Community.
Norwell, MA, Kluwer Law International, 2001. (Immigration and asylum law and policy in Europe, v.2) ISBN 9041115935. $100.00.
CLOTH.
Emigration and immigration law.
L.C. 2001029555. KJE6044.G854 2001.
C.I.P.

William S. Hein & Co., Inc. Littleton, Colorado 80127
bookorders@wshein.com or Toll-Free (888) 361-3255

APPENDIX B

The profile set up by the Law Library in 1997 is a liberal one, having few restrictions within Blackwell's law division. We have selected an earliest publication date of 1995 since our profile was set up in 1997 and we wanted to be sure we received notice of recent titles published just prior to that date. While it seemed appropriate to include here a duplicate of our exact profile as supplied by Blackwell's, that copy was too compressed to reproduce in any readable fashion. The main criteria are the non-subject parameters, which I've outlined below using Blackwell's language. All of these parameters are considered when Blackwell's selects titles for our profile, except where noted.

Non-Subject Parameters

Academic difficulty level

Lower undergrad textbook
Upper undergrad textbook
Graduate text
Professional/practitioner
University/research library
Undergraduate library
Highly specialized collection
Popular collection

Readership Level

Specialist reader
Non-specialist reader
General reader
Reference

Type of Book

General
Encyclopedic work
Selected/collected works
Symposium proceedings
Collected articles–npp (*not previously published*)
Collected articles–pp (*previously published elsewhere*)
Anthology
Miscellaneous/reference
Bibliography
Dictionary
Concordance/commentary
Directory
Handbook
Data book/tables
Atlas
Exam preparation
Pocket reference
Dissertation
Journal monograph
Musical score
Readings & cases
Hardware/software specific
Documentary collection
Facsimile
Art exhibition catalog

APPENDIX B (continued)

Type of Edition

Critical edition
Heavily illustrated book
Original & translation
Translation
General edition
Photo collection

Language of Book

English
All other thirteen categories of languages not selected
All English translations of other language titles included

Printing History

New
Subsequent editions
Reprints not selected

Format of Publication

Paper
Hardbound
Spiral/ring/portfolio
Pamphlet
Book with media/software

Time Character of Subject

All date ranges selected: second century B.C.E.–'future'
'No time' also selected
Note: a total of fifteen time ranges are listed in this category

Treatment of Subject

History of
Practical
Clinical
Political/governmental
Teaching of/pre-college
Computer/programming aspects
Religious aspects
Biological treatment
Statistical/mathematical treatment
Legal aspects of
Economics of
Medical aspects of
Social aspects of
Teaching of/college level
Business/management/administration of
Law as a subject related to art
Law as a subject related to literature
General or no specific treatment
Psychological aspects of

Type of Publisher

University press
Trade
Societal
University/university department
Small press
Governmental publisher
Art museum
Personal author
Corporate body
Importer/distributor

List Price Limitations

We have not selected any price limitations

Country of Original Publication *(country location of editorial office responsible for the intellectual content of the book)*

All (other) countries considered

Country of Source Publication (*location of the publisher or distributor from whom Blackwell's acquired the book*)

Canada
United States
No other countries

Geographic Character of Subject

All (other) countries
General–no specific place

APPENDIX C

The following table lists contact information for the handful of slip service providers used by responding AALL law libraries:

Vendor	Web Address/Telephone
Blackwell's Book Services (US)	www.blackwell.com/ (800) 547-6426 (OR) (609) 228-8900 (NJ)
Gaunt, Inc. (GauntLetter)	www.gaunt.com (800) 942-8683 (FL)
W.S. Hein & Co. (Green Slips)	www.wshein.com (800) 828-7571 (NY)
Midwest Library Service	www.midwestls.com (800) 325-8833 (MO)
Yankee Book Peddler	www.ybp.com (800) 258-3774 (NH)

Changes in the Courthouse–Electronic Records, Filings and Court Dockets: Goals, Issues and the Road Ahead

Julie C. Turner

SUMMARY. This article describes the electronic revolution that is currently taking place within court systems across the nation. Digital archiving of documents is becoming a well-established practice. Electronic filing of documents is gathering momentum as a viable method of conducting the daily business of the courts. Although court functions remain relatively the same, the manner in which their daily business is being affected is changing dramatically. *[Article copies available for a fee from The Haworth Document Delivery Service: 1-800-HAWORTH. E-mail address: <getinfo@haworthpressinc.com> Website: <http://www.HaworthPress.com> © 2002 by The Haworth Press, Inc. All rights reserved.]*

KEYWORDS. Court technology, state and county courts, digital signatures, electronic court filing

INTRODUCTION

This article will discuss a number of the far-reaching effects that recent electronic technological advances will have upon court systems.

Julie C. Turner is affiliated with the University of Washington Law School Library.

[Haworth co-indexing entry note]: "Changes in the Courthouse–Electronic Records, Filings and Court Dockets: Goals, Issues and the Road Ahead." Turner, Julie C. Co-published simultaneously in *Legal Reference Services Quarterly* (The Haworth Information Press, an imprint of The Haworth Press, Inc.) Vol. 21, No. 4, 2002, pp. 275-299; and: *Law Library Collection Development in the Digital Age* (ed: Michael Chiorazzi, and Gordon Russell) The Haworth Information Press, an imprint of The Haworth Press, Inc., 2002, pp. 275-299. Single or multiple copies of this article are available for a fee from The Haworth Document Delivery Service [1-800-HAWORTH, 9:00 a.m. - 5:00 p.m. (EST). E-mail address: getinfo@haworthpressinc.com].

The vast changes that are being implemented within the courts, particularly in the areas of electronic records, filings and court dockets, will touch upon court personnel at all levels–lawyers, law librarians, government personnel, and indeed, any member of the public seeking information from or dealing with the court system in any way. Courts at all levels are moving towards computer technology as an alternative to paper. Most courts now use computer case-processing systems to perform their docketing, indexing, calendaring, notice generation, and financial operations. Courts supplement this with word processing to produce orders, letters, and other documents. Some even have integrated these capabilities. While these types of systems have addressed the basic case-processing needs, they have not solved the record-keeping problem.[1] Many clerks admit that lost or misplaced paper files are chronic problems. Most courts handle constantly increasing volumes of paper. Many courthouses have file cabinets occupying every inch of wall space.

As an alternative to paper files, electronic records (files) have many advantages. More than one person can see a document at a given time. The "original" or "official copy" of the document is never touched because it is kept in the electronic "file room" in a storage device (usually in a "jukebox"–a huge CD player filled with disks or platters–or an array of magnetic hard disks). An electronic document has to be indexed, usually twice: (1) to track the document to its location in the electronic file system and (2) to identify the document with its case number or other basic identifying information. Electronic documents are available over connections with the computer file room systems (e.g., the Internet, an office-wide computer network). The costly steps of paper processing go away: case files don't have to be retrieved by a file clerk and they never have to get reshelved after use. They rarely if ever get lost.[2]

THE COURTS AND THE INTERNET

An ever-increasing number of courts use the World Wide Web to enhance their technological abilities. Internet access to public court records is the number one technology issue in the courts, followed closely by the use of the Internet to file electronic court documents. Connecticut, Oklahoma, and Wisconsin have recently joined the growing number of states that offer free public access to their court records via the Web. Courts have attempted to adopt new court rules to accommodate the new technology and have scrutinized privacy and security implications of the electronic court environment. The economic benefits of filing court documents electronically are considerable. A study in Shawnee County, Kansas, reported that the time involved to accomplish nine identified steps in the filing of 100 court documents was reduced from 9.75 hours to 8.8 minutes.[3]

In addition to posting court calendars and appellate opinions and paying traffic fines via the Internet, courts are becoming more imaginative in their use of this electronic medium. Many courts including Orange County, Florida; Wise County, Virginia; and Delaware County, Ohio, stream videos of courtroom activities to the Internet. Additionally, in Delaware County, not only are complete judgment entries of domestic violence offenders available for all to see on the Website, but the offenders' photographs are displayed as well.[4]

In August 1997, the Seattle Municipal Court unveiled a credit card payment option for traffic tickets and other court fines. They became the first court in the country to use Internet based electronic commerce. To use the system, the public goes to the Website and chooses the link for payment of fines. The system accepts credit cards, both Visa and Mastercard. The court had previously accepted credit card payments made in person at the downtown Seattle courthouse. Thus, the Internet payment option was not such a large jump in business practices for the court.

The court collects approximately $21 million annually in tickets and fines issued in the state's largest city, with a population of roughly one million. The convenience of the service accrues to the public who can pay fines without having to travel downtown. Parking is a perennial problem in the downtown district so this is a significant advantage. Additionally, the transaction can be done outside of normal business hours, or on weekends. For people who work during the day, this will prove helpful. The greater ease of payment should improve collection of fines and assist the courts in maximizing revenue.[5]

Many courts use the Internet to increase customer service, especially for pro se litigants. New York State provides over 20 forms, complete instructions, and a glossary of terms in a uniform, uncontested divorce packet via the Web; California's Statewide Office of Family Court Services provides information to assist pro se litigants in handling a divorce or separation, as well as for applying for or responding to a domestic violence restraining order. The Tucson City Court, Arizona, supplies a complete explanation of an order of protection and an injunction against harassment, while the self-service center in Maricopa County, Arizona offers comprehensive tips on self-representation. The

Clerk of Courts in Hamilton County, Ohio, provides an excellent small claims guide. Many states have initiatives to provide public Internet access terminals in convenient locations, such as libraries, for persons without personal computers.[6]

THE ELECTRONIC COURT

In moving courts toward an electronic environment, the concept of Judicial Electronic Document and Data Exchange (JEDDI) is gaining importance. The JEDDI concept, which was first conceived in the early nineties, will have profound consequences for the way in which courts and the entire justice community operate.[7]

The vision for an ideal JEDDI implementation includes:

- Electronic documents
- Electronic case files
- Electronic signatures
- Electronic filing
- Electronic noticing
- Electronic public access
- Integration of case management, document management, electronic filing, and public access systems.[8]

Electronic record-keeping systems are essential to the court's ability to keep and manage the papers and records involved in the cases before the court. They have the added advantage of being more accessible to the public. Courts that are converting from paper files to electronic files have several options. Some courts have chosen imaging, a process in which paper documents are scanned into electronic files. Imaging is ideal for converting older paper files into electronic files and can provide a solution to a court's filing and storage problems.

Imaging is a well-developed way to incorporate hard copy source documents into an electronic filing system. Imaging is a lot like faxing. When a document is passed through an electronic scanner, each page is converted to computer code that represents the patterns of light and dark that make up the page (the result is called a "bit map"). The resulting computer code is compressed and stored electronically (in a fax, the code is transmitted across telephone lines to the recipient's fax machine). An imaged or faxed electronic document acts more like paper than like a word-processed electronic document. An image viewer uncompresses and interprets its code to reconstruct a viewable picture of what was scanned, displaying it on a computer screen or printing it on paper. Even though it can be shown on a computer screen, an image cannot be spell-checked, text searched, or edited like a word-processed document, because it is merely a picture of the shapes which made up the source document from which it was made. An image has to be "read" by a human to find and use the data within it.

Paper will almost certainly continue to make up for some part of what is presented for inclusion in the court file. Therefore, document imaging needs to be a part of a full-service electronic court filing system.[9]

ELECTRONIC DOCUMENTS IN THE COURTS

In addition to imaging, courts have begun experimenting with electronic documents. Imaging is already in use by many courts. It is a well-established technique with a mature service industry ready to provide quality systems and support. For an existing document management system, imaging speeds up many processes and saves time eaten up by paper manipulation, physical storage, and unavailability/loss of documents. Often, imaging is purchased with a "workflow" product that allows redirections and redesign of how information moves and how work is sequenced. Imaging will not in itself fix a bad workflow or document management system, but it provides a wonderful opportunity to do so.

Paper will almost certainly continue to make up some part of what is presented for inclusion in the court file. The text of the document can be manipulated to allow editing, unlike a scanned document, which is simply a reproduction of an original document. The creation of an electronic document includes the use of a standardized language, called a mark-up language, which uses tags to identify and describe it.

The formal specification of mark-up languages is accomplished through Standard Generalized Mark-up Language (SGML). SGML is an ISO (International Standards Organization) specification that determines how a mark-up language should be defined and what rules documents must follow if they employ a particular mark-up language. SGML is a very broad and powerful language. Unfortunately, because it is so broad in scope, its direct application has been too complex for most purposes, although (like EDI) it has been used by many large corporations in high-volume applications.

The most widespread example of a mark-up language is Hypertext Mark-up Language (HTML)–the language of the World Wide Web.[10] HTML is a special mark-up language defined by SGML for describing the format of Web documents. HTML uses tags to specify how a Webpage is to be displayed by the user's browser software. The tags identify the boundaries of each component of the document (e.g., title, heading, paragraph), and the rules that apply to the HTML specification determine how that component is to be formatted for display (e.g., centered, larger font). The tags themselves are not displayed in the browser window, even though they are contained in the document as ordinary ASCII text. The browser software follows the HTML conventions to recognize the tags as formatting commands instead of content. By selecting "View/Source" on the browser menu bar, the user can view the actual Web document "behind the scenes" complete with tags.

As powerful as HTML is in instructing a computer how to display a Webpage, it is of no help in defining the meaning of the information contained on the page. A different mark-up language is needed to describe what a document contains. The language that has evolved in recent years for this purpose is called Extensible Mark-up Language (XML). Whereas HTML is concerned with the viewing of information, XML provides a standard method for working with data. It is "extensible" in the sense that as powerful as HTML is in instructing a computer how to display a Webpage, it is of no help in defining the tagging scheme, is somewhat open-ended, and can be defined to suit a variety of different purposes involving the exchange of information electronically.

XML can be thought of as a much simpler version of SGML. XML permits standardized data exchange using the Hypertext Transport Protocol (HTTP) over the Internet. Just as Web document authors can use HTML to tag a word or phrase to be displayed in bold or italic characters, they can use XML to tag structured data to indicate that a particular phrase represents the description of a retail catalog item, the name of the manufacturer, or the street address of a defendant. Adopting a data-tagging scheme to complement a formatting scheme adds powerful capabilities for processing electronic documents.

The benefits of tagging data through XML include:

- Improved Searching;
- Automatic Recognition and Extraction of Information; and,
- Multiple Data Views.

Tagging the data content of a Web document through the use of XML can enable a search engine to locate that information more accurately. For instance, a search for opinions or articles written by a particular author, such as a judge, could be instructed to retrieve only those Web pages on which the author's name appeared after the "<author>" data tag. The search engine would skip over extraneous occurrences of the same name in other documents, including occurrences in which the name appeared after the "<subject>" tag, as in the case of a biography. Perhaps more important, XML can enable the automatic extraction and processing of relevant data once the data have been located and retrieved. In addition, XML permits the same set of data to be viewed differently by different users. In this context, different users are permitted to view different fields out of the entire document. Because individual fields are recognized, for example, court software displaying an electronic brief could show court staff all data, while blocking out address information in the view accessible by the general public.

XML STANDARDS FOR JEDDI PROJECTS

A Legal XML mark-up language, Document Type Definitions (DTDs) for use in the courts is being developed that will specify the data elements to be tagged (pointed to) within documents, so the data can be located by a parser and copied for use in a table, another document, another computer system, etc. Examples of such diverse data are: Case Number, amount of Court Costs, months of incarceration, names of participants, Courtroom Number, plaintiff's attorney's Bar ID Number, date/time of hearing. A Legal XML DTD will show how data elements are related to each other. For example, under an element called <PersonIdentity> there could be nested sub-elements such as <FirstName>, <MiddleName>, <LastName>, <DateOfBirth>, <IdentificationNumber>, <Tattoos>, <StreetAddress>, etc. Documents called "Namespaces" will provide rules and guidance for collecting information on the various roles a person may have in relation to a case, e.g., judge, prosecutor, defendant, clerk, juror, reporter, witness.

The task before those who want to use XML will be to identify and assign clear definitions to terms and relationships so they can be used consistently in the electronic documents filed in a court. The tasks for technical experts in XML will be to help the courts develop standard DTDs and build other tools they will need to set up documents and forms. Another technical task is to build the software to capture data from filed documents and carry the copied data to mainframe, case management, or other systems, where data is now transferred by hand or perhaps not at all. These tools are still being developed.[11]

Pioneering work in the practical implementation of XML for JEDDI projects is being accomplished in several state court systems. In Utah the AOC (Administrative Office of the Courts) has developed preliminary DTDs for court documents and is using them in a criminal JEDDI system operating in the Third District Court. These standards can be spread throughout the state as the JEDDI system expands, potentially enabling the entire state court system to use a standard set of XML documents in the near future. Yet the Utah AOC recognizes the desirability of national standards and would prefer to adapt its systems to those standards, once they are developed.

In the State of Washington, Superior Court clerks read documents filed with them to identify data, including at least the document's case number, serial number in the case, and title. Clerks then re-type this information into the State's Office of the Administrator for the Courts' mainframe system, SCOMIS (Superior Court Online Management Information System). If data elements were tagged using DTD, software could copy data from a document and put the data into corresponding data fields in SCOMIS. No one would have to re-key that information.[12]

To date, such efforts in all courts have been following an individual approach to setting up DTDs and developing other conventions for the use of XML. Fortunately, however, a concerted effort to address these issues is now in its formative stage. The National Center for State Courts is working with the Joint Technology Committee (JTC) of the Conference of State Court Administrators (COSCA) and the National Association for Court Management (NACM) to develop national court technology standards. The National Consortium for Court Automation Standards, operating with oversight by the JTC and staffing by NCSC, currently is focusing on functional standards for case management systems. However, it is undertaking a court XML standards initiative, as well as working in cooperation with Legal XML, a non-profit organization consisting of volunteers from private industry, non-profit organizations, government, and academia, which is sponsored by Georgia State University (see www.legalxml.org). In addition, the NCSC has conducted a project to compile data exchange requirements and definitions as a preliminary step toward identifying XML DTD requirements for courts. Courts planning JEDDI implementations should monitor these activities closely and participate in the standards development efforts whenever possible.

STATE COURT FILING PROJECTS

Within state courts, there are three comprehensive systems planned and a number of smaller projects operating. Many courts are currently experimenting with filing systems and have portions of a total system operating. Each discrete project has added to the understanding of what a system will look like.

The state courts in Utah are implementing a comprehensive filing project. A private company, Digital Signature Trust Company, a subsidiary of Zions First National Bank, was hired to set up the system. Criminal cases are being used for the pilot phase. The primary advantage of criminal cases is that there is a self-contained community among prosecutors and public defenders, with a few private defense lawyers. The group can receive training in the system, and feedback about wrinkles in the software is easily gathered.

The approach in Utah is essentially the vision articulated by Alan Asay in a 1994 report that studied the issue.[13] The documents will use SGML (Standard Generalized Mark-up Language) to provide docket information. Imaging is bulky, while SGML is elegant; parsing docket data works best with SGML fields while simply emailing documents in their original word processing format leaves clerks making docket entries much as before. Finally, SGML is platform neutral, as easily done on a Macintosh as a PC. For states with a high rate of technical literacy, where lawyers know HTML, the burden of using SGML templates are minimal and the advantages significant. Whether attorneys and the public have the requisite comfort level to use the SGML approach is a matter of adequate training.[14]

The approach that most busy urban courts will adopt is likely to be a mixture of imaging and electronic document submission, as is occurring in King County, Washington. In King County, the court will image paper archives and new documents submitted in paper. The court will immediately begin to accept electronic documents in a variety of word processing formats, and plans to receive a larger portion of filings in this manner each year. There are tradeoffs to the King County approach. On the one hand, by letting go of the SGML model, King County will bear a greater burden for docket entry than the court in Utah. On the other hand, the King County system will be easier for attorneys to submit documents to since they won't need to use the SGML template.

Long-term storage of case file documents has also been addressed in a comprehensive fashion by the King County Superior Court. At present, the plan is to use microfiche imaging for long-term storage of documents. Courts should adopt the approach of King County until solutions are provided for storage.[15] In the future, the technology for long-term storage of documents on a hard drive will undoubtedly advance, given the economic advantages of keeping electronic documents in their electronic format. With the advent of large hard drives, organizations will begin to move into the field of long-term storage. Today, a desktop computer with a four-gigabyte hard drive can hold so many documents that small courts possess the essential raw tools for long-term electronic storage.[16]

The Electronic Court Records (ECR) program in King County is a very large, advanced, multi-phased effort to eliminate paper and institute electronic filing for all cases before the Superior Court. The Superior Court Clerk, also known as the Department of Judicial Administration (DJA), is the agency whose responsibility includes managing all of the Court's case records. By law, those records must be retained indefinitely. The directors and managers of DJA have been responsible for the planning and implementation of all phases of ECR.

King County is following a three-step strategy:

Pre-ECR:	Archive Scanning
Phase 1:	Core Electronic Court Records Project
Phase 2:	ECR Connectivity Project
Phase 3:	Electronic Filing Project[17]

DJA's leaders defined the phases of the ECR program in a Master Plan written in April of 1998.[18] In November of 1997, DJA had begun scanning files for cases that had been archived, i.e., which were inactive for prescribed periods ranging from 18 months to 2 years. Accordingly, the name "Phase I: of ECR" was given to "Core ECR," which was to bring imaging of active court case files, with workflow for document processing within DJA by late 1999. That project is now done. Imaging is in place for documents for all cases filed on or since January 3, 2000. Including both active and archived cases, over 50,000 pages per day are now being scanned. Over 12 million pages of images are on file, 10 million of which were converted from a different imaging system DJA used for the archived cases from 1997 to 1999.

The final phases of ECR will extend image connectivity within the County and, ultimately, will bring the online case file and electronic filing to the community. "Phase II" brings images to the courtrooms, Judges' chambers, courtroom clerks, and case file users, all within the County's wide area network (WAN). This "connectivity" phase was completed at the end of 2000. "Phase III" will extend connectivity to file users over the Internet and, most significantly, will introduce electronic filing, a substantial change for the King County Superior Court and, by example, the state. Remote access to the case files over the Internet, along with electronic filing, will constitute "the online case file."[19]

A number of barriers had to be overcome, including:

- a relatively recent introduction of desktop technology into the Court and Clerk's office,
- a lack of standards to define data elements and build internally consistent legal documents,
- a lack of technological readiness among most law firms and sole practitioners, and
- a general uncertainty about the still-developing infrastructure within which successful systems would have to be built.

Other serious issues that would have to be tackled on the way to the online court file, include:

- reviewing and revising statutes and court rules,
- assessing the privacy consequences of online files, and
- addressing how different it is to work with electronic, rather than paper files and documents.[20]

The underlying key to this transformation is replacing the paper file with an electronic official court file. The King County vision statement, dated February 6, 1995, provides a clear picture of the magnitude of the King County Superior Court's long range goals.

Reengineer Washington's Courts

Rethink, redesign, reengineer our judicial system.

Restructure how courts do their work to deliver better service to customers (litigants and public):

- undertake a zero-based reexamination of court functions,
- reconsider jurisdictional levels,
- remove organizational and hierarchical barriers,
- expedite cases to their earliest feasible completion, with issue identification at entry,

- enable simultaneous processes that avoid delay,
- expedite and manage appeals and revisions, and
- ensure enforcement of judgments, to
- give finality, certainty, and predictability to the judicial process.

Build Tomorrow's Information Infrastructure Now

Build a statewide data web, enabling electronic data and document interchange, to make needed information readily accessible to support judicial decision-making and enforcement.

A modernized information infrastructure is necessary to gain maximum benefit from reengineering. Even before reengineering is done, essential features of this infrastructure are discernible:

- a seamless, statewide data web in which all courts and associated agencies share information and data entry,
- electronic data/document interchange, imaging, and multi-media supplanting hard copy as the principal medium for active records,
- judicial information accessible to the court and associated agencies when needed (eliminating organizational and geographical barriers),
- timely access to judicial records available for litigants, the bar, and the public, both in the courthouse and remotely, and
- protection of personal privacy and confidential/sealed information ensured.[21]

SECURITY AND AUTHENTICATION TECHNOLOGIES

In almost any discussion of electronic documents and JEDDI systems, the topics of security and authentication issues and methods are sure to arise. Understandably, court leaders and attorneys are concerned about maintaining the integrity of electronic documents in the absence of traditional paper originals, handwritten signatures, and embossed seals. Fortunately, many of these same issues also affect the commercial world, which has been well out in front of the courts in the pursuit of electronic commerce and information interchange. Banking, insurance, and other industries have invested countless hours and millions of dollars addressing security needs.[22]

Initially, most commercial transactions were accomplished via secure, private networks and direct high-speed telecommunications between organizations. However, the phenomenal global expansion of the Internet has changed the playing field dramatically, establishing the Internet as the information highway of choice. Organizations all the way from mom and pop enterprises to Fortune 100 corporations are turning to the Internet for transmission of critical business documents and for transactions collectively worth billions of dollars. *But, the*

Internet is a public, unregulated, and inherently unsecured network. Ensuring the security of corporate-to-corporate exchanges is enough of a challenge, but it pales by comparison with the challenge of conducting electronic transactions with millions of individual consumers.

Courts already are finding the Internet invaluable for exchanging information by e-mail, conducting legal research, locating a variety of other information helpful to their staffs or operations, and making information available to the public. The Internet also is the most practical and useful communications infrastructure for JEDDI systems. Consequently, it is essential that all aspects of sound system and data security principles be applied faithfully to JEDDI systems. For example, disaster recovery plans, good backup procedures including off-site storage, comprehensive system logging and audit functions, redundant or fault-tolerant servers, robust Internet firewalls, stringent anti-virus measures, and other standard techniques are critical to establish a firm technology foundation for JEDDI. If a computer system goes down for an hour or two today because of a component failure or breach of access security, most courts can continue to operate to a certain extent, because they have the paper case records available for court proceedings. With totally electronic records, a court is much more likely to grind to a halt if a computer failure or damage from a system intrusion cannot be remedied almost immediately.

SECURITY ISSUES FOR ELECTRONIC DOCUMENT TRANSMISSION

Being able to rely on the integrity and authenticity of court documents is fundamental to the judicial process. To be legally acceptable, documents must satisfy several conditions, regardless of whether they are in paper or in electronic form:

Authenticity: There must be some method for the recipient to identify the actual sender as the same one indicated by the document as the individual authorized to send the document on behalf of the organization.

Integrity: There must be some method for the recipient to determine that the document is intact and has not been altered since it was sent.

Non-repudiation: There must be some method to ensure that the sender cannot falsely claim that he or she did not send the document at all or that the contents are different from what was sent.

In the world of paper, these conditions have been satisfied through a variety of accepted techniques or practices. Preprinted letterhead, watermarks, embossed seals, handwritten signatures in permanent ink, and sealed envelopes are all intended to help ensure the integrity and authenticity of a message or document. Even though letterhead can be imitated, signatures can be forged, and envelopes can be resealed, these conventions are sufficient to generate the level of trust needed for paper transactions. Certain assumptions are made regarding the authenticity and integrity of documents meeting the accepted standards, with the force of law and its associated penalties for fraudulent activities undergirding the entire process. In the world of electronic documents, a similar kind of system is needed to establish the level of trust required to conduct transactions or exchange information between parties at opposite ends of the wire. The first challenge–and the one that has received the most attention in the security field–is to establish the authenticity of the sender of data or documents. It is of paramount importance for a JEDDI system to provide a means to ensure that only authorized, identifiable users can create and transmit electronic documents.[23]

PRIVACY ISSUES FOR COURTS WITH ELECTRONIC DOCKET/FILING SYSTEMS

The growing use of electronic filing and imaging technology makes it possible for courts to offer broader public access to case files, including electronic access from locations outside the courthouse. There is increasing awareness, however, of the personal privacy implications of electronic access to court case files, especially access through the Internet. In the court community, some have begun to suggest that case files–long presumed to be open for public inspection and copying unless sealed by court order–contain private or sensitive information that should be protected from unlimited public disclosure and dissemination in the new electronic environment. Others maintain that electronic case files should be treated the same as paper files in terms of public access, and that existing court practices are adequate to protect privacy interests.[24]

The public currently has open access to a majority of court records, but in order to see the records, one has to go to the relevant courthouse. However, because of the Internet, all of those records could be made available online, greatly widening the likelihood of public access. By 2005, the federal judiciary hopes to have electronic case filings replace current docketing and case management systems in more than 200 bankruptcy, district, and appellate courts. Currently, there are nine federal courts (four U.S. district courts and five federal bankruptcy courts) that offer electronic filing of court documents. Those nine courts have been formulating a policy to deal with what could become greater public access to documents since they can be made available on the Internet. A conference committee held a hearing in March 2001, where all sides of the issue were aired. The committee's three month public comment period attracted 240 comments from lawyers, privacy advocates, and other interested individuals. The conference has not set a date for deciding on the proposals that were submitted.

The two distinct camps that have emerged on the privacy issue were very evident during the public comment process. For the public access camp, court case files are open records, and putting them on the Internet is a new and better way of allowing the public to monitor what the courts are doing. The privacy camp believes that putting a sensitive document online is much more revealing than letting it sit in the back of a courthouse filing cabinet.[25] Privacy groups, such as Privacy Rights Clearing House, have submitted comments to the conference committee stating serious concerns about dishonest individuals obtaining personal information. The group points out that there are a rising number of organized criminal enterprises and gangs that specialize in identity theft.[26]

Bankruptcy cases, which typically include financial information such as credit card account numbers, Social Security numbers, loan account details, dates of birth, bank account numbers and even inventories of the possessions of the bankrupt, are of particular concern. In fact, a federal study released in January, 2001, said that even traditional, paper-based bankruptcy filings reveal too much information about the people involved. The federal court system plan would allow all its member courts, including bankruptcy courts, to post documents on the Internet within the next few years. Under the proposed system, lawyers would file documents electronically instead of on paper. Before searching the online database, users would have to register. Unlike the documents currently now posted on some court Web pages, documents filed under this system would not pop up when using Internet search engines.

Putting court records online would make life easier for judges, lawyers and journalists who need to access files. From the lawyer's standpoint, they can avoid the necessity of physically reproducing copies of their pleadings. Judges can access the entire court file right from their desk or remotely.[27] Coming at the issue from both sides is the *Electronic Privacy Information Center* (EPIC), a Washington-based group that advocates on behalf of both privacy and open access.

"EPIC is devoted to civil liberties and we post many electronic documents, so it's very important that there be robust and inexpensive and convenient access to public records," says EPIC staff counsel Chris Hoofnagle. "We recommend access be provided at no cost. But on the flip side, access should be limited in certain ways to accommodate privacy." EPIC recommends for both electronic and paper documents that in criminal cases, no preindictment information about an individual should be made public. Sensitive information should be protected in civil cases and in bankruptcy cases; for example, specific financial information such as Social Security numbers or bank accounts and credit card numbers should not be open to the public.[28]

Recognizing the need to review judiciary policies in the context of new technology, the Judicial Conference Committee on Court Administration and Case Management has formed a subcommittee to consider privacy and access issues and provide policy guidance to the courts. The subcommittee is reviewing these issues and has not reached any binding conclusions.

The Administrative Office of the United States Courts is developing the *Case Management/Electronic Case Files* ("CM/ECF") system to replace current federal court docketing and case management systems. As a Web-based system, CM/ECF will allow access to electronic case files through the court's network, or as appropriate from outside the court via the Internet. The system, however, will permit a court to limit electronic access to case files and to individual documents within each file. Nine courts currently are using the prototype CM/ECF system, and national implementation is set to begin in mid-2000, continuing until late 2003. In addition, many courts currently create electronic case files by imaging filed documents.[29]

Some courts, such as King County, in Washington State, already have policies of only allowing those who are authorized to see certain categories of paper files, such as cases in the subject areas of Juvenile (civil and criminal); domestic violence; parentage-juvenile dependency; mental illness. Washington State has proposed new legislation, which would provide for the sealing of sensitive electronic filings. The areas considered include those listed above. The electronic document would be "sealed," using current encrypting technology, and only available for limited authorized use.[30]

The following section has been reproduced from a paper by the staff in the Office of Judges Programs of the Administrative Office of the United States Courts. The full text is available on the Web.[31] The paper also includes detailed analysis of case law on access to case files and privacy interests; a survey of the federal statutes and rules of procedure that affect access to case files; and a survey of present day judicial policy.

National policy alternatives on access to electronic case files

Three broad alternatives merit consideration in fashioning a national policy on access to electronic case files. Outlined below, they include:

1) providing the broadest possible access to electronic files;

2) taking a more narrow and cautious approach by excluding all, or most, sensitive information from case files altogether;

3) devising a "middle-ground" approach that would provide access to the complete public case file at the courthouse, but would limit remote electronic access to certain private or sensitive case file information.

Alternative 1: Extend current open access policies to cover electronic case files

This approach would implement the philosophy that the public case file should not be treated differently simply because it is in electronic rather than paper form. Electronic case files would be "open" for public access to the same extent as paper case files. There would be no restrictions on remote access. Litigants and others would be expected to assert their privacy interests through the regular motions process, and disputes over access would be addressed on a case-by-case basis.

Alternative 2: Review the elements of the "public" case file to better accommodate privacy interests

This alternative would focus on evaluating the need to include particular information or documents in the public case file, whether in paper or electronic format. The goal would be to develop a new definition of the "public case file" that would better accommodate privacy interests. Like Alternative 1, this approach assumes that the entire public file would be made available electronically without restriction. It would recognize privacy interests by excluding certain private or sensitive information from the public case file. Many state court systems essentially follow this approach, even for paper files, by sealing all files in specific types of cases.

Alternative 3: Provide limited access to certain electronic case file information to address privacy concerns

Like Alternative 2, this alternative would focus on identifying categories of case file information or specific documents that may implicate privacy concerns. But rather than redefining the contents of the public case file, it would involve limiting *remote* electronic access to certain private or sensitive information. Remote electronic access to case files might be limited depending on the level of access granted to a particular individual. Several levels of access may be appropriate, including:

- Judges and court staff presumably would have unlimited remote access to all electronic case files.

- Similarly unlimited access might also be extended to certain other key participants in the judicial process, such as the U.S. Attorney, the U.S. Trustee, and bankruptcy case trustees.

- Litigants and their attorneys would be given unrestricted access to the files relevant to their own cases.

- The general public would have remote electronic access to a subset of the entire case file, including pleadings, briefs, orders, and opinions.

This approach assumes that the complete case file would be available for public review *at the courthouse*, just as the entire paper file is available for inspection in person. Certain documents, however, would be excluded from unlimited remote electronic access. It is important to recognize that this approach would not limit how case files may be copied or disseminated once obtained at the courthouse. Documents that may be candidates for limited electronic access might include medical records, tax records, employment records, third-party sensitive information, or financial information in bankruptcy cases.[32]

DIGITAL SIGNATURES

In order to authenticate the record of an electronic communication, courts must adhere to strict standards. A court must be satisfied that the following conditions have been met: the contents of the record have remained unchanged since it was sent, the sender of the communication must be identifiable, the identified sender must have agreed to the contents of the communication, and in certain instances, extraneous information, such as the apparent date of the transmission, must be verifiable. This last condition becomes extremely important when a considerable amount of time has elapsed between the time of communication and the time when the particular case is heard in court.[33]

Images of hand written signatures that are transferred electronically do not meet court standards for adequate assurance of the authenticity of record. Digital signatures do provide a high level of security and practicality. Vastly different than an image of a handwritten signature, digital signatures are based on a mathematical encoding methodology known as cryptography. Digital signatures make it possible to determine not only who sent the document, but also whether that document has been tampered with after it was signed.[34]

ENCRYPTION FOR AUTHENTICATION PURPOSES

Since the majority of court documents are a matter of public record, the most important security concern when transmitting these documents is authentication of the sender and the actual message itself. This can be best achieved through the use of a digital signature. When a sender signs a message with a digital signature, the sender's computer performs a mathematical operation involving both the sender's private key (a replacement for a normal written signature) and the message itself. The most common replacements for the normal written signature are either a password or a numerical pin number.[35]

The original message is put through an operation called a hashing algorithm that generates a fixed length code called a message digest. The message digest is much smaller than the message, but has a unique mathematical relationship to it. Then the message digest and the sender's private key are used together in an encryption computation. The result of this second computation is a digital signature, which is attached to the message and sent along with it.

To verify the signature, the recipient's computer performs a computation involving the message and the signature that was attached to it. If the result is correct according to the prescribed mathematical relationship, the signature is verified as genuine, and both the sender and the message are authenticated. If the computed result does not match, then either the signature is fraudulent, or the message may have been altered after signing.[36]

PRIVATE AND PUBLIC KEY CRYPTOGRAPHY

Private key cryptography involves identical keys at each end of an electronic submission. There is only a single unique secret key known to both parties. This limits its usefulness for widespread exchange because each pair of senders and receivers needs a unique key. The situation becomes impossible to manage as the number of potential senders and receivers increases. Each time a sender wanted to exchange a document with a new party, that sender would have to generate, catalog and store a unique key. Further, that secret key would have to be securely transmitted to the other party, which creates a kind of security "catch-22."[37]

For more widespread secured electronic exchanges, such as the workings of the courts, a solution has been developed called public key cryptography. This process involves a pair of keys, not a single shared key. The pair is comprised of one private and one public key. Each individual user is assigned a secret private key and a public key that can be freely given to any other user to whom the sender wishes to send information. In fact, a public key can be publicly posted so that anyone can obtain it as needed. Each pair of private and public keys is mathematically related to each other. Distribution of the public key does not endanger the security of the private key because it is not possible to calculate the private key from the public key. It is deemed to be "computationally infeasible."[38]

The trend to combine signature validity with proof of the identity of a signatory has recently gained momentum. Current proposals in legal and electronic technology circles are leaning towards the setting up of a Certification Authority, which would perform the function of ensuring that digital signatures effected with a signatory's secret key are verifiable using the public key. Once the Certification Authority has successfully verified the digital signature, it would issue an ID Certificate, which would include a certification of the signatory's identity and their matching key.[39]

Once the identity requirement has been satisfied, the very fact that an electronic signature has been affixed to a document should raise the same presumptions as manuscript signatories: the signatory intended to sign the document in order to verify its contents. In the case of a manuscript signature, the signatory must be present and have the document signed in front of them. In the case of an electronic signature, a third party with access to the computer or to the storage device would be able to make the signature. Courts seeking to rely on the validity of an electronic signature may well have to develop new extrinsic evidentiary rules. One possibility is that the courts may be prepared to presume that a third party who is given access to the signature technology has been authorized by the signatory to sign on his or her behalf. However, safeguards built into any new laws would play a crucial role in protecting bona fide signatories. Lawmakers in many states are currently grappling with this kind of dilemma.[40]

THE FUTURE

Alameda County, California attorney Donald Kirby daydreams about filing court papers from the porch of his Sierra County house near the banks of the Yuba River. Court officials say his fantasy will come true. Alameda County Superior Court, like a growing number of courts around California and the nation, is preparing to launch a pilot project that will allow attorneys to file court documents via the World Wide Web.[41] King County, Washington also has a pilot project in process in which selected Seattle law firm attorneys will each submit electronic filings, on a trial basis, from their firms' personal computers. This project is in the very early stages. At the very beginning of the project, it is uncertain whether participating attorneys will actually be able to view the documents they have filed electronically. This will be a period of experimentation, which has been eagerly anticipated by the Seattle legal community.[42]

THE FUTURE FOR LAW LIBRARIANS

Many courts house law libraries or utilize the services offered by law libraries nearby. Just as the impacts of technology are affecting the daily business of the courts, the impacts of technological innovation have changed the role of law librarians no matter what the setting. Although law libraries still hold many books, a new concept has emerged–the law library as an information transfer network.[43] Many professional law librarians are already heavily involved in electronic document storage and computerized information retrieval systems. It has become essential for law librarians to possess a good working knowledge of online databases, such as Lexis and Westlaw; as well as the many legal resources available on the Internet. Much of their own research will utilize the new tools available and will be carried out online. Many law libraries now offer their catalogs online, which allows for ease of access to the library's collection.[44]

Advances in technology have expanded the teaching component of the jobs of professional law librarians. The general public needs assistance in the use of the new electronic research tools. Many academic law librarians are required to teach Legal Research to students in a formal setting; law firms often require their librarians to provide ongoing legal research assistance and training to lawyers at the firm. County law libraries provide assistance to a diverse group of patrons, some of whom do not have access to online materials elsewhere. Many law libraries now offer e-mail reference via the Web, responding to patron's questions electronically, in conjunction with handling the queries of patrons who chose to visit the law library in person.[45]

Internet commerce, with its underlying profit motive, has provided impetus for fast moving technological innovation. Most online users now expect sophisticated sites that offer ease of access and speedy delivery of search materials. The same user expectations are reflected when patrons use law libraries. Planning for new equipment and services must involve seeking out quality products that are easy to use.[46]

New services offered by libraries invariably require additional training for librarians and staff. New services almost always require additional funding. One example of a new project that may well pave the way for similar projects in other law libraries is beginning to take shape in the King County Law Library in Seattle. The Director, Jean Holcomb, believes that within five years her library will be able to offer "one stop shopping." This will be a direct result of the King County Electronic Records Program, discussed earlier in this article. Phase I should be in place within two years and will allow patrons to look up court records online. Phase II is expected to take place within five years. Patrons will be able to file documents for the purposes of pro se litigation, especially in the areas of family law and bankruptcy law. PCs will be set up for these purposes in the library as each phase is put into place.

Budget planning for the new services being offered in law libraries presents an enormous challenge. For Directors, such as Jean Holcomb, the fundamental question underlying the provision of the planned new services is the cost. Staff will need additional training, and new computers and equipment will have to be purchased. An important question is what may have to be cut from the current library budget in order to incorporate the cost of the new services.[47]

CONCLUSION

Much of the real labor of creating and maintaining an electronic filing system lies with the courts. However, there are unique advantages that have served to drive court electronic filing programs forward. While reducing storage costs and staff requirements, a successful electronic filing system would make it easier to work at locations away from the courthouse. The court's files would be "open" 24 hours a day, and accessible over the Internet from any location in the world. The instant most documents are filed, they would be available for view. Courts would retain their traditional right to determine the categories of persons entitled to search records online, as well as the right to restrict access to "sensitive" documents as they see fit.[48]

Technological innovation in the courtroom has afforded lawyers the opportunity to add sophistication to trial practice. Currently, there are approximately 50 integrated high-tech courtrooms in the United States and many more are in the design or construction stage. A new era has opened for such key trial elements as presentation of evidence and opening statements. The traditional idea of an attorney standing at a lectern and speaking to the jury using, for example, charts, photographs, or sketches as props, is already starting to be replaced by counsel standing before a control podium, speaking to the jury, 'clicking through' a well-illustrated slide show, pausing only to circle key portions of images displayed on a state-of-the art screen, using an electronic light pen.[49]

The task of implementing technological innovation in the courthouse, which, in turn, affects the functioning of the entire legal system, has fostered the coming together of professionals from diverse disciplines and backgrounds. The spirit of cooperation that has arisen between those involved in law, technology and commerce has served to add momentum to the enormous advances in progress. Only a few years ago, who could have anticipated the far reaching effects and the increasing speed with which technological advances are transforming courts as we know them?[50]

NOTES

1. National Center for State Courts, *Trends in Court Technology*, 2000, at *http://www.ncsc.dni.us/KMO/Projects/Trends/99-00.*
2. *Id.*
3. *Id.*
4. National Center for State Courts, *Trends in State Court Technology*, 2000, at *http://www.ncsc.dni.us/KMO/Projects/Trends/99-00.*
5. Interview with Roger Winters, Electronic Court Records Program Manager, King County, Washington (March 2001).
6. Brad Hillis, *Critique of Existing Electronic Court Filing Projects*, 2001, at *http://www.wolfenet.com.*
7. J. Douglas Walker, *Electronic Court Documents*, 29-34 (National Center for State Courts, 2000).
8. *Ibid.*
9. National Center for State Courts, *Trends in State Court Technology*, 2000, at *http://www.ncsc.dni.us/KMO/Projects/Trends/99-00.*
10. J. Douglas Walker, *Electronic Court Documents*, 46-51 (National Center for State Courts, 2000).
11. *Id.*
12. J. Douglas Walker, *Electronic Court Documents*, 46-51 (National Center for State Courts, 2000).
13. *Id.*
14. National Center for State Courts, *Trends in Court Technology*, 2000, at *http://www.ncsc.dni.us/KMO/Projects/Trends/99-00.*
15. Roger Winters and Robert Cary, *Finding the Way to Electronic Court Records*, 2000, at *http://www.aiim.org/edocdis.cfm.*

16. National Center for State Courts, *Trends in Court Technology*, 2000, at *http://www.ncsc.dni.us/KMO/Projects/Trends/99-00.*
17. King County Judicial Administration, *Electronic Master Plan*, 1998, Seattle, Washington.
18. *Id.*
19. National Center for State Courts, *Trends in Court Technology*, 2000, at *http://www.ncsc.dni.us/KMO/Projects/Trends/99-00.*
20. Brad Hillis, *Critique of Existing Electronic Court Filing Projects*, 2001, at *http://www.wolfenet.com.*
21. King County Judicial Administration, *King County Vision Statement*, 1995, Seattle, Washington.
22. Robert Deyling, Attorney Adviser, Administrative Office, the Judicial Conference of the United States, *Privacy and Access to Electronic Case Files*, December, 1999, at *http://www.uscourts.gov/privacyn.htm.*
23. Robert Deyling, Attorney Adviser, Administrative Office, the Judicial Conference of the United States, *Privacy and Access to Electronic Case Files*, December, 1999, at *http://www.uscourts.gov/privacyn.htm.*
24. Elizabeth Hurt, *Opening Up the Courts: Internet Access to Court Documents Sparks Privacy, Security Concerns*, 2001, at *http://www.business2.com/content/channels/ebusiness/2001.*
25. Robert Deyling, Attorney Adviser, Administrative Office, the Judicial Conference of the United States, *Privacy and Access to Electronic Case Files*, December, 1999, at *http://www.uscourts.gov/privacyn.htm.*
26. Kate Marquess, *Open Court?*, 87 ABA Journal 56-57 (2001).
27. *Id.*
28. Elizabeth Hurt, *Opening Up the Courts: Internet Access to Court Documents Sparks Privacy, Security Concerns*, 2001, at *http://www.business2.com/content/channels/ebusiness/2001.*
29. Robert Deyling, Attorney Adviser, Administrative Office, the Judicial Conference of the United States, *Privacy and Access to Electronic Case Files*, December, 1999, at *http://www.uscourts.gov/privacyn.htm.*
30. Interview with Roger Winters, Electronic Court Records Program Manager, King County, Washington (March 2001).
31. *Id.*
32. *Ibid.*
33. Chris Reed, *Legally Binding Electronic Documents: Digital Signatures and Authentication*, GP Solo (2001) 18:6, 54-55.
34. J. Douglas Walker, *Electronic Court Documents*, 49-66 (National Center for State Courts, 2000).
35. McBride, Baker and Coles, *E-Commerce Spotlight: Electronic Commerce and Digital Signatures*, (2001) at: *http://www.mbc.com/ecommerce/ecommerce.asp.*
36. supra, note 34.
37. *Id.*
38. Reed, supra note 33.
39. *Id.*
40. McBride, Baker and Coles, *Summary of E-Commerce Legislation* (2001) at: *http://www.mbc.com/ecommerce/summary.asp?states.*
41. Jahna Berry, *First Came Home Office, Now Comes Home Courtroom*, January 3, 2001, at *http://www.law.com/cgi-bin/gx.cgi/AppLogic/.*

42. Interview with Roger Winters, Electronic Court Records Program Manager, King County, Washington (March 2001).

43. Julius J Marke & Richard Sloane (Editors), *Legal Research and Law Library Management*, American Lawyer Media (1990, supp. 2000), Section 44.10.

44. *Id.*, Section 44.02.

45. Ronald J. Heckart, *Imagining the Digital Library in a Commercialized Internet*, Journal of Academic Librarianship 25:4 (July 1999) 274-280.

46. Martha K. Heyman, *Building Successful Relationships with IT Professionals*, Information Outlook (April 2001) 34-42.

47. Interview with Jean Holcomb, Director of the King County Law Library, Seattle, Washington (April 2001).

48. Tobe Liebert, *Electronic Filing*, GP Solo (2001) 18:6, 32-33.

49. Luke M. Pittoni, *Using Technology During Trial to Persuade the Jury*, GP Solo (2001) 18:6, 34-35.

50. Interview with Roger Winters, Electronic Court Records Program Manager, King County, Washington (March 2001).

The Changing Role of Law Library Vendors: The William S. Hein & Company Perspective

Kevin M. Marmion
Richard J. Spinelli

SUMMARY. The authors present their perspective on changes in library-vendor relationships over the past two decades. It finds four basic changes in these relationships: the transformation of the legal publishing world; tighter budgets, but more choices of products in a variety of formats; increases in librarians' responsibilities; and, finally, the use of computers to manage library systems. The authors then discuss how these changes have impacted the William S. Hein & Company in its various roles as subscription agent, book jobber, publisher of book reprints, microform provider, and provider of online legal information. They conclude by analyzing what the future may hold for library vendors. *[Article copies available for a fee from The Haworth Document Delivery Service: 1-800-HAWORTH. E-mail address: <getinfo@haworthpressinc.com> Website: <http://www.HaworthPress.com> © 2002 by The Haworth Press, Inc. All rights reserved.]*

KEYWORDS. Library vendors, book jobbers, subscription agents, legal publishing

---

Kevin M. Marmion is President, William S. Hein & Company.
Richard J. Spinelli is Vice President, Sales & Marketing, William S. Hein & Company.

[Haworth co-indexing entry note]: "The Changing Role of Law Library Vendors: The William S. Hein & Company Perspective." Marmion, Kevin M., and Richard J. Spinelli. Co-published simultaneously in *Legal Reference Services Quarterly* (The Haworth Information Press, an imprint of The Haworth Press, Inc.) Vol. 21, No. 4, 2002, pp. 301-306; and: *Law Library Collection Development in the Digital Age* (ed: Michael Chiorazzi, and Gordon Russell) The Haworth Information Press, an imprint of The Haworth Press, Inc., 2002, pp. 301-306. Single or multiple copies of this article are available for a fee from The Haworth Document Delivery Service [1-800-HAWORTH, 9:00 a.m. - 5:00 p.m. (EST). E-mail address: getinfo@haworthpressinc.com].

William S. Hein & Co., Inc., incorporating the Fred O. Dennis Company and Fred B. Rothman & Co., has been serving academic, public, and private law libraries for more than 80 years. Our position–as both a multi-media information publisher and a full-service agent for all formats of legal materials worldwide–gives us a unique perspective from which to comment on the changing role of the library vendor over the past few years.

In this essay, we will look at the various library services our company provides as a specialized law agent and trace the changes we have witnessed in these services over the last twenty or so years. We will also look toward the future to try to predict what may be in store for the library-vendor relationship.

Changes in both technology and information management have accelerated over the past twenty years, affecting workflow between libraries and vendors. Furthermore, the recent advent of the Internet has dramatically altered the playing field and will forever change the "rules" and "tools" of the library-vendor relationship. Despite all these "dramatic changes," the core function of the library vendor remains fundamentally the same–that is, to simplify the process of the libraries' acquiring multi-media information for its staff and users. Simply stated, the vendor's job is to make the librarian's life easier.

While there have been very specific changes in the past two decades, it is safe to say that the following changes are universally seen in most library-vendor relationships:

1. Many of the traditional publishers and vendors have changed, merged, or ceased to exist. There are now fewer vendors, and they are, as a rule, larger and more powerful than their predecessors. Often they are not as attuned to the needs of the library market as smaller, more specialized vendors can be.
2. Most librarians are faced with tighter budgets to pay for more choices of products offered in more formats that are being updated more frequently than in the past. With this proliferation of materials, sometimes similar in nature and possibly with less editorial control than in times past, librarians must exercise even greater judgment in acquisitions. The increase in offerings came about mainly because advances in word processing and computerization gave publishers an economic way to publish more titles, supplements, and updates. Conversely, the merger of smaller publishers into larger publishing groups in some cases decreased competition and increased supplementation prices, while also introducing

alternative media that has made the librarians' choices more complex.

3. The scope of librarians' responsibilities has broadened dramatically, while in many cases the size of the staff has decreased. In addition to having to deal with traditional duties, including those related to acquisition and maintenance of library materials, librarians are now taking on additional jobs related to their changing roles in administering new technologies.
4. The development of computers and sophisticated library management and cataloging tools, as well as the centralization of information within a library, have changed how vendors receive orders, claims, and communications from the libraries they serve.

Throughout the core areas of our business, we have noticed specific changes as well. As a subscription agent, we have seen computerization dramatically change how information is transferred between the agent and library. For instance, a significant number of our customers now place orders electronically, and a growing number of larger law libraries even receive their invoices electronically, which eliminates the need to re-key all the invoice data into their library systems. The majority of libraries, however, still require paper copies of their invoices (interestingly, including those who also request an electronic invoice).

Claiming missing issues and volumes has been greatly impacted by the automated library system. Surprisingly, a majority of serial claims are still received in paper, while only a handful of our customers send their claims to us electronically. The automation of the claiming process has been a double-edged sword. On their part, the libraries' use of computers allows for claims to be sent out on a more timely and consistent basis, but because the human element has been removed from the claiming process, there is less control over the inevitably increasing number of claims for material not truly overdue. Before the automation of the claiming process, we estimated that more than 50% of the claims we received were for legitimate issues. Today, we receive more than 300,000 claims each year for missing material, and our staff estimates that nearly 75% of the claims are for material not yet published or never published.

As a book jobber, we have seen a dramatic change in the landscape of services for libraries. Many smaller book suppliers have gone out of business or have been bought out, leaving Baker & Taylor, Blackwell, and Midwest Library Services as the major book distributors. Amazon.com has also entered into the fray, and offers librarians a quick and easy way to order and pay for rush titles from a variety of publishers. These changes have, again, been a mixed blessing for the library customer. The larger jobbers have been able to compile acquisition profiles to simplify ordering and offer better discounts to libraries. What can be lost when dealing with large distributors, however, is the hallmark of smaller vendors: personal relationships, individualized problem solving, and customized service. Our customers at Hein have remained with us precisely because they value the fact that they can speak to experienced representatives who have been meeting their needs for years.

Receiving accurate bibliographic information on new materials, in multiple media, in the ever-changing landscape of academic and professional publishing is very important to libraries. A recent survey of the original Rothman "Green Slip" bibliographic service customers indicates that a majority of them still prefer to receive new book information in a print version, which is how the service has been delivered since its inception in the 1960s. We do, however, see a growing interest in having the option of receiving this type of information via e-mail and Web pages in the future.

The role of the book reprinter has evolved over the past few decades. With a large number of academic and research libraries opening from 1965 to 1980, there was a great demand for books and journals that had long been out-of-print and unavailable in the secondhand market. Reprinters found these titles and made them available again to those who needed to build their collections or fill in their holdings. This role continues, but reprinting is important today for still another reason. Preservation concerns have fueled the need to provide acid-free reprints with long-life bindings as more and more libraries are looking to replace older print materials with copies in a format that will ensure long-term availability and usability.

As a microfilm provider, we have not seen any significant downturn in the use of this medium by our customers, but the primary reason for acquiring microforms has changed. When originally introduced in the late 1960s and early 1970s, libraries acquired microforms strictly as a preservation alternative to deteriorating paper collections, such as the *Federal Register*, *Congressional Record*, and other large print sets. However, as limited budgets and space problems face more librarians, microforms are seen as an economic and space-saving alternative to print subscriptions. A majority of larger research libraries collect sets such as state attorney general opinions, state session laws, and other large, lesser-used material in a micro format. We have received many recommendations about what other sets we should be converting to microform. This conversion allows libraries both to save space and preserve historically significant collections.

These changes in the availability of alternative formats have also had a significant impact on our role in helping new law school libraries develop their collections. Decades ago, with few exceptions, new libraries primarily ordered print materials, buying microforms only when print was not available. During the last ten years, however, new academic law libraries have relied more heavily on both microforms and electronic resources to constitute a significant part of their primary collection. No longer are new libraries automatically acquiring complete print sets of retrospective or current legal periodicals, government documents, and treatises when the same material can be found in microform or electronic formats.

There are a number of reasons for these changes, both philosophical and practical. Because research processes and patrons' usage have shifted more and more to electronic rather than print sources, many libraries no longer need to purchase and house extensive print sets to support their main mission to users. Also, with the ease of using interlibrary loan, it is generally not a problem to decrease the library's dependence on print materials. In many cases, then, the librarians have to decide whether it makes sense for their particular libraries to collect original print material to act as a repository of historical, but not mission-critical, titles. Of course, practical considerations play a role in choosing from multi-media offerings as well, such as space and budgetary constraints or the condition of the print copies when titles are available in more than one format.

The most recent change in the way our company delivers legal information to its customers concerns our entry into the world of the digital delivery of legal journals in our *Hein-On-Line* service. Last year, *Hein-On-Line* was awarded the 2001 American Association of Law Libraries Best New Product Award. Just twenty years ago, it seemed inconceivable that anyone could afford to put large collections of legal journals or other legal classics online because of the technical costs in relationship to the size of the market for this specialized information. Technological changes over the last ten years, however, have allowed us to introduce a "new vision" to the library researcher. While the future of other electronic delivery methods, such as e-books, appears cloudy at this point, we are convinced that this innovative offering of retrospective collections of journals and legal classics online is a viable and indispensable product.

What does the future hold? We believe that all types of libraries will continue to need the support and services provided by the library subscription agent. Most libraries will continue to subscribe to print material, but as more titles are offered in electronic format as well, subscriptions to the print version will decline. Electronic usage will determine which titles libraries duplicate in hard copy. As e-mail and library management software continue to develop, the agent will play a larger role in aggregating information from small publishers and from larger publishers that are not concerned with the library market, in order to deliver the information to the libraries in formats that best meet their needs.

Libraries will continue to use the book jobbers who can best combine good service and good prices. Librarians will always appreciate the ease of going to a single source for their acquisitions rather than having to deal with myriad suppliers. This frees up staff members to concentrate their time and efforts less on the administrative problems of maintaining their collections and more on patron usage and education, technology integration, research, and so on.

As a larger percentage of information becomes available digitally, the libraries' role in the preservation of primary materials will become even more significant than it has been in the past. Self-selected libraries will become part of only a few repositories of the physical print version of much research material. In fact, large research libraries will evolve into the "museum of law book publishing," accentuating the need for preservation printing and microforms.

As we've said, the librarians' job, although increasingly complex and constantly changing in processes and details, at its core remains unchanged. Librarians provide information to library users in the most sensible formats while balancing space, budgetary and technical limitations in a fast-changing environment. We see our company continuing to fill the role that it has played for the past 80 years. We at William S. Hein & Co. listen intently to what our customers tell us they want and need. In our role as liaison between the information providers and the law library staff, we act as an advocate while simplifying, as much as possible, the processes involved.

Change is occurring more quickly, more often, and more dramatically than ever before. Therefore, it is essential to have a personal relationship with friendly, knowledgeable, and experienced agents whom librarians can count on to solve their problems and meet their ever-changing needs. William S. Hein & Co., Inc. will continue to provide that friendly, personal service our library friends have come to expect.

Index

AAAS. *See* American Association for the Advancement of Science (AAAS)
AALL. *See* American Association of Law Libraries (AALL)
AALS. *See* Association of American Law Schools (AALS)
ABA. *See* American Bar Association (ABA)
Academic Press, 192,210-211
Access issues
intellectual property (access *vs.* ownership), 153-171. *See also* Intellectual property (access *vs.* ownership) issues
long term access, 88-92. *See also* Long term access issues
open access, 289
open access site archives, 96-97
remote access, 231-232
scholarly information resource access, 219-223
Accreditation standards, 14-15
Acquisition issues, 207-212
Administrative Office of the United States Courts, Office of Judges Programs, 291-292
Aggregator and consortia issues, 212-214. *See also* Consortia and cooperative networks
ALA. *See* American Library Association (ALA)
ALCTS, Electronic Serials Institutes, 209
ALWD. *See* Association of Legal Writing Directors (ALWD)
American Association for the Advancement of Science (AAAS), 192
American Association of Law Libraries (AALL), 1,25,30-31,35,97-98, 134-135,208-209,214-220, 235-236
American Bar Association (ABA), 13-16,23-25,70,74-75,77-81, 97-98,124,216-217,260
American Library Association (ALA), 90,191-193,200, 207-208,221
Archival-related issues, 232-235
ARL. *See* Association of Research Libraries (ARL)
ARL-EJOURNAL, 244
ASCII text, 207-208
Association of American Law Schools (AALS), 25,190-191,208-209
Association of American Universities, 196-197
Association of Legal Writing Directors (ALWD), 235-236
Association of Research Libraries (ARL), 33,192,196-197,201,205, 213-218,231,233-234
Authentication and security technologies
authenticity issues and, 89-90
digital signatures, 292
document transmission, 287-288
encryption, 292-294
introduction to, 286-287
private and public key cryptography, 292-294
Authorization issues, 290-292
Availability, resources. *See* Resource availability
Axtmann, M. M., 177-188

Bankruptcy cases, 289-290
Bath Profile, 229
Blackwell North America (BNA), 8, 16-19,261-267,270-274
BNA. *See* Blackwell North America (BNA)
Book jobbers. *See* Vendors, changing roles of
Book selection services
  American Bar Association (ABA) and, 260
  case studies of
    Blackwell North America (BNA), 261-267,270-274
    data collection, 261-262
    goals, 261
    Green Slips, 261-267,270-274
    introduction to, 259-261
    processes, 261
    profile creation, 271-273
    service comparisons, 262-267
    slip service providers, listing of, 274
  future perspectives of, 267-268
  historical perspectives of, 260-261
  introduction to, 259
  reference and research literature about, 268-269
  vendors, changing roles of. *See* Vendors, changing roles of
Boston Library Consortium, 214
Bradford's Law, 4
Butterworths, 198-199

Canadian publishing industry, 133-134
Canick, S., 55-67
CARL. *See* Colorado Alliance for Research Libraries (CARL)
Case Management/Electronic Case Files (CM/ECF) system, 290-291
Cataloging issues, 46-47,167-168, 219-223
CCH. *See* Commerce Clearing House (CCH)
Chaos *vs.* control issues, 165-168
Chiorazzi, M., 1-28
Citation styles, 235-236
CLIR. *See* Council on Library and Information Resources (CLIR)
CM/ECF system. *See* Case Management/Electronic Case Files (CM/ECF) system
Coalition of Library Consortia (COLC), 211-212,218-219
Cognitive Sciences Eprint Archive (CogPrints), 239-240
CogPrints. *See* Cognitive Sciences Eprint Archive (CogPrints)
COLC. *See* Coalition of Library Consortia (COLC), 211-212, 218-219
Collection management issues
  acquisition issues and, 207-212
  aggregator and consortia issues and, 212-214
  historical perspectives of, 206-207
  introduction to, 206-207
  selection issues and, 207-212
Collection use issues
  accreditation standards and, 14-15
  bibliometrics, 5
  Blackwell North America (BNA) and, 8,16-19
  Bradford's Law and, 4
  costs, digital *vs.* paper, 13-16
  electronic discussion lists and
    Law-lib, 1
    Lawlibdir-l, 1-3
  future perspectives of, 23-25
  Garfield's Law of Concentration and, 5
  Government Printing Office (GPO) and, 17
  interlibrary loan (ILL) and, 11-12
  introduction to, 1-4
  LEXIS-NEXIS and, 6-7,10-12,16,23-24

Parento Principle and
digital collection development and, 5-7
digital libraries, viability of, 7-10
hybrid libraries, longevity of, 16-19
introduction to, 4
storage and, 19-23
use measurements and, 11-13
reference and research literature about, 25-28
societies and professional organizations and
American Association of Law Libraries (AALL), 1,25
American Bar Association (ABA), 13-16,23-25
Association of American Law Schools (AALS), 25
WESTLAW and, 6-7,10-12,17,23-24
Colorado Alliance for Research Libraries (CARL), 209
Commerce Clearing House (CCH), 128
Commercialization issues, 242-243
Conglomerates *vs.* imprints, 127-138. *See also* Publishers
Consortia and cooperative networks
Boston Library Consortium, 214
Council on Library and Information Resources (CLIR), 218, 233-234
Legal Scholarship Network (LSN), 206
New England Law Library Consortium (NELLCO), 213-214,218-219
OCLC, 38-40,192,220-221,226-229
OhioLink, 195,214
PALS, 219
Research Libraries Group (RLG), 33
Scholarly Publishing and Academic Resources Coalition (SPARC), 205
Social Science Research Network (SSRN), 206
Southeastern Library Network (SOLINET), 37,213-214
for web mirror sites, 98-99
Control *vs.* chaos issues, 165-168
Conversions, print-to-electronic, 237-238
Cooperative networks. *See* Consortia and cooperative networks
Cooperative projects
Cognitive Sciences Eprint Archive (CogPrints), 239-240
Jointly Administered Knowledge Environment (JAKE), 224-226
JSTOR, 33-35,60,66,190-191, 194,205, 212-213,243
Legal Education Document Archive (LEDA), 234-235,240-241
Open Journal Project, 239-240
Project MUSE, 33-35,205,209, 212-213
Project Open Book, 33-35
for web mirror sites, 98-99
Copyleft and general public licenses (GPLs), 238-239
Copyright issues
Copyright Act (1976), 170
Digital Millennium Copyright Act (DMCA), 163-164,215-216
models of, 159-161
vs. non-copyright models, 161-165
terminology, copyright *vs.* patent, 158
Uniform Commercial Code (UCC) and, 164-165
Uniform Computer Information Transactions Act (UCITA), 164-165,215-216
Cost-related issues
digital *vs.* paper collections, 13-16
fixed, 168-171
hidden, 200
journals, 196-198
technology, 171
Council on Library and Information Resources (CLIR), 218, 233-234

Court dockets and digital information
electronic courts
electronic *vs.* paper documents, 279-281
imaging technology and, 278-279
introduction to, 278
Judicial Electronic and Data Exchange (JEDDI), 278-282, 286-288
formats and standards for
Document Type Definitions (DTDs), 281-282
Extensible Mark-up Language (XML), 280-282
Hypertext Mark-up Language (HTML), 280-284
Hypertext Transport Protocol (HTTP), 279-281
International Standards Organization (ISO), 279-281
Standard Generalized Mark-up Language (SGML), 279-284
future perspectives of, 294-297
Internet, use of, 276-278
introduction to, 275-276
library-related issues of, 295-296
privacy issues
Administrative Office of the United States Courts, Office of Judges Programs, 291-292
authorization, 290-292
bankruptcy cases and, 289-290
Case Management/Electronic Case Files (CM/ECF) system and, 290-291
Electronic Privacy Information Center (EPIC) and, 290-291
imaging technology and, 288-289
introduction to, 288-289
open access, 289
Privacy Rights Clearing House and, 289
reference and research literature about, 297-299
security and authentication technologies for
digital signatures, 292
document transmission, 287-288
encryption, 292-294
introduction to, 286-287
private and public key cryptography, 292-294
state court filing projects
introduction to, 283-284
in Utah, 283-286
in Washington State, 283-286
Court filings and transcripts, 65
Cryptography, key, 292-294
Current awareness services, 229-230

Danner, R. A., 69-85
DC. *See* Dublin Core Metadata Element Set (DC)
Delegalization, law, 243-244
Dethman, J., 123-151
Digital delivery issues, 305-306
Digital libraries, viability of, 7-10
Digital Millennium Copyright Act (DMCA), 163-164,215-216
Digital signatures, 292
DIGITAL-COPYRIGHT, 244
Digitalization issues
collection growth, effect of, 35-40
collections and, 32-35
Early Canadiana Online and, 33-35
JSTOR and, 33-35
LegalTrac and, 35-36
Making of America project and, 33-35
netLibrary model and, 36-40
Project MUSE and, 33-35
Project Open Book and, 33-35
shelf life and, 36
Discussion groups, electronic. *See* Electronic discussion groups
Disintermediation, 241-242
Distance learning, strategic planning for

American Bar Association (ABA) and, 70,74-75,77-81
educational technology and, 71-73
introduction to, 69-71
library-related issues
information access, 81
information environments, 79-81
introduction to, 79
licensing, 79-80
online services, 81
new markets
alumni and others, 75-76
introduction to, 73-74
J.D. curricula, 71,73-76
LL.M. curricula, 71,75,80-81
M.B.A./executive education programs, 76-78
reference and research literature about, 82-85
vs. residential programs, 81
Temporary Distance Education Guidelines, American Bar Association (ABA), 80-81
DMCA. *See* Digital Millennium Copyright Act (DMCA)
Dockets, courts. *See* Court dockets and digital information
Document delivery issues, 230-231
Document Type Definitions (DTDs), 234
DTDs. *See* Document Type Definitions (DTDs)
Dublin Core Metadata Element Set (DC), 222-223

Early Canadiana Online, 33-35
Edmonds, E. P., 177-188
Educational technology issues, 71-73
E-journals. *See* Electronic journals
Electronic courts, 279-281. *See also* Court dockets and digital information
Electronic discussion groups
ARL-EJOURNAL, 244
DIGITAL-COPYRIGHT, 244
LAW-ACQ, 217
Law-lib, 1
Lawlibdir-l, 1,208
Liblicense-l, 211,214-215
NewJour, 244
SERIALIST, 244
VPIEJ-L, 244
Electronic journals
collection management issues of
acquisition issues and, 207-212
aggregator and consortia issues and, 212-214
historical perspectives of, 206-207
introduction to, 206-207
licensing, 214-216
selection, 207-212
consortia and cooperative networks and
Boston Library Consortium, 214
Council on Library and Information Resources (CLIR), 218,233-234
Legal Scholarship Network (LSN), 206,240-241
New England Law Library Consortium (NELLCO), 213-214,218-219
OCLC, 192,220-221,226-229
OhioLink, 195,214
PALS, 219
Scholarly Publishing and Academic Resources Coalition (SPARC), 205
Social Science Research Network (SSRN), 206
Southeastern Library Network (SOLINET), 213-214
cooperative projects and
Cognitive Sciences Eprint Archive (CogPrints), 239-240
Jointly Administered Knowledge Environment (JAKE), 224-226

JSTOR, 190-191,194,205, 212-213, 243
Legal Education Document Archive (LEDA), 234-235, 240-241
Open Journal Project, 239-240
Project MUSE, 205,209,212-213
electronic discussion groups about
ARL-EJOURNAL, 244
DIGITAL-COPYRIGHT, 244
LAW-ACQ, 217
Lawlibdir-l, 208
Liblicense-l, 211,214-215
NewJour, 244
SERIALIST, 244
VPIEJ-L, 244
formats and standards for
ASCII text, 207-208
Bath Profile, 229
Document Type Definitions (DTDs), 234
Dublin Core Metadata Element Set (DC), 222-223
Extensible Mark-up Language (XML), 234
Hypertext Mark-up Language (HTML), 207-208, 218
Internet Engineering Task Force (IETF) standard, 207-208
Open Archives Initiative (OAI), 204-205,222-223,235,240-241
Portable Document Format (PDF), 192,207-208
reference linking and, 226-229
Standard Generalized Mark-up Language (SGML), 234
Z39.50, 229
future perspectives of
delegalization, law, 243-244
disintermediation, 241-242
general public licenses (GPLs) and copyleft, 238-239
introduction to, 236
librarian roles, 241-242
library commercialization, 242-243
print-to-electronic conversions, 237-238
publishing industry directions, 239-241
resource access, 236-237
introduction to, 189-191
LEXIS-NEXIS and, 191,198-199, 212-213,217
Library of Congress and, 221-222
licensing issues and
Digital Millennium Copyright Act (DMCA), 215-216
introduction to, 214-216
Liblicense-l, 211,214-215
Uniform Computer Information Transactions Act (UCITA), 215-216
National Serials Data Program, 221-222
publishers and
Academic Press, 192,210-211
Butterworths, 198-199
Cambridge, 192
Gale Group, 229
High Wire Press, 205,209-211
Little Brown, 198-199
Oxford, 192
Reed Elsevier, 192,198-200,209, 211,214,220
Springer, 192
Thompson/West, 191-192,198-200
Wiley, 192
William S. Hein & Company/ Hein-On-Line, 190-191, 217-221
Wolters Kluwer, 192,198-200
reference and research literature about, 245-258
scholarly communication and serials-related issues of
archives, 232-235
Bath Profile, 229
cataloging, 219-223
citation styles, 235-236
collection development, 201

collection statistics, 216-219
current awareness services, 229-230
document delivery, 230-231
expectations *vs.* reality, 193
hidden costs, 200
historical perspectives, 192-193
impact of, 194-196
interlibrary loan (ILL), 230-231
interoperability, 229
introduction to, 192-193
IP filtering, 231-232
journal costs, 196-198
law reviews, 201-204
licensing, 214-216
Open Archives Initiative (OAI) and, 204-205,222-223,235
pay-per-views (PPVs), 230-231
preprints, 189-190
publisher mergers, 198-200
reasons for, 193-194
reference links, 226-229
remote access, 231-232
resource access, 219-226
scholarly communication initiatives, 204-206
use statistics, 216-219
Z39.59 standard, 229
societies and professional organizations and
ALCTS, Electronic Serials Institutes, 209
American Association for the Advancement of Science (AAAS), 192
American Association of Law Libraries (AALL), 208-209, 214-220,235-236
American Bar Association (ABA), 216-217
American Library Association (ALA), 191-193,200,207-208, 221
Association of American Law Schools (AALS), 190-191, 208-209
Association of American Universities, 196-197
Association of Legal Writing Directors (ALWD), 235-236
Association of Research Libraries (ARL), 192,196-197,201,205, 213-218,231,233-234
Coalition of Library Consortia (COLC), 211-212,218-219
Colorado Alliance for Research Libraries (CARL), 209
WebCT course management software and, 242-243
WESTLAW and, 191,199,212-213, 217
XanEdu and, 243
Electronic Privacy Information Center (EPIC), 290-291
Encryption issues, 292-294
Environments, information, 79-81
Executive education/M.B.A. programs, 76-78
Extensible Mark-up Language (XML), 234,280-282

Federal Depository Library Program Electronic Collection (FDLP/EC), 91-92
Filing projects, state courts. *See* State court filing projects
Foreign law, 65
Formats and standards
ASCII text, 207-208
Bath Profile, 229
Document Type Definitions (DTDs), 234,281-282
Dublin Core Metadata Element Set (DC), 222-223
Extensible Mark-up Language (XML), 234,280-282
Hypertext Mark-up Language (HTML), 207-208,218, 280-284

Hypertext Transport Protocol (HTTP), 279-281
International Standards Organization (ISO) and, 279-281
Internet Engineering Task Force (IETF) standard, 207-208
Open Archives Initiative (OAI), 204-205,222-223,235,240-241
Portable Document Format (PDF), 192,207-208
reference linking and, 226-229
Standard Generalized Mark-up Language (SGML), 234,279-284
Z39.50, 229
Fragility issues, 89
Future perspectives
of book selection services, 267-268
of collection use issues, 23-25
of court dockets and digital information, 294-297
of electronic journals, 236-244
of intellectual property (access *vs.* ownership) issues, 171-173
of new library creation issues, 186-187
of resource availability, 66
of resource re-engineering issues, 47-48
of scholarship and research issues, 113-114
of trust *vs.* antitrust issues (legal publishing industry consolidation), 145-146
of vendors, changing roles of, 306
of web mirror sites, 99

Gale Group, 130,229
Garfield's Law of Concentration, 5
Garmon, M., 259-274
General public licenses (GPLs) and copyleft, 238-239
Germain, C. M., 87-104
Government Printing Office (GPO), 17
GPL. *See* General public licenses (GPLs) and copyleft
GPO. *See* Government Printing Office (GPO)

Hein-On-Line. *See* William S. Hein & Company/Hein-On-Line
Hierarchical arrangements, resources, 43-44
High Wire Press, 205,209-211
Historical perspectives
of book selection services, 260-261
of collection management issues, 206-207
of scholarly communication and serials-related issues, 192-193
of scholarship and research issues, 108-110
of trust *vs.* antitrust issues (legal publishing industry consolidation)
consolidation by foreign invasion, 127-128
legal documents as history, 125-127
HTML. *See* Hypertext Mark-up Language (HTML)
HTTP. *See* Hypertext Transport Protocol (HTTP)
Hybrid libraries, longevity of, 16-19
Hypertext Mark-up Language (HTML), 207-208,218,280-284
Hypertext Transport Protocol (HTTP), 279-281

ICJ. *See* International Court of Justice (ICJ) web site
IETF. *See* Internet Engineering Task Force (IETF) standard
ILL. *See* Interlibrary loan (ILL) issues
ILO. *See* International Labour Organization (ILO) web site

Imaging technology issues, 278-279, 288-289
Imprints *vs.* conglomerates, 127-138. *See also* Publishers
Information environments, 79-81
Infrastructure, impact of, 187
Integrity issues, 89-90
Intellectual property (access *vs.* ownership) issues
  chaos *vs.* control, 165-168
  copyright
    Copyright Act (1976), 170
    Digital Millennium Copyright Act (DMCA), 163-164
    models of, 159-161
    vs. non-copyright models, 161-165
    terminology, copyright *vs.* patent, 158
    Uniform Commercial Code (UCC) and, 164-165
    Uniform Computer Information Transactions Act (UCITA), 164-165
  future perspectives of, 171-173
  introduction to, 153-155
  LEXIS-NEXIS and, 154,163, 168-171
  library *vs.* user concerns
    cataloging, 167-168
    fixed costs, 168-171
    interlibrary loan (ILL), 171
    licensing, 169-170
    permanence, 168-171
    preservation, 169-170
    technology costs, 171
  paradigm shifts in, 155-159
  reference and research literature about, 173-176
Interlibrary loan (ILL) issues, 11-12,171, 230-231
International Court of Justice (ICJ) web site, 87-104
International Labour Organization (ILO) web site, 87-104
International Standards Organization (ISO), 279-281
Internet Archives, 96-97
Internet Engineering Task Force (IETF) standard, 207-208
Interoperability issues, 229
IP filtering issues, 231-232
ISO. *See* International Standards Organization (ISO)

J.D. curricula, 71,74-76
JAKE. *See* Jointly Administered Knowledge Environment (JAKE)
JEDDI. *See* Judicial Electronic and Data Exchange (JEDDI)
Jobbers. *See* Vendors, changing roles of
Jointly Administered Knowledge Environment (JAKE), 224-226
Journals, electronic. *See* Electronic journals
JSTOR, 33-35,60,66,190-191,194,205, 212-213,243
Judicial Electronic and Data Exchange (JEDDI), 278-282,286-288

Key cryptography, private and public, 292-294

Law of Concentration, Garfield's, 5
LAW-ACQ, 217
Law-lib, 1
Lawlibdir-l, 1, 208
LEDA. *See* Legal Education Document Archive (LEDA)
Legal Education Document Archive (LEDA), 234-235,240-241
Legal Scholarship Network (LSN), 206
LegalTrac, 35-36
LEXIS-NEXIS, 6-7,10-12,16,23-24, 29-35,55-66,90,111-113,128, 133-135,154,163,168-171, 191,198-199,212-213,217

Liblicense-l, 211,214-215
Library of Congress, 88,98-99,221-222
Library-related issues
book selection services, 259-269. *See also* Book selection services
cataloging, 46-47,167-168,219-223
collection use, 1-28. *See also* Collection use issues
for court dockets and digital information, 295-296
distance learning, 79-81
for electronic journals, 189-258. *See also* Electronic journals
fixed costs, 168-171
information access, 81
information environments, 79-81
intellectual property (access *vs.* ownership) issues. *See* Intellectual property (access *vs.* ownership) issues
interlibrary loan (ILL), 11-12,171, 230-231
library commercialization, 242-243
library-vendor relationships, 302-303
licensing, 79-80,169-170,211-216. *See also* Licensing issues
online services, 81
permanence, 168-171
preservation, 169-170
resource re-engineering and, 46-48
technology costs, 171
vs. user issues, 167-171
Licensing issues, 79-80,211-216
Linking, reference, 226-229
Listservs. *See* Electronic discussion groups
Little Brown, 198-199
LL.M. curricula, 71,75,80-81
Long term access issues
authenticity and integrity, 89-90
current information, availability of, 90
digital law concerns, 89-90
Federal Depository Library Program Electronic Collection (FDLP/EC) and, 91-92
fragility, 89
introduction to, 88-89,93
National Archives and Records Administration (NARA) and, 91-93
National Commission on Libraries and Information Science (NCLIS) and, 91
web content, disappearance of, 90-81
LSN. *See* Legal Scholarship Network (LSN)

M.B.A./executive education programs, 76-78
Making of America project, 33-35
Marmion, K. M., 301-306
Matherson, S., 153-176
Matthew Bender, 138
Microformats, expanding roles of, 40-42
Minerva Project, 96
Most, M., 189-298

NARA. *See* National Archives and Records Administration (NARA)
National Archives and Records Administration (NARA), 91-93
National Association of Court Management, 97-98
National Commission on Libraries and Information Science (NCLIS), 91
National Serials Data Program, 221-222
NCLIS. *See* National Commission on Libraries and Information Science (NCLIS)
Neacsu, E. D., 105-122
NELLCO. *See* New England Law Library Consortium (NELLCO)
netLibrary model, 36-40
New England Law Library Consortium (NELLCO), 213-214,218-219

New library creation issues
collection development plans, creation of, 181-186
future perspectives of, 186-187
historical perspectives of, 178-179
information resources and, 181-186
infrastructure, impact of, 187
introduction to, 177-178
processes of, 179
reference and research literature about, 188
staffing issues and, 179-180
New markets
alumni and others, 75-76
introduction to, 73-74
J.D. curricula, 71,74-76
LL.M. curricula, 71,75,80-81
M.B.A./executive education programs, 76-78
NewJour, 244
Non-copyright *vs.* copyright models, 161-165

OAI. *See* Open Archives Initiative (OAI)
OCLC, 38-40,192,220-221,226-229
Office of Judges Programs, 291-292
OhioLink, 195,214
Open access, 289
Open access site archives
Internet Archives, 96-97
introduction to, 96
Minerva Project, 96
Open Archives Initiative (OAI), 204-205,222-223,235,240-241
Open Journal Project, 239-240
Ownership *vs.* access issues. *See* Intellectual property (access *vs.* ownership) issues

PALS, 219
Paradigm shifts, 155-159
Parento Principle. *See also* Collection use issues
digital collection development and, 5-7
digital libraries, viability of, 7-10
hybrid libraries, longevity of, 16-19
introduction to, 4
storage and, 19-23
use measurements and, 11-13
Patent *vs.* copyright terminology, 158
Pay-per-views (PPVs), 230-231
Periodicals, electronic. *See* Electronic journals
Permanence issues, 168-171
Portable Document Format (PDF), 192,207-208
PPVs. *See* Pay-per-views (PPVs)
Preprints, 189
Preservation issues, 169-170
Print-to-electronic conversions, 237-238
Privacy issues
Administrative Office of the United States Courts, Office of Judges Programs, 291-292
authorization, 290-292
bankruptcy cases and, 289-290
Case Management/Electronic Case Files (CM/ECF) system, 290-291
Electronic Privacy Information Center (EPIC) and, 290-291
imaging technology and, 288-289
introduction to, 288-289
open access, 289
Privacy Rights Clearing House and, 289
Privacy Rights Clearing House, 289
Private and public key cryptography, 292-294
Professional organizations. *See* Societies and professional organizations
Project MUSE, 33-35,205,209,212-213
Public and private key cryptography, 292-294
Publishers
Academic Press, 192,210-211
Butterworths, 198-199

Cambridge, 192
Canadian publishing industry, 133-134
Commerce Clearing House (CCH), 128
conglomerates *vs.* imprints, 127-138
Gale Group, 130
High Wire Press, 205,209-211
Little Brown, 198-199
Matthew Bender, 138
mergers of, 198-200
Oxford, 192
Random House, 36
Reed Elsevier, 127-128,130-132, 135-136,192,198-199,209,211, 214,220
Simon & Schuster, 36
small legal publishers, 132-133
Springer, 192
Thompson/West, 124,128-130, 135-138,191-192,198-200
William S. Hein & Company/ Hein-On-Line, 33-34,190-191, 217-221,301-306
Wolters Kluwer, 192,198-200

Random House, 36
Reading online, legal analysis and, 41-43
Reed Elsevier, 127-128,130-132, 135-136,192,198-199,209, 211,214,220
Re-engineering, resources. *See* Resource re-engineering issues
Reference and research literature
about book selection services, 268-269
about collection use issues, 25-28
about court dockets and digital information, 297-299
about distance learning, strategic planning for, 82-85
about electronic journals, 245-258
about intellectual property (access *vs.* ownership) issues, 173-176
about new library creation issues, 188
about resource availability, 67
about resource re-engineering issues, 48-54
about scholarship and research issues, 114
about trust *vs.* antitrust issues (legal publishing industry consolidation), 146-151
about web mirror sites, 99-104
Reference linking, 226-229
Reliability issues, 106-108
Remote access issues, 231-232
Research Libraries Group (RLG), 33
Residential programs *vs.* distance learning programs, 81
Resource availability
in books, 61
in court filings and transcripts, 65
in federal law, 63-63
in foreign law, 65
future perspectives of, 66
introduction to, 55-56
JSTOR and, 60,66
in legal periodicals, 59-60
in LEXIS-NEXIS, 55-66
in non-legal periodicals, 60-61
reference and research literature about, 67
in reports and working papers, 62
in state law, 63-64
studies of
data collection, 56-58
findings, 58-66
introduction to, 55-56
methods, 56-58
in uniform laws, 64
in WESTLAW, 55-66
Resource re-engineering issues
consortia and cooperative networks and
OCLC, 38-40
Research Libraries Group (RLG), 33
Southeastern Library Network (SOLINET), 37

digitalization
collection growth, effect on, 35-40
of collections, 32-35
Early Canadiana Online and, 33-35
JSTOR, 33-35
LegalTrac and, 35-36
Making of America project and, 33-35
netLibrary model and, 36-40
Project MUSE and, 33-35
Project Open Book and, 33-35
shelf life and, 36
future perspectives of, 47-48
hierarchical arrangements, 43-44
introduction to, 29-32
LEXIS-NEXIS and, 29-35
library-related roles in
acquisitions, 46
cataloging, 46-47
collection management, 46-48
introduction to, 44-48
microformats, expanding roles of, 40-42
publishers and
Random House, 36
Simon & Schuster, 36
William S. Hein & Company/Hein-On-Line, 33-34
reading online, legal analysis and, 41-43
reference and research literature about, 48-54
societies and professional organizations and
American Association of Law Libraries (AALL), 30-31,35
Association of Research Libraries (ARL), 33
WESTLAW and, 29-35
RLG. *See* Research Libraries Group (RLG)
Russell, G., 29-54
Scholarly communication and serials-related issues
archives, 232-235
Bath Profile, 229
cataloging, 219-223
citation styles, 235-236
collection development, 201
collection statistics, 216-219
current awareness services, 229-230
document delivery, 230-231
expectations *vs.* reality, 193
hidden costs, 200
historical perspectives, 192-193
impact of, 194-196
interlibrary loan (ILL), 230-231
interoperability, 229
introduction to, 192-193
IP filtering, 231-232
journal costs, 196-198
law reviews, 201-204
licensing, 214-216. *See also* Licensing issues
Open Archives Initiative (OAI), 204-205,222-223,235
pay-per-views (PPVs), 230-231
preprints, 189
publisher mergers, 198-200
reasons for, 193-194
remote access, 231-232
resource access, 219-223
scholarly communication initiatives, 204-206
use statistics, 216-219
Z39.59 standard, 229
Scholarly Publishing and Academic Resources Coalition (SPARC), 205
Scholarship and research issues
digitalization, 110-113
future perspectives of, 113-114
historical perspectives of, 108-110
importance of, 107-108
introduction to, 105-107
LEXIS-NEXIS and, 111-113

reference and research literature about, 114
reliability, 106-108
WESTLAW and, 113
Security and authentication technologies
digital signatures, 292
document transmission, 287-288
encryption, 292-294
introduction to, 286-287
private and public key cryptography, 292-294
Selection issues
book selection services, 259-269. *See also* Book selection services
introduction to, 207-212
SERIALIST, 244
SGML. *See* Standard Generalized Mark-up Language (SGML)
Shelf life issues, 36
Signatures, digital, 292
Simon & Schuster, 36
Slip services, 259-269. *See also* Book selection services
Small legal publishers, 132-133
Social Science Research Network (SSRN), 206
Societies and professional organizations
ALCTS, Electronic Serials Institutes, 209
American Association for the Advancement of Science (AAAS), 192
American Association of Law Libraries (AALL), 1,25, 30-31, 35,97-98,134-135,208-209, 214-220,235-236
American Bar Association (ABA), 13-16,23-25,70,74-75,77-81, 97-98,124,216-217,260
American Library Association (ALA), 90,191-193,200, 207-208,221
Association of American Law Schools (AALS), 25,190-191,208-209
Association of American Universities, 196-197
Association of Legal Writing Directors (ALWD), 235-236
Association of Research Libraries (ARL), 33,192,196-197,201, 205,213-218,231,233-234
Coalition of Library Consortia (COLC), 211-212,218-219
Colorado Alliance for Research Libraries (CARL), 209
National Association of Court Management, 97-98
Southeastern Library Network (SOLINET), 37,213-214
Sovereignty issues, 145
SPARC. *See* Scholarly Publishing and Academic Resources Coalition (SPARC)
Spinelli, R. J., 301-306
Springer, 192
SSRN. *See* Social Science Research Network (SSRN)
Staffing issues, 179-180
Standard Generalized Mark-up Language (SGML), 234, 279-284
State court filing projects
introduction to, 283-284
in Utah, 283-286
in Washington State, 283-286
Statistics, collection, 216-219
Storage issues, 19-23
Strategic planning, distance learning. *See* Distance learning, strategic planning for
Subscription agents. *See* Vendors, changing roles of

Temporary Distance Education Guidelines, American Bar Association (ABA), 80-81

Thompson/West, 124,128-130,
135-138,191-192,198-200
Trust *vs.* antitrust issues (legal publishing industry consolidation)
antitrust issues, 134-136
cost, 143-144
database protection
effective dates, 142-143
enforcement, 141-142
exclusions, 140-141
introduction to, 136-139
legislation (H.R. 354 and H.R. 1858), 138-143
permitted actions (differences), 140-141
prohibitions, 139-140
protections, 139
reasonable use, 141
future perspectives of, 145-146
historical perspectives of
consolidation by foreign invasion, 127-128
legal documents as history, 125-127
introduction to, 123-124
publishing conglomerates *vs.* imprints
Canadian publishing industry, 133-134
Commerce Clearing House (CCH), 128
Gale Group, 130
LEXIS-NEXIS and, 128-129, 133-135
Matthew Bender, 138
Reed Elsevier, 127-128,130-132, 135-136
small legal publishers, 132-133
Thompson/West, 124,128-130, 135-138
WESTLAW and, 134-135
Wolters Kluwer, 124,128,131-132
reference and research literature about, 146-151
societies and professional associations and
American Association of Law Libraries (AALL), 134-135
American Bar Association (ABA), 124
sovereignty, 145
Turner, J. C., 275-299

UCC. *See* Uniform Commercial Code (UCC)
UCITA. *See* Uniform Computer Information Transactions Act (UCITA)
Uniform Commercial Code (UCC), 164-165
Uniform Computer Information Transactions Act (UCITA), 164-165,215-216
Use measurements, 11-13

Vendors, changing roles of
business-related changes, 303-305
digital delivery issues, 305-306
future perspectives of, 306
information management, impact of, 302
introduction to, 301-302
library-vendor relationships, 302-303
reasons for, 305-306
service-related changes, 303-305
technology, impact of, 302
William S. Hein & Company/ Hein-On-Line and, 301-306
VPIEJ-L, 244

Web mirror sites
consortia and cooperative projects
consortial activities, 98-99
digital preservation projects, 97-98

introduction to, 97
creation and maintenance of, 95
future perspectives of, 99
goals of, 93-94
importance of, 93
International Court of Justice (ICJ) site, 87-104
International Labour Organization (ILO) site, 87-104
introduction to, 87-88
LEXIS-NEXIS and, 90
Library of Congress and, 88,98-99
long term access issues of
authenticity and integrity, 89-90
current information, availability of, 90
digital law concerns, 89-90
Federal Depository Library Program Electronic Collection (FDLP/EC) and, 91-92
fragility, 89
introduction to, 88-89,93
National Archives and Records Administration (NARA) and, 91-93
National Commission on Libraries and Information Science (NCLIS) and, 91-92
web content, disappearance of, 90-81
open access site archives and
Internet Archives, 96-97
introduction to, 96
Minerva Project, 96
reference and research literature about, 99-104
societies and professional organizations and
American Association of Law Libraries (AALL), 97-98
American Bar Association (ABA), 97-98
American Library Association (ALA), 90
National Association of Court Management, 97-98
WESTLAW and, 90
WebCT course management software, 242-243
WESTLAW, 6-7,10-12,17,23-24, 29-35,55-66,90,113,134-135, 191,212-213,217
William S. Hein & Company/ Hein-On-Line, 33-34, 190-191,217-221,301-306
Wolters Kluwer, 192,198-200

XanEdu, 243

Z39.50, 229

For Product Safety Concerns and Information please contact our EU representative GPSR@taylorandfrancis.com
Taylor & Francis Verlag GmbH, Kaufingerstraße 24, 80331 München, Germany

www.ingramcontent.com/pod-product-compliance
Lightning Source LLC
Chambersburg PA
CBHW050449051126
54379CB00003B/70
9780789020222